Bhagavad Gītā

Home Study Course

(Text in Sanskrit with transliteration, word-to-word and verse meaning, along with an elaborate commentary in English based on Śaṅkara-bhāṣyam)

Volume 6

Summary of Chapters 1-7

Chapters 8-9-10

Swami Dayananda Saraswati
Arsha Vidya

Arsha Vidya
Research and Publication Trust
Chennai

Published by :
Arsha Vidya Research and Publication Trust
4 ' Srinidhi' Apts 3rd Floor
Sir Desika Road Mylapore
Chennai 600 004 INDIA
Tel : 044 2499 7023
Telefax : 2499 7131
Email : avrandpt@gmail.com
Website: www.avrpt.com

ISBN : 978-93-80049-35-9
ISBN : 978-93-80049-39-7 (Set of 9 Volumes)

New Edition & Format :	July	2011	Copies : 1200
1st Reprint :	July	2012	Copies : 1000

Design & Layout :
Graaphic Design

Printed at :
Sudarsan Graphics
27, Neelakanta Mehta Street
T. Nagar, Chennai 600 017
Email : info@sudarsan.com

Preface

I am very happy that the 'Bhagavad Gītā Home Study Course' will now be available in nine compact volumes so that one can carry a given volume while travelling. As I said in my foreword for the last edition, I want the readers to be aware that these books do not constitute another set of books on the *Bhagavadgītā*. They are different in that they are edited transcript-pages of classroom discussions; they are presented to the reader as a program for self-study. If this is borne in mind, while reading, one can enjoy the same attitude of a student in the classroom, making oneself available to the whole process of unfoldment of the content of the words of Bhagavān. The study will then prove to be as rewarding as directly listening to the teacher. This attitude would prove to be *ātma-kṛpā*. Once this *kṛpā* is there, the other two, *śāstra-kṛpā* and *īśvara-kṛpā* would follow.

The enormous job of patient editing of the pages, thousands of them, and presenting them, retaining the original words and content without any compromise, was done by Dr. Martha Doherty. These books have created a number of committed students of the *Bhagavadgītā*, thanks to Martha's invaluable contribution to the teaching tradition of Vedanta. I also congratulate the staff of our Publication division ably led by Ms. K. Chandra, a dedicated student of Vedanta.

Swami Dayananda Saraswati
Arsha Vidya
June 19 2011

Key to Transliteration and Pronunciation of Sanskrit Letters

Sanskrit is a highly phonetic language and hence accuracy in articulation of the letters is important. For those unfamiliar with the *Devanägari* script, the international transliteration is a guide to the proper pronunciation of Sanskrit letters.

अ	*a*	*(but)*	ट	*ṭa*	*(true)**3
आ	*ā*	*(father)*	ठ	*ṭha*	*(anthill)**3
इ	*i*	*(it)*	ड	*ḍa*	*(drum)**3
ई	*ī*	*(beat)*	ढ	*ḍha*	*(godhead)**3
उ	*u*	*(full)*	ण	*ṇa*	*(under)**3
ऊ	*ū*	*(pool)*	त	*ta*	*(path)**4
ऋ	*ṛ*	*(rhythm)*	थ	*tha*	*(thunder)**4
ॠ	*ṝ*	*(marine)*	द	*da*	*(that)**4
ऌ	*ḷ*	*(revelry)*	ध	*dha*	*(breathe)**4
ए	*e*	*(play)*	न	*na*	*(nut)**4
ऐ	*ai*	*(aisle)*	प	*pa*	*(put)* 5
ओ	*o*	*(go)*	फ	*pha*	*(loophole)**5
औ	*au*	*(loud)*	ब	*ba*	*(bin)* 5
क	*ka*	*(seek)* 1	भ	*bha*	*(abhor)**5
ख	*kha*	*(blockhead)**1	म	*ma*	*(much)* 5
ग	*ga*	*(get)* 1	य	*ya*	*(loyal)*
घ	*gha*	*(log hut)**1	र	*ra*	*(red)*
ङ	*ṅa*	*(sing)* 1	ल	*la*	*(luck)*
च	*ca*	*(chunk)* 2	व	*va*	*(vase)*
छ	*cha*	*(catch him)**2	श	*śa*	*(sure)*
ज	*ja*	*(jump)* 2	ष	*ṣa*	*(shun)*
झ	*jha*	*(hedgehog)**2	स	*sa*	*(so)*
ञ	*ña*	*(bunch)* 2	ह	*ha*	*(hum)*

ं	*ṁ*	*anusvāra*	(nasalisation of preceding vowel)
ः	*ḥ*	*visarga*	(aspiration of preceding vowel)
*			No exact English equivalents for these letters

1.	Guttural	–	Pronounced from throat
2.	Palatal	–	Pronounced from palate
3.	Lingual	–	Pronounced from cerebrum
4.	Dental	–	Pronounced from teeth
5.	Labial	–	Pronounced from lips

The 5th letter of each of the above class – called nasals – are also pronounced nasally.

Contents

Chapter 9

Chapter 10

Summary of chapters 1-7

Enquiry into tvaṁ-pada – chapters 1-6

The whole subject matter of Vedanta is covered by the statement, '*tat tvam asi.*' *Tvam* refers to the *jīva*, the individual and *tat* denotes Īśvara, the Lord. And there is an equation between them, which is revealed by *asi*. An equation does not reveal something that is going to happen later. It reveals a fact that exists now. The *śāstra* does not say, '*tat tvaṁ bhaviṣyasi*, you will become that.' It says '*tat tvam asi*, you are that.' It is an important fact to note.

Once I say, '*tvam asi*, you are,' an expectation is created as to, 'What am I?' The speaker has something to convey; something is expected. This *ākāṅkṣā*, expectation, created by the statement, '*tvam asi*' is fulfilled by the word '*tat*'. Since the word '*tat*' is a pronoun, it refers to something already explained in the *śāstra*. *Tat-pada* was presented as *sat-vastu*, the existent reality, which is the cause of creation.

Since *tat-pada* stands for Īśvara, in order to understand the *tat tvam asi* equation, the *tvaṁ-pada* has to be understood properly. In an equation there are two things that are equated. The necessity for an equation is that one side of the equation seems to be different from the other. If one is totally different from the other, there is no equation. Only if they are the same, but not recognised, can there be an equation.

If a chair is told, 'You are wood, that of which the whole wooden world is made,' the chair has to understand this statement. Naturally, it has to die to the notion that it is just a chair. It has to acknowledge that it is wood in the form of chair and it can be in the form of a table too. The chair has to recognise this and so, it is given an equation. When there is a possibility of an equation, it means there is an already existent fact.

Here too, this equation states an existent fact. The *jīva* happens to be Īśvara. To recognise this, what the *tvaṁ-pada* implies must be understood and the nature of Īśvara must also be understood; only then can the equation be understood. In the process of understanding the nature of *tvaṁ-pada*, and the nature of the *tat-pada*, the meaning of the equation is discovered. As a result of this enquiry, the discovery 'I am that' takes place.

In the first six chapters of the *Gītā*, the subject matter is predominantly *ātmā*, the *jīva*. Arjuna was confused. And one who is subject to confusion is a *jīva*, an individual, which is the meaning of the word *tvam*. The first part of the *Gītā* is enquiry into the *tvaṁ-pada*.

Chapter 1

In the first chapter it was shown that Arjuna was confused. It means that a *jīva* is subject to confusion. Arjuna was not an ordinary *jīva*. Born a prince with the blessings of Indra, Arjuna was a man of great character and valour. In his day, he was invincible. Bhīṣma waited for Arjuna to fight and Droṇa, his teacher, was anxious to see him fight. Arjuna who was also highly accomplished in music and dance found himself in a state of depression. What does it mean? An individual, *jīva*, no matter what his or her accomplishments may be, is subject to sorrow. This was presented in the very first chapter.

Chapter 2

Next was Arjuna's *puruṣārtha-niścaya*, ascertainment of what is to be pursued in life. He found himself in a no-win situation, exactly the situation where one can discover what one really wants. If he is victorious, he loses those that are dear to him. If he does not gain victory, yet he is a loser. In this unenviable situation is born his desire to solve the problem of sorrow in a way that requires no further solution. Arjuna addresses the human problem. He did not address his topical problem but saw a fundamental problem of the human heart that needs to be addressed. To do so, in the situation he was in, he needed support. And Kṛṣṇa was the greatest support possible. Whenever you address a fundamental problem, you cannot do it alone. You do require help. The subject matter here being what it is, you require not just support, but a teacher. Arjuna finds in Kṛṣṇa a teacher.

The discovery of the human problem is the subject matter of *tvaṁ-pada*, the meaning of 'you.' And seeking a solution is done by *jīva, the tvaṁ-pada-artha*, as is finding a teacher and asking for this knowledge. Arjuna discovered the teacher in Kṛṣṇa and surrendering to him asked him to teach, *śiṣyaste'haṁ śādhi māṁ tvāṁ prapannam.*[1] Kṛṣṇa accepts Arjuna as a student and

[1] *Gītā* 2.7

teaches him immediately, as though he was waiting for such a situation. He starts with the statement, *aśocyān anvaśocastvam*, you are grieving over that which does not deserve grief.[2] And then he talks about *ātmā* and how it is not subject to death at all. He says, 'Your conclusion about *ātmā* is not true; it is not born nor does it ever die, it was never non-existent nor will it ever not be there; it is unborn, eternal, and so on, *na jāyate mriyate vā kadācit, nāyaṁ bhūtvā bhavitā vā na bhūyaḥ, ajaḥ nityaḥ* and so on.[3] Kṛṣṇa talks about *ātmā* in entirety right in the second chapter. It is the analysis of the *tvaṁ-pada*. This is the whole style of teaching. The exposition of *tat-pada* comes and goes, but the predominant topic in the second chapter is the analysis of *tvaṁ-pada*. Then Kṛṣṇa gives Arjuna different arguments as to why he must fight and how *karma* is not opposed to knowledge if it is backed by proper attitude.

Chapter 3

In the third chapter, Arjuna wanted to know whether to pursue self-knowledge. In response to Arjuna's question at the end of the second chapter, Kṛṣṇa had described a wise man as one who is happy with himself, without requiring any addition or subtraction. Arjuna's thinking now is that he should pursue this wisdom. Since *sannyāsa* as a lifestyle was available exclusively for this pursuit, Arjuna considered it as a possibility for himself. Yet Kṛṣṇa was encouraging him to fight this battle. So, Arjuna asked Kṛṣṇa, which was better – a life of

---

[2] *Gītā* 2.11

[3] *Gītā* 2.20

karma or a life of renunciation in pursuit of self-knowledge. 'You seem to praise both of them. So, please teach me again clearly. They must have different results because one seems to be a life of activity and the other, a life of non-activity. Both cannot have the same result. Action will produce result that will necessarily bind me. It means I will continue in *saṁsāra*. But *sannyāsa* is supposed to deliver me from *saṁsāra*. How can both be the same?' So, Arjuna wanted to know in unequivocal terms what the means for *mokṣa* is – a life of *karma-yoga* or a life of *sannyāsa*. And for whom is the life of *karma-yoga* and *sannyāsa*, for Īśvara or for the *jīva*?

There is a lot said about *karma-yoga* in the third chapter but it was meant for the *jīva*. That is the predominant topic. Later, in the fourth chapter, Kṛṣṇa talked about knowledge again. Having pointed out that it is not *karma* that is a binding factor, but a lack of attitude and knowledge, he then talked about real *sannyāsa*.

Chapter 4

Sannyāsa as a lifestyle is one, but *sarva-karma-sannyāsa*, total renunciation by knowledge is quite another. In the fourth chapter, Kṛṣṇa unfolded this total renunciation of action, which is possible only through knowledge. And for whom is this? It is for the *jīva*. The Lord says, 'I am always performing actions and yet I do not perform any action; the system of the four *varṇas* was created by me. Understand me to be the creator of that system and yet as someone who is not a doer at all, *cāturvarṇyaṁ mayā sṛṣṭaṁ guṇa-karma-vibhāgaśaḥ tasya kartāram api māṁ viddhi akartāram avyayam.*'[4] Even though he is very active, the Lord is released from *karma* because of his knowledge. Therefore, knowledge is required, not for Īśvara but for *jīva*.

The one who is able to see actionlessness, which is the nature of *ātmā* in every activity, and the one who sees action in inactivity, he alone sees; he is the most knowledgeable among men; he is the successful one who has accomplished all that has to be accomplished, *karmaṇi akarma yaḥ paśyet akarmaṇi ca karma yaḥ sa buddhimān manuṣyeṣu sa yuktaḥ kṛtsna-karmakṛt.*[5] If you think you are a *kartā*, you perform action, even if it is refusal to act. It is the doership that is the kingpin of all actions. Therefore, the one who is able to see the absence of doership in the midst of activities is a real *sannyāsī*.

Chapter 5

After talking about *jñāna-karma-sannyāsa*, renunciation of action through knowledge, Kṛṣṇa talked about *sannyāsa* again – *jñeyaḥ sa nitya-sannyāsī yo na dveṣṭi na kāṅkṣati*, he is to be known as always a *sannyāsī* who has neither aversion nor longing.[6] ...*ekaṁ sāṅkhyaṁ ca yogaṁ ca yaḥ paśyati sa paśyati*, the one who sees knowledge and *karma-yoga* as the same, he sees.[7] *Sannyāsastu mahābāho duḥkham āptum ayogataḥ yoga-yukto munirbrahma na cireṇa adhigacchati*, renunciation of action,

---

[4] *Gītā* 4.13
[5] *Gītā* 4.18
[6] *Gītā* 5.3
[7] *Gītā* 5.5

Arjuna, the mighty armed! is difficult to accomplish without *karma-yoga*. Whereas, one who is committed to a life of *karma-yoga* and is capable of reasoning, gains Brahman quickly.[8] By these words Bhagavān shows the nature of knowledge in the fifth chapter. Gaining this knowledge one becomes *sannyāsī* and in order to gain it, one takes to a life of *sannyāsa*. The nature of knowledge was again pointed out by the word *sannyāsa* and so the chapter was called *sannyāsa-yoga*. Again, for whom was this pointed out? For the *jīva*. There, *tvaṁ-pada-artha*, the nature of *ātmā* was talked about only for the *jīva* – *tadbuddhayaḥ tadātmānaḥ tanniṣṭhāḥ tatparāyaṇāḥ gacchanti apunarāvṛttiṁ jñāna-nirdhūta kalmaṣāḥ*, those whose intellect is awake to that (Brahman), for whom the self is that (Brahman), who are committed only to that (Brahman), for whom the ultimate end is that (Brahman which is already accomplished), whose impurities have been destroyed by knowledge – they attain a state from which there is no return.[9] These are, then, the nature of *pratyagātmā*.

Chapter 6

In this chapter, the main topic is *dhyāna*, contemplation, in which Kṛṣṇa tells how to sit, what exactly should one do, and what kind of a lifestyle should one live, and so on. He says, *... ātmasaṁsthaṁ manaḥ kṛtvā na kiñcid api cintayet*, making the

---

[8] *Gītā* 5.6

[9] *Gītā* 5.17

[10] *Gītā* 6.25

mind abide in the self, may one not think of anything else.[10] He also says, *yukta-āhāra-vihārasya, yukta-ceṣṭasya karmasu, yukta-svapna-avabodhasya, yogo bhavati duḥkhahā,* for one who is moderate in eating and other activities, who is mindful in all activities, (and) to one's sleeping and waking hours, (for such a person) meditation becomes the destroyer of sorrow.[11] Thus, Kṛṣṇa talked about what is necessary for a contemplative life including the emotional life and attitudes that constitute *yoga,* a mature lifestyle. The chapter ended with *dhyāna,* contemplation of *pratyagātmā.* In the contemplation, even though he mainly talked about *pratyagātmā,* he also brought in Īśvara, when he said, *mat-cittaḥ yukta āsīta mat-paraḥ,* and so on.

In these six chapters the *jīva* was presented as the seeker, the one who has to undergo changes. And it is the *jīva* whose *ātmā* was presented there, mainly. This is *tvaṁ-pada-vicāra,* enquiry into the *tvaṁ-pada.*

Then, from chapter 7 onwards the whole teaching and the approach is different because the enquiry into Īśvara, the *tat-pada* begins and is discussed primarily.

Enquiry into tat-pada begins

Summary of chapter seven

Here we shall briefly see the meaning of each verse of the seventh chapter.

---

[11] *Gītā* 6.17

Verse 1

The first verse begins with *mayyāsaktamanāḥ... mayi* means in me, Īśvara; so in the very first verse Īśvara is brought in. He says, 'Pārtha (Arjuna)! With a mind committed to me by taking to *yoga*, and having surrendered to me, please listen to the way in which you will know me totally, without any doubt.'

Verse 2

This verse he says. 'I will teach you without any omission, this knowledge, along with immediate knowledge, knowing which there remains nothing else to be known here.' Whatever *parokṣa*, indirect knowledge you have, because Īśvara is involved here, I am going to convert it into *aparokṣa*, immediate knowledge. We saw how Kṛṣṇa presents this knowledge in *parokṣa* and also in an *aparokṣa* form. Once this is known, there is nothing else to be known.

Verse 3

To encourage Arjuna, Kṛṣṇa says, 'Among thousands of people, a rare person makes effort for *mokṣa*. Even among those seekers making effort, (only) a rare person comes to know me in reality.'

Verse 4

Here, Kṛṣṇa began talking about what he had promised. He divides everything into *parā* and *aparā-prakṛti* and begins with *aparā* describing the eight-fold *prakṛti*.

Verses 5&6

Here, Kṛṣṇa talks about *aparā-prakṛti*. And he points out the *parā* in the second half of this. *Parā-prakṛti* is consciousness, the very meaning of the word *jīva*, and is not a mere thought. That is indeed the *yoni*, the cause for everything. I am the *caitanya-ātmā* that is the cause for everything, from which everything comes, by which everything is sustained and unto which everything goes.

Verse 7

Kṛṣṇa says there is no other cause superior to me and there is nothing besides me. There is no cause for me. In fact, there is nothing that is separate from me. The great canvas of this world is woven (has its being) in me, like the beads in a string. Then he says, I am the cause of all of them, the truth of everything, Īśvara is understood as *parokṣa*.

Verse 8

Kṛṣṇa starts by saying I am the taste in the water and then goes on in detail talking about name and form and the very content of it. I am the material cause of everything. A thing is there only because of me; I am the very essence of everything. All the glories belong to me. In the sun and moon, I am the light that is there. I am the essence of the Vedas, which is reduced to *om*. I am the sound in space, and in a human being, his strength.

Verse 9

Kṛṣṇa continues – I am the sweet fragrance in the earth and the brilliance and heat in the fire. I am the very life in all beings.

I am the one because of whom a great ascetic is called an ascetic, because I am in the form of the result of all his austerities and remain as his very austerity.

Verse 10

Here he says, Pārtha (Arjuna)! Understand me as the one who is the eternal seed from which all living beings come into being. I am the intellect of those that have the capacity to discriminate; I am the brilliance in the brilliant.

Verse 11

Kṛṣṇa says, Arjuna, in the strong I am the strength that is free from desires, likes and dislikes and attachment. Even your desire is me as long as it is in conformity with *dharma* because *dharma* is me.

Verse 12

Kṛṣṇa continues to talk about the indirect knowledge of Īśvara. The *bhāvas*, beings born of *sattva-guṇa, rajo-guṇa* or *tamo-guṇa* are born only of me. Or here, the word *bhāva*s could mean the various thought process born of *sattva, rajas* or *tamas;* they exist in me, but I do not exist in them. I do not depend on them but they depend entirely upon me. I give them their very existence. And whatever features they have are me; they are all my glory.

Verse 13

Here Kṛṣṇa says that even when this is so, people do not recognise me because they are deluded by the three *guṇa*s, *sattva-rajas-tamas,* and their products.

Verse 14

And, therefore, he says, 'This *māyā*, which is the modification of the three *guṇa*s, which belongs to me, is very difficult to cross.' Deluded by the modifications of the mind you are not able to recognise your identity with Īśvara. So Arjuna, you have to go to a *māyāvī*, magician. When you are under the spell of magic, you cannot see the trick. So, you have to stand by the side of the magician and watch how he does it. Then you find that there is no magic at all. Therefore Kṛṣṇa says, 'I am that *māyāvī*, the magician. You come to my side, directly seek me. Under the spell of magic, you are a seeker. If you know the magic, you find there is no seeking. Therefore, those who seek me directly cross over this *māyā*.'

Verse 15

Kṛṣṇa says that people do not seek me because they are given to lifestyles that do not even allow them to think. There are even devotees who do not come to me. Although they are devotees, they do not seek me directly; only a few seek.

Verse 16

In the next verse, Kṛṣṇa describes the four types of devotees. An *ārta*, devotee in distress, an *arthārthī* is a devotee both when he is in distress and when he wants something. For the sake of accomplishing that end, he seeks my help. Then there is the *jijñāsu* who is interested in the very truth of Īśvara; he wants to know what Īśvara is. The last, of course, the *jñānī* is also a devotee. A successful *jijñāsu* is a *jñānī*.

Verse 18

All of them are my devotees and are great. Yet, the *jñānī* is myself, says Kṛṣṇa in the eighteenth verse. He becomes one with me. Now, is this indirect or direct knowledge? It is here Kṛṣṇa converts it to *aparokṣa-jñāna*, direct knowledge. He went on saying, I am the strength in the strong, and so on, and now he says, you also can say the same. You are everything. This is what he meant by *vijñāna* in the second verse of this chapter.

Verse 19

Here Kṛṣṇa says that after a number of births, the one who has knowledge gains me and such a *mahātmā* is not easy to find. 'After a number of births' means that when one comes to study *Gītā*, a number of births have already been taken care of. But it does not mean that one gains knowledge only after a number of births after coming to *Gītā*.

Verse 20

Kṛṣṇa says here that people go to other *devatā*s because they do not recognise me at all. These are *ārta*s or *arthārthī*s, and I establish their *śraddhā*.

Verses 21&22

Here he says such a person, endowed with *śraddhā* gains the result of his *karma*s ordained by me.

Verse 23

In this verse Kṛṣṇa comes to the point. All the results are *antavat*, limited and finite. If devotees are only invoking the deities, they get very limited results. But if they seek me, they become me.

Verse 24

Those who lack discrimination – who do not know my limitless, changeless nature beyond which there is nothing greater – look upon me only as Kṛṣṇa as one endowed with a manifest form, as though I am another person who has come down from heaven.

Verses 25&26

In these verses Kṛṣṇa talks about his nature, which is found in all the *Upaniṣads*. I know everything and I am not subject to time. People do not recognise me, whereas I know all that has gone before and what comes later.

Verse 27

Here Kṛṣṇa says even as they are born they are deluded. They are born with *icchā, rāga-dveṣa*, because of which there is *dvandva*, the opposites, and these oposites cause delusion. The delusion does not allow them to see properly. Even the knowledge of the external world is vitiated by these *rāga-dveṣa*s and things are not understood as they are, which is why there is no chance of recognising me.

Verses 28&29

Those who are freed from the spell of these opposites, that is, for whom *rāga-dveṣa*s and *pāpa*s are neutralised by *puṇya-karma*, seek me for release from old age and death. People of good actions, firm in their commitment come to know Brahman which is *pratyagātmā*. They also know and understand *karma* in its entirety, and so they have no more problems.

Verse 30

In this last verse, Kṛṣṇa says that they come to know me not only as the truth of themselves but as the entire creation, all that is centred on the world, the *devatā*s and the rituals. They know me even at the time of death, as the efficient and material cause, the one from whom nothing is separate. Those who know me in this particular form are not separate from me. This is *vijñāna*.

Chapter 8

अक्षर-ब्रह्म-योगः

Akṣara-brahma-yogaḥ

Topic of imperishable Brahman

Introduction

This chapter is called *akṣara-brahma-yoga* or *tāraka-brahma-yoga*. *Tāraka-mantra* is that which helps you cross over *saṁsāra*. *Om* is a *tāraka-mantra*. Another *tāraka-mantra* is '*rāma, rāma*'. Here *om* is the *tāraka-mantra* and therefore, *oṁkāra-upāsana* is talked about in great detail.

The predominant topic of this chapter is *upāsana*. In the sixth chapter the topic was *nidhidhyāsana* as an *aṅga* of *śravaṇa*. Whereas here real *upāsana*, *mānasa-karma* is talked about. *Upāsana* means *saguṇa-brahma-viṣaya-mānasa-vyāpāra*. The words *upāsana*, *dhyāna*, *vidyā* and *jñāna* all mean the same.

The whole teaching, '*ayam ātma brahma*' is *śābda*, that is, the whole thing is conveyed by words alone. Other means of knowledge such as direct perception and inference have no scope here at all. The words do their job by knocking off the ignorance. Some say that reality cannot be revealed through words. It is not true. In fact, through words alone can the reality be revealed. Therefore, the only *pramāṇa* for self-knowledge is *śabda- pramāṇa*, words of the *śāstra*. *Dhyāna* prepares the person for self-knowledge. So, it is indirectly useful, *ārat upakāraka*. If it is so, and if any *upāsana* is *karma*, a *mānasa-karma*, then why is it placed here in the middle of the *Gītā* and also in the *Upaniṣads* and not in the *karma-kāṇḍa*? Why is it that the varieties of *upāsanas* discussed in the *śāstra* are often found in various *Upaniṣads?* This is the question we have to answer now.

Between *karma* and *jñāna* there is a connection. *Karma* is indirectly useful because it helps in preparing the person for *jñāna*. The *kāyika-karma*s in the form of *nitya- karma*s and *naimittika-karma*s are useful in giving *citta-śuddhi* when done with the right attitude and is thus a *bahiraṅga-sādhana*. *Upāsana* is an *antaraṅga-sādhana* and it gives *citta-naiścalya*, an absorption of the mind which is necessary for removing the *pratibandhaka*s, obstacles that prevent one from owning up this knowledge. And *citta-naiścalya* is gained through *upāsana*s. Therefore, they are relevant here in the *jñāna-kāṇḍa*. Moreover, knowledge can take place only in the mind. So *upāsana*s and knowledge have a common factor, *mānasatva*, which is another reason why these are placed in the *jñāna-kāṇḍa*.

Ātmā is *sat-cit-ānanda-svarūpa*, Brahman. The *jīva* does not know this fact. It means there is ignorance, which is the first *pratibandhaka* towards this knowledge and is called *āvaraṇa*. And to eliminate this *pratibandhaka*, one requires a means of knowledge which is *vedānta-pramāṇa*. The knowledge that I am Brahman will take care of the ignorance once it is understood. But to understand this fact about oneself, the mind has to be ready. If the mind is not ready, this *āvaraṇa* does not go away even after exposure to *vedānta-pramāṇa*. Then one has to conclude that there are other *pratibandhaka*s. Therefore, we say that preparedness is required and that involves the removal of the *pratibandhaka*s.

*Pratibandhaka*s are divided into two. One is *mala* and the other is *vikṣepa*. *Mala* means impurity and that is nothing but *rāga-dveṣa*s. So for the sake of removal of these impurities one has to do *karma*, both *kāyika* and *vācika* with the attitude of *karma-yoga* as we have seen before, *mala-nivṛttyarthaṁ karma*. *Vikṣepa* means restlessness or non-abidance of the mind. And for the removal of *vikṣepa*, *upāsana* is the means. *Upāsana* is in the form of *japa*, visualisation, and so on. The various *upāsana*s prescribed by the *śāstra* are meant for creating a mind that is steady and abiding. Taking the cue from this, even modern psychology uses various techniques of meditation and visualisation as forms of therapy to calm down the mind. A person may be free of conflicts, may live a life of *dharma*, may have the right attitude and yet can have *vikṣepa* because there is an unconscious part of the mind that throws up these disturbances.

For this *vikṣepa-nivṛtti* we require the various types of *upāsana*s such as *saguṇa-brahma-dhyāna*, *ahaṅgraha-upāsana*, *sampat-upāsana*, and so on. Therefore, for *vikṣepa-nivṛtti* and *citta-naiścalya*, for gaining a steadiness of mind, *upāsana* is advised. Even though meditation is a *karma*, a mental *karma*, it is relevant in this area where knowledge is discussed. The knowledge of Īśvara, *saguṇa-brahma*, has been talked about in the seventh chapter and will also be addressed later in the tenth chapter. Thus it is very relevant to talk about meditation. Because meditation is only with *saguṇa-brahma* as the object for the meditation, *saguṇa-brahma-viṣaya-jñāna* is necessary for meditation. So, the discussion on *upāsana* is relevant in the *Upaniṣad*s and the *Gītā*.

There are many kinds of *upāsana*s with different *upāsya-devatā*s or *iṣṭa-devatā*s. It is because each person has his or her own unique *saṁskāra*s that make it easy for the person to relate to a particular *iṣṭa-devatā*. Because of the uniqueness of these *saṁskāra*s there are varieties of *upāsana*s discussed by the *śāstra* and there are different types of results for them. But if a *mumukṣu* has no interest in the result, that is, *adṛṣṭa-phala*, in terms of going to *brahma-loka*, etc., then *citta-naiścalya* alone is the *dṛṣṭa-phala* that he gains through these *upāsana*s.

Even if you are interested in going to *brahma-loka*, when you reach *brahma-loka* through these *upāsana*s, there, being taught by Brahmaji, you gain *ātma-jñāna*, and this is called *krama-mukti*. But it is very difficult to reach *brahma-loka*. Within *saṁsāra*, if there is the highest *karma-phala* that you can gain, beyond which there is nothing, that is *brahma-loka*. This *brahma-loka-prāpti* is through *upāsana*. And there, if you have a special *puṇya* then you will be taught by Brahmaji and gain the knowledge, '*ahaṁ brahma asmi*, I am Brahman' and you will gain *mokṣa*. Otherwise you have to be born again on this earth.

So, the *upāsana*s are *āntaraṅga-sādhana*s for this knowledge in that they give the *citta-naiścalya* needed for *nidhidhyāsana* that is necessary for assimilating this knowledge. Therefore, they are mentioned here in this chapter. This chapter also talks about the results of *upāsana*s done for the sake of results other than *mokṣa*. And the chapter ends by stating the two *mārga*s or *gati*s the *jīva*s take after death.

In the *Gītā*, at the end of a chapter there are often one or two verses that introduce new ideas which are expanded in the subsequent chapter. They either create a question in Arjuna's mind or are addressed by Kṛṣṇa directly.

In the last two verses of the seventh chapter, Kṛṣṇa talked about the understanding of a wise man even at the time of death and in doing so, introduced several new words. This forms the basis for the questions, which are formulated by Arjuna in the first two verses of chapter eight. Before we get into the chapter we have to see the relevance of this chapter.

Verses 1&2

Arjuna's questions introduce the entire topic of the chapter

अर्जुन उवाच ।
किं तद्ब्रह्म किमध्यात्मं किं कर्म पुरुषोत्तम ।
अधिभूतं च किं प्रोक्तमधिदैवं किमुच्यते ॥ १ ॥

arjuna uvāca
kiṁ tadbrahma kim adhyātmaṁ kiṁ karma puruṣottama
adhibhūtaṁ ca kiṁ proktam adhidaivaṁ kim ucyate (1)

arjuna – Arjuna; *uvāca* – said;
kiṁ tadbrahma – what is that Brahman; *kim adhyātmam* – what is that which is centred on the self?; *kiṁ karma* – what is *karma*?; *puruṣottama* – O the one beyond whom there is none!; *ca* – and; *adhibhūtaṁ kiṁ proktam* – what is spoken of as centred on beings?; *adhidaivaṁ kim ucyate* – what is said to be centred on gods?

Arjuna said:

Puruṣottama[12] (Kṛṣṇa)! What is that Brahman? What is centred on the self? What is *karma*? What is spoken of as centred on beings? And what is said to be centred on gods?

अधियज्ञः कथं कोऽत्र देहेऽस्मिन्मधुसूदन ।
प्रयाणकाले च कथं ज्ञेयोऽसि नियतात्मभिः ॥ २ ॥

adhiyajñaḥ kathaṁ ko'tra dehe'smin madhusūdana
prayāṇakāle ca kathaṁ jñeyo'si niyatātmabhiḥ (2)

madhusūdana – O the one who destroyed the demon Madhu (Kṛṣṇa)!; *atra asmin dehe* – here in this body; *adhiyajñaḥ kathaṁ kaḥ* – how and who is that which is centred on ritual?; *ca* – and; *prayāṇakāle* – at the time of death; *kathaṁ jñeyaḥ asi* – how are you known?; *niyata-ātmabhiḥ* – by those whose minds are steady

Madhusūdana (Kṛṣṇa)! How and who is that which is centred on ritual here in this body? At the time of death, how are you known by those whose minds are steady?

Arjuna asks what is that Brahman, which you say the wise men know. The word '*brahma*' has many meanings. It can mean the Veda, a *brāhmaṇa* or Brahmaji. It can also mean something big that can be anything. So, what is that Brahman? Then you mentioned *akhilaṁ karma*. What does it mean? Is it past *karma*, present *karma*, or future *karma*?

---

[12] *Puruṣebhyaḥ uttamaḥ puruṣottamaḥ* – the one who transcends all beings is Puruṣottama.

What is this *adhyātma* and what is said to be *adhibhūta*? What is it that is called *adhidaiva*? Is there an *adhiyajña* in this body? Who is the *adhiyajña* to be understood?

Arjuna addresses Kṛṣṇa here as Puruṣottama. *Puruṣa* means person and *uttama* means the highest, so Puruṣottama can mean the most exalted among persons. But Kṛṣṇa is not the most exalted among persons; he is the only person, as *paraṁ-brahma* he is the only *vastu*. Here, Puruṣottama means he is *puruṣa* and he is the one beyond whom there is none. We will see the meaning of Puruṣottama in more detail in the fifteenth chapter.

The Lord had said that those people whose minds are steady, *niyata*, know me even at the time of their departure from the body. How is it possible? At the time of death people will either worry about their survival or think of what is beloved to them. This is the basis of Arjuna's question. At the time of death, when they have so many urgent concerns, how do they remember you? How are you recognised? How do you become the object of their knowledge? Thus Arjuna asked many questions in the first two verses of this chapter.

Verses 3-6

Bhagavān answers every question and elaborates them

श्रीभगवानुवाच ।
अक्षरं ब्रह्म परमं स्वभावोऽध्यात्ममुच्यते ।
भूतभावोद्भवकरो विसर्गः कर्मसंज्ञितः ॥ ३ ॥

śrībhagavān uvāca
akṣaraṁ brahma paramaṁ svabhāvo'dhyātmam ucyate
bhūtabhāvodbhavakaro visargaḥ karmasañjñitaḥ (3)

śrībhagavān – the Lord; *uvāca* – said;
akṣaram – that which does not change; *paramam* – limitless; *brahma* – Brahman; *svabhāvaḥ* – (its) manifestation; *adhyātmam* – that which is centred on the body,[13] (that is, the *jīva*); *ucyate* – is called; *karma-saṁjñitaḥ* – known as *karma*; *visargaḥ* – offering (the act of offering an *āhuti* in the fire in a *yajña*); *bhūta-bhāva-udbhava-karaḥ* – the one which causes the production of bodies for the beings

Śrī Bhagavān said:
Brahman is limitless and not subject to change. Its manifestation, centred on the body is called the *jīva*. What is known as *karma* is an offering, which causes the production of bodies for the beings.

अधिभूतं क्षरो भावः पुरुषश्चाधिदैवतम् ।
अधियज्ञोऽहमेवात्र देहे देहभृतां वर ॥ ४ ॥

adhibhūtaṁ kṣaro bhāvaḥ puruṣaścādhidaivatam
adhiyajño'ham evātra dehe dehabhṛtāṁ vara (4)

deha-bhṛtāṁ vara – O the most exalted one among the embodied!; *adhibhūtam* – what is centred on beings; *kṣaraḥ bhāvaḥ* – is that which is subject to decline; *adhi-daivataṁ ca* – and what is centred on the *devatās*; *puruṣaḥ* – (is) *hiraṇyagarbha*;

---

[13] The word '*ātmā*' here refers to the physical body.

atra dehe – here in this body; *adhi-yajñaḥ aham eva* – I alone am what is centred on ritual

> Arjuna, the most exalted among the embodied! What is centred on beings is that which is subject to decline. What is centred on *devatā*s is *hiraṇyagarbha*. Here in this body, I alone am what is centred on ritual.

Brahman is limitless and is myself

Akṣaraṁ brahma paramam, Brahman is limitless and not subject to change. *Akṣara* means that which does not decline. Anything that declines is within time and therefore subject to *ṣad-bhāva-vikāra*s, the six-fold modifications.[14] So, what does not decline is also free from these modifications. Brahman is *akṣara*, not subject to any change whatsoever. It can only be *parama*, not conditioned by place, time, or a given attribute. An object like a pot is limited in space by its own dimension, limited by time because there was a time when it was not, there will be a time when it will not be and being a pot, it is distinct from everything else, including other pots.

Brahman is not limited in any of these respects. It has no dimension and so, it does not exist in space. But, one may ask, is space also not free of this limitation since there is no place where space is not? It is true that space is all-pervasive within creation but it does not pervade Brahman, rather Brahman pervades space.

---

[14] *jāyate* – born; *asti* – is; *vardhate* – grows; *vipariṇamate* – undergoes changes; *apakṣiyate* – decays; *vinaśyati* – is destroyed. Every object has these six-fold modifications.

Space is limited with respect to time; it does not exist in *pralaya* or deep sleep. Further, it is only space, distinguishable from all other things, that is, it is not air, fire or time.

Brahman has no limitation with respect to objects because it has no particular quality of its own. Yet it is the truth of everything. Nothing stands separate from Brahman and that *paraṁ-brahma* can only be *sat-cit-ānanda-ātmā*.

The word '*akṣara*' is used later[15] to refer to the single syllable word *om*. So, Śaṅkara raises the question as to why the word *akṣara* does not mean *om* here and he himself answers it. He says that the adjective *parama* negates that possibility. And further, *om* is not the topic here. Even though it is a name for Brahman, *om* is not Brahman. Therefore, *akṣara* is Brahman here.

Svabhāvaḥ adhyātmam ucyate – svabhāva, the manifestation of this *paraṁ-brahma* is said to be *adhyātma*, *jīva*. *Ātmā* here means body. So, *adhyātma* is that which is centred on the physical body. It can be anything – the body itself, *buddhi*, sense organs, mind, *prāṇa* and finally the *pratyagātmā*. So, Arjuna wants to know what is this *adhyātma* which the wise men know.

The word *adhyātma*, meaning the *jīva*, can refer to any of these. Contextually, here it is *pratyagātmā* that obtains in this and every physical body in the form of consciousness. This is the nature of the *jīva*. Recognising the *jīva* in its essence is the final reality, consciousness called *adhyātma* here. *Akṣaraṁ-brahma* is also called the essence of the *jīva*, *adhyātma*.

---

[15] *Gītā* 8.13

The meanings of the word Brahman and *adhyātma* are identical but are used in different contexts. Only Brahman, not *ātmā*, is used when we talk about the cause of the world. That Brahman is equated to this *jīva* who is *adhyātma* centred on a given physical body. Because Bhagavān said the wise knows Brahman, the cause of everything, the word *adhyātma* is used here to dismiss the notion that Brahman is an object. They know Brahman, but not as something remote from themselves but as themselves; to point this out he says *adhyātma*. By knowing Brahman they know *ātmā*, and by knowing *ātmā* they know Brahman. It is because Brahman and *ātmā* are the same.

Karma is also Bhagavān

Visargaḥ karma-sañjñitaḥ – Arjuna wanted to know what is meant by *karma*, which it was said, the wise men know in its entirety. *Karma-sañjñita*, what is known as *karma* is *visarga*, offering, the act of offering an *āhuti* in the fire in a *yajña*. Śaṅkara says it is an offering intended for a given *devatā*. Even though the word *karma* can mean any type of action, in the *śāstra* it specifically means the ritual in which there is an offering. The ritual stands for other *karma*s. Therefore, he calls *karma* as *visarga*. And it is the *karma-phala* that causes one to be born in a particular body. So Bhagavān calls this *karma* as *bhūta-bhāva-udbhava-karaḥ*, the one that causes the birth of the existence of beings. In order to be born, a being needs a body. *Karma* is the cause for it. It produces a two-fold result, *dṛṣṭa* and *adṛṣṭa*. The *adṛṣṭa* produces bodies for you.

Bhūta can be taken as the already existent *jīva*s. They are not created, only the body is created. When you say a son is born, what is really born? Is it a *jīva* or a body? It is a given physical body with a given parentage at a given place and time. It is creating the bodies for the already existent beings that are created.

It is important to know that the *jīva* is not created. If it were to be created, then *ātmā* would also be created and there would be no possibility of *mokṣa*. The *jīva*'s essential nature is eternal and therefore it is not created. Even the *jīva* who exists as an individual is not created because his cause, ignorance, is beginningless. A particular form is created and the cause for it is *karma*.

Karma also is non-separate from Brahman. The one who knows Brahman knows this. The action, the agent, and other things connected to the action are Brahman as we saw in the fourth chapter.[16] They are *mithyā* and depend upon Brahman which is *satya*. Therefore, the wise men know the entire *karma*, *akhilaṁ karma*.

So forms are born because of this *karma*. When a person performs a ritual, he is propitiating the *devatā*s. Rain and food and other things necessary for creation are provided because of the *devatā*s. Ultimately the ritual is the cause for a person's birth. We saw this in the third chapter,[17] and Śaṅkara reminds us of that here.

---

[16] *Gītā* 4.24

[17] *Gītā* 3.14-15

The beings that are subject to change are also Bhagavān

Adhibhūtaṁ kṣaraḥ bhāvaḥ, an existent being that is subject to destruction is called *adhibhūta*. All beings are subject to change and destruction. Anything that exists is called *bhāva*, and anything that exists is subject to change, *kṣaraḥ bhāvaḥ*. All that is born, the whole world that exists in time, is *adhibhūta*. Kṛṣṇa says that all the physical bodies that exist here and are subject to the changes of birth, existence, growth, development, decline and death are also me. Even though something changes, it does not disappear. So, wherever there is change, there is dependence upon a changeless basis. The essence, the existence of a given object, which is undergoing change, is never destroyed. And that, Kṛṣṇa says, is me.

Brahman, which is *akṣara*, is itself *adhyātma* with reference to the person who is making an enquiry. With reference to other bodies that he confronts, it is *adhibhūta*. 'Thus not only is *adhyātma* me, *adhibhūta* is also me,' says Kṛṣṇa.

अन्तकाले च मामेव स्मरन्मुक्त्वा कलेवरम् ।
यः प्रयाति स मद्भावं याति नास्त्यत्र संशयः ॥ ५ ॥

antakāle ca mām eva smaran muktvā kalevaram
yaḥ prayāti sa madbhāvaṁ yāti nāstyatra saṁśayaḥ (5)

anta-kāle ca – and at the time of death; *mām eva smaran* – remembering me alone; *muktvā* – giving up; *kalevaram* – the body; *yaḥ prayāti* – the one who departs; *saḥ* – he; *madbhāvaṁ yāti* – gains my nature; *atra* – here, regarding this; *saṁśayaḥ na asti* – there is no doubt

At the time of death, the one who departs giving up the body, remembering me alone, he gains my nature. Regarding this, there is no doubt.

A wise man knows he is Brahman even at the time of death

Anta-kāle ca, and at the time, which is the end, the last moment, *māṁ smaran*, remembering me, *sa madbhāvaṁ yāti*, he gains my nature. The time of one's departure from a given physical body in a given incarnation is called *anta-kāla*, that is, it is the time of one's death. It is not that only at the time of departure he remembers Īśvara and such a person reaches Īśvara. Throughout his life too, the one who knows he or she is Brahman will remember 'me,' Brahman. One's knowledge will not go away. The word '*smaran*' meaning 'remembering,' is used figuratively here. What is actually meant here is that one who has the knowledge of Brahman will have that knowledge even at the end of his or her life.

If Brahman is an object of thought kept in the memory, then at the time of death Brahman will not be of any use to the person because it will not come to mind. When one faces death, what is going to be thought of, is what concerns one the most. If Brahman is an object of thought and one has to rely upon thinking about it at the time of death, then one is taking a chance. One may think of it or one you may not. Even if one does think about Brahman at that time, it does not mean that one will know Brahman because thinking about Brahman is not the same as knowing Brahman.

Brahman is the very nature of oneself. 'I am Brahman' is not just a statement; it is assimilated knowledge. Can it ever be a matter of memory? No. One can remember hundred different things but Brahman can never be one of them because the one who remembers everything is Brahman. On the other hand, the one who knows oneself as Brahman can never forget that one is Brahman because it is one's very nature and not an object of memory.

Kalevaraṁ muktvā yaḥ prayāti, giving up the physical body, the one who departs. Where does he go? He reaches me, gains my nature, the nature of *paramātmā* – *saḥ mad-bhāvaṁ yāti*. This person is a *jīvan-mukta*. Even while alive, one knows the identity between oneself and Brahman. What happens when one dies? If the person is not a *jñānī*, when the physical body dies, his subtle body continues to exist because the causal body, ignorance, still exists. Since there is self-ignorance, all his *karma*s are waiting to fructify. So, at the time of death one assumes a body appropriate for those *karma*s and travels to a place suitable for their fulfilment. What happens when a wise man dies?

For a jīvan-mukta there is no jīva – there is only Brahman

For a *jīvan-mukta*, such a travel does not take place because at the time of death his subtle body disintegrates. The same *śāstra* that tells us that a person travels after death also tells us that the *jñānī* does not have any subtle body with which to travel. It has disappeared because its cause, ignorance, is gone. The causal body is ignorance and knowledge of *ātmā* being

Brahman amounts to removal of that ignorance. When the cause is gone, naturally, the effect is not there. Once the threads are burnt, the piece of cloth cannot remain. Similarly, once ignorance is gone, the subtle body cannot remain. Therefore, there is no travel.

The Lord says, 'Giving up this body he reaches me alone.' 'Reaching' is purely figurative here. Kṛṣṇa has already said what he means by 'me'– *paraṁ-brahma. Paraṁ-brahma* is non-separate from *ātmā*. Therefore, there can be no real reaching. Reaching is only in the sense of being non-separate from Īśvara.

However, a particular thing cannot assume the nature of another.[18] A given object, which has its own nature, cannot give it up and still exist in its original form. But here, the nature of *ātmā* is already Brahman. The *jīvan-mukta* knew this even while alive; dead, there is nobody, no separate individual.

While one was alive there was a seeming doer and enjoyer. Now that too is not there. Before knowledge one was performing actions. After knowledge one was seemingly performing actions. After death, meaning when the body is no more, there is no one to even seemingly do; one is gone, once and for all.

Atra na asti saṁśayaḥ, here there is no doubt. *Atra*, here, means 'with reference to this.' It is not an assurance but purely a statement of fact. The *vastu* being eternal, there is no question of it being born. Once one knows oneself as that *vastu*, how can one be born? What is eternal cannot be born. Even before this

---

[18] See pages 69-72 – the discussion under the heading, 'one recognises one's identity with Īśvara.'

knowledge, one was eternal but one did not know this fact about oneself. Therefore, there was a false entity that accumulated *karma-phala* and required further births. Now one knows one's nature as *akartā*, and so there is no question of any future birth for him.

There is not one Īśvara before knowing and another one after knowing. All that is there is one *vastu*. The one who knows that reaches my nature, *mad-bhāvaṁ yāti*. There is no doubt or question whether one goes to *paramātmā* or not because one already is *paramātmā*. Where is then the question of his going to *paramātmā*?

Examining some popular concepts of mokṣa

The expression, '*mad-bhāvaṁ yāti*' has been subject to various interpretations. We need to understand the *śāstra* well and, to do so, we must be very clear about what *mokṣa* is.

One commentator interprets this verse as saying, 'The one who gives up the body thinking of me, Nārāyaṇa, goes to *vaikuṇṭha*.' According to him, going to heaven is *mokṣa*. *Vaikuṇṭha* can be replaced by any other concept of heaven. Since it is a popular concept, it is worth examining here.

Brahma-sāyujya is not mokṣa

The contention is that one goes to heaven and there he or she becomes one with Īśvara. If it is so, the following questions arise – who goes to *vaikuṇṭha*? If the one who goes is an individual, does he or she have a body? If one does not, it will be like sleep where there is no time or space and therefore, no travel at all. There is no possibility of going anywhere without a body. Besides this, different worlds are presented in the *śāstra* as physical places. Therefore, when one goes there, one must have a physical body. It may be a celestial body but it has got to be a body. A mere physical body will not be enough because it would be insentient. So, one must also have a subtle body; it is important. How can one become Nārāyaṇa with one's own subtle and gross bodies? With one's own body, one is entirely different from Nārāyaṇa. On the other hand, if one does not have one's own *sthūla-sūkṣma-śarīra*s, then where is the individual who is to become one with Nārāyaṇa?

Again, if the individual becomes a part of the Lord, then does the individual retain his or her individuality? If so, there is no *mokṣa*. The Lord is the Lord and the individual is the individual. If the individual dissolves in the Lord, how can the individual be real? Individuality must be *mithyā* in order to disappear. If that is so, then one is already not separate from the Lord. And the discovery of this fact is *mokṣa*. It is the real *brahma-sāyujya*, being one with Brahman. It is only a figure of speech. One is Brahman always even when one is ignorant of that fact.

Sāmīpya – nearness to Bhagavān – is not mokṣa

In another concept of *mokṣa*, the contention is that if one is pure enough, one is almost equal to the Lord and can therefore, go very near him. It is called *sāmīpya*. Nearness to Bhagavān is considered to be *mokṣa*. However, it cannot be *mokṣa*. Even though one may be near the Lord, someone else may be nearer.

One would naturally compare oneself with the other and experience pain. In other words, as long as one is a separate individual, one will be subject to degrees of pleasure and pain. This concept of *sāmīpya* again does not dissolve the individuality and therefore there is no possibility of total freedom.

Going to heaven is not mokṣa

Going to heaven of any denomination is not *mokṣa*. Sometimes the gain of heaven is referred to by the words *amṛta*, *mokṣa*, etc. But it is obvious that these words only point out a relative freedom from pain. Heaven, being a place reached by a person at a given time, the life therein is going to be within a time frame determined by one's own *puṇya*. That there is a heaven, one comes to know through the *śāstra*; and that very *śāstra* makes it clear that a sojourn in heaven is only a sojourn. It will be over when the cause, the *puṇya*, is exhausted. For a serious *mumukṣu*, heaven holds no attraction. When one is already free, that one should go to heaven is nothing but a confirmation of the original error. Even going to *brahma-loka* which is considered to be the greatest achievement in *saṁsāra*, is meaningless in the light of the fact that all the *loka*s are non-separate from Brahman and that Brahman is oneself. So, there is no *mokṣa* in any becoming that implies a change of body, place, and time. *Mokṣa* is here and now, not at another place, another time. This body-mind-sense complex does not in anyway stand opposed to *mokṣa*. In fact, the human *śarīra* is adequate enough to gain this *mokṣa*, which is in the form of knowing, 'I am Brahman.' And, Brahman is always free.

Mokṣa means freedom. That can only mean giving up something one already has. The body, mind and so on can be given up; but if they are given up, for whom is *mokṣa*? If it is for the physical body, from what does it require *mokṣa*?

Śruti says that the person who is free from a body is free from the desirable and the undesirable. None of the opposites touch him or her. If *mokṣa* means being free from the opposites, then it is not possible for anyone who has a body. Even if one has only a subtle body, one cannot have freedom from pleasure and pain. In a dream there is no physical body but there is pleasure and pain. In sleep it is not so. Only in the absence of a physical or subtle body is there no pleasure or pain. In their presence, there is *sukha* and *duḥkha*. This is the truth of the *jīva*. *Mokṣa* is to get rid of *sukha* and *duḥkha*. So, how can one call going to heaven *mokṣa*?

You may argue that once you make it to *vaikuṇṭha* you will experience only the desirable. But when the mind is active, all the properties of the mind will be there; desires will be there and depending on whether they are fulfilled, there will be varying degrees of *sukha* and *duḥkha*. Even though the present may not be affecting you, guilt and hurt lingering from past experiences will always be recollected. Such memory cannot be avoided and that alone is enough to create pleasure and pain.

To be unhappy, all you have to do is look around and see, who is next to you, who is in front of you, and so on. Then, comparison will be there, which is enough to make you feel miserable. At the very least you will be bored.

How can you call heaven a place of liberation? Even though the *śāstra* talks about *loka*s that are desirable, it does not say that going to one of them is *mokṣa*. It says that wherever you go, you will come back.

A serious *mumukṣu* will not wish for heaven but for a better chance next time. If he finds that in this body he is not able to understand, in this situation things are not conducive for him, he is going to wish for improved conditions for *mokṣa*, and not for heaven.

The *śruti* shows us that, in spite of having a body-mind-senses, we are free from them. *Ātmā* is not touched by *sukha* or *duḥkha*; its nature is *ānanda*. Since it is already free, *mokṣa* is knowledge, the knowledge, 'I am free from being the body.'

Impossibility of mokṣa when a form is involved

Madbhāva does not mean a form. *Bhāva* here means the essence of a thing. The essence of Īśvara is formlessness and *ātmā* is *sat-cit-ānanda*, also formless. Only then can there be identity. Two forms can never be identical.

One who knows the truth will understand Īśvara as having no particular form, the one to whom all forms belong. You know you are non-separate from Īśvara because the whole cannot be separate from anything. It is partless, limitless. Nor can there be any kind of relation between the individual and the whole because the whole is the individual; the individual is the whole. It is just like how between number 'one' and 'infinity' there is no relationship. 'One' can be divided into infinity and infinity includes all ones; so there is no relationship. If the Lord is whole, he cannot be separate from you. If he is separate from you, he becomes finite, not whole.

Any form you attribute to Īśvara is going to be less than Īśvara, because a given form will exclude all others. Generally one form is given and other forms are superimposed upon it. One name is given and other names are superimposed upon it.

We have varieties of *devatā*s and forms of worship. By all of them you can accomplish only *karma-phala*. So, there is no such thing as liberation through Īśvara with a form. There can only be the required grace whereby you can get a result within *saṁsāra*.

Mokṣa is knowledge

If the words of the *śāstra* are understood properly, the whole vision reduces itself to *ātmā*, *sat-cit-ānanda*. The one who knows this, knows the truth. To know something, you must see it as it is. If you know a rope as a rope you know the truth of it. Similarly, knowledge of the truth of Īśvara makes you a knower of Īśvara, rather than knower of a particular form. If you superimpose Bhagavān on a particular form, then it is for the purpose of worship. It is fine, but it is not knowing the truth. And without knowing the truth, there is no question of reaching Īśvara. Bhagavān says, only the *jñānī* reaches me; his *ātmā* is myself alone. This knowledge is *mokṣa*.

We need not give up meditation because its result can provide situations conducive to gaining knowledge of the nature of Parameśvara. You are a devotee in order to be free from being a devotee. It is true of any type of devotion. If you are devoted to getting into the White House, your devotion will end only when you are elected to the White House. When will you, the devotee of the Lord, fulfil your devotion? Only when you are the Lord. Therefore, the Lord says, 'The one who seeks me, who thinks of me at the end of his life, gains me.'

In the previous verse it was said that the one who thinks of Īśvara at the time of death reaches Īśvara. This logic is extended in the next verse to other objects.

यं यं वापि स्मरन्भावं त्यजत्यन्ते कलेवरम् ।
तं तमेवैति कौन्तेय सदा तद्भावभावितः ॥ ६ ॥

yaṁ yaṁ vāpi smaran bhāvaṁ tyajatyante kalevaram
taṁ tam evaiti kaunteya sadā tadbhāvabhāvitaḥ (6)

kaunteya – O son of Kuntī!; *ante* – at the time of death; *yaṁ yaṁ vā api bhāvam* – whatever thing; *smaran* – remembering; *kalevaram* – the physical body; *tyajati* – one gives up; *sadā* – always; *tadbhāva-bhāvitaḥ* – having thought about it; *taṁ tam eva* – that alone; *eti* – one reaches

Kaunteya (Arjuna)! At the time of death, remembering whatever thing one gives up the physical body, having thought about it always, one reaches that alone.

Whatever you are thinking of at the time of death, that alone you reach. It seems to be a very good arrangement. Suppose you want to go to heaven. According to the *śāstra*, you have to do good *karmas* your entire lifetime and avoid a lot of things. You want to go to heaven but do not want to give up anything or spend your time and energy doing the required rituals. You want to enjoy here and then go to heaven. So, you will do what you want here and at the time of death you will just think of heaven. Someone could think in this manner.

However, this thinking is not valid. The problem is, after living such a life, you will not think of heaven at the time of death. Whatever thought has dominated throughout your life, that alone will come to the forefront at the time of death. The thought patterns are conditioned. At the time of death, the deepest impressions in your psyche created by your own love and commitment to an object will bring that object to your mind. It will be in keeping with your cumulative thought life. Mere thinking is not enough; there should also be a relevant action. *Karma* is very important here. It is the result of the *karma* along with *saṁskāra* that produces the result. The idea is, if you have been working for a particular end, that end alone you achieve.

If you live your entire life for the sake of money, all that will occur in your mind at the time of death is the thought of money. In the next birth you will work for money again. It also applies to worship of a *devatā*. If you repeatedly invoke Indra, you will go to *indra-loka*. Whatever you think about, you work for and that alone you get. When you pursue Īśvara you become Īśvara because you are Īśvara. But if you think of any other end, you may gain that only if everything goes well.

Verse 7

Remember me at all times and do what is to be done

तस्मात्सर्वेषु कालेषु मामनुस्मर युध्य च ।
मय्यर्पितमनोबुद्धिर्मामेवैष्यस्यसंशयः ॥ ७ ॥

tasmāt sarveṣu kāleṣu mām anusmara yudhya ca
mayyarpitamanobuddhirmām evaiṣyasyasaṁśayaḥ (7)

tasmāt – therefore; *sarveṣu kāleṣu* – at all times; *mām anusmara* – remember me; *yudhya ca* – and fight; *mayi arpita-mano-buddhiḥ* – being one whose mind and intellect are offered unto me; *mām eva eṣyasi* – you will reach me alone; *asaṁśayaḥ*[19] – there is no doubt

Therefore, remember me at all times and fight. Being one whose mind and intellect are offered unto me, you will reach me alone. There is no doubt (in this).

Tasmāt sarveṣu kāleṣu mām anusmara, therefore at all times think of me. Here *kāla* is used in plural as *kāleṣu*, to indicate the seasons, and the day and night. In winter, summer, autumn and spring, throughout this year and the next, may you think of me.

Bhagavān says, *anusmara* and not merely *smara*. *Anu* means 'in keeping with something.' Therefore, Śaṅkara has commented on this word by adding '*yathā śāstram*, in keeping with the *śāstra*.' Thus the Lord says, 'Please think of me as you have learned from the *śāstra*.' There is no other way. You cannot

---

[19] असंशयः न संशयः अत्र विद्यते । (शङ्कर भाष्यम्)

think of Bhagavān unless you know something of him. Since it is a question of knowing Parameśvara as it is taught by the *śāstra*, may you pursue him all the time by *śravaṇa*, *manana* and *nididhyāsana*.

Yudhya ca, and fight. Think of me and fight. This is for Arjuna, but we have to extend it to ourselves. Arjuna's situation is a battle therefore, the Lord says, '*yudhya ca*, and fight.' But in our context this mandate refers to anything that is expected out of us under our circumstances, such as the daily prayers or whatever that needs to be done. 'Do your duty, play your roles and pursue me. In the process, you will come to know me,' says the Lord.

Let us assume Arjuna has come to know that *ātmā* is Brahman. Then he knows he is not a doer and will spontaneously do what has to be done. He does not need advice, nor does he need teaching. But Arjuna knows and does not know.[20] In this situation, *yoga* is important. So, Kṛṣṇa is telling Arjuna to be a *karma-yogī*.

If you are a *jñānī*, nothing is going to affect you. You can easily do what is to be done even though you have the freedom to do or not do anything. If you are an *ajñānī*, you had better follow the script of your role. It is the motive that is important here.

---

[20] Arjuna knows because the Lord has taught him in detail and has given the full vision that *ātmā* is indestructible. Therefore, one cannot say that he does not know. Yet he has doubts as is evident by the fact that he is asking questions. The doubts arise because he has not yet assimilated the knowledge.

It is like a servant performing his duties. Even though he is requested to do something he does not like, he will do it because his master motivates his actions. His own personal intentions and motives are relegated to the background and he does what is to be done. If the action is a pleasant one, there is no problem. But if it is a battle, as it was for Arjuna, it definitely requires an appreciation of *dharma*. For a *kṣatriya* like Arjuna, there is nothing better than a battle, which is in keeping with *dharma*, as Kṛṣṇa reminded him in the second chapter.[21] So may you do what is to be done. It is due to *dharma* alone that you are acting and *dharma* is the Lord. When you conform to *dharma*, you are with the Lord.

Mayi-arpita-mano-buddhiḥ, the one whose mind and intellect are offered unto me, Parameśvara. The seeker here is referred to as *mayi-arpita-mano-buddhiḥ*, the one whose mind and intellect are offered unto the Lord. How do you offer your mind and intellect to the Lord?

Situations call for certain actions. What is to be done becomes very obvious and relevant to that situation. There is a *saṅkalpa* in your mind, 'This is to be done.' It is because you did not create the situation nor did you create the sense of propriety that dictates the action. This was not the case with Duryodhana. He created this situation. But Arjuna has to meet it with proper action. That propriety is the order that is uncreated by man. This is what we call *dharma*. It is not Arjuna's creation, much

[21] *Gītā* 2.31

less Duryodhana's. That order creates the *saṅkalpa* in Arjuna that Duryodhana has to be punished. Against that is a *saṅkalpa* of his own that says, 'Why should I fight my own people?' It is not Bhagavān's *saṅkalpa*. It is a personal *saṅkalpa* born of Arjuna's affection. If it is offered unto *īśvara-saṅkalpa*, then he becomes a *mayi-arpita-manas*, the one whose mind has been offered unto the Lord. The *manas* here stands for the *saṅkalpa-śakti*.

What is referred to here by the word *buddhi* is your sense of doership – that I am a doer, I am doing something, I am the cause of some action and so on. Certain things are to be done, and in doing them you surrender your *ahaṅkāra*. *Buddhi*, here, can also mean your personal prejudices. The *buddhi* is also offered unto 'me' when one is engaged in the pursuit of 'me,' according to the *śāstra*. This person is a *mayi-arpita-buddhi*, the one whose *buddhi* has been offered unto the Lord. Thus, *buddhi* here stands for the sense of doership.

When the *buddhi* is offered in the pursuit of the truth of the Lord or in surrendering the notion of doership and the mind is offered unto the Lord in the form of *saṅkalpa*s conforming to *dharma*, one becomes *mayi-arpita-mano-buddhi*, the one whose mind and *buddhi* are offered unto the Lord. Such a person is not in conflict. One gains *antaḥ-karaṇa-śuddhi*, and it is not going to take time for such a person to understand that he or she is essentially non-separate from Īśvara.

Further, the Lord says, '*mām eva eṣyasi*, you will come to me alone.' How? You will come to recognise me and thereby become me. As already pointed out, the *jñānī* is non-separate from Parameśvara. When the Lord says, 'Those who think of me, reach me,' this is what he means. They discover their identity with Īśvara.

The Lord says, '*asaṁśayaḥ mām eṣyasi*, there is no doubt that you will reach me.' Although there is a promise here, it is not a prediction; it is a simple logical consequence. There is no way of it not happening. Unlike trying to reach a mountain, where anything can happen, it is you. So, it is only a question of clarity of the knowledge.

However, in the process of gaining clarity if one were to die, what would be the lot of this person? Kṛṣṇa has already promised that such a person will definitely pick up the thread in the next life and continue from where he left, *na hi kalyāṇakṛt kaścit durgatiṁ tāta gacchati*.[22] Even if one dies without understanding, there is nothing more valuable that one could have been doing. From the standpoint of an onlooker it is a tragedy. The person gave up everything in pursuit of this knowledge and then he or she did not get it. But one had grown out of everything else and was doing that which was most valuable to him or her.

One was happy that one was doing it, while one died. It is true of everyone. People pursue something or other and may die without completing what he or she set out to do. Someone who was making money does not die thinking, 'I have made all the money that I had set out to make. Now I can die.' Nobody dies thinking everything is over. Only a *jñānī* dies

---

[22] *Gītā* 6.40

having completed everything. He is the only one who dies in fullness because he knows he is non-separate from Parameśvara. There is no doubt about this.

Removal of three possible obstructions to mokṣa:

Ignorance

There are three possible obstructions for *mokṣa*. One is *āvaraṇa*, ignorance. The self is already free. So, you must only recognise the fact that you are identical with Brahman and therefore, free. Knowledge of this is *mokṣa* and what denies it is ignorance.

Impurity

For any knowledge to take place, the mind must be prepared. For knowledge of *ātmā*, lack of preparedness may be in two forms. One is *mala*, impurities gathered in previous births, which unfold as difficult situations in this birth. To neutralise these, you do daily duties and prayers. Powerful *rāga-dveṣa*s, likes and dislikes, also obstruct this knowledge and *karma* is again advocated to neutralise them.

Agitation

The other obstruction is agitation. Without a composed mind, enquiry cannot be done properly. The mind has to be rendered steady by meditation. Some of the more complicated forms of meditation require great concentration and will bring about steadiness. You also understand the ways of the mind as it keeps moving from one thing to another and you have to bring it back. In the process you gain steadiness.

Purity and steadiness of mind go together. As one increases, so does the other. *Karma* produces purification of the mind; meditation produces steadiness of mind. *Karma*, meditation and enquiry into the *śāstra* are the three means of dealing with the three obstructions.

In the next two verses, Kṛṣṇa talks about a person who meditates upon Parameśvara. There are different types of meditation apart from *nididhyāsana*, contemplation.

Two types of meditation – upāsana:

When a form is involved in meditation it is called *upāsana*. There are two types of *upāsana* – *sampat-upāsana* and *ahaṅgraha-upāsana*.

Sampat upāsana

In *sampat-upāsana*, a given object is looked upon as something more than it is. Two objects are involved, the one you know and the other you impose upon it. You may look upon the mind as Īśvara. In this form of meditation you impose upon an ordinary object something greater. This *sampat-upāsana* gives you steadiness of mind, a general result of any meditation. By this we mean absence of agitation, a state of mind wherein there is a capacity for absorption and a degree of inner composure. It is an immediate gain, *dṛṣṭa-phala*, a result that is seen.

Besides this, being a prayer, *sampat-upāsana* produces *adṛṣṭa-phala*, an unseen result. According to the *śāstra*, this is generally in the form of the gain of other *loka*s.

Ahaṅgraha-upāsana

In this second type of *upāsana*, Brahman, the cause of everything, is equated to *aham*, 'I.' But it is not pure knowledge because there is a *vṛtti* involved connecting two things. It is something like contemplation. So, it is at the level of *ahaṅkāra*. Since the *ahaṅkāra* is not negated, the recognition has not yet taken place.

The next two verses can be taken as *ahaṅgraha-upāsana* or as *nididhyāsana*. Let us look at them as *nididhyāsana*.

Verses 8&9

The meditator reaches the limitless self-effulgent parama-puruṣa

अभ्यासयोगयुक्तेन चेतसा नान्यगामिना ।
परमं पुरुषं दिव्यं याति पार्थानुचिन्तयन् ॥ ८ ॥

abhyāsayogayuktena cetasā nānyagāminā
paramaṁ puruṣaṁ divyaṁ yāti pārthānucintayan (8)

pārtha – O son of Pṛthā (Arjuna)!; *abhyāsa-yoga-yuktena cetasā* – with a mind endowed with the practice of *yoga*; *na anya-gāminā* – that does not stray to anything else; *anucintayan* – reflecting in keeping with the teaching; *paramaṁ divyaṁ puruṣam* – the limitless self-effulgent person; *yāti* – he reaches

Pārtha (Arjuna)! Reflecting in keeping with the teaching, with a mind endowed with the practice of *yoga* that does not stray to anything else, he reaches the limitless self-effulgent person.

The meditator goes to the limitless self-effulgent person, *paramaṁ divyaṁ puruṣaṁ yāti*. *Puruṣa* means a person, and he is *parama*. So, there is no possibility of him being anything less than the limitless person who is everything, from whom nothing is separate.

He is *divya*. Two meanings are possible here for the word *divya*. One who is born in heaven, a celestial, is called *divya*. Or it means the one who is all-effulgent Parameśvara who is essentially the meaning of the word 'I.' The meditator goes for that. How does he achieve it?

Anu-cintayan, by contemplating. *Cintayan* means doing enquiry, contemplating, or meditating. *Anu* means 'according to the *śāstra*.' Contemplating on the words of the *śāstra* in keeping with what is understood through the *śāstra-pramāṇa* is *anu-cintana*. As a student listens to the words of the teacher, his mind follows the thought process that takes place, he is doing *anu-cintana*. The teacher is also doing *anu-cintana* because he follows the *śāstra*.

The object of this contemplation is also shown by the words, *paramaṁ puruṣaṁ divyam*. And the result is that he goes to that same *puruṣa* because *ātmā* happens to be that *paramaṁ puruṣam*. He contemplates upon the infinite, and there is no contemplation upon the infinite minus the person or anything else.

Here, thinking, contemplating is just seeing a fact that you have already come to know through the *śāstra*. It may be preceded by a few steps of thinking given by the *śāstra*, which are conducive to arriving at its vision. Seeing naturally implies a mind. So, he points out the kind of mind that is required.

Abhyāsa-yoga-yuktena na anya-gāminā cetasā. Cetasā means 'by the mind.' Two adjectives are given to describe the mind, *abhyāsa-yoga-yuktena cetasā,* by a mind that is endowed with *abhyāsa,* practice, which itself is *yoga. Na anya-gāminā cetasā,* by a mind that does not go to anything else.

Only the chosen object is allowed to occupy the mind; anything else is dismissed as it arises. It is important to note that the meditation does not cease when other thoughts arise. If that were to be the case, meditation would not be possible. When you meditate upon a given object, there is always the possibility of getting distracted, which is why you meditate. As we saw in the sixth chapter, whenever the mind strays from the chosen object of meditation, you bring it back, *yato yato niścarati... tatastato niyamyaitat...,*[23] bringing the mind back to the object of meditation is also part of meditation.

When Arjuna told Kṛṣṇa that the mind itself is agitation and he did not think he could do anything about it,[24] Kṛṣṇa agreed with him. Then he told him that it could be managed by *vairāgya* and *abhyāsa.*[25] This is the *abhyāsa* meant here. He emphasises it by saying *yoga,* which is another word that means the same thing. *Yoga* is *abhyāsa* and *abhyāsa* is *yoga,* a means for gaining mastery over the mind.

This meditator contemplates upon the *puruṣa,* who is limitless and all effulgent. And he comes to identify himself as that *puruṣa.*

---

[23] *Gītā* 6.26

[24] *Gītā* 6.34

[25] *Gītā* 6.35

कविं पुराणमनुशासितारमणोरणीयांसमनुस्मरेद्यः ।
सर्वस्य धातारमचिन्त्यरूपमादित्यवर्णं तमसः परस्तात् ॥ ९ ॥

kavim̐ purāṇam anuśāsitāram
aṇoraṇīyām̐sam anusmared yaḥ
sarvasya dhātāram acintyarūpam
ādityavarṇam̐ tamasaḥ parastāt (9)

kavim – the one who is omniscient; *purāṇam* – the most ancient; *anuśāsitāram* – the one who rules (everything); *aṇoḥ aṇīyām̐sam* – the one who is subtler than the subtlest; *sarvasya dhātāram* – the one who ordains all; *acintya-rūpam* – whose form cannot be conceived of; *āditya-varṇam* – whose form is effulgent like the sun; *tamasaḥ parastāt* – the one who is beyond ignorance (and knowledge); *yaḥ anusmaret* – the one who contemplates upon; (*saḥ* – he; *paramam̐ puruṣam̐ divyam* – the limitless self-effulgent person; *yāti* – reaches)[26]

> The one who contemplates upon the being who is omniscient, the most ancient, who is the ruler, who is subtler than the subtlest, ordainer of all, whose form cannot be conceived of, who is effulgent like the sun, who is beyond ignorance (and knowledge), (he reaches the limitless self-effulgent person.)

Yaḥ anusmaret, the one who properly meditates upon. *Smaraṇa*, recalling, is only possible when you have come to know something. *Anu-smaraṇa* is in keeping with what is

---

[26] This verse connects to the previous verse in this manner. The words that connect are taken from the previous verse.

already known to you. So, the meaning of this statement is 'the one who contemplates after *śravaṇa* and *manana.*'

He meditates upon Parameśvara who is described by the following words:

Kavi, the one who sees through. *Kavi* is an excellent word for Parameśvara. It also means poet because a poet sees something more than what meets the eye. Here Bhagavān is called *kavi* not because he sees something more; but because he sees everything – past, present and future. *Kavi* here means the one who is all-knowledge.

Purāṇa, the one who is ancient, in fact, who is eternal.

Anuśāsitā, the one who rules the whole creation, because of whom the law of *dharma* and other laws in the creation exist.

Aṇoḥ aṇīyān, the one who is subtler than the subtlest thing you can ever conceive of. Anything that you can conceive of, even the subtlest concept, is an object of thought, but what is contemplated upon here is the one because of whom that subtlest of thoughts is known.

Sarvasya dhātā, the one who is the ordainer of everything. A person who meditates upon Īśvara in this manner comes to recognise oneself as the upholder of this cause-effect relationship, the giver of the fruits of all actions. Previously he was only an agent, subject to ups and downs of the results of his actions as they were given by Īśvara's law of *karma*. By contemplating upon the *svarūpa* of Parameśvara, he identified himself as Parameśvara who is *sat-cit-ānanda-ātmā*.

Acintya-rūpa, the one whose form cannot be thought of. What you cannot think about can also be non-existent. But here it is existent. If you take it as the one who is in the form of creation, how are you going to think about him? There is the known as well as the unknown.

How are you going to imagine or even appreciate omniscience or all-pervasiveness, the one whose form is the whole creation? Your mind is capable of thinking of only one thing at a given time. It is not possible for a human mind to imagine everything at the same time. If you look at Īśvara's own *svarūpa* as *ātmā*, he is not available for objectification. It is *caitanya*, as the next word reveals.

Āditya-varṇa, the one who has the appearance of the sun. The form of the sun is nothing but light. It is not a light that comes and goes; it is always in the form of light; and it illumines everything. Similarly, this *puruṣa* is in the form of consciousness, which is not subject to increase and decrease. Like the sun, it always illumines without any motive or intention. When we say it illumines everything, we are using a verb. It implies an agent. But here there is no agency involved; its essential nature is to shine. Like the sun, it illumines anything in front of it. Without doership, self-shining *ātmā* illumines the entire creation. Everything shines after it. It is *asaṅga*, untouched by what happens in its light.

Tamasaḥ parastāt, it is above darkness. It illumines both light and darkness. It illumines particular knowledge as well as ignorance. It is pure consciousness.

The difference between contemplation and meditation

The verb '*yāti*' is carried through from the previous verse. Everything else in this verse talks of the object of meditation, and also what you gain.

In contemplation there is no difference between what you meditate upon and what you get. If you are doing *upāsana*, the result is not going to be the same as what you meditate upon. If you invoke Indra, you will not become Indra. You will only go to another *loka*.

However, here the one who meditates upon *parama-puruṣa* reaches *parama-puruṣa*. This is not meditation wherein there is a knower-known difference. However small the difference may be, if there is a difference, it would be *upāsana*. If there is no difference, the knower is recognised as Parameśvara; therefore, there is no knower in reality.

All these words are appellations of Īśvara and that indeed I am. This is pure *jñāna*, which is why *nididhyāsana* is entirely different from *upāsana*. In *upāsana*, *jīva* and Īśvara are two different things, whether it is *sampat-upāsana* or *ahaṅgraha-upāsana*, where you superimpose Īśvara's attributes on the *jīva*. Even so, it can pave the way for *jñāna* and is therefore considered a fruitful meditation. Contemplation, however, based on *śravaṇa* and *manana* is entirely different from any type of meditation.

If what you have understood is somehow contradicted by experience, *nididhyāsana* is to be done. *Śāstra* says that you are *sat-cit-ānanda*. If you do not think so, you are making a judgement about yourself on the basis of your mind; you require further enquiry. Until you understand, you must study the *śāstra* which is the *pramāṇa*. Vedanta reveals that you are the whole. So, you cannot say that you have studied Vedanta and are now turning your attention to something else to fulfil yourself.

If you say that in spite of knowing *ātmā*, you do not see that you are *ānanda*; logically it cannot be true. But experientially there seems to be a condition wherein there is knowledge and at the same time, some problem in owning up the knowledge. You cannot say you do not know, nor can you say you know that you are Brahman, because you have problems. You have to eliminate the obstruction, which is a condition of the mind that seems to stand against the very knowledge that you are free. That knowledge seems to be affected by a process of habitual thinking which you take care of in a variety of ways; the main way is *nididhyāsana*.

Contemplation upon the knowledge, 'I am Īśvara' is not an action. Wherever a statement of fact is repeated or contemplated upon, no result is produced because it is *siddha-viṣaya*, an already accomplished fact. This is important to know. An already accomplished fact is not the result of an action because it is not produced. *Karma* can produce, modify, cleanse, or help you reach something.[27] The fact is *ātmā* is Brahman. It is a

[27] *Karma* can be of the following four types – *utpādya*, that which produces something; *vikārya*, that which modifies something; *saṁskārya*, that which cleanses something; *āpya*, that which helps one to reach something

statement of fact like saying, 'Fire is hot.' This fact is not produced, and therefore not a result of *karma*. As a statement of fact, it is to be merely understood. Similarly the statement, 'I am Brahman,' is a statement of fact that needs to be understood. There is nothing to be accomplished by *karma* here. *Śravaṇa, manana* and *nididhyāsana* are the three-fold means to understand this and it is adequate. *Nididhyāsana* is contemplation in keeping with the *śāstra*. Therefore, Kṛṣṇa says here that the one who contemplates on Parameśvara in this manner, that is, in keeping with what is said in the *śāstra*, reaches that Parameśvara, *yaḥ kaviṁ purāṇam... anusmaret saḥ paramaṁ puruṣaṁ yāti*. This is knowledge.

Kṛṣṇa starts by saying that the one who knows him as Īśvara, being always in him, comes to him after death. There is no rebirth for this person. And another person who contemplates upon him as Īśvara, having gained from *śāstra* the knowledge that *ātmā* is Parameśvara, contemplates upon that. He is the *parama-puruṣa* that he is contemplating upon and he too does not come back after death.

Then there is another person for whom the contemplation is coupled with *yoga*, specifically *prāṇāyāma*. He is discussed in the next verse. He also reaches Īśvara because of his contemplation.

All these possibilities are mentioned because there are obstructions which are different for different people. And they have to be tackled differently depending on the person. A seeker uses *yoga*, various forms of *upāsana*, and anything else that is necessary to remove obstructions.

Verse 10

The lot of a yogī at the time of death

प्रयाणकाले मनसाचलेन भक्त्या युक्तो योगबलेन चैव ।
भ्रुवोर्मध्ये प्राणमावेश्य सम्यक् स तं परं पुरुषमुपैति दिव्यम् ॥ १० ॥

prayāṇakāle manasācalena
bhaktyā yukto yogabalena caiva
bhruvormadhye prāṇam āveśya samyak
sa taṁ paraṁ puruṣam upaiti divyam (10)

prayāṇa-kāle – at the time of death; *acalena manasā* – with a steady mind; *bhaktyā yuktaḥ* – endowed with devotion; *yoga-balena ca* – and with the strength gathered by *yoga*; *bhruvoḥ madhye* – between the brows; *prāṇam āveśya samyak* – placing the breath properly; *saḥ* – he; *taṁ paraṁ puruṣaṁ divyam* – that limitless effulgent person; *upaiti* – reaches

> At the time of death, with a steady mind, endowed with devotion and the strength gathered by *yoga*, placing the breath properly between the brows, he indeed reaches that limitless effulgent person.

This entire discussion deals with the lot of a seeker at the time of death. A *yogī* is someone who can give up his life at will. Because of the strength of his *yoga*, he is able to stop the flow of *prāṇa* when he wishes to die. While he lives, he leaves the *prāṇa*, that is, stops the functioning of the *prāṇa* while contemplating upon *ātmā*. It was very clear to him while he was alive that he was *sat-cit-ānanda-ātmā*, and therefore he was free. But he still had *kartṛtva* because he used his will for death.

So, he will go to *brahma-loka* and will be taught by Brahmaji and gain *mokṣa*. This is called *krama-mukti.*

Prayāṇa-kāle means 'at the time of travel or departure.' Death is referred to as departure here. How does he die? *Acalena-manasā,* with a mind that does not waver, that is not distracted. And he is *bhaktyā yuktaḥ,* endowed with devotion to the *puruṣa* he is contemplating upon. This is a person who has great love for the *ātmā* he contemplates upon. For him there is no other love.

How does he wilfully stop his *prāṇa*? *Yoga-balena ca eva,* with the strength of his *yoga* practice alone. Śaṅkara says, *yoga-bala* is steadiness of mind born of his practice of absorption, the culmination of his practice of *aṣṭāṅga-yoga.*

The object of meditation produces a *saṁskāra* in the mind and with repeated meditation, the *saṁskāra* deepens. For a *mumukṣu,* the only object of meditation is *ātmā*. Here he has a *yoga-bala* that is due to the *saṁskāra* arising from repeated practice of absorption. This is a person who has lived his life in the practice of *yoga* along with the pursuit of knowledge. At the time of death, what does such a person do?

Bhruvoḥ madhye prāṇam āveśya samyak. First he brings his mind to his heart, the core of the self. He imagines a location on the right side of the heart that is looked upon as the seat of *ahaṅkāra*. It is purely a visualisation; but it does bring the mind to a state of absorption. Even when chanting a *mantra,* if you imagine that the *mantra* comes from there, the chanting is much more absorbing.

Then he stops his *prāṇa,* that is, stops breathing. He inhales and does not exhale. Śaṅkara supplies the word *nāḍī,* a technical term from *yoga* for a kind of nerve. He visualises a *nāḍī* going through the heart to the place between the eyebrows. Emitting the *prāṇa* through this *nāḍī*, placing it between the brows, he stops it there and does not exhale. And thus gives up his life.

When he does so, *paraṁ puruṣam upaiti*, he reaches the limitless person. Because of this expression we understand that he is a *vidvān* and a *yogī*.

So far, Bhagavān has talked about those who contemplate upon Brahman directly. There are others who use a symbol to arrive at contemplation. This he introduces in the next verse.

Verse 11

The end which does not decline – the knowers of Veda talk about this

यदक्षरं वेदविदो वदन्ति विशन्ति यद्यतयो वीतरागाः ।
यदिच्छन्तो ब्रह्मचर्यं चरन्ति तत्ते पदं सङ्ग्रहेण प्रवक्ष्ये ॥ ११ ॥

yadakṣaraṁ vedavido vadanti
viśanti yad yatayo vītarāgāḥ
yadicchanto brahmacaryaṁ caranti
tatte padaṁ saṅgraheṇa pravakṣye (11)

yat akṣaram – that which does not decline (about which); *vedavidaḥ* – the knowers of Veda; *vadanti* – talk about; *yat* – that which; *yatayaḥ* – those who make effort (renunciates); *vīta-rāgāḥ* – who are free from desire; *viśanti* – enter; *yadicchantaḥ* – desiring which; *brahmacaryaṁ caranti* – people follow a life of study and discipline; *tat padam* – that end; *saṅgraheṇa* – briefly; *te pravakṣye* – I will tell you

I will tell you briefly about that end, which does not decline, about which the knowers of Veda talk about, which the renunciates, free from desire, enter, and desiring which people follow a life of study and discipline.

The first quarter of this verse is similar to the one in *Bṛhadāraṇyakopaniṣad*[28] and the second quarter to one in *Kaṭhopaniṣad.*[29] That end, which the Vedas talk about, desiring which people take to a life of discipleship, I am going to tell you briefly. That is *om*. The same thing is going to be said here in three verses.

Yad-akṣaraṁ vedavido vadanti. Vedavit means those who know the Veda, not merely how to recite but the meaning of the Veda. There is a mandate that everyone should study one's own Veda, either the *Ṛgveda, Sāmaveda, Yajurveda* or *Atharvaveda – svādhyāyo adhyetavyaḥ*. Mere recitation of the Veda is also called *adhyayana*. But a *vidhi*, rule, is only complete when the result is realised. Veda is a *pramāṇa* and has the capacity to reveal knowledge which has a result. After learning to recite, one must analyse the sentences until one understands the entire *śāstra*, especially *vedānta-śāstra*. Until that time, one has not fulfilled the *vidhi*. Its force applies until one knows, '*ahaṁ brahma asmi*, I am Brahman.' So, *vedavit* is the one who knows the meaning of the Veda.

Brahman is *akṣara*, that which is not subject to destruction, not being bound by time. Those who know the Veda talk about this.

---

[28] 3.8.8

[29] 1.2.15

In the *Bṛhadāraṇyakopaniṣad*, Yājñavalkya teaches Gārgī what *akṣaraṁ-brahma* is.[30] It is neither big, nor small, nor short, nor tall; thus it is free from all attributes. *Akṣaraṁ-brahma* is not an object, nor is it something to be gained in the usual sense. It is not to be experienced, but to be known.

Yadicchantaḥ brahmacaryaṁ caranti, desiring to know this, people live a life of *brahmacarya*, a life of discipline in the presence of the teacher. That discipline implies study, meditation, *mantra-japa* and so on.

*Yat yatayaḥ vīta-rāgāḥ viśanti. Yati*s are those who are capable of right effort. One of the principal things that is required for this knowledge is renunciation. So, a person who gives up all other pursuits and dedicates his life to this pursuit is called a *yati*; he is a *sannyāsī*. They are free from powerful likes and dislikes because they are not interested in security and pleasure. They are committed to *mokṣa*.

Tat te padaṁ saṅgraheṇa pravakṣye, I will tell you briefly that end which is to be accomplished in terms of knowledge. *Padam* means the end that is to be accomplished. It also means that which is the most worshipful. Here, *mokṣa* is the ultimate end and also the most worshipful.

Śaṅkara introduces the next two verses discussing *oṁkāra, praṇava*. It is introduced for the first time in the *Bhagavadgītā*. So, Śaṅkara makes a note here.

---

30 एतद्वै तदक्षरं गार्गि ब्राह्मणा अभिवदन्ति । (3.8.8)

Om as a word for contemplation

Om is a word for Brahman. Just as when you hear the word pot, a meaning strikes you, so too with *om*. If you know the meaning, it registers when you hear the word *om*. Then *om* becomes a *vācaka,* name, and Brahman becomes *vācya,* what is named.

In general, between a word and its meaning, there is a permanent connection, *vācya-vācaka-sambandha*. For example, the word apple is a *vācaka* and the object apple, the *vācya*. It is not quite the same with the name of a person. Like John can mean anybody. John is not a *vācaka* in the same sense that apple is. It has no real *vācya* in that, there is no permanent *vācya vācaka sambandha*. John is a word that brings to mind a given person whom you know. It serves as a *vācaka* if you know it is the name of a person you know. Similarly, the *śāstra* has named Brahman as *om*. If you have studied the *śāstra*, you recognise Brahman by the name *om*. The *śāstra* says that *ātmā*, the conscious being, is Brahman and that Brahman is *om*. You contemplate upon the meaning of *om* as yourself being everything. Then *om* takes the mind to contemplation, not meditation. But if you contemplate upon the meaning of *om* as Īśvara, then it becomes *dhyāna,* meditation, *saguṇa-brahma-upāsana*.

In meditation there are two types of symbols. One is *pratīka,* verbal, the other is *pratīmā,* a tangible physical form. Upon either of these you can superimpose a concept of Īśvara and worship that symbol as Īśvara. In this type of meditation Īśvara is always *parokṣa*.

Meditation with om as a pratīka

Om can also be a sound symbol, a *pratīka*. Then it means *aparaṁ-brahma*. It is purely a symbol upon which you superimpose your indirect knowledge of Īśvara. Because there is no knowledge, it is no longer a *vācaka*; it is purely for *upāsana* which has the result of taking you to *brahma-loka*. There, Brahmaji may teach you if you are a *mumukṣu* and if you have enough *puṇya*. Or you will return to a human birth and pick up the thread.

In the *Praśnopaniṣad,* [31] Satyakāma asks his *guru* what kind of *loka* a person will gain if he meditates upon *om* and he is told that *oṁkāra* can represent both *paraṁ-brahma* and *aparaṁ-brahma*. It is *apara* if it is a *pratīka,* a symbol for *parokṣa-īśvara*. It is *para* if it is contemplated upon as *paramātmā* who is identical with *pratyagātmā*.

Each letter, as we have seen, represents one of the three states of experience. When *oṁkāra* is chanted, the last letter, *makāra*, resolves into silence, which is pure consciousness, neither waker, dreamer nor sleeper. From that silence the *akāra* rises. When you chant *om*, the word is pervaded by consciousness, which itself is not affected by *akāra, ukāra* or *makāra*; A, U or M. Everything resolves in that which is neither waker-consciousness, nor dreamer-consciousness, nor in between-consciousness, nor sleeper-consciousness, nor unconsciousness; this is what is called consciousness which is *ātmā*, *om*, the *vācaka* for Brahman.

---

[31] 5.1 to 5.5

In *Kaṭhopaniṣad*, Naciketas asks about that which is above *dharma* and *adharma*, above cause and effect. Lord Yama answers in a way that is similar to what is mentioned here. But in other places, *oṁkāra* is presented as a symbol for *upāsana* for those who do not understand *paraṁ-brahma* as it was taught to them.

Since the *Gītā-śāstra* is dealing with the various forms of departure here, the one who meditates upon *om* is discussed. If he meditates on *om* as a symbol, there is travel and further birth; if he contemplates and understands it, there is no further travel.

Verses 12&13

Meditation upon om and its result

सर्वद्वाराणि संयम्य मनो हृदि निरुध्य च ।
मूर्ध्न्याधायात्मनः प्राणमास्थितो योगधारणाम् ॥ १२ ॥

ओमित्येकाक्षरं ब्रह्म व्याहरन्मामनुस्मरन् ।
यः प्रयाति त्यजन्देहं स याति परमां गतिम् ॥ १३ ॥

sarvadvārāṇi saṁyamya mano hṛdi nirudhya ca
mūrdhnyādhāyātmanaḥ prāṇamāsthito yogadhāraṇām (12)

omityekākṣaraṁ brahma vyāharan mām anu-smaran
yaḥ prayāti tyajan dehaṁ sa yāti paramāṁ gatim (13)

sarva-dvārāṇi – all the gates of perceptions (sense organs); *saṁyamya* – closing; *manaḥ* – the mind; *hṛdi* – into the heart; *nirudhya ca* – and withdrawing; *ātmanaḥ prāṇam* – one's breath; *mūrdhni* – at the top of one's head; *ādhāya* – placing; *yoga-*

dhāraṇām āsthitaḥ (*san*) – being the one who remains holding (breath) by *yoga; om iti eka-akṣaraṁ brahma* – the single syllable *om* (which is) Brahman; *vyāharan* – chanting; *mām anu-smaran* – remembering me; *dehaṁ tyajan* – giving up the body; *yaḥ prayāti* – the one who departs; *saḥ* – he; *paramāṁ gatiṁ yāti* – goes to the most exalted end

> Closing all the gates of perception (sense organs), withdrawing the mind into the heart, placing one's breath at the top of one's head, being the one who remains holding (one's breath) by *yoga*, chanting the single syllable *om*, which is Brahman, giving up the body, the one who departs remembering me, goes to the most exalted end.

This is the *yogī* who meditates on *oṁkāra.*

Sarva-dvārāṇi saṁyamya, having closed all the gates. The gates are the ways through which the world enters into you, the sense organs. The person discussed here is a *yogī*, not a *jñānī*. A *yogī* has to shut out everything and then concentrate. A *jñānī* may shut out the world or may not; because he knows his vision has changed. Here the meditator is sitting in a relaxed posture with all his senses withdrawn.

Mano hṛdi nirudhya ca, and taking the mind inward. In fact, this is all you really have to do, to withdraw the senses from their pursuits. Just turn the mind towards yourself.

Ātmanaḥ prāṇam mūrdhni ādhāya, placing one's *prāṇa* at the top of one's head, one does not allow the breath to be exhaled.

Om iti eka-akṣaraṁ brahma vyāharan, chanting the single syllable *om*, which is the name of Brahman, *mām anu-smaran*, thinking of me, Īśvara, one continues to hold one's breath at the top of one's head. And continuing to hold one's breath in this way, *yoga-dhāraṇām āsthitaḥ dehaṁ tyajan*, giving up one's body, *yaḥ prayāti*, the one who departs, *saḥ paramāṁ gatim yāti*, he goes to the most exalted end.

Death is only for the body, not for the *jīva*. The *jīva* keeps travelling until he knows he is *ātmā*, which is eternal. Then the *jīvatva*, the superimposition upon *ātmā*, dies. The *jīva* does not die at any time because the truth of the *jīva* is *ātmā*.

So, the one who leaves his body in this manner, goes to the most exalted end. The word '*prayāti*' can indicate travel. Kṛṣṇa says, 'Because of his great meditation, holding his breath, thinking of me and chanting *om*, he leaves this body and goes straight to *brahma-loka*.' There he asks Brahmaji for this knowledge. Brahmaji teaches him the *ātma-jñāna* and he is released. *Paramā gati* is the end, which is the discovery of the self being Brahman. This is *mokṣa*, but gained in *brahma-loka* and it is called *krama-mukti*.

Verse 14

I am easily gained for the one who constantly remembers me

अनन्यचेताः सततं यो मां स्मरति नित्यशः ।
तस्याहं सुलभः पार्थ नित्ययुक्तस्य योगिनः ॥ १४ ॥

ananyacetāḥ satataṁ yo māṁ smarati nityaśaḥ
tasyāhaṁ sulabhaḥ pārtha nityayuktasya yoginaḥ (14)

pārtha – O Pārtha!; *ananya-cetāḥ* (*san*) – being the one whose mind sees no other; *yaḥ* – the one who; *nityaśaḥ* – for a length of time; *satatam* – constantly; *mām* – me; *smarati* – remembers; *tasya yoginaḥ* – for that *yogī*; *nitya-yuktasya* – who is always united with me; *ahaṁ sulabhaḥ* – I am easily gained

> Pārtha (Arjuna)! The one who has a mind that sees no other, who remembers me constantly, for a length of time, for that *yogī* who is always united with me, I am easily gained.

Ananya-cetas, the one whose mind is not in any object or *devatā* other than oneself. This particular expression is used throughout the *Gītā*. *Anya* means another. So, *anya-cetas* is one whose mind is committed to an object other than himself whether it is *dharma, artha, kāma* or even Īśvara as someone other than oneself. The one who does not look upon Īśvara or anything else as other than oneself is *ananya-cetas*. How long must one contemplate?

The Lord says *satatam*, constantly. *Satataṁ yaḥ māṁ smarati*, the one who always remembers me. The word '*smaraṇa*' is used here because you can only bring back to mind what you already know. This *smaraṇa* is always preceded by *śravaṇa*. It means dwelling upon something and implies contemplation, *satsaṅga, manana* and even *śravaṇa*. The person spoken of here has undergone exposure to the *śāstra* and analysed it but still has the orientation that he is the body, *deha-ātma-buddhi*.

We have seen the difference between confusion and an orientation.[32] A simple confusion requires clarification only once. An orientation or habitual error requires repeated correction.

---

[32] See Vol 5 - page 399, under ' An orientation can persist after knowledge.'

Here the *deha-ātma-buddhi*, the notion that the body is 'I,' and 'I' am the body, is such an orientation, which is why even when the confusion is resolved by the *śāstra*, you continue to have problems that are due to this identification. It is because, this notion has prevailed for a long time. When you have lived your entire life with the notion that you are the body, how are you going to remove it just because somebody said, '*tat tvam asi*?' The orientation has to go, and for that constant *smaraṇa* of the fact that 'I am Brahman' or *brahma-abhyāsa*, as we saw before, is necessary. You must constantly dwell upon this knowledge until the orientation is corrected.

Since *satatam* means 'always,' the question arises as to why has Bhagavān used *nityaśaḥ*, which also means 'always.' It is because the word *satatam* is used in the sense of 'constantly, without any interval.' So, by using this word the one who constantly remembers Īśvara, that is, the one who spends one's time in contemplation, thinking, teaching, discussing, the one who is thus constantly in *satsaṅga* is being indicated here. But 'constantly' can be for one day, a week, or longer. So, Bhagavān adds another word, '*nityaśaḥ*,' which also means 'always.' The affix '*śas*' conveys either the sense of abundance or limitation. Therefore, the use of the word *nityaśaḥ* indicates that one contemplates until one requires no more contemplation, which is why the meaning given for this word is 'for a length of time,' instead of 'always.'

Bhagavān continues and says, '*tasya yoginaḥ ahaṁ sulabhaḥ*, for that *yogī* I am easily gained. *Sulabha* means the one who is gained without any difficulty. A number of arguments can be given as to why the Lord is easily gained.

Anything that you want to accomplish requires effort. No matter how small the effort, if at all it requires effort, it is not considered *sulabha*. Now the gain of Brahman is the maximum possible gain. You cannot exceed limitlessness. Your orientation is, greater the gain, greater the effort required to achieve it. But here, the greatest possible gain is said to be easily gained.

To gain Brahman, Bhagavān says here, you must dwell upon Brahman, the source of all love. What effort do you require to dwell upon what you love? Loving does not require any effort; it is very natural. At least, if it is an object, you have to bring it to your mind. But here it is you; *ātmā* is Parameśvara. Therefore, there is nothing to be desired. *Ātmā*'s nature is fullness; so, dwelling upon that is joyous.

Nothing new is produced either. So, it is not born of any effort. It is born purely of recognition of the fact because it is an already accomplished fact. No production is involved. Nothing new is added. Nothing old is removed. Who is that *yogī*?

A nitya-yukta's mind is always tranquil

A *nitya-yukta* is one who is endowed with a mind that is always tranquil. It is under control, in the sense that, it does not have any problem in dwelling upon Bhagavān. It is something that is natural to him. Whenever the mind is free it goes towards Bhagavān.

It is like a person who is in love. His mind always goes naturally towards the beloved. Here the mind naturally goes towards *paramātmā* because he has understood it, as the word *smaraṇa* indicates. Where else will the mind go? Until he gains such a mind, he continues to do *śravaṇa* and uses his will to dwell upon the Lord. Later the very subject matter takes over and he does not require any will. All that is required is the initial choice. Being one who is *ananya-cetas*, whose mind is committed to Parameśvara, he remains absorbed.

Verse 15

One recognises one's identity with Īśvara

मामुपेत्य पुनर्जन्म दुःखालयमशाश्वतम् ।
नाप्नुवन्ति महात्मानः संसिद्धिं परमां गताः ॥ १५ ॥

mām upetya punarjanma duḥkhālayam aśāśvatam
nāpnuvanti mahātmānaḥ saṁsiddhiṁ paramāṁ gatāḥ (15)

mahātmānaḥ – the wise men; *upetya* – having reached; *mām* – me; *duḥkha-ālayam* – the abode of misery; *aśāśvatam* – finite; *punar-janma* – another birth; *na āpnuvanti* – do not gain; *paramāṁ saṁsiddhim* – the ultimate success; *gatāḥ* – (they) have reached

Having reached me, the wise men do not gain another birth, which is the abode of misery and is finite; they have reached the ultimate success.

Mām upetya, gaining me. Here *upetya* means reaching in the sense of being of the same nature. How is it possible?

If there are two objects, one cannot assume the nature of the other. Each has its own attributes. If one becomes the other, the nature of one or both of them is destroyed. For example, if you add water to milk, you will have a liquid of a different density from either of the original components. Therefore, one object cannot gain identity with another. An object enjoying its own attributes cannot enter into another and remain the same object.

Suppose one *bhāva*, object, is indeed the other *bhāva*. Then the separation is only due to ignorance. It is the situation here. Ignorance is the cause of separation between Īśvara and *jīva*. And there is an orientation, which is also a product of ignorance. Therefore, dwelling on Parameśvara is only to attack that ignorance and to remove that orientation. Gaining identity with Bhagavān is possible because it is an already accomplished fact.

Undesirability of further births

Kṛṣṇa says further, '*punar-janma na āpnuvati*, they do not gain rebirth.' Two more words tell us the nature of this *punar-janma*.

You may think it would be desirable to be born again, in a better situation, of course. The problem is, you will have the same struggle in one form or another because, to be born, you must necessarily be ignorant. No one is afraid of another birth, but only the pain. So, Bhagavān makes it clear here.

He says that every birth is an abode of pain, *duḥkha-ālayam*. *Ālaya* is a place, and *duḥkha* means pain. There are three types of pain, as we have seen. *Ādhyātmika,* pain caused by your own body-mind-senses; *ādhibhautika,* by the beings around you; and *ādhidaivika,* by unknown forces over which you have no control whasoever. Another definition of the physical body is therefore, *duḥkha-ālaya,* an abode of pain. One thing or another is always in trouble. If everything else is all right, you need at least some dental work! Like even a car the body requires constant maintenance. You have to make sure it has fuel and water. You have to check the parts and if there is some problem you have to take it to the garage, the hospital. And you need insurance in case of accidents.

Suppose you go to heaven where there is no *duḥkha,* because the physical body you will have there, would not be subject to any pain. To cover that, Bhagavān has another word, *aśāsvatam;* it is not eternal. Even if you gain a celestial body, it is not eternal, and you have to reincarnate with a body that is subject to pain. Although in a celestial body, there will not be predominance of pain, there will be some kind of pain. As long as you are an individual, some trace of pain will be there because of the isolation of being a *jīva.* Eventually, even a celestial body has to be given up because the *puṇya* that has taken and kept you there is exhausted or the abode, heaven, which is also a part of creation, is itself destroyed.

Who are freed from this kind of birth and rebirth? *Mahātmānaḥ* are those whose *ātmā* is *paraṁ-brahma.* They gain the ultimate success, *paramāṁ saṁsiddhiṁ gatāḥ. Saṁsiddhi* is success. The only real success is *mokṣa* and this they have gained. *Paramā* means it is the most exalted among the *puruṣārtha*s. Those who have gained this freedom will not come back again.

Even though gaining the Lord is easy, the result is the maximum. On the other hand, gaining a *loka* is difficult and the result is *duḥkha-ālaya*. To choose the latter is a bad bargain. In the next section Bhagavān talks about what a bad bargain it is.

In the previous verses, Kṛṣṇa said that those wise men who have recognised me as their own self do not attain another birth. They do not assume another body, which is by nature subject to pain. But, what about the others who do not have this recognition? Where do they go and what is their lot?

Verse 16

All lokas are limited by time but having gained me there is no rebirth

आब्रह्मभुवनाल्लोकाः पुनरावर्तिनोऽर्जुन ।
मामुपेत्य तु कौन्तेय पुनर्जन्म न विद्यते ॥ १६ ॥

ābrahmabhuvanāllokāḥ punarāvartino'rjuna
mām upetya tu kaunteya punarjanma na vidyate (16)

arjuna – O Arjuna!; *ābrahma-bhuvanāt lokāḥ* – (all) the worlds (where beings exist) upto the world of Brahmaji; *punarāvartinaḥ* – are subject to return; *tu* – however; *mām upetya* – having reached me; *kaunteya* – O son of Kuntī!; *punarjanma* – rebirth; *na vidyate* – is not there

Arjuna! All the worlds (where beings exist) up to the world of Brahmaji are subject to return. However, having reached me, Kaunteya (Arjuna)! there is no rebirth.

Ābrahma-bhuvanāt lokāḥ punarāvartinaḥ, the worlds where beings exist, up to *brahma-loka,* lead back. The prefix '*ā*'[33] has the meaning of 'up to,' that is, it indicates the 'limit' of something. It may or may not include the point of demarcation. Therefore, the expression, '*ābrahma-bhuvanāt lokāḥ,* all the worlds up to *brahma-loka*' either include *brahma-loka* or may not include *brahma-loka.* We have to analyse the context and see if *brahma-loka* is included or not. In this section, Bhagavān is saying that anything created, which is everything other than *paramātmā,* is by nature something from which you will return, *punarāvartinaḥ.* Since all the *loka*s including *brahma-loka,* are created, *brahma-loka,* otherwise called *satya-loka* or *kṛta-loka,* is also included in the description, *punarāvartinaḥ.* So here, the meaning of '*ā*' is 'up to and including.'

Bhuvana means a world in which beings exist. *Brahma* in this verse is *hiraṇya-garbha,* Brahmaji, who resides in *brahma-loka.* Therefore, *brahma-bhuvana* refers to *brahma-loka* where Brahmaji resides. When the Lord says, all the worlds up to and including *brahma-loka* are *punarāvartinaḥ,* what it means is that they are subject to destruction. This world, the very ground on which you are standing, is perishable as is your physical body. If this world is destroyed, there is no possibility of you remaining to witness the destroyed world because your body is part of it. Nor is there any question of you retaining this physical body, no matter where you go. The physical bodies and the worlds in which they exist, are subject to destruction. There is a time when everything must dissolve in the cause,

---

33 आङ्-मर्यादा-अभिविधौ

and there is not a single place in the creation, which is going to survive *mahā-pralaya*, the final dissolution. Therefore, the Lord says, 'Arjuna, if you are planning to go to *brahma-loka* or any other *loka*, you will have to return because all the *loka*s, including *brahma-loka*, are subject to destruction.'

There is one possible exception to this in the case of some people. *Śruti* allows that; those who go to *brahma-loka* may not come back. This is not merely because they have gone there, but being there, if Brahmaji teaches them, they come to understand that *ātmā* is Parameśvara; they are thereby freed and they do not come back. Therefore, even those people are freed and do not come back, not by virtue of going to *brahma-loka*, but because of knowledge.

Mām upetya tu kaunteya punar-janma na vidyate, but having reached me, Kaunteya, there is no further birth. How do they reach Parameśvara who is not located in this or any other *loka*? And if they have to go somewhere to reach Parameśvara, they have to come back. They reach him in terms of knowledge; as *sat-cit-ānanda-ātmā*, they are non-separate from Parameśvara. They reach him by knowing he is Brahman, which is *sat-cit-ānanda-ātmā* out of which this creation has come, and which is the very truth of everything. Reaching Īśvara in this manner, by knowledge, they do not have rebirth.

Otherwise, all *loka*s are subject to time and for that reason alone one has to return from there. How long one remains there does not matter. It is still not eternal.

Here, two questions are implied. Why are all the *loka*s such that one must return from them? Because they are subject to time.

Verse 17

The day and night of Brahmaji

सहस्रयुगपर्यन्तमहर्यद्ब्रह्मणो विदुः ।
रात्रिं युगसहस्रान्तां तेऽहोरात्रविदो जनाः ॥ १७ ॥

sahasrayugaparyantam aharyad brahmaṇo viduḥ
rātriṁ yugasahasrāntāṁ te'horātravido janāḥ (17)

(*ye*) *janāḥ* – (those) people; *aho-rātra-vidaḥ* – who know about the day and night; *te* – they; *yat brahmaṇaḥ ahaḥ* – that which is the day of Brahmaji; (*tat* – that;) *sahasra-yuga-paryantam* – as that which consists of one thousand *yugas*; *viduḥ* – know; (*brahmaṇaḥ*) *rātrim* (*ca*) – and night of Brahmaji; *yuga-sahasra-antām* – measuring one thousand *yugas*; (*viduḥ* – know)

Those people who know about the day and night, know that a day of Brahmaji consists of one thousand *yugas* and a night (of Brahmaji), measuring one thousand *yugas*.

People, who know about Brahmaji's day and night, know that Brahmaji's one day consists of one thousand *yugas*. Here the word '*yuga*' refers to a *mahā-yuga*. So, the day of Brahmaji is one thousand *mahā-yugas* and the night of Brahmaji is one thousand *mahā-yugas*. One *mahā-yuga* consists of four *yugas*, *satya*, *dvāpara*, *tretā*, and *kali*. *Kali-yuga* is four hundred and thirty-two thousand years in length. *Dvāpara-yuga* is twice that, that is, eight hundred and sixty-four thousand years. *Tretā* is three times *kali-yuga*, that is, one million two hundred and ninety-six thousand years. Then *satya-yuga* is four times *kali-yuga*, that is, one million seven hundred and twenty-eight thousand.

So, complete *mahā-yuga* is four million three hundred and twenty thousand years in length. One thousand of these is one day of Brahmaji, four billion three hundred and twenty million years.[34] When Brahmaji's night begins, all the *loka*s are destroyed. So, after four billion three hundred and twenty million years, all of creation except *brahma-loka* is destroyed. Night comes and Brahmaji goes to sleep. When you go to sleep, your world is dissolved; so, it is logical that when Brahmaji goes to sleep, the entire creation is gone except for *brahma-loka*. Then creation remains dissolved for four billion three hundred and twenty million years. Again it begins when Brahmaji wakes up and his day begins.

Brahmaji's longevity is one hundred years, called a *kalpa*, and at the end of it, there is the destruction of *brahma-loka* too. This is what those people who calculate time with reference to Brahmaji's day and so on, know. The purpose of saying

---

34

Kali-yuga		432,000	or	432	thousand years
Dvāpara-yuga	(*kali-yuga* x 2)	864,000	or	864	thousand years
Tretā-yuga	(*kali-yuga* x 3)	12,96,000	or	1296	thousand years
Kṛta-yuga	(*kali-yuga* x 4)	17,28,000	or	1728	thousand years
Mahā-yuga or *catur yuga*	(*kali-yuga* x 10)	43,20,000	or	4320	thousand years

One day of Brahmaji consists of 1000 *mahā-yuga*s, that is, 4,32,00,00000 years, four billion three hundred and twenty million human years. And one night of Brahmaji is again the same number of human years. Thus 1000 *mahā-yuga*s constitutes one day and 1000 *mahā-yuga*s constitute one night, that is, 2000 *mahā-yuga*s constitute one complete day of Brahmaji. With this as one unit for a day comprising of a day and night 100 years form Brahmaji's life. Please note – One human year is equal to one day of the *deva*s. Thus one year of the *deva*s is equal to 360 human years.

this here is to indicate that even though they are four billion three hundred and twenty million years, they are still countable. Because they are limited by time in this way, they are all places from which one must return. So, going to a *loka*, including *brahma-loka* is not going to help.

Such a long length of time is still subject to time. There is no eternal heaven because in time there is no eternity. Then what is eternity? Only 'now,' which is not subject to time. There is no other eternity and that indeed is *ātmā*, which is Parameśvara.

Verse 18

अव्यक्ताद्व्यक्तयः सर्वाः प्रभवन्त्यहरागमे ।
रात्र्यागमे प्रलीयन्ते तत्रैवाव्यक्तसंज्ञके ॥ १८ ॥

avyaktād vyaktayaḥ sarvāḥ prabhavantyaharāgame
rātryāgame pralīyante tatraivāvyaktasañjñake (18)

aharāgame – at the beginning of the day (of Brahmaji); *avyaktāt* – from the unmanifest; *sarvāḥ vyaktayaḥ* – all things that are manifest; *prabhavanti* – arise; *rātri-āgame* – at the beginning of the night (of Brahmaji); *avyakta-saṁjñake* – in that which is called unmanifest; *tatra eva* – in that alone; *pralīyante* – they resolve

At the beginning of the day, all things that are manifest arise from the unmanifest. At the beginning of the night, they resolve in that alone which is called unmanifest.

Avyaktāt vyaktayaḥ sarvāḥ prabhavanti aharāgame, from the unmanifest, come all the manifest forms when the day of Brahmaji breaks. From the sleep of Brahmaji arise the manifest individuals, sun, moon, stars, the mobile, immobile, sentient and insentient entities and the places where they exist. Just as from our sleep, our day or dream manifests, similarly from Brahmaji's sleep the whole creation has come about.

Brahmaji is nothing but Parameśvara. This is one step further. Everything is Parameśvara and Brahmaji is not an entity other than him. Only from the standpoint of creation do we say that from Brahmaji alone everything has come. Brahmaji is non-separate from Īśvara and from Īśvara everything comes. When does this happen? At the break of day. In other words, when Brahmaji wakes up, the creation arises, comes into manifestation.

Rātri-āgame pralīyante tatra eva avyakta-sañjñake. Similarly *rātri-āgame,* when Brahmaji's night comes – after four billion three hundred and twenty million years – all things that are manifest dissolve, *pralīyante*. Where? They go back to the cause, the condition called unmanifest, *avyakta-sañjñake,* which is Brahmaji's sleep. Like even our own world that resolves into us in sleep, night after night, and comes back again day after day, so too, when Brahmaji's day comes, there is creation and when his night begins, there is dissolution. This goes on thirty six thousand times. Then Brahmaji's life is over and *brahma-loka* is also destroyed; only Parameśvara remains. That Parameśvara, Kṛṣṇa says, is me. If you reach me, you do not get into this cycle. I am the only survivor, the only one who is *nitya*, eternal, *sat-cit-ānanda*.

From this we understand Brahman is *satya*, the world is *mithyā*. Anything subject to the three periods of time is *mithyā*. It is not that it did not exist in the past and is existent now. It is not that it existed in the past and is not existent now. Again it is not that it is not existent now but will be existent in the future. All the *loka*s, their residents and lords can be negated in all three periods of time. They are other than Brahman, meaning Brahman is independent of them, while they are not independent of Brahman. Anything that Brahman is independent of is called *loka*. Within the *loka*s are many *jīva*s, including the *devatā*s who are in charge. But, being subject to time, they are subject to death.

Then what is *satya*? What is not subject to the three periods of time. In the past it was, in the present it is, in the future it will be, and it can only be one *caitanya-ātmā*. Being the very basis of time, *satya-ātmā* is *nitya*. What is eternal, what exists is only one; that is Brahman, which is *ātmā*. And the creation, which is by nature an observable object, is *mithyā*. Anything seen is *mithyā*, it is perishable. The seer, however, can objectify even time and is therefore, the basis of time, eternal, which is *ātmā*, Brahman, the only one not subject to time. Kṛṣṇa says that alone is *nitya* and it is himself. This is what Bhagavān means when he says here, '*mām upetya punar-janma...na āpnuvanti...*, reaching me they do not gain another birth.'[35]

---

[35] *Gītā* 8.15

Whenever Kṛṣṇa uses the first person singular with reference to himself, he means *paramātmā* and not the historical Kṛṣṇa. It can be argued that if this is so, why should he say, 'Reaching me you are freed from birth?' If it is *ātmā* that you must know, then why should Kṛṣṇa not say, 'Knowing oneself, *ātmānaṁ jñātvā*?' He did not say so, because that is not enough. You have to know that Īśvara is *ātmā*. By the statement 'knowing me,' Kṛṣṇa equates Īśvara and the *jīva*. This equation is the whole teaching. Pointing out that *pratyagātmā* is consciousness alone is not the *upadeśa*, teaching. That *pratyagātmā* and Parameśvara are identical is the teaching, which is why Bhagavān frequently says, 'Reaching me you are freed,' meaning 'recognising me as *ātmā* you are freed.' Only with this kind of equation does it become a teaching equivalent to *tat tvam asi*. Otherwise it will be experiential. Dismissal of thoughts is not what is being taught here; it is the knowledge that, 'I am everything,' which is being taught.

To point out this identity, Bhagavān says, '*mām upetya punar-janma...na āpnuvanti*, this *jīva* reaching me, does not gain another birth. Knowing he is Brahman, he knows that he is eternal. Knowing *ātmā* is knowing Brahman, because there is no Brahman other than *ātmā*. Those who recognise *ātmā* as *nitya-brahma* do not return to another birth.

Those who go to *brahma-loka* etc., however, do come back to assume another birth. And to go to *brahma-loka*, the effort required is extraordinary. It involves elaborate *karma* backed with complex *upāsanas*. Even if you achieve it, you have to come back again unless Brahmaji has taught you, for which you require some extra *puṇya*. Everyone who goes to *brahma-loka* does not get a chance to be taught.

Gaining Brahman, on the other hand, is easy because it is your nature. 'Since I am so easily available, why do you turn away from me and make efforts to reach *loka*s? It is the intention here.

Sṛṣṭi and laya of creation

In this verse Bhagavān says that every day when Brahmaji goes to sleep, the whole cosmos including the physical and subtle bodies resolve. Then again the whole creation arises when Brahmaji wakes up. On the other hand, if you consider that the whole creation is totally dissolved and an absolutely new creation comes up, then there are three possible problems which Śaṅkara raises here.

They are *kṛta-vipraṇāśa*, the total destruction of something created, *akṛta-abhyāgama*, the coming into being of something that is not created, and *niṣphalatva* of the *śāstra*, the purposelessness of the *śāstra*. *Kṛta-vipraṇāśa*, the total destruction of something created. If all the *jīva*s in various *loka*s resolve into Brahmaji, they will be gone. Since they were ignorant, in endless births, they accumulated endless *karma*. These *karma*s will also be gone now and have no possibility of fructifying. The *karma* done by these *jīva*s without being completely fulfilled, are destroyed because they also dissolve when Brahmaji goes to sleep. So, we have the complete destruction of something that is already created. This would be a logical defect in Īśvara's creation.

Akṛta-abhyāgama, the coming into being of something that is not created. Every time when Brahmaji wakes up, new *jīva*s are created. But these new *jīva*s have no *karma*s. It means Bhagavān creates varieties of new *jīva*s for his own amusement or for no purpose at all. There is no rhyme or reason to the creation. This is a second logical defect, the coming into being of something that is not created.

The *karma*s in the account of the *jīva*s get destroyed if the *jīva*s are destroyed. And if new *jīva*s are created, then they have come into being without any past *karma* and so on. So, what is created is destroyed and what is not created is brought into being. The next verse will dismiss both these defects.

The third difficulty is *niṣphalatva*, the purposelessness of the *śāstra*. There is a *vidhi-niṣedha-śāstra* which enjoins certain actions and prohibits other actions. You will gain *puṇya* by performing the prescribed actions, and incur *pāpa* by doing the prohibited actions. Then there is the *bandha-mokṣa-śāstra*, which says that if you keep performing such actions you will be in bondage, whereas, if you know the truth, you will be released.

If the *jīva*s totally disappear in *pralaya,* they will not enjoy the results of their many actions, good and bad. Without that, and without any knowledge, they will get liberated. So, both *vidhi-niṣedha-śāstra* and *mokṣa-śāstra* will have no meaning. All you have to do to get liberated is to wait for the *kalpa* to end. It is something like amnesty. If you wait long enough, it will come. You just keep living in *śāstra* and you will get liberated anyway because everything is going to end one day. You need only to wait for Brahmaji's night and it will all be over. The next verse removes this difficulty also.

In the next verse Bhagavān shows that the *jīva* is helplessly caught in the cycle of creation and dissolution. *Karma* has its source in a five fold affliction – *avidyā*, ignorance; *asmitā*, ego; *rāga*, likes; *dveṣa*, dislikes; and *abhiniveṣa*, attachment or even mistaking something, which is non-eternal as eternal. Why does a person perform *karma*? It is only due to *abhiniveṣa*, a fondness or preoccupation with something. For instance, one has confusion that by going to heaven, one will get *mokṣa* or simply by getting a thing one will achieve a given end and thereby better one's lot. Similarly, *rāga dveṣa* is a source of *karma*. And to do any action, there must be a subject, the agent, *asmitā*. All these are possible due to *avidyā*, ignorance. Together these five are the basis for a *karma*. Since they exist in the mind of a *jīva*, *karma* has its abode in the *jīva*. Because of the force of this *karma*, necessarily, without one's willingness, the *jīva* is forced to perform action.

Verse 19

Repeatedly coming back to assume birth is saṁsāra

भूतग्रामः स एवायं भूत्वा भूत्वा प्रलीयते ।
रात्र्यागमेऽवशः पार्थ प्रभवत्यहरागमे ॥ १९ ॥

bhūtagrāmaḥ sa evāyaṁ bhūtvā bhūtvā pralīyate
rātryāgame'vaśaḥ pārtha prabhavatyaharāgame (19)

sa eva ayam – that is indeed this; *bhūta-grāmaḥ* – group of beings; *avaśaḥ* – necessarily; *bhūtvā bhūtvā* – having repeatedly come into being; *rātri-āgame* – when the night comes; *pralīyate* – dissolves; *pārtha* – O son of Pṛthā!; *aharāgame* – when the day comes; *prabhavati* – it arises

> Pārtha (Arjuna)! The same group of beings indeed (which), having repeatedly come into being necessarily dissolves when the night (of Brahmaji) comes. When the day comes, it necessarily arises.

Without any personal volition, by the law of *karma*, a person comes into being again and again. Every time the day breaks for Brahmaji, all the beings emerge. Then again, having existed, they resolve.

Bhūta-grāmaḥ sa evāyaṁ bhūtvā bhūtvā pralīyate. Bhūta-grāma means all forms of life, mobile and immobile. *Saḥ* and *ayam* used together indicate that which was before, is the one now mentioned. The same group of beings that went into *pralaya* in the previous *kalpa* is the group spoken of here. It means *pralaya* is not a real dissolution but an unmanifest condition. *Ayam* tells us that the same group of *jīva*s, and not any other, comes back again. The group of beings that existed in the previous cycle, the previous day of Brahmanji returns in the next cycle. The repetition of the word *bhūtvā*, as '*bhūtvā bhūtvā*' is meant to show the cyclic nature of the *kalpa*s and also that the same beings come, go into *pralaya*, then again come back.

Since the same ones who became unmanifest return to fulfil their *karma*, there is no destruction of the created *karma*.

New *jīva*s are not created; the old ones are coming back. Both logical defects are dismissed by this verse.

The exception to this are those *jīva*s who got liberated. They do not exist as *jīva*s; all that is there, is *paraṁ-brahma*. Only those who go into *pralaya* come back.

When do they resolve?

Rātri-āgame avaśaḥ pralīyate, when the night of Brahmaji comes, they necessarily resolve. *Avaśaḥ,* necessarily, means they have no say over the matter at all. They are forcefully pushed into dissolution.

Prabhavati aharāgame, then, the entire group of beings appears again when the day breaks for Brahmaji. Since the *jīva*s are infinite in number, their *karma*s are countless and they can, therefore, appear in any form. Sometimes you find more animals on this earth and fewer human beings, or fewer animals and more human beings. It is the nature of the process. But they are all there somewhere in creation. In time, they all come into being.

The big bang or the biological theories of evolution are in keeping with this because they are processes. We do not accept an immediate simultaneous creation of everything but we consider it to be a process. First, the infrastructure comes into being, then everything else comes about as part of a process within that. So, it is said here, again and again they come back.

Bhagavān says this explicitly to help you develop *vairāgya* towards *saṁsāra*. You are not going to solve the problem of *saṁsāra* by being in it. Repeatedly coming back to assume a birth is *saṁsāra*. Then, in a given life there are ups and downs of *sukha-duḥkha*. This is *saṁsāra*; it repeats itself. Do not have the illusion that you can just go on living and one day, when the *kalpa* ends, you will gain *mokṣa*. There is no such amnesty. When the *kalpa* ends, it is like sleep. As soon as Brahmaji wakes up the following morning, you come back. When this is the case, *mokṣa-śāstra* is necessary.

Vidhi-niṣeda-śāstra also becomes meaningful. Your *puṇya-pāpa*s have to be accounted for in terms of experiences. The *pāpa*s have to be gone through; the *puṇya*s have to be enjoyed. You can neutralise some of your *karma*s but you cannot totally eliminate all of them because there is an inviolable cause effect relationship between an action and its result, which is why *karma-phala* is called *ṛta, satya,* it is true. It can wait, even for one *kalpa*, but if not now, later, in one form or another, here or elsewhere, the *jīva* will reap his results. Once Brahmaji is awake, the subtle bodies are going to experience their own *puṇya-pāpa*s in some form. It means both the *vidhi-śāstra* and the *niṣeda-śāstra* become meaningful. This is within *saṁsāra*. Then *mokṣa-śāstra* also becomes meaningful. Through knowledge there is freedom, *jñānāt mokṣaḥ*.

This verse shows us that the *jīva*s do not disappear in *pralaya*; they continue to exist even there and then they return. By saying this, Bhagavān emphasises what he pointed out before, that is, there is no way of getting rid of *saṁsāra* except by reaching him.[36] That reaching is identifying yourself to be Parameśvara, which is the one thing that is eternal, *nitya*.

---

[36] *Gītā* 8.15-16

Earlier, in verses 13 and 14 of this chapter, *oṁkāra upāsana* as a means for gaining Brahman was pointed out. *Om* can be a name for Brahman, in which case it is to be understood. Knowing that, you are free. Or it can be meditated upon as a symbol of Parameśvara. By this, you go to *brahma-loka* and can gain the knowledge of Brahman. Now, if *oṁkāra* is *vācaka*, the name, then what is *vācya*, the named? What is it that is revealed by *oṁkāra* essentially? It is shown in the next three verses.

Since there seems to be a repetition, Śaṅkara introduces these verses saying that they are taught with a desire to unfold the meaning of *akṣaraṁ-brahma*, which was referred to as *om–om iti ekākṣaraṁ brahma.*[37] What is the real nature or meaning of *oṁkāra*, which stands for *akṣaraṁ-brahma*? What is the nature of that Brahman for which *oṁkāra* is *vācaka* the name? By knowing this, you can gain Brahman; in other words, *mokṣa*. It is the purpose of the next three verses.

Verses 20&21

The unmanifest – avyakta-ātmā – is never destroyed

परस्तस्मात्तु भावोऽन्योऽव्यक्तोऽव्यक्तात्सनातनः ।
यः स सर्वेषु भूतेषु नश्यत्सु न विनश्यति ॥ २० ॥

parastasmāt tu bhāvo'nyo'vyakto'vyaktāt sanātanaḥ
yaḥ sa sarveṣu bhūteṣu naśyatsu na vinaśyati (20)

tu – but; *yaḥ* – that which is; *tasmāt avyaktāt paraḥ* – distinct from that unmanifest; *anyaḥ avyaktaḥ* – another unmanifest; *bhāvaḥ* –

[37] *Gītā* 8.13

existent; *sanātanaḥ* – eternal; *saḥ* – that; *sarveṣu bhūteṣu naśyatsu* – when all beings are destroyed; *na vinaśyati* – is not destroyed

> But, distinct from that unmanifest is another unmanifest, which is existent and eternal. That is not destroyed when all beings are destroyed.

In the previous verse, Bhagavān showed that everything becomes unmanifest and from that unmanifest condition, everything comes back. This must be clearly understood. When we say the *jīva* is *anitya*, it is not like saying a pot is *anitya*. The name form pot is finite. From the standpoint of the pot, its cause, the clay is not. The pot form is destroyed but not its cause, the clay. Similarly, when we say the *jīva* is *anitya*, it is only the name form, the *upādhi* that is *anitya*. When the physical body dies, the subtle body remains and when *pralaya* comes, even the subtle body goes and what remains is the causal body. Unlike clay which is the cause of pot, here the causal body is also *anitya* with reference to *paraṁ-brahma*.

Only *ātma-vastu* is *nitya*. When you say I am a *jīva*, the 'I' is really *ātmā*. Just as when you say this is a pot, there is clay plus the name form pot, similarly when you say, 'I am a *jīva*,' there is *ātmā* plus *jīvatva*, the individuality, which is only a superimposition upon *ātmā* caused by *avidyā*. If in saying I am a *jīva*, *ātmā* is mistaken for the individual, that 'I' is *mithyā* because *jīvatva* is *anitya*, superimposed on what is real, the *ātmā*; *ātmā*'s *svarūpa* is *nitya*.

We need to understand this well; otherwise, there will be a problem of a mix up between what is *vastu*, and what is *avastu*. This mix up exists in every situation. Only the *vastu* is real, *avastu* being dependent upon the *vastu* for its existence. Since, it draws its existence from the *vastu*, the *avastu* is not another object; it is non-separate from the *vastu*. Therefore, there is only *vastu*. This entire world is nothing but *paraṁ-brahma*. All that you see, the seer, and the sight, are nothing but *vastu*. If this is understood, you know that at the time of *pralaya*, the *jīva*s resolve into the unmanifest, the *avyakta- upādhi* otherwise called *ajñāna-upādhi*.

When Brahmaji goes to sleep, it means that Brahmaji is in that particular state where he does not see that he is omniscient; this is what they call the avyakta-avasthā, unmanifest state.

Paraḥ tu tasmāt avyaktāt anyaḥ avyaktaḥ bhāvaḥ sanātanaḥ, distinct from or superior to that *avyakta* is another *avyakta*, which is eternal. '*Tasmāt paraḥ*' is similar to the expression '*avyaktāt puruṣaḥ paraḥ*' in *Kaṭhopaniṣad*, which describes the Lord as the one who is distinct from all causes.[38]

We always try to accomplish an end within *saṁsāra* but *puruṣa* himself is expressed here as the end to be accomplished. *Puruṣa* is non-separate from myself and that is also the limit, the end to be accomplished. That *puruṣa* is Parameśvara who is non-separate from *ātmā*. Recognition of that is the end and the recognition is the very nature of *mokṣa*.

---

[38] महतः परम् अव्यक्तम् अव्यक्तात् पुरुषः परः ।
पुरुषान्न परम् किञ्चित् सा काष्ठा सा परा गतिः ॥ (कठोपनिषद् १ .३.११)

mahataḥ param avyaktam avyaktāt puruṣaḥ paraḥ, puruṣānna param kiñcit sā kāṣṭhā sā parā gatiḥ (*Kaṭhopaniṣad* 1.3.11)
The unmanifest is higher than *mahat; puruṣa* is higher than the unmanifest. There is nothing higher than *puruṣa*. He is the end; he is the highest goal.

The nature of *mokṣa* is described in various ways. Freedom from bondage, freedom from self-ignorance, freedom from *saṁsāra,* reaching the abode of Viṣṇu, not as a place, but as recognition that I am one with Īśvara, or gaining *ānanda,* are some of the expressions describing *mokṣa.*

The most interesting one is that you gain the *puruṣa.* This is only possible if you are already *puruṣa* and do not know it. Then you can gain the *puruṣa* by knowledge; to be the *puruṣa* is, to know, which is why a *brahmavit* is sometimes described in terms of Brahman. The knower of Brahman is Brahman, *brahmavit brahma eva bhavati.*

The uniqueness of Vedanta is that the description of *mokṣa* is description of the *vastu.* The different descriptions in terms of result, freedom from bondage, gaining of *ānanda,* etc., are confusing for some people. If *ānanda* is understood as bliss, some experience of happiness that is out of the ordinary, a person becomes a seeker of that bliss. Like any other thing in *saṁsāra, mokṣa* becomes one of the things sought after. But this gain of *ānanda* is the gain of one's own nature. It is not experiential *ānanda,* but the essence of every experience of *ānanda.* That recognition is gaining *ānanda.*

Significance of the word 'tu'

Tasmāt tu paraḥ. The word '*tu*' is always to distinguish between two things and can be translated as 'but,' 'so,' 'whereas,' etc. It is a word that introduces a new topic, bringing in a condition, whereby something already stated is to be distinguished from what is to come. *Tu* here is to distinguish *parā-vastu* from everything else. Everything else has been reduced to *avyakta*, but superior to that, *tasmāt tu paraḥ*, is something else. The word *tu* here shows the distinction of the *vastu* that is going to be talked about. It conveys the idea that there is no other thing like the *vastu*.

Avyakta, the cause of everything that is manifest, is not the final cause after all; it is only another *upādhi*. The true cause is the basis of the *avyakta*. That is Brahman.

When everything is reduced to *avyakta*, the cause, and if it is even other than that, you may think it is non-existent. It is like asking what, on this planet, is to the north of the North Pole? Once you are on the North Pole, there is nothing to the north of that.

To show that the *vastu* under discussion is not non-existent, Bhagavān uses the word *bhāva*, existent. It always is. That is the nature of *akṣaraṁ-brahma*. It has no *abhāva*, non-existence, and does not change at all. What is distinct from *avyakta* and is an existent being is *paraṁ-brahma*.

Dismissal of being a member of a set – sālakṣaṇya

Anyaḥ, a thing that is different from another thing can still belong to the same group as the thing it is distinguished from. This is called *sālakṣaṇya*, having the same characteristic. For example, chair, table, sofa, etc., even though different from each other, are characterised as furniture. All of them are of the same class. Similarly, when you say, it is other than the unmanifest cause, *avyaktāt paraḥ*, it may be one of the many things in the world even though it is different from everything else. It is true that Brahman is different from everything else, but nothing is different from Brahman. Because it is not like any other thing, it is necessary to dismiss the possibility of *sālakṣaṇya*. Brahman cannot be characterised under any group, including *loka* or *devatā*. To show this, Bhagavān uses the word '*anya*,' meaning, it is quite another. It is distinct in an entirely different way from what we normally understand. It is not non-existent; it is not momentarily existent; it is existent and at the same time distinct from everything else. What is that?

It is *avyakta*, that is, it is not known as an object of the sense organs. Since Bhagavān has used the word *bhāva*, it can be understood as an existent thing. *Avyakta* makes it clear that it is something that is not available for objectification. It is the cause of the very sense organ; so, it is not going to be available as a sound, or a form or colour. Then how are you going to know that Brahman?

It is manifest in the mind because it is the very nature of the mind. It is recognised there. Even in the sense organs it is present. It is the ear of the ear, the eye of the eye – not the object of the eye, but that because of which the eyes see, ears hear, and so on.[39] Even though it is not an object of perception, it is always manifest as the very truth of every sense organ, every thought; it is you. Further, it is the very basis of *avyakta*, the unmanifest, which is the seed of all beings.

Sanātanaḥ means that which always exists. It is beyond cause and effect and not bound by time. It existed before, exists now, and will exist later; it is timeless. Even though we use the word beyond, there is nothing beyond; everything we can

---

[39] *Kenopaniṣad* 1.2

reach or even imagine is within this *avyakta*. This means it is *dṛk-svarūpa*, the very nature of the seer, which is *paraṁ-brahma*.

Brahma-loka etc., are all within your knowledge and within time and space, which are manifest from *avyakta*, the unmanifest. What is beyond that is *ātmā* which is always immediately available as the self of all beings, purely in the form of consciousness, which is the truth of 'I.' And this, not being limited by time, is never destroyed. *Sarveṣu bhūteṣu naśyatsu na vinaśyati*. The one who remains in all perishable forms, never getting destroyed, is indeed the *ātmā*.

Verse 21

अव्यक्तोऽक्षर इत्युक्तस्तमाहुः परमां गतिम् ।
यं प्राप्य न निवर्तन्ते तद्धाम परमं मम ॥ २१ ॥

avyakto'kṣara ityuktastam āhuḥ paramāṁ gatim
yaṁ prāpya na nivartante taddhāma paramaṁ mama (21)

avyaktaḥ – the unmanifest; *akṣaraḥ iti uktaḥ* – that was spoken of as the one that is not subject to destruction; *tam akṣaram* – that *akṣara; paramāṁ gatim* – as the highest end; *āhuḥ* – they say; *yaṁ prāpya* – gaining which; *na nivartante* – (people) do not return; *tat* – that; *mama* – (is) my; *paramam* – the highest; *dhāma* – abode

The unmanifest that was spoken of as the one that is not subject to destruction, is the highest end, they say. That abode of mine, gaining which (people) do not return, is the highest.

Avyaktaḥ akṣaraḥ iti uktaḥ tam āhuḥ paramāṁ gatiṁ. The *avyakta-ātmā* is *akṣara*, not subject to destruction. Because it is not subject to time, it is not subject to any kind of change. It is that which people who know the *śāstra* call *paramā gati.* A place that we reach or any accomplishment we achieve is called *gati,* the end. *viṣṇu-loka* and *brahma-loka* are ends for the *jīva,* the *saṁsārī.* But here, *ātmā,* the self who wants to go to places is itself said to be the end.

How is this possible? How can I be a *gati* to myself? How can there be two *ātmā*s, one who reaches and the other who is reached? The answer is, for the confused person, truth is the *gati,* end. All other ends are within *saṁsāra* and they are for the confused *jīva.* So, when he wants to be released from *saṁsāra, ātmā* itself, the truth of the confused *jīva,* becomes the *gati.*

That is what they say is the most exalted end, *paramā gati.* Any other *gati* is reached only after death and can be either bad or good. *Paramā gati* has no equal; it is *mokṣa.* So, the *ātmā* itself becomes *mokṣa* here. Freedom, the *puruṣārtha,* is non-separate from oneself. Therefore, the seeker of *mokṣa* is not separate from *mokṣa.* Since the seeker and the sought are one and the same, the seeking stems from ignorance. If I am the end and I am the seeker, the means for accomplishing that end can only be *viveka,* discernment. *Viveka* is the means, *ātmā* is the end. The *avivekī* becomes the seeker, the *avyakta-ātmā,* the end, and *viveka,* the means.

Yaṁ prāpya na nivartante taddhāma paramaṁ mama. Why is it called the *paramā gati*? It is because, gaining this, they do not come back. There is no coming back because it is not an end other than yourself. Generally from any end you certainly come back; but when the end is yourself, how can you come back? You can come back only from an experience. For instance, simple *nirvikalpa-samādhi,* without the knowledge that *ātmā* is *nirvikalpa,* is an experience from which you will come back. When it is knowledge, coming back is not possible. With the mind you are *sat-cit-ānanda-ātmā,* and without the mind you are still *sat-cit-ānanda-ātmā*. What is to be gained? Before a thought there is *sat-cit-ānanda-ātmā*; when a thought is there it is the same. A thought does not displace *sat-cit-ānanda-ātmā*; it is nothing but an expression of the *sat-cit-ānanda-ātmā*. Even if you have a thought, if you know you are *sat-cit-ānanda-ātmā,* there is no question of losing that knowledge. Once there is no ignorance of *ātmā,* which does not change, there is no return.

Bhagavān says, '*Ātmā* is indeed my abode, *dhāma*.' It is *paramā gati,* the highest end. The expression *paramā gati* can give rise to the notion that there is a place that you have to reach. *Śāstra* does talk about heaven as a desirable place. But Bhagavān says here that the highest end is 'you.' There is no heaven beyond 'you.' All other places are places from where you will return. This is the heaven entering which you will never return. Everybody is generally committed to go to a place where they can be free from the troubles of life. That desirability is expressed by using the word *dhāma*. At the same time it is made clear that even though it is heaven like, it is non-separate from you and there is no coming back. That is the greatest abode. Bhagavān says, 'I have no abode, other than you. I reside in your own intellect.' Achieving this *ātmā* by knowledge, which is the only way to achieve it, is *mokṣa*.

Now Bhagavān shows the only means for achieving this and it is none other than committed *vicāra,* enquiry into the nature of *ātmā*.

Verse 22

The word puruṣa indicates both taṭastha-lakṣaṇa and svarūpa-lakṣaṇa

पुरुषः स परः पार्थ भक्त्या लभ्यस्त्वनन्यया ।
यस्यान्तःस्थानि भूतानि येन सर्वमिदं ततम् ॥ २२ ॥

puruṣaḥ sa paraḥ pārtha bhaktyā labhyastvananyayā
yasyāntaḥsthāni bhūtāni yena sarvam idaṁ tatam (22)

puruṣaḥ sa paraḥ – that *puruṣa* is limitless; *pārtha* – O Pārtha (Arjuna)!; *labhyaḥ tu* – but can be gained; *bhaktyā ananyayā* – by devotion in which there is no other; *yasya antassthāni* – in whom all the beings have their being; *yena* – by whom; *sarvam idam* – all this; *tatam* – is pervaded

> That *puruṣa* who is the limitless, Pārtha (Arjuna)! can be gained by devotion in which there is no other. (He is) the one in whom all the beings have their being, the one by whom all this is pervaded.

Puruṣaḥ sa paraḥ pārtha bhaktyā labhyaḥ tu, Arjuna, that *puruṣa* is to be gained; it can be gained through *parā-bhakti*. Śaṅkara says here that *puruṣa* means the one who seems to sleep in the body, who resides there without performing any action, which is why Viṣṇu is depicted as lying down. He is not sleeping but is very much awake as *caitanya-svarūpa*. *Ātmā*, which is *caitanya-svarūpa* is resting in this physical body. This is the *taṭastha-lakṣaṇa* of *puruṣa*, the definition that defines a thing in terms of its connection to something, as we saw before. When we say that out of which the world has come, by which it is sustained and unto which it returns is Brahman, it is *taṭastha-*

lakṣaṇa of Brahman. It indicates that Brahman is not to be sought as name and form or beyond name and form. It is to be sought as that out of which all names and forms have come, by which they are sustained and unto which they return. Your own physical body is a name and form, and therefore, non-separate from Brahman. So, you need not search for Brahman. You need not wait for certain conditions or go to a place or be in a situation where you can see Brahman. Any place and time is Brahman. It is a matter of recognising what is already existing now. The very knower is non-separate from Brahman as is everything he knows. From this you understand that everything is Brahman. This is *taṭastha-lakṣaṇa*.

Puruṣa can also mean *pūrṇa*, limitless. This is *svarūpa-lakṣaṇa*, a definition which tells the nature of Brahman. It is not limited by space, time or any attribute, even though all qualities belong to it. *Pūrṇamadaḥ pūrṇamidam...*, that is whole this is whole; and this whole coming into being is only a manifestation of name and form. If this whole is removed from that whole, what remains is that whole.[40] Any way you look at it, it is *pūrṇa*. Therefore, it is *para*. The one who obtains in the physical body is *para*, limitless. *Para* becomes the reason for it being *puruṣa*, or we can say *puruṣa*, the *jīva*, is nothing but *para*. Either way it has the same meaning.

How are you going to reach this *para-puruṣa* when it is already the nature of yourself? Bhagavān says, *ananya-bhaktyā*

---

[40] पूर्णमदः पूर्णमिदं पूर्णात् पूर्णमुदच्यते । पूर्णस्य पूर्णमादाय पूर्णमेवावशिष्यते ॥

pūrṇamadaḥ pūrṇamidaṁ pūrṇāt pūrṇamudacyate, pūrṇasya pūrṇamādāya pūrnamevāvaśiṣyate.

tu labhyaḥ, it is gained only by devotion in which there is no other. Śaṅkara says here, it is devotion that is characterised by knowledge. If he is already non-separate from yourself, the only way you can pursue him is through the committed pursuit of knowledge. Usually, there is love when two people are involved, and a fusion takes place. In the devotional literature, the *jīva*s represented by the *gopīs*, are totally absorbed in the pursuit of Kṛṣṇa, who is Parameśvara. This can be called *ananya-bhakti,* devotion to one object and only that object. But when another object is involved, it is *anya-bhakti.* Here, Bhagavān says *ananya-bhakti,* a devotion in which there is no other, a devotion to *ātmā,* which is not other than yourself.

Generally, the result of devotion is to go to other *loka*s and the commitment is for that purpose. But in *ananya-bhakti,* the commitment is to one's *ātmā. Bhakti* here implies an enquiry that is imbued with *śraddhā* and longing. Because of that, only a *jijñāsu* or a *mumukṣu* can gain this knowledge.

Anything knowable that is other than yourself, you can stumble upon, but not *ātmā.* There are many reasons for this but the most important one is that *ātmā* is not an object. It is well hidden because the person who looks for it is really looking for oneself. So, the problem of seeking should be reduced to simple *jijñāsā.* All desires are reduced to one dominant consuming desire to know the *ātmā.* That is what is meant by the word, *ananya-bhakti* here.

About that *ātmā* he says, *yasya antaḥ sthāni bhūtāni yena sarvam idam tatam,* the one within whom are all beings and things in the world and by whom all beings are pervaded, that is *ātmā.* Just as an effect is pervaded by its material cause, all names and forms which are effects are pervaded by *ātmā*, the cause.[41] Śaṅkara uses the word, *kārya-bhūtāni*, in the form of a product, to describe these beings. Like even a product like pot that exists within its cause, the clay, so too, all things exist within or are comprised of *puruṣa*; this entire world is pervaded by *puruṣa*. Like the pot that is pervaded by space and within space alone all pots exist, this *ātmā*, being the cause of everything, is the one in whom all have their being and by whom all are pervaded. Being the cause of everything, there is nothing that is away from it. The existence of everything belongs only to *sat-cit-ātmā*.

What we call creation is nothing but name and form. Upon analysis, every name and form is reducible to further name and form until the entire *nāma-rūpa* is reduced to *sat-cit-ānanda-ātmā*. Wherever there is name and form, understand that there is *ātmā*, which is non-separate from it. This *ātmā* is to be gained by *ananya-bhakti*. *Bhakti* implies something that you love. In *ananya-bhakti*, all objects of desire are reduced to one, *ātmā*. The desire to know that *ātmā* is *jijñāsā*, and the love to know that *ātmā* is *bhakti*. Any form of *bhakti* is meant to discover Īśvara and the discovery of Parameśvara as *ātmā* is the end of the *jijñāsā*.

In these verses, Bhagavān points out two types of seekers. One seeker is directly and totally committed to Brahman. For such a seeker there is no travel after death because there is no subtle body. Its cause, the causal body, ignorance has been

---

[41] Like the rope for the snake, *ātmā* is the *vivarta-upādāna-kāraṇa*, the material cause that does not undergo any change.

destroyed along with all its products. The *karma* standing in the account of the *jīva* is no longer separate from Brahman. Therefore, in effect there is no causal body. So, there is no more birth.

The other seekers are the *upāsaka*s, meditators. They go to *brahma-loka* and there, being taught by Brahmaji, gain liberation. Then there are those who are doing good *karma* desiring for a better life later. They do gain a better life. But they have to come back again. All this is pointed out here.

Keeping this in mind, Śaṅkara introduces the next four verses.

These verses discuss the *upāsaka*s, meditators, who impose the concept of Brahman upon *oṁkāra* as a symbol in order to invoke or gain Parameśvara. For them, liberation is only after death. Such people, the *śruti* says, can go to *brahma-loka*. They travel through the *uttara-mārga*, one of the routes followed after death. Those who perform good *karma*s desiring a better life later, follow the *dakṣiṇa-mārga*, southern route, when they depart from this life. Both paths are shown to point out that there are two different directions – *uttara-mārga* goes to a place from where there is no possibility of return; the other, *dakṣiṇa-mārga*, goes to a place from where you will return. The south stands for *saṁsāra* or death and north for *mokṣa*. Everyone is attracted to *mokṣa*, even those who strive for the other *loka*s. Because of ignorance and confusion they pursue lesser things thinking that those will solve the problem. The northern route is also called the solar or bright path, and the other one the smoky or cloudy path. Both are pointed out here only to praise the *uttara-mārga*.

Verses 23&26

Praising the uttara-mārga by using dakṣiṇa-mārga as a background

यत्र काले त्वनावृत्तिमावृत्तिं चैव योगिनः ।
प्रयाता यान्ति तं कालं वक्ष्यामि भरतर्षभ ॥ २३ ॥

yatra kāle tvanāvṛttim āvṛttiṁ caiva yoginaḥ
prayātā yānti taṁ kālaṁ vakṣyāmi bharatarṣabha (23)

tu – however; *yatra kāle* – at which time (by which route); *yoginaḥ* – *yogī*s; *prayātāḥ* – who have departed; *yānti* – go; *taṁ kālaṁ* – that time; *anāvṛttim* – of no return; *āvṛttiṁ ca* – and of return; *eva* – indeed; *vakṣyāmi* – I will tell; *bharatarṣabha* – O the foremost in the clan of Bharata!

> Arjuna, the foremost in the clan of Bharata! I will tell you what is the time (route) of no return and also the time (route) of return by which the departed *yogī*s go.

Just as in a herd of cattle, there is usually one bull that stands out, so too, Arjuna cannot be missed among the members of the Bharata family. Therefore, he is addressed as *bharatarṣabha*.

Prayātāḥ means travellers and the word is connected to *yoginaḥ*, which refers to those who are either meditators or *karmaṭhas*. After death, some of the *yogī*s travel the path from which they will return while others depart through a path from which there is no return. I will now tell you about both these *mārgas*, says Bhagavān. The word *kāla* in this verse stands for *mārga*, path, by which people depart after death. The *mārga* is mentioned through the *kāla*. The word *kāla* also indicates the *devatā*s identified with time.

Since the world is not separate from Īśvara, every phenomenon in the world is Īśvara. When you look at through a given phenomenon, Īśvara becomes a *devatā*. All things – earth, trees, rivers, besides being objects, are looked upon as *devatā*s.

Īśvara, the efficient cause of creation is viewed from the standpoint of a given effect. If the Lord is the material cause, the world becomes the very form of Īśvara. When you view Īśvara through a given form in the creation, Īśvara becomes the presiding deity of that form. If you look at Īśvara through *karma*, he becomes the one who presides over the law of *karma* and gives the results of actions. Any number of *devatā*s are possible because there are varieties of phenomena. When you can look at Īśvara from any given aspect in the creation, there are many gods and they are nothing but one Īśvara viewed from different standpoints.

This is said not only to show where these meditators go but to praise the meditators who go to *brahma-loka* and do not return, a description of the others and where they go is also given. The intention of Kṛṣṇa is to praise the *uttara-mārga* by using *dakṣiṇa-mārga* as a background. There is no better background than a good contrast. It is not said to belittle the other, but as an aid to understanding.

अग्निर्ज्योतिरहः शुक्लः षण्मासा उत्तरायणम् ।
तत्र प्रयाता गच्छन्ति ब्रह्म ब्रह्मविदो जनाः ॥ २४ ॥

agnirjyotirahaḥ śuklaḥ ṣaṇmāsā uttarāyaṇam
tatra prayātā gacchanti brahma brahmavido janāḥ (24)

(*yatra* – where in which path); *agniḥ* – the deity of fire or time;[42] *jyotiḥ* – the deity of light; *ahaḥ* – the deity of the day; *śuklaḥ* – the deity of the bright fortnight (of the waxing moon); *ṣaṇmāsā uttarāyaṇam* – the deity of the six months of the sun's northward travel; (*santi* – are present); *tatra prayātāḥ* – those who have departed through that path after death; *brahma-vidaḥ janāḥ* – the people who meditate on Brahman; *brahma* – to *brahma-loka*; *gacchanti* – go

> Departing there (through that path) in which the deity of fire, the deity of light, the deity of the day, the deity of the bright fortnight (of the waxing moon), the deity of the six months of the northern solstice (the sun's travel towards the north) are present, the meditators of Brahman go to *brahma-loka*.

A blazing and beautiful route to brahma-loka

This is a blazing and beautiful route. On the way all the *devatā*s are there. *Agni,* the fire god is there to welcome you. *Jyotiḥ*, the presiding deity of time is there as is *ahaḥ*, the *devatā* of the day. *Śukla* is the fortnight of the bright half of the moon, represented by the *śukla-devatā*. The idea here is to indicate all that is bright. And these *devatā*s are present along the route to *brahma-loka*. *Uttarāyaṇa* is the period of six months when the

---

[42] Here the word '*agni*' refers to the *devatā* and that too the *devatā* of time. So too, with the others mentioned in this verse and the next. As Bhagavān Śaṅkara says,

अग्निः कालभिमानिनी देवता तथा ज्योतिरपि देवता एव कालाभिमानिनी । (शङ्कर भाष्यम्)

sun is travelling northwards, to the north of the equator. The north symbolises *mokṣa*; therefore, when the sun is travelling northward, it is considered to be a *puṇya-kāla*, a better period of time than *dakṣiṇāyana*, the six months when the sun is travelling southwards, to the south of the equator. *Ṣanmāsā uttarāyaṇa* literally means the six months of *utarāyaṇa*, but here, it refers to the deity presiding over the six months of *uttarāyaṇa*. All these bright *devatā*s invite the *jīva* on the path and take him to *brahma-loka*.

Brahmavidaḥ janāḥ brahma gacchanti, those people who meditate upon Brahman through *oṁkāra* go to *brahma* – *brahma-loka*. The word *brahma* here stands for *brahma-loka*. Having reached there, they can gain knowledge of themselves as Brahman and are free. Thus there is no return for them. We are only talking about those meditators who are successful enough to go to *brahma-loka*. We know that the word *brahma* stands for the gain of *brahma-loka* rather than Brahman because it is said that they follow a path with *devatā*s on the way. Śaṅkara says they go to *brahma-loka* and gain knowledge of Brahman, *krameṇa*, gradually. This is called *krama-mukti*. Then he adds that for the knowers of Brahman, there is no travel. The intention of Lord Kṛṣṇa is not to describe various paths but to point out that meditators go to *brahma-loka* and the path is brighter for them. So, Śaṅkara says that we have to take the word *brahmavidaḥ* here to mean meditators on Brahman and not knowers of Brahman. There is no going or coming for those who have clear knowledge of Brahman. As you come to know that you are Brahman, you have gained liberation. We are not talking about such people here. Since there is a route mentioned, it is only for the meditators.

For the wise man, there is no subtle body to depart when the physical body dies. All the *prāṇas* have resolved in Brahman. There is no person, no nucleus to which the *karma* can adhere. Since there are no *karma-phalas*, there is no travel. For the wise there is no going or coming because he or she is Brahman.

धूमो रात्रिस्तथा कृष्णः षण्मासा दक्षिणायनम् ।
तत्र चान्द्रमसं ज्योतिर्योगी प्राप्य निवर्तते ॥ २५ ॥

dhūmo rātristathā kṛṣṇaḥ ṣaṇmāsā dakṣiṇāyanam
tatra cāndramasaṁ jyotiryogī prāpya nivartate (25)

(*yatra* – where, in which path;) *dhūmaḥ* – the presiding deity of clouds; *tathā rātriḥ* – similarly the deity of night; *kṛṣṇaḥ* – the deity of the dark fortnight; *ṣaṇmāsā dakṣiṇāyanam* – the deity of the six months of the sun's southward travel; *tatra* – there (on the path); (*gatvā* – going) *yogī* – the *yogī*, the meditator; *cāndramasaṁ jyotiḥ* – the world of the moon; *prāpya* – having gained; *nivartate* – returns

The *yogī*, (travelling by the route) where the presiding deity of clouds, the deity of night, the deity of the dark fortnight (of the waning moon), and the deity of the six months of the southern solstice (the sun's travel towards the south) (are present), having gained the world of the moon, returns.

The dhūma-mārga is for the one who is not a karma-yogī

There is a *mārga*, route, for the one who is not a *karma-yogī*, but who does rituals to gain some merit. Even though he is a *karmaṭha*, he is called a *yogī*, because he does only the enjoined *karma*s, not those which are considered sinful. Thereby he gains a *deva-loka* called *candra-loka*. Again, the description of this path is given only to praise the bright path. For both, travel is involved. On the bright path, there is no return once the knowledge is gained in *brahma-loka*. Here, on the other hand, the *karmaṭha*s follow the path called *dhūma-mārga*, smoky path. The *devatā*s on this path preside over things that represent darkness – the god of the night; the god of the waning or dark side of the moon, the god of the six months of the sun's southward travel, are there on this path. *Jyotiḥ* here refers to *karma-phala* and not light because light cannot be enjoyed. A person who has done the enjoined *karma*s enjoys the fruit of those actions for some time and then returns back to the earth. The *jīva* is not released from *saṁsāra* just because he or she has done good *karma*s.

The idea of the verse is that you travel; death does not give you *mokṣa*. Only knowledge can do it, and if it is not gained, you embark upon these two paths after death. But these are only the good paths. There are others which are not so good. There is even a *naraka*, a place where you undergo certain pain. That is also *karma-phala* and when it is exhausted, you return. *Karma-phala* cannot be eternal; so, even from a painful *loka* you will return. Here only the desirable ends are talked about and even from them, you return.

शुक्लकृष्णे गती ह्येते जगतः शाश्वते मते ।
एकया यात्यनावृत्तिमन्ययावर्तते पुनः ॥ २६ ॥

śuklakṛṣṇe gatī hyete jagataḥ śāsvate mate
ekayā yātyanāvṛttim anyayāvartate punaḥ (26)

hi – as is well known; *jagataḥ* – of the world; *ete gatī* – these two paths; *śukla-kṛṣṇe* – the bright and the dark; *śāsvate mate* – are considered eternal; *ekayā* – (travelling) by one; *anāvṛttiṁ yāti* – one goes to a place of no return; *anyayā* – by the other; *āvartate punaḥ* – one returns again

As is well known in the *śāstra*, these two paths of the world, the bright and the dark, are considered eternal. By the one (path), one goes to a place of no return, by the other, one returns again.

Śukla-kṛṣṇe gatī hi ete jagataḥ, these two paths by which one gains various ends are called as *śukla*, the bright path, and *kṛṣṇa*, the dark path. *Hi* here indicates 'as it is known in the *śāstra*.' *Śāstra* is the only means of knowing them. *Jagat* means 'world' and here it stands for the world of people – the meditators and those who do good actions. For such people who are qualified to do *karma*, there are these two paths available.

The two paths are relatively eternal

Śāśvate mate, they are considered eternal. These paths are relatively eternal because *saṁsāra* can go on indefinitely. Unless you gain *mokṣa*, it does not come to an end. You have to put an end to it by knowing the truth about yourself. So, when it is said that these two paths are eternal, the idea is that there is no natural liberation. You must have a desire to know; and until that happens, *saṁsāra* continues. For the *jīva* who is ignorant, *saṁsāra* seems eternal.

Ekayā yāti anāvṛttim anyayā āvartate punaḥ, by one path, he goes to an end from where there is no return, *anāvṛtti*. That is the *śukla-gati* whereby he reaches *brahma-loka* and there being taught by Brahmaji, gains *mokṣa*. If he goes by the other, the *dhūma* or *kṛṣṇa-gati*, he comes back. Between the two paths, one would naturally want to choose the bright one, which leads to *mokṣa*. *Mokṣa*, however, is gained not by a *gati*, path, but by knowledge, which Bhagavān shows in the next verse.

Verse 27

The yogī knows that mokṣa is not gained by gati but by knowledge

नैते सृती पार्थ जानन्योगी मुह्यति कश्चन ।
तस्मात्सर्वेषु कालेषु योगयुक्तो भवार्जुन ॥ २७ ॥

naite sṛtī pārtha jānan yogī muhyati kaścana
tasmāt sarveṣu kāleṣu yogayukto bhavārjuna (27)

pārtha – O son of Pṛthā, Arjuna!; *kaścana yogī* – a *yogī*; *ete sṛtī* – these two paths; *jānan* – knowing; *na muhyati* – is not deluded; *tasmāt* – therefore; *arjuna* – O Arjuna!; *sarveṣu kāleṣu* – at all times; *yoga-yuktaḥ* – united to *yoga*; *bhava* – may you be

Knowing these two paths, Pārtha (Arjuna)! a *yogī* is not deluded. Therefore, Arjuna! at all times may you be united to *yoga*.

Na ete sṛtī pārtha jānan yogī muhyati kaścana, O Arjuna! knowing these two paths, a *yogī* does not get deluded. The *yogī* here is a *vivekī* or a *jijñāsu*. He is not at all deluded about these two paths because he knows one is for *saṁsāra*, the other is for *mokṣa*. He has no confusion about the fact that gaining another *loka* does not give him liberation. Freedom comes only by knowledge, which can be gained here or in *brahma-loka*. The whole of humanity suffers from this delusion that going to heaven is *mokṣa*. It is methodically propagated by all religions and is so prevalent in humanity that Kṛṣṇa had to state it explicitly as a delusion. A *vivekī* or *yogī* is not deluded about this at all.

Tasmāt sarveṣu kāleṣu yoga-yuktaḥ bhava arjuna, therefore, O! Arjuna, equip yourself for this knowledge at all times. Whatever is necessary for knowledge, please do. *Yoga* here is knowledge, preceded by *antaḥ-karaṇa-śuddhi*, purification of the mind. Knowledge is *yoga* and any means that helps you gain it is also called *yoga*.

Verse 28

Such a yogī crosses all that and gains the status of Īśvara

वेदेषु यज्ञेषु तपःसु चैव दानेषु यत्पुण्यफलं प्रदिष्टम् ।
अत्येति तत्सर्वमिदं विदित्वा योगी परं स्थानमुपैति चाद्यम् ॥२८ ॥

vedeṣu yajñeṣu tapaḥsu caiva
dāneṣu yatpuṇyaphalaṁ pradiṣṭam
atyeti tatsarvam idaṁ viditvā
yogī paraṁ sthānam upaiti cādyam (28)

yogī – the *yogī*; *idaṁ viditvā* – knowing this; *yat puṇya-phalam* – the result of good actions; *vedeṣu* – with regard to Veda (study of the Vedas); *yajñeṣu* – in rituals; *tapaḥsu* – in disciplines; *ca eva* – and as well; *dāneṣu* – in charities; (*śāstreṇa* – by the *śāstra*);[43] *pradiṣṭam* – is ordained; *tat sarvam* (*puṇya-phalam*) – all that *puṇya-phalam*; *atyeti* – goes beyond; *ādyam* – the primal cause; *paraṁ sthānam* – which is the highest state; *upaiti ca* – and he reaches

> The *yogī* knowing this, (the answers to Arjuna's questions here) goes beyond all things taught by the *śāstra*, with reference to the result of good actions, which abides in the (study of the) Veda, the rituals, disciplines, and charities. And he reaches the primal cause (of creation), which is the highest state.

There are two sentences here. Knowing this, the *yogī* crosses all that, *yogī idam viditvā, tat sarvam atyeti*, is one sentence. The other is, *param ādyam sthānam upaiti*, he reaches the highest place, the primal cause (of creation).

Vedeṣu yajñeṣu tapaḥsu ca eva dāneṣu pradiṣṭam yat puṇya-phalam, the *puṇya* that is ordained by the *śāstra* as a result of the study of the Vedas, performing of various rituals, austerities and charities. These are the ways by which one gathers *puṇya-phala*. Simply studying the Veda is a *puṇya-karma*. Besides, there are many rituals mentioned there, which, if performed, bring *puṇya-phala*. The emphasis is both on the study of the Veda and the performance of rituals. *Tapas* is following various religious disciplines. *Dāna* is giving time, expertise or money

[43] This word is understood here and is therefore added to complete the meaning.

to others. All these produce *adṛṣṭa-phala* that is not immediately seen by you, but is credited to your account and reaped either in this life itself or later in another life.

Yogī idam viditvā tat sarvam atyeti, knowing this, the answers to Arjuna's questions in the first and second verses of this chapter, the *yogī* grows out of the limited means and ends. He goes for the total freedom, that is knowing oneself as the limitless Brahman which is the Lord.

Paraṁ sthānam upaiti ca ādyam, and he gains the status of Īśvara, which is the highest status one can reach. *Ādya* is what is in the beginning, the cause of creation. Only Brahman was there in the beginning; then Brahman created the entire world and is in the form of this world. The cause is very important here. If it is *satya,* the product becomes *mithyā* because there is no product separate from its cause. When the cause is *satya,*the product continues to be Brahman. Therefore, if one understands this–the nature of Brahman, the creation, which includes oneself, Īśvara, the *ādyaṁ kāraṇam,* first cause, and knowing 'I am everything'– all these *loka*s have no meaning. Then, one understands that 'I am that Brahman.' And understanding that, one gains that ultimate end.

ॐतत्सत् ।

इति श्रीमद्भगवद्गीतासूपनिषत्सु ब्रह्मविद्यायां योगशास्त्रे श्रीकृष्णार्जुन-
संवादे अक्षर-ब्रह्म-योगो नाम अष्टमोऽध्यायः ॥ ८ ॥

oṁ tat sat.

iti śrīmadbhagavadgītāsūpaniṣatsu brahma-vidyāyāṁ yoga-śāstre śrīkṛṣṇārjuna-saṁvāde akṣara-brahma-yogo nāma aṣṭamo'dhyāyaḥ (8)

Om, Brahman, is the only reality. Thus ends the eighth chapter called *akṣara-brahma-yoga* – having the topic of imperishable Brahman – in the *Bhagavadgītā* which is in the form of a dialogue between Śrī Kṛṣṇa and Arjuna, which is the essence of the *Upaniṣads*, whose subject matter is both the knowledge of Brahman and *yoga*.[44]

[44] Here the word *yoga* refers to anything a person needs in terms of *antaḥ-karaṇa-śuddhi*, preparation of the mind and so on, that is needed for the assimilation of this knowledge. Since the *Gītā* discusses all these along with *brahma-vidyā*, it is also referred to as *yoga-śāstra*.

Chapter 9

राजविद्या-राजगुह्य-योगः

Rājavidyā-rājaguhya-yogaḥ

Topic of the king of knowledge, the king of secrets

In the previous chapter, a number of topics were discussed ending with the gain of *brahma-loka* and the possibility of *krama-mukti*. It was said that a person meditating upon a form of the Lord for the sake of *mokṣa*, reaches *brahma-loka* where Brahmaji can teach him that he is limitless Brahman, the cause of creation. Knowing that he is free, he does not come back, that is, there is *anāvṛtti* for him, an end to the cycle of birth and death that characterises *mokṣa*. It is possible only with the knowledge that 'I am Brahman.' Only then, is there no longer an individual, an entity that can assume a body and travel.

All this was pointed out, and you may conclude that by meditation upon the Lord, *saguṇa-brahma*, you gain *mokṣa*, though not in this life. To show that there is no such thing, Bhagavān reveals here that *mukti* is always immediate. This has to be said explicitly to eliminate any notion that by going to heaven you will gain liberation. For that purpose, Bhagavān begins the ninth chapter of the *Gītā* with the following verse.

Verse 1

Kṛṣṇa reveals this most secret knowledge gained right now

श्रीभगवानुवाच ।
इदं तु ते गुह्यतमं प्रवक्ष्याम्यनसूयवे ।
ज्ञानं विज्ञानसहितं यज्ज्ञात्वा मोक्ष्यसेऽशुभात् ॥ १ ॥

śrībhagavān uvāca
idaṁ tu te guhyatamaṁ pravakṣyāmyanasūyave
jñānaṁ vijñānasahitaṁ yajjñātvā mokṣyase'śubhāt (1)

śrībhagavān – the Lord; *uvāca* – said;
tu – whereas; *idam* – this; *guhyatamaṁ jñānam* – most secret knowledge; *vijñāna-sahitam* – together with immediate knowledge; *te anasūyave* – to you who are without calumny; *pravakṣyāmi* – I will explain clearly and in detail; *yat jñātvā* – knowing which; *mokṣyase* – you will be released; *aśubhāt* – from all that is inauspicious

Śrī Bhagavān said:
Now, I will clearly explain to you (who are) without calumny, this most secret knowledge together with immediate knowledge, knowing which you will be released from all that is inauspicious.

Vakṣyāmi means 'I will explain.' The prefix '*pra*' enhances the meaning of the verb. Therefore, *pravakṣyāmi* means I will explain in detail, clearly.

Explain what? *Idam*, this. Since Bhagavān is just starting this chapter, how can he use the pronoun 'this,' which usually refers to something directly in front of you? Here, while introducing the topic, he says 'this.' But the pronoun can also be used to refer to a topic already begun, which is now being further discussed. And it can be used when you have something in mind, which you are going to explain, just as when you say, 'When I went to New York today, I met this man.' 'This' man is someone you have in your mind, whom you are going to talk about. Śaṅkara says, having brought to his mind, *tadbuddhau sannidhī-kṛtya*. What he is going to tell has already crystallised in his mind. *Idam* is *brahma-jñāna*, the knowledge of Brahman that was unfolded from the second chapter through to the eighth and is now going to be elaborated further. Bhagavān is saying, 'I am going to tell you what I have already talked about before,' knowing full well what he is going to talk about later in this chapter.

The word 'tu' distinguishes this knowledge as immediate

'*Tu*' indicates that he is distinguishing the topic he is now introducing from the one he has just discussed, *brahma-loka-prāpti* and the subsequent gain of knowledge, *krama-mukti*. To distinguish that kind of accomplishment from this, he uses the word *tu*, the distinction being that the knowledge he is unfolding here is to be gained right now, and not later. If you are already Brahman why should you wait to go to *brahma-loka* to know that?

The vision of the *Gītā* is that you are Brahman, and once you know it, you are free. Everyone wants to be free. If you claim to be interested in something else, you are only confused about what you really want. This confusion has to be resolved so that you can understand right now that you are Brahman. You are already Brahman and that is exactly what you want to be. In the vision of the *śāstra*, you are totally acceptable. If you think that you are not, it is a mistake, and to correct it knowledge is necessary. If you are already Brahman, postponement of gaining this knowledge is silly.

It is like a rich person who wants to be rich, not knowing that he has great wealth. To be rich, he has only to know that he is rich; anything else postpones it. Between who he wants to be and who he is, the ideal and the actual, what is the distance? There is no physical distance nor is there any temporal distance. He will not become rich later; he is already rich. Nor is the rich person away from him. The only thing separating him from being rich is ignorance. It has to be removed.

Right now you are Brahman. Why should you postpone knowing that by making efforts to go to *brahma-loka* and gain this knowledge there? If you want to do a few things here like making some money etc., my question would be, 'Why do you want that money?' If you say, 'it is for some security, some happiness,' I say, 'that is exactly what Brahman is.' You first discover that you are secure and happy and you can also earn money happily. Otherwise, after earning money you will discover that you are still unhappy. Solve the problem of being unhappy, and then happily do whatever you want. You need to solve this problem first and understand that you are Brahman; you are what you are seeking. This is the significance of the word *tu*. It distinguishes this knowledge that Bhagavān is now going to talk about as something to be gained right now.

Śaṅkara explains that clear knowledge is the only means for immediate liberation. It is simple knowledge. There is no experience involved here, no particular condition to be achieved. He quotes a number of *śruti*s and *smṛti*s to describe the knowledge distinguished by the word *tu*, knowledge that is the direct means for freedom, *sākṣāt mokṣa-prāpti-sādhana*.

It was said earlier, *vāsudevaḥ sarvam iti*, all that is here is nothing but Vāsudeva, the Lord.[1] This entire creation is non-separate from the Lord. Since nothing is separate from that Lord, you are the Lord; you are the total. This knowledge liberates you. *Vāsudevaḥ sarvam* is not a belief; it is knowledge, a fact to be understood.

The *Chāndogyopaniṣad* says, *ātmaiva idam sarvam*, this is *ātmā*, yourself.[2] The whole world – sun, moon, stars, known and unknown – is not separate from you. What else can be said about you? You are everything, you are limitless, infinite; everything is you. And again the *Chāndogyopaniṣad* says, *ekam eva advitīyam*, one that is non-dual alone.[3] And knowing, 'I am that *ātmā* which is everything,' there is freedom from any sense of limitation and one is free. This is *mokṣa*.

The same idea is also expressed negatively by the *śruti* when it says, those who do not know this fact about *ātmā*, suffer a life of limitation, *atha te anyathā ato viduḥ anya-rājānaḥ te kṣayalokaḥ bhavanti*, those who look upon themselves as other (than Brahman), are subject to experiences that perish.[4]

When you describe *mokṣa*, bondage is very clear. Even then it is spelled out. In English we say it is expressed unequivocally. In clear terms the *śāstra* says that the one who looks upon

---

1 *Gītā 7.19*

2 *Chāndogyopaniṣad* 7.25.2

3 *Chāndogyopaniṣad* 6.2.1

4 *Chāndogyopaniṣad* 7.25.2

himself as other than Brahman, delivers himself into the hands of death and one who understands that he is Brahman is free.

This knowledge alone is the direct means for *mokṣa*, nothing else. Not meditation, *karma*, attitude, or values, though all of them are indirectly helpful to gain a mind that can grasp this knowledge. It is like the fuel, vessels, and so on that are needed for cooking, but all of them together cannot cook. For that you require fire. Similarly, for liberation, the direct means is the knowledge, 'I am Brahman.' Hence Śaṅkara says clear knowledge is the direct means for gaining liberation, not anything else.

In knowledge, preparedness is what accounts for whether that knowledge takes place. The equation 1+1=2 is impossible for an infant to understand, because, he is not yet prepared. For the knowledge 'I am Brahman' to sink in, the required preparation is certain maturity or assimilation of the experiences of life.

Therefore, Kṛṣṇa says here, '*arjuna te anasūyave idaṁ pravakṣyāmi*, Arjuna unto you, who is free from *asūyā*, I will tell you this clearly.' The word *asūyā* has no real equivalent in English. The definition of this word in Sanskrit is, *guṇeṣu doṣa-darśanam*, seeing a defect where there are virtues. Saying of a great man that he is lame is *asūyā*. It is an expression of not being able to accept good qualities or accomplishments in others. This is one of the worst problems a person can have. Karṇa,[5] a man of great virtues, had this problem. Even though

[5] Refer to footnote 11 in Volume 1- page 101

he had all the princely qualities, because he thought he was the son of a driver, he suffered from a complex that expressed itself as *asūyā*. Arjuna had no such complex and therefore, no such problem. So, he is called *anasūyā*. Wherever there was some good quality, he recognised it, giving the qualified person his due. He accepted the person without *asūyā*. Absence of *asūyā* represents all other qualities which Bhagavān is going to talk about in the twelfth and thirteenth chapters – *adveṣa, amānitva, adambhitva, ahimsā, kṣānti, ārjava* and so on. All are implied by this one word, *anasūyā*, and they qualify Arjuna for this knowledge.

This knowledge is the greatest secret

About this knowledge, Bhagavān says further that it is *guhyatama*, the greatest secret. *Guhya* means secret and the affix *tama* added to it makes it a superlative – the greatest secret. Why is it the greatest secret? There are various reasons.

The fact about it is that no matter how many times you may teach, rarely does anyone understand. It remains a secret in spite of being revealed. And even if it is understood, there are certain things that inhibit the assimilation of the knowledge. Therefore, it is *guhyatama*, the greatest secret. The preparedness for it is the greatest thing you can accomplish in life. You require maturity, which does not come by itself; you have to work on it. That is why it has been said that you need not protect Vedanta. It guards itself like the formula on relativity, $E = mc^2$.

You can write it down a hundred times and yet not understand what it means. You need to reach a point from where you can understand, and this requires a lot of preparation. Therefore, this knowledge is *guhyatama*.

It is outside the known means of knowledge

Another reason it is the most secret is that, it is not something that can be gained by the known means of knowledge like perception, inference, or by your experience. There are two types of perceptions, *indriya-pratyakṣa*, perception by the sense organs, and *sākṣi-pratyakṣa*, witness perception, which is a direct perception by the mind. Seeing the printed word on the page is *indriya-pratyakṣa*, perception through a sense organ. The conditions of your mind like *sukha, duḥkha* are known by you as a *sākśī*, witness. That the witness that witnesses everything is Brahman is not a perception of either of the above, not *pratyakṣa*. It is not an object of experience, that is, perception through a sense organ or a perception directly by the mind. Nor is it a matter for inference. Therefore, there is no way of knowing, 'I am Brahman,' unless you have another *pramāṇa*, means of knowledge. And that *pramāṇa* by which this knowledge is gained is *śabda*, the words of the *śāstra*. Because it is not available for any known *pramāṇa*, and because it is only through the teaching that you can gain this knowledge, it is *guhyatama*.

It is the most valuable

Another thing that makes it the greatest of secrets is its worth. What is sacred or precious is always a secret. You cannot keep a large emerald as a table weight! It will disappear in no time. Anything that is precious or rare is kept secret. So, saying that it is the most secret is saying that it is the most precious.

Jñānaṁ vijñānasahitaṁ te pravakṣyāmi, this knowledge I am going to give you, which is the knowledge of Brahman as yourself, is also *vijñāna-sahita*. I am not simply going to state that there is Brahman. I am going to prove that you are Brahman. That is what is meant by the statement *vijñāna-sahita*. I will bring to you an immediate appreciation of this knowledge as yourself.

You may ask, 'What will I gain from it?' Suppose I tell you a secret like the crows have no teeth. What do you get out of it? When I say you are Brahman, you can say, 'If I am Brahman, let it be so. What difference does it make to me?' The fact is, knowing that you are Brahman you are everything, you will be free from all things that are inauspicious, *mokṣyase-aśubhāt*. You will be free from *aśubha*, what is not auspicious, not desirable You will be released from sorrow, from inadequacy, smallness, and from the bondage of the self – in short, from *saṁsāra*. You will be free from a life of becoming.

Śubha means something that is ultimately good. It is often written at the end of a letter or book to indicate an auspicious conclusion. *Aśubha* means it is not an auspicious end. When a person dies and is released from the body, although the end takes place, it is not auspicious because it begins again. That is *saṁsāra* and from which you will be liberated, *mokṣyase*. *Aśubha* can also mean doubt. Then the meaning of these words will be – you will be released from doubt.

Verse 2

Bhagavān praises this knowledge to draw the attention of Arjuna

राजविद्या राजगुह्यं पवित्रमिदमुत्तमम् ।
प्रत्यक्षावगमं धर्म्यं सुसुखं कर्तुमव्ययम् ॥ २ ॥

rājavidya rājaguhyaṁ pavitram idam uttamam
pratyakṣāvagamaṁ dharmyaṁ susukhaṁ kartum avyayam (2)

idam – this; *rājavidyā* – the king of all-knowledge; *rājaguhyam* – the king of secrets; *pavitram uttamam* – is the greatest purifier; *pratyakṣa-avagamam* – directly appreciated; *dharmyam* – in keeping with *dharma; susukhaṁ* – easy to accomplish; *avyayam* – imperishable

This is the king of all-knowledge, the king of secrets, the greatest purifier, directly appreciated, not opposed to *dharma*, easy to accomplish and imperishable.

The *jñāna*, knowledge, that was spoken of in the first verse is called *vidyā* here. The roots of both words have the same meaning, to know. This knowledge that liberates you from *saṁsāra,* is necessarily different from any other type of knowledge and is therefore called *rāja-vidyā*, the king among all disciplines of knowledge.

It is rāja-vidyā because it is self-shining

As in a kingdom, among the many inhabitants, the one who is the *raja*, the king, is the final authority, similarly here, this knowledge is the king among the various disciplines of knowledge. Śaṅkara gives the meaning of the word drawn from its root, *rāj,* which means to shine. So, *rājā* is the one who shines by himself, who does not depend upon anything else. Among the people in the kingdom, the king is glorious, great in his own right. Similarly, *ātmā* is the only one who is self effulgent.

Knowledge of this self-shining self is the king of all-knowledge because all other forms of knowledge depend upon this *ātmā,* the illumining factor. Every other piece of knowledge is revealed by your *buddhi,* but this one is self revealing, *svayam rājate,* it shines of its own accord.

Ātma-vidyā resolves all divisions

All other forms of knowledge perpetuate the *jñātṛ- jñāna-jñeya-bheda,* the division of the knower-knowledge,[6] and the object of knowledge. They confirm the notion of division that makes you experience yourself as limited. This *jñātṛ-jñāna-jñeya-bheda,* division, accounts for all differences. It is not really the differences that we are concerned about here, but the division. Knowing that there are these differences is not a problem. But the sense of division creates self-inflicted limitations. When you say that the *jñātā,* the knower, is other than the *jñeya,* the known, then one limits the other. Thus the division causes a sense of limitation in the knower. It is because what you are not, that is, the entire world is overwhelmingly big; whereas you are small and insignificant.

---

[6] Here the word '*jñāna,* knowledge' refers to the instrument of knowledge.

As we have seen, all *bheda*s, divisions, fall under three categories. They are – *vijātīya-bheda,* the division between species, *sajātīya-bheda,* the division within a given group, and *svagata-bheda,* the division within a member of a given group. Once you say things are divided, you become one among the divided. You are a distinct entity qualified by a few attributes living in and transacting business with the world, which is other than yourself. You find you are a limited individual with your own problems that seem very legitimate. You become a mortal, limited in terms of sex, age, colour, race, and a whole host of other attributes. All of these are brought about by the original division, that of *jñātā, jñāna* and *jñeya*. This division is not ordinary; it creates *saṁsāra*. It is the villain of the drama called *saṁsāra*.

It exists in every other *vidyā*, even in psychology. If you examine your own psychology, even though it is 'your' psychology, you begin with a symptom, which you attempt to trace to its roots. The connection is inferred based on a pattern that emerges from the study of the behaviour and background of many people. That pattern becomes the basis for further deduction and you make a conclusion. This inferred piece of knowledge implies a *jñātā*, knower, who has *jñāna*, knowledge, of *jñeya*, something known. Even though psychology seems very much connected to you, it is still a discipline of knowledge, which only confirms *saṁsāra*.

Any knowledge is true to its object. The knowledge of the crystal is as true as the crystal, in the sense, all the properties of the crystal are contained in your knowledge of the crystal. But in knowing a crystal, you are the knower of it and different from the crystal. The self, however, is not a known object. The 'object' of the self is the self that knows. So, the knower of the self and the object are one. Once this is known, ignorance is removed and the *vṛtti* that removed the ignorance goes away leaving the *phala*, the resolution of the *jñātṛ-jñāna-jñeya-bheda*, the division of knower-knowledge-known. When these are destroyed, all other differences are also destroyed. You see that every piece of knowledge is nothing but you, every object of knowledge is non-separate from you, and the knower, of course, is non-separate from you. All three of them depend entirely upon the self, consciousness, as such. How is it so?

Jñātā, the knower, is a *caitanya-ātmā*, conscious being, with reference to something known. The knowledge, the *vṛtti*,[7] is also nothing but *caitanya-ātmā*. And the object of knowledge is not separate from *caitanya-ātmā*. If you say the object is outside *sat-cit-ānanda-ātmā*, how is it outside? If you consider the world from the *sat-aṁśa*, the existence-aspect, there is nothing away from it. All that exists in this world has its being in *sat*, which happens to be *ātmā*. From the knowledge aspect, there is no piece of knowledge that is separate from consciousness, the very nature of the subject, *ātmā*. The knowledge of the self implies all these. *Aham ekam advitīyaṁ brahma*, I alone am everything, one non-dual Brahman – knower-known-knowledge;

---

[7] This *vṛtti* is the instrument of knowledge and the word *jñāna* in the *tripuṭī*, *jñātā*, *jñāna* and *jñeya* refers to this.

the cause of the whole creation – and at the same time the *jagat-kāraṇa*. This is *ātma-vidyā*. Definitely, it is *rāja-vidyā*, the king among all forms of knowledge. While every other *vidyā* maintains divisions, this *vidyā* devours all divisions.

Going one step further, only *ātma-vidyā* can be called as *vidyā*. Everything else is *avidyā* because the division is *avidyā*. The division – I am the knower, this is an object of knowledge and I have knowledge of it – is all *avidyā* There is no knower-known-knowledge separate from Brahman. These divisions are created by *avidyā* and depend entirely upon *ātma* being taken as a knower. Based on that are the knower-known pursuits.

'Does it mean that if I have knowledge of *ātma* I will have no knower-known pursuits? Will there be no more seer-seen, hearer-heard?' All these will remain but the division is *bādhita*, negated. There is an apparent knower-known pursuit, but between the knower and known, there is no division. Then for whom is the pursuit? Everything is '*iva*, as though.' There is a seeming knower-known pursuit.

Moreover, in every other pursuit of knowledge, there is always something more to be known, which is invariably much greater than what is known. Sometimes what you think you know is also falsified later. And, your definition of knowledge is *abādhitaṁ jñānam*, that which is not subject to negation. Any knowledge you have is negatable because from another standpoint, it changes completely. If you say this is a table, from another standpoint it becomes wood. The table is *bādhita*.

The previous knowledge is completely negated by knowledge of the *kāraṇa*, cause. And if a new discovery takes place, a given piece of knowledge also becomes *bādhita*. Furthermore, no knowledge is ever complete. Because the universe is a whole, every piece of knowledge is connected to every other piece of knowledge. In the whole, how can you have a piece of knowledge and yet call it knowledge? Knowing an aspect of something you cannot say you know it completely. Unless you know the whole, you will not know the part as a part.

There is no other knowledge, knowing which everything is as well known. Every other *vidyā* leaves behind a bit of ignorance because knowledge without the vision of the whole is never understood completely. The whole happens to be the self. Therefore, you are the whole in which there are no details because *ātmā* is free from attributes; *nāma-rūpa* is superimposed upon *ātmā*. To know that the self is Brahman as something that is whole, is to have complete knowledge because it has no attributes. If there are attributes, you have to know them and it is not possible to know them completely. So, any piece of knowledge is really *avidyā*, it cannot be called *jñāna*.

Whereas in knowledge of the self, Brahman, partial knowledge is not possible because there is no part. It is the partless whole and therefore, either you know it or you do not. 'I,' the *ātmā* is free from any form of limitation. It is one limitless consciousness, free from any attributes. There is no possibility of partial knowledge here. Therefore, only one *jñāna* is possible, *ātma-jñāna*.

So, *abādhita-jñāna* means not just that it cannot be negated; it means this alone can be considered as knowledge.

In any other *vidyā*, after knowing it how do you feel about it? Every Ph.D. is grateful when he or she is awarded his degree because the person alone knows how little one knows. One knows how much one had to study and how little one has understood. Even what one has written, one has not understood completely. Every sentence can be research material for another Ph.D. This goes on and on. No one is satisfied with one's knowledge even in a given field. What to talk of the ignorance one has in so many other disciplines of knowledge. In terms of simple satisfaction, *ātma-vidyā* has the last word among the disciplines of knowledge.

Every dissatisfaction implies an 'I' as *ahaṅkāra* which is the knower. It is not the brain that is dissatisfied with itself. 'I' am dissatisfied. This dissatisfaction is centred on *ahaṅkāra*, the ego. How are you going to eliminate that? You cannot remove it, you can only understand that *ahaṅkāra* is only an apparent form, a *mithyā* form of *sat-cit-ānanda-advaya-brahma*. This knowledge that removes the notion of limitation of the self is therefore, *rāja-vidyā*.

This rāja-vidyā is rāja-guhyam – the greatest secret

What we saw in the last verse for *guhyatama* can be said again here. *Ātma-vidyā* is the greatest secret. Any secret can be stumbled upon but this one can remain a secret for eternity. Any other secret is available for disclosure because as a knower you have the means to know, that is, your perception and inference. But the self is the secret of the very knower; how can you know it? About the knower who goes about unravelling all secrets, there is a great secret. The knower is the sought. What you seek is exactly what you are. You are not going to figure it out. You need to be told by some other source.

It is like wanting to see your eyes. It is an illegitimate desire. If you see, you know that you have eyes; in fact, if you want to see the eyes, it is a problem. That you exist and you are conscious is no problem. But if you have to know the nature of that self, you have a problem. To see the eyes you need a mirror. So too, words are like a mirror to show you exactly what you have to know. You must see the fact, 'I am Brahman.' Until then, it is *rāja-guhya*, the greatest secret.

As we saw in the last verse, because of its sanctity, *ātma-vidyā* is also *guhya*. Anything that is precious is *guhya*. Among all the precious things, the most precious is *ātma-vidyā*, self-knowledge, because anything else, no matter how precious it is, makes you more insecure. Even if a woman has a necklace, which has a value of one million dollars, she will wear an imitation of it and keep the real one locked up. Why, because it is precious. Does this precious thing make her secure or insecure? She is insecure because someone may take it from her and even harm her in the process. All precious things in this world make us insecure. Only *ātma-vidyā*, the real precious one, makes you secure, which is why it is *rāja-guhya*; no one can take it away from you.

Ātma-jñāna is the greatest purifier

Further the Lord says, *pavitram idam uttamam*, this knowledge is the greatest purifier. *Pavitra* means something that purifies. There are many purifying agents, the most well known of which is *agni*, fire, who is also called *pāvakaḥ*, the one who purifies. Even so, there is nothing so purifying as *ātma-jñāna* because it removes the very concept of purity and impurity. It is, therefore, *uttama*, the most exalted. Śaṅkara says it is the greatest purifier because in an instant it burns away countless births, along with their cause, *puṇya* and *pāpa*.

Suppose a person commits a regrettable action that leaves one feeling guilty. One knows the action was wrong. Others also know that it was wrong and may even point it out. How are you going to remove that sense of guilt? You can try to shift the attention, look for a scapegoat, a justification. To an extent you can free yourself from guilt by focusing on your parents or the planets or even confessing about the whole thing; but the guilt will not completely go. Once it is entertained, you cannot remove it. Similarly, you cannot totally remove hurt. Some traces are always left behind. Psychologically, astrologically, or even religiously you can deal with it but the guilt remains as long as you think you are the *ahaṅkāra*. This is the nucleus that holds all the imprints of guilt. Total elimination is not possible unless you understand *ātmā* is *akartā*.

That I never perform any action at any time is the truth about the self. It is not self-hypnotism. I cannot hypnotise myself into a belief that I did not do any action. But that I never performed any action is a fact from the standpoint of *ātmā* – *naiva kiñcit (karma) karomi.*[8]

A story illustrating this is told of Lord Kṛṣṇa. It seems there was a big discussion going on among the *gopī*s about Kṛṣṇa having many wives. He wanted to make the *gopī*s understand something. One day, when he was on the banks of the Yamuna he told them that there was a *ṛṣi* on the other bank who had not eaten for a number of months and they must go and feed him. All the *gopī*s prepared food and taking it on several plates, went to the banks of the Yamuna to cross. They found the Yamuna in spate and no boatman would come. So, they came back to Kṛṣṇa and asked him how they were to get to the other bank. Kṛṣṇa told them to go to the Yamuna and address it saying, 'If Kṛṣṇa is a *brahmacārī*, then O Yamuna! Please subside.' The *gopī*s laughed, went to the Yamuna, not believing what Kṛṣṇa had said but simply following his orders. No sooner did the *gopī*s address the Yamuna, it dried up as instructed. What is this? In great wonder – thinking Kṛṣṇa is not a *brahmacārī*, he has Rādhā, Rukmiṇī, Satyabhāmā, and others – they went to the other bank to feed the *ṛṣi*.

They marvelled as he ate everything they had brought – plates and plates of food. When they went back to the Yamuna, they were again unable to cross and went back to the *ṛṣi* to seek his help to cross to the other side. He told them to go to the Yamuna and say, 'If the Swami had never eaten in his life,

---

[8] *Gītā*5.8

O Yamuna! Please go down.' They went and said so to Yamuna and she dried up. What does this story mean?

The story shows that *ātmā akartā, abhoktā,* it is neither the doer nor the enjoyer. The status of enjoyer or doer is only an incidental attribute imputed to the self from a standpoint. From the standpoint of the senses and organs of actions, an action is imputed to the self and you consider it as a *kartā*. Once you take it as *kartā*, all limitations are imposed upon it. There is no possibility of a perfect action and so there will always be remorse and guilt. If you are a perfectionist, you are constantly plagued with a sense of defeat. You remember the actions you did not do properly. The whole world may praise you but you can still feel that you have not achieved anything. As a *kartā*, there is no way you can escape such a feeling. The only way out is to understand that the self performs no action.

Anything that helps you resolve your problem is *pavitra*, something that purifies. Prayer, rituals, disciplines, therapy, any kind of help you seek to get rid of guilt, hurt, laziness, frustration, procrastination and so on, can be called *pavitra*. Among all possible things that can be called *pavitra* the most *uttama*, exalted is only *ātma-jñāna* because that alone calls the bluff of the *ahaṅkāra*, the nucleus of all these problems. *Ahaṅkāra*, ego, is 'I,' the *ātmā*; but 'I' the *ātmā* is not ego. 'I' is *paraṁ-brahma*. It not only cleanses you of the things done in this life, it eliminates all the *puṇya* and *pāpa* of previous lives that is standing in your account. By prayer and so on, you neutralise some of the *pāpa-karma*s to an extent and also eliminate some guilt. But any amount of expiatory action can only neutralise a finite number of *pāpa-karmas*. *Brahma-jñāna* wipes out everything. As Śaṅkara says, it burns along with its root the entire *sañcita-karma* that has been accumulated in thousands of births.

The root is ignorance whose product is *ahaṅkāra*. The complete elimination is instantaneous because knowledge does not take time. If you know clearly, 'I am Brahman' that is the end of it. It is something like waking up from a dream. In dream you may have committed multiple murder but upon waking up, you are completely exonerated. You are not responsible for it because you did not do it. When it is so, what is there to be said about the purifying capacity of this knowledge? It is *pavitram idam uttamam*, the most purifying. And what kind of knowledge is it?

It is dharmyam – enjoined by the śāstra

And it is *dharmya*, something that is enjoined by the *śāstra*. *Śāstra* talks about various *karmas* that help you gain a number of results for yourself. This is all *dharma*. But this knowledge is something that destroys *puṇya* and *pāpa* and so you may conclude that it is outside *dharma*. No. It is something enjoined by the *śāstra* even though it destroys *dharma* and *adharma* taking you beyond them. *Śāstra* is divided into two sections. One is meant for *abhyudaya*, the prosperity and well being of the *jīva* within *saṁsāra*. The other gives the utmost well being, *mokṣa*. So, from the standpoint of being a *mokṣa-śāstra*, this is *dharmya*. Because we see statements in *śāstra* such as, '*ātmā vā are draṣṭavyaḥ śrotavaḥ mantavyaḥ nididhyāsitavyaḥ* – *ātmā* is to be recognised, heard about, thought about, and meditated upon,'[9] we understand this knowledge is *śāstra-vihita*, enjoined by the *śāstra*.

In the above *śruti* statement, the suffix '*tavya*' indicates the imperative. It is a *vidhi*, command. When there is a command in the *śāstra*, you should be able to fulfil it because it is based upon your will. The *puruṣa* using his will fulfils the *vidhi*. But when it comes to *ātma-jñāna* in *mokṣa-śāstra*, the *vidhi* does not apply in the way you normally understand because it is yourself. The statement, '*tat tvam asi*, you are Brahman' is not a command. *Śāstra* is not saying that you better become Brahman if you want *mokṣa*. It is a simple statement of fact. In a statement of fact, where is the pursuit? Even though there is no pursuit of action, because you cannot undertake any activity to be yourself, here too there are certain things to be done. As with any fact, it has to be understood. So, it has to be enquired into as directed by the *śāstra*. Therefore, it is said in the form of an injunction, '*ātmā vā are draṣṭavyaḥ śrotavaḥ mantavyaḥ nididhyāsitavyaḥ*.' Because it is enjoined by the *śāstra*, this knowledge is said to be *dharmya*. This is one meaning for *dharmya*, not outside the *śāstra*.

Another meaning is that it is never opposed to *dharma*. If you analyse *dharma*, you will find that it is order which is Īśvara and you are not separate from that order at any time. Your notion of being separate, your *ahaṅkāra*, is negated; so, you are no longer frightened and isolated. Once you understand, 'I am Brahman,' you have no need to prove yourself.

---

9 *Bṛhadāraṇyakopaniṣad*4.5.6

At the beginning of the *Gītā* we see that Arjuna is overwhelmed by his situation and confused about right and wrong. Because of his prior *saṁskāra*s and the knowledge from his culture that there is a *mokṣa-śāstra,* he decides to solve his problem for good and asks Kṛṣṇa to teach him.

Since the knowledge is of yourself, the *buddhi* has to turn its attention towards the self. If it is unenlightened, it cannot, because it has no *pramāṇa* for that. Since you require *pramāṇa,* you expose your *buddhi* to the *śāstra* coming from teacher. In any learning, if a teacher has to convey something, the *buddhi* of the teacher and student should become one. Only then can you gain the knowledge that is in the *buddhi* of the teacher. Here, Kṛṣṇa's *buddhi* will become Arjuna's or your *buddhi*. So, the real *guru* is your own *buddhi* that is exposed to the teacher.

Then he can say, '*tat tvam asi,* you are that Brahman, from which everything has come.' In this process the *ahaṅkāra* goes completely because 'I' does not reside in the mind and body. You know it continues even after knowledge because you see Kṛṣṇa talking. But the difference now is that the *ahaṅkāra* is enlightened. It is the *bādhita-ahaṅkāra,* the *ahaṅkāra* that has been negated cognitively, which continues. It has no need to prove itself because it is no longer insecure, frightened, mortal, and possessed of a number of attributes all of which merely define its limitations. Before this knowledge you wanted to be somebody bigger than what you were. But now, you have discovered that you are *jagat-kāraṇa,* the very cause of the creation.

With this knowledge, what kind of action will you do? Is your self-knowledge opposed to *dharma*? Is it opposed to the virtues such as *amānitva, adambhitva, ahimsā, kṣānti, ārjava, ācāryopāsana, śauca, sthairya, ātmavinigraha*? No. They are all very natural to you. What is a value if it is not natural and universal? Love, sympathy, compassion, friendliness, sharing, and so on, are all natural. They are not something created by you but the very order of the creation. That order is Parameśvara. So, with this knowledge, the values you have will be *dharmaya, dharmāt anapetam,* not opposed to *dharma,* the order. They will be spontaneous virtues.

Previously you tried to be sympathetic, to be loving. In order to be mature, you tried to be understanding. You tried to be giving so that you could become more than what you were. As a mature person, you recognised and responded to the needs of others. There was alertness, an attempt on your part that was necessary. But now after knowledge, all these are natural to you. What was a *sādhana* before becomes an embellishment now. Because you are fullness, you have no need to go against *dharma*. You have nothing more to gain.

Generally behind every wrong action is a person who is frightened or greedy. One is greedy because one feels small, and frightened because one feels overwhelmed by the world – all because of ignorance. When that ignorant person is gone, where is the possibility of *adharma*? *Dharma* becomes natural. Self-knowledge and *dharma* go together; so, the knowledge is *dharmāt anapetam,* that is, *dharmya.*

It is the easiest if one is ready for it

Because Bhagavān has described this knowledge as *rāja-vidyā, rāja-guhya, pavitra,* etc., you can be afraid that it is beyond your capacity to attain. This notion is a deterrent to even undertaking the pursuit; so it needs to be addressed. If you are asked to lift a thing that is beyond your capacity, even its mere sight will make you feel weak. Similarly, you can think that there is a lot of effort involved in gaining this knowledge and get discouraged. In fact, it is *susukhaṁ kartum,* very easy to pursue because you need not make any effort; you have simply to know. The *pramāṇa,* means of knowledge, is available, the teacher is there; all you have to do is expose your *buddhi.* The *śāstra* makes the *ahaṅkāra* drop. It is like your seeing these words right now. What effort do you make? Your eyes are open, the printed page is right in front of you, and you see the words. You are not doing something; your eyes are open, and you happen to see. Even if you do not want to see, you will see if the eyes are open and are backed by your mind. It is the same for any piece of knowledge. *Ātmā* is *sat-cit-ānanda,* and all you have to do is expose yourself to the teaching and see exactly what the words say. Your will or effort is not involved. This is what is called surrender. You need not do anything; the words take care of the job of revealing what the self is. This is the teaching. And therefore, it is *susukhaṁ kartum.*

Any knowledge is like that. But for it to be easy, you need to have *adhikāritva,* adequate preparation. For *ātma-jñāna* the preparedness that is required is maturity. Daily experiences are good enough to make you a mature person, if you are ready to learn. Take cognisance of your behaviour and that of others. Maturity does not require any special experience; it requires just understanding your experiences. Nor do you have to be someone special in order to be mature. It depends entirely upon just how much attention you pay to your own behaviour and thinking. Anybody's experiences are good enough for this. Society provides enough frustrations, invokes enough anger. It does not deny you the material that is necessary for growth. You simply have to understand it and thereby maturity is assured. For such a mature person, this knowledge is *susukhaṁ kartum*.

From the standpoint of the result, it looks as though gaining this knowledge is going to be an enormous task, because what is taught is, 'I am everything, the whole.' Typically, you think that for a small result, there will be little effort, and greater the result, more the effort. For an absolute result, what can be the effort? There is no such thing as absolute effort, nor is it required. To be Brahman, you simply have to know, 'I am Brahman.' It is very easy, *su-sukham*, because it is just knowing. Śaṅkara says it is like discerning a ruby, *ratna-vivekaḥ iva*. For a person who has the expertise, it does not require any time to know whether a ruby is real or not. Just by looking at it, he can tell. Śaṅkara uses the example of a *ratna* because here too certain expertise is required. It is as easy for a *jñānī* to understand that he or she is Brahman because one has the expertise, *ātma-jñāna*, the knowledge.

If it is very clear that *nāma-rūpa* is *anātma* and *ātma* is the consciousness in whose presence all things are known, there is no problem. Knowing this is *susukham*, very easy, while everything else, especially *brahma-loka-prāpti*, takes a lot of time and effort. It is better to strive for *ātma-jñāna* and thereby *mokṣa*. Therefore, recognising the self is Brahman is *susukhaṁ kartum*, easy to accomplish. All the other *karma*s also have a place here because they give you *puṇya*, which will lead you to this knowledge. The *puṇya* is *karma-phala* but the real benefit of all *karma-phala*s is that it gives you the *adhikāritva*, qualification, and thereby knowledge. After gaining the *adhikāritva* all you require is *viveka*. Once there is *viveka* you are pushed towards *ātma-jñāna* and *mokṣa*.

This knowledge is pratyakṣa avagamam

'If I am to gain this knowledge, how am I to gain it? It is not like *vaikuṇṭha* or any other place about which I hear I can gain some indirect knowledge, hoping to verify it later.

Bhagavān says, this knowledge is *pratyakṣa-avagamam*, known to you directly, immediately. For instance, if you have to know a crystal, what you need is immediate knowledge. When you are told, 'This is a crystal,' to know it as such, you must have a *vṛtti*, thought, corresponding to the crystal, which removes your ignorance of the crystal. To have this thought, you must be able to see the crystal. Similarly, for self-knowledge, the self already being available for appreciation, you must have a *vṛtti* that can remove your ignorance about the self. That *vṛtti* is what is created by the teaching. It gives immediate knowledge, and having destroyed ignorance about the self, it goes away.

Ātma-jñāna is avyayam – never lost

The *vastu* of that knowledge is *avyaya*, imperishable. *Jñāna-vṛtti* is *vyaya*, perishable, whereas *ātma-jñāna* is *avyaya* because knowledge is as true as its object. *Ātmā* is not subject to time. It is *nitya* and so knowledge of the *ātmā* is also *nitya*. Since the object of knowledge is yourself and because it is *nitya* you do not require memory to retain the knowledge. You can remember hundred different things but never *ātmā* because you are that *ātmā* because of which all memory takes place. If you are ignorant about that self, you need only have that ignorance destroyed. The knowledge that takes place is *avyaya* because it is you and you can never lose sight of yourself. When you see the world you are *sat-cit-ānanda*; when you do not see the world you are *sat-cit-ānanda*. You do not need to repeat it to yourself. The words are meant to reveal, not for repetition. *Sat* is a *lakṣaṇa* to understand that *ātmā* is not time bound; *cit* is a *lakṣaṇa* for knowing that *ātmā* is not subject to ignorance. That it is *ānanda-svarūpa* is to show that *ātmā* is *ananta*, free from any limitation. These words are used to convey the knowledge of the reality and not for *japa*. We are not invoking the grace of the *sat-cit-ānanda* by saying *sat-cit-ānando'haṁ*. If you repeat these words, you try to see the implied meaning of *sat*, of *cit*, and of *ānanda*. It is a different type of *śraddhā* leading to *nididhyāsana*.

Another question can be asked here. Suppose a *jñānī* has thrombosis in the area of the brain, which stores memory. When he regains consciousness, he has no memory of his name or the people he knew. He previously knew all the

Upaniṣads but now he remembers none of them. How can you say this knowledge is *avyaya*? Will he know he is *sat-cit-ānanda*? Yes, he will. He will not remember the words but since his original ignorance is gone, there will be no more birth for him. It is like the situation in sleep. If you have understood that you are Brahman, when you are asleep, that knowledge is not available to you. It does not mean ignorance has come back. Similarly here, the *antaḥ-karaṇa* is not functioning as it should. But once he has gained the knowledge, he no longer has any self-ignorance. So, there is no question of his returning to this world. That knowledge is *avyaya* because the result of it is yourself, which is *avyaya*. There is no question of it being lost.

The description of this knowledge is not really praise. If you introduce me to a very rich man saying that he can buy this town, you are not flattering him. It happens to be true. Similarly, the words that are used here to describe this knowledge such as *rāja-vidyā, rāja-guhyam, pavitram, uttamam, pratyakṣa-avagamam, susukhaṁ kartum* are true descriptions of this knowledge. In fact, all these words are not enough. No matter what you say, you always fall short of the Lord. Bhagavān is never flattered and whatever you say about this knowledge of him is always less than what it is. It deserves all this and a little more.

So, why are these words used? It is only to make Arjuna, and other students who read this, more attentive. After hearing this, Arjuna will be all attention and ready to listen. This is the purpose. Moreover, by such words, the nature of the knowledge is told, and to know about the learning is a part of the learning.

Most of the problems in the spiritual field are that people do not know exactly what they are seeking. Not understanding the nature of this knowledge, they are looking for some extraordinary experience, which will leave them entirely transformed. In short, they are looking for an event to take place. The self is not an event. It is something because of which all events take place, which is why the nature of this knowledge has to be told.

You do not have to do something, or transform yourself, in order to become Brahman, which is why I used the example of the rich man. If you are rich, all you have to do to lose your sense of being poor is to discern that you are rich. For that you must be ready to listen. If you are conditioned to being a pauper, it is difficult even to listen. Take the case of a man who has been poor from birth. If he suddenly comes into an inheritance that makes him rich, it is going to take him a while to get used to the fact that he is a rich man. He is very much used to considering himself a pauper – his grandfather was a pauper, his father was a pauper, his maternal grandfather was also a pauper, his brother is a pauper, all his friends are paupers! Naturally, when you tell him he is rich, is he going to believe it? He will think you are deluded and will continue to beg.

In the same way, as far as happiness and fulfilment are concerned, we all think that we are paupers. We always beg for happiness at the altar of life, waiting for the hands of chance to shape a moment of joy. We keep on praying or manipulating so that some situation will become so conducive that we are happy for the moment. And we can never be sure that even after manipulating we are going to be happy. We can be so exhausted that we cannot even enjoy what we worked for. This is the lot of a pauper. So, when one is told one is *ānanda*, limitless, fullness, etc., it is too much even to believe. To make one stop and listen, *śraddhā*, trust, is required. And it takes a lot of *śraddhā*.

After introducing the subject matter as *rāja-vidyā* and *rāja-guhya*, now Kṛṣṇa says that gaining this you will be released from bondage. Therefore, you have enough reason to have *śraddhā* in the pursuit of knowledge. You must have *śraddhā* in both the nature of the knowledge and the result in order to listen, which is why they both have been told in these two verses.

Verse 3

Those who do not have śraddhā remain in saṁsāra

अश्रद्दधानाः पुरुषा धर्मस्यास्य परन्तप ।
अप्राप्य मां निवर्तन्ते मृत्युसंसारवर्त्मनि ॥ ३ ॥

aśraddadhānāḥ puruṣā dharmasyāsya parantapa
aprāpya māṁ nivartante mṛtyusaṁsāravartmani (3)

parantapa – O scorcher of foes, Arjuna!; *asya dharmasya* – in this self-knowledge; *aśraddadhānāḥ puruṣāḥ* – those people who have no faith; *māṁ aprāpya* – not gaining me; *mṛtyu-saṁsāra-vartmani* – on the road of *saṁsāra*, which is fraught with death; *nivartante* – they return to/ remain in

Arjuna, the scorcher of foes! Those people who have no faith in this self-knowledge, not gaining me, they return to/remain in the road of *saṁsāra*, which is fraught with death.

Kṛṣṇa addresses Arjuna as Parantapa, the one who destroys enemies, a warrior.

Aśraddadhānāḥ puruṣāḥ, one who has *śraddhā* is called *śraddadhāna*. And the one who does not have *śraddhā* is *aśraddadhāna*. *Śraddhā* is giving the benefit of doubt to the veracity of words of the *śāstra*, and the teacher regarding the nature and result of this knowledge. You have *śraddhā* in the nature of this *ātma-jñāna*, self-knowledge, that the self is identical with Brahman, the cause of creation. Even though you have not yet understood this, you believe that what the *śāstra* says is true. And you have *śraddhā* in the result of this knowledge, which is freedom from any sense of bondage. If you have understood properly, you would not require *śraddhā*. But until you understand, you need *śraddhā* so that you can pursue this knowledge.

Asya dharmasya. The word '*dharma*' has a number of meanings. It is used in the sense of knowledge, duty, the order of Īśvara, religion, and also in the sense of a property or nature of a thing. Therefore, whenever this word is used, in order to understand its meaning, we need to see the context. Here the word *dharma* means *ātma-jñāna*, self-knowledge. It is because in the previous verse the word *dharmya* was used to introduce this knowledge. There the word *dharmya* meant that it is enjoined by the *śāstra* and also that it was not opposed to *dharma*.

The one who has this knowledge is not going to express oneself against *dharma*. So, this knowledge is called *dharma*.

In this verse Bhagavān is talking about *aśraddadhāna*s, people who have no *śraddhā* either in the nature of the knowledge or its result. Because of this, they cannot even begin to pursue this knowledge.

For a person who has *śraddhā*, the *śāstra* is a *pramāṇa*, means of knowledge. The *śraddhā* that the *śāstra* is a *pramāṇa* is very important here. For a *nāstika* who does not look upon the *śāstra* as a means of knowledge, there is no *puṇya* or *pāpa*. There may be people who are very ethical in spite of this lack of *śraddhā*. But generally, a person who does not have *śraddhā* in the *śāstra* will have a tendency towards *pāpa-karma* because one's whole pursuit will be directed towards one's own comfort. Happiness is equated to satisfying the senses. After all, the senses will age anyway. Even if a person lives a very disciplined life, one's senses will still age. After seventy years of age, one's sight and hearing will further decline; so, what is the difference? There is an interesting statement by a total materialist, who has no *śraddhā* in any thing other than what is available to his senses. He says, 'Incurring debt, feed the senses and enjoy yourself as long as you live. If the body is reduced to ashes who will reap the results of its action?'[10] What is the lot of these people who have such conclusions? The Lord says, '*aprāpya*

---

[10] यावज्जीवेत् सुखं जीवेत् ऋणं कृत्वा घृतं पिबेत्। भस्मीभूतस्य देहस्य पुनरागमनं कुतः॥

yāvajjīvet sukhaṁ jīvet ṛṇaṁ kṛtvā ghṛtaṁ pibet, bhasmībhūtasya dehasya punarāgamanaṁ kutaḥ.

mām, not gaining me, *mṛtyu-saṁsāra-vartmani nivartante*, they keep returning to the cycle of birth and death.'

There is no doubt about whether these people reach Parameśvara by recognising the *ātmā* as Brahman. It is not possible. When they have no *śraddhā* even in *puṇya-pāpa*, *dharma-adharma*, where is the question of their seeking identity with Parameśvara? Not gaining this, what happens to a person?

Mṛtyu-saṁsāra-vartmani nivartante, they come back to the cycle of life and death. The word *nivartante* has two meanings, 'they come back' or 'they remain.' *Mṛtyu-saṁsāra* is really *mṛtyu-yukta-saṁsāra*. It is a compound in which the middle word is dropped. It means, it is a *saṁsāra* that is fraught with *mṛtyu*, death. Death is coupled with birth, so *saṁsāra* is fraught with death and change. Even empires that once flourished have all been levelled. What remains are few remnants beneath the earth, some pots, some coins, etc. And the demolition squad is none other than Lord *mṛtyu*, time. *Vartman* means road, the road through which you reach pain; we are talking about the one who does not believe. Even *svarga* is within *saṁsāra*; but here, he is talking about *aśraddadhānāḥ puruṣāḥ*, the people of no *śraddhā* at all. Such people are on those routes that lead them to *naraka*, a place of pain and births in lesser wombs like those of animals, etc. In these tracks they remain, *mṛtyu-saṁsāra-vartmani nivartante*.

This particular verse is said only to create *śraddhā*. The first two verses praise *ātma-jñāna* as *rāja-vidyā* to positively create *śraddhā*. This verse tells how much you miss if you do not have *śraddhā* in this knowledge.

Having drawn Arjuna's attention, Lord Kṛṣṇa begins the topic of this chapter in a very big way.

Verse 4

This entire world is pervaded by me

मया ततमिदं सर्वं जगदव्यक्तमूर्तिना ।
मत्स्थानि सर्वभूतानि न चाहं तेष्ववस्थितः ॥ ४ ॥

mayā tatam idaṁ sarvaṁ jagad avyaktamūrtinā
matsthāni sarvabhūtāni na cāhaṁ teṣvavasthitaḥ (4)

mayā – by me; *avyakta-mūrtinā* – whose form cannot be objectified; *idaṁ sarvaṁ jagat* – this entire world; *tatam* – is pervaded; *sarva-bhūtāni* – all beings; *matsthāni* – have their being in me; *na ca aham* – and I am not; *teṣu avasthitaḥ* – based in them

> This entire world is pervaded by me whose form cannot be objectified. All beings have their being in me and I am not based in them.

It is important to note here that in this and the following verses, the word *bhūta,* being, is used in the sense of *jīva*. The word *bhūta* also covers the entire *jagat*. When it is said that the *jīva* is created, sustained and destroyed, you should know that by *jīva* is meant an embodied being. The *jīva,* being non-separate from *ātmā*, is never created or sustained or destroyed. But the subtle and physical bodies, born of subtle and gross elements, are created, sustained and destroyed. So, for the *jīva*, creation, sustenance and destruction are only with reference to these bodies. At the destruction of the entire *jagat*, which includes bodies of all *jīva*s, all *jīva*s as well as the *jagat* become unmanifest. From this unmanifest state, when all these become manifest, that manifestation is called creation. As long as the *jīva* does not recognise his identity with Īśvara this process of manifestation and unmanifestation continues for the *jīva*.

The Lord says, '*mayā jagad avyaktamūrtinā tatam idaṁ sarvam*.' There is an adjective to 'me,' *avyakta-mūrtinā*. A form or the truth of a given thing is called *mūrti*. *Avyakta-mūrti* is a form that is beyond objectification. Something that cannot be objectified may be hastily construed as non-existent. To avoid such problem, Bhagavān has used the word *mūrti*. *Avyakta-mūrti* is the one who exists and is available for appreciation. That is me, and by that me, this entire creation is pervaded. It is not Kṛṣṇa's body that is pervading everything but his real nature, *paro-bhāva*. When Kṛṣṇa says here '*mayā*, by me' he uses the first person and that refers to the real being, *sat-cit-ānanda*. By me, Brahman, *sat-cit-ānanda*, in the form of existence, consciousness, not limited by time, space, or any object, *mayā tatam idaṁ sarvaṁ jagat*, this entire world is pervaded.

All beings have their being in me.

Matsthāni sarvabhūtāni. Things that are born are called *bhūta*s. Because they are born, they are subject to change. *Ākāśa, vāyu, agni, āpaḥ, pṛthivi*, are all *bhūta*s. Then out of these *bhūta*s a number of systems, *loka*s, were born. And in any *loka* there are many forms of physical bodies, each with their own subtle body, made of *pañca-bhūta*s, the five elements, according to our five elemental model. Out of these five *bhūta*s, subtle and gross, come all the *loka*s and the embodied beings within them.

Together they are called *sarva-bhūtāni*. Even the *ahaṅkāra* is included in these *bhūta*s. All thoughts are created and have their being in one uncreated *ātmā*. Therefore, Kṛṣṇa says, *matsthāni sarva-bhūtāni*, all beings have their being in me.

And without me there will be no being at all. Śaṅkara says, '*na hi nirātmakaṁ kiñcit bhūtaṁ vyavahārāya avakalpate*, anything without an existential status is not available for empirical transaction. He introduces this sentence to illustrate an important point. All beings, upon enquiry, prove to be *mithyā*. When you analyse any object, it is reduced to something else; therefore it is purely *nāma-rūpa*. If you stop here, there is only a void, *śūnya*. If at the bottom of everything there is *śūnya*, there will be no *vyavahāra*, transaction, at all. But because there is one thing that 'is,' everything is understood as existent; space 'is,' time 'is,' everything 'is.'

However, you may argue, there are certain things that are understood as non-existent like the rabbit's horn. Even so, the rabbit is existent, only the horn is not existent. And even though the rabbit's horn is non-existent, how do you know of the non-existence of the rabbit's horn? It is very important to note. To know this, there must be a person who knows. That person knows '*aham asmi*, I am,' and then he uses a means of knowledge to know that rabbits do not have horns. That rabbits have no horns is purely a piece of knowledge and to acquire that, there must be a means of knowledge.

You cannot say it is perception because eyes can capture only form and colour, not non-existence. They detect presence, not absence. So, the means of knowledge is not perception.

Then how do you know that the rabbit's horn does not exist? It is not inference because any inference is based on perception. Nor is it presumption. You do not arrive at the fact that rabbits do not have horns by presuming it from the fact that rabbits never hit you with their horns. You do not conclude, 'Rabbits do not hit me with their horns, therefore, they do not have horns.' It is not knowledge born of perception, inference or presumption but an independent means of knowledge known as *anupalabdhi*, a negative means of knowledge based upon the knowledge you have. You know what a rabbit is like but you do not really see the absence of the horn. When you question whether a rabbit has horns you determine that it does not have horns. That is arrived at by *anupalabdhi*, a means of knowledge employed by the person who is existent. The person uses a means of knowledge to determine the fact that the rabbit has no horn. But the fact 'is' and the person who knows 'is,'exists.

The orientation is – existence is an attribute of an object

Generally, existence is considered as an attribute of the object. For example you say, 'This pot is existent.' Here, existence becomes an attribute that distinguishes this pot from an absent or a destroyed pot. This existent pot you will later call a destroyed pot. So, when you say, 'This is an existent pot,' 'existent' is used as an opposite to 'non-existent' or destruction. Since there is such a thing as an absent or a destroyed pot, you can say, 'This is an existent pot.' The knowledge that you have of existence is always opposed to non-existence. The fact that it exists only means that it is not yet destroyed. This is how your *buddhi* grasps existence and because of that, it is always an attribute imputed to an object.

Vedanta just reverses this orientation

Vedanta's whole intent is only to dismiss this orientation of existence being an attribute. It says existence is not an attribute. It is unlike anything that you know. To this existence it is the objects that are so called attributes. Let us look at it in a simple form. Suppose I say, 'This is a gold chain.' Here the gold becomes the attribute and the chain substantive. It is not a mere linguistic orientation, it reflects an orientation in your vision, your way of looking at the world and yourself. It means you see myself as a mortal being who is existent now, subject to ageing, to time, and is going to be destroyed one day. All these are involved in this simple statement. In Vedanta, we reverse this vision.

If we say, 'gold chain,' chain has the status of a substantive and the gold, an attribute. Do we add some gold to the existent chain? If we do, it is a gold-plated chain, not a gold chain. I am talking of a gold chain. In fact, all that is there is gold; chain being purely a *nāma-rūpa*. It is an entirely different vision. The gold becomes *satya*, existent, and the chain becomes *nāma-rūpa* seemingly added to gold. Why seemingly? Any real addition should bring an addition to the gold. But here we find the chain's appearance does not bring any addition or change to the gold. The gold substance, the *svarūpa*, its weight and other properties remain the same. Even with the appearance of the chain, the gold retains its own nature. So, we say the appearance of the chain is a kind of addition, a seeming creation. We cannot totally deny a creation because we see the chain. Even so, it is only a seeming creation because there is no beginning of a substantive. The gold has been, the gold is, and gold will be. There is no real chain at all. It is nothing but an incidental *nāma-rūpa* attributed to the gold. Therefore, it is a sort of addition to the gold. If the gold could talk, it would say, 'All these golden ornaments – the gold chain, the gold bangle, gold ring, gold earring, gold nose ring, gold ring – have their being in me.' The existence of the chain is entirely dependent upon the gold. Therefore, in Vedantic language, we will not say 'gold chain' but 'chainy gold.' I have to completely change my language just to express this vision. In fact, it is not really the language we have to change but our vision. When we say, 'gold chain,' we must know that what we are saying is that the chain is gold.

Similarly if this entire creation is Īśvara, it means the creation is the attribute, Īśvara is *vastu*, the substantive. *Paramātmā* is *satya* and the entire creation is nothing but *nāma-rūpa*. Therefore, Kṛṣṇa says, *matsthāni sarva-bhūtani*, all beings are in that existence, which is 'I,' the *ātmā*. *Sarva-bhūta*s include my body, my senses, all that I know, my *ahaṅkāra* and even ignorance. Ignorance 'is.' That 'is' is *ātmā*, consciousness – the thought **is**, the knower **is**, seer **is**, hearer **is**, thinker **is**, thinking **is**, emotion **is**, memory **is**, and so on. Then anything that you say **is**, that **is**, is *ātmā*. And that **is**, which is qualified by whatever you say, is itself unqualified. So, the statement, *matsthāni sarva bhūtani* is meaningful.

Now it is clear what was meant by '*mayā tatam idaṁ sarvaṁ*, everything is pervaded by me.' It means nothing is away from me.

In anything that is, that 'is,' consciousness, is the *ātmā*. In any piece of knowledge there is consciousness involved and that consciousness is *sat-cit-ānanda-ātmā*.

And it is *avyakta* because it is not an object. The means of knowledge you have can only bring the objects to light. The object is, and that 'is,' is you. This is something you appreciate not in the way you are used to because the one who appreciates is also pervaded by *ātmā*, as is the knowledge of the object and the object itself. *Ātmā* is self-evident, not an object that is to be known.

First the Lord said, '*mayā tatam idaṁ sarvam*, by me all this is pervaded.' It means *ātmā* is in every being. Next by saying, '*matsthāni sarva-bhūtani*, all beings are in me,' he completely changes the situation. In this particular expression, there is a potential problem.

While everything has its being in me – I am not in any of them

There is a common notion that in every heart there is a divine spark. *Ātmā* is looked upon as something located in the *buddhi* of every being. According to this, the *buddhi* can be construed as the basis, the *ātmā* as the based, with a basis-based relationship between the *buddhi* and *ātmā*.

To eliminate any such notion Bhagavān says, '*na ca aham teṣu avasthitaḥ*.' While all of them have their being in me, I am not in any of them. We have hundreds of such paradoxes. The meaning is simple – all of them are in me, but because you may think that I am located in them, I say that I am not.

They are all located in me, that is, I am the *sat* of everything, like even gold is the *sat* of all things golden. In every gold chain there is gold. Gold is not located in the chain; chain is gold. The gold does not exist in chain, in the sense it does not depend upon the chain, which is only the *nāma-rūpa*. The very existence of chain is because of gold. If the chain is, the 'is ness' is nothing but the 'is ness' of gold. Therefore, gold does not exist in chain, whereas the chain exists in gold. One is *satya,* the other, *mithyā*. *Satya* does not exist depending upon *mithyā* but *mithyā* cannot exist without *satya*. This is the whole intent here.

So, *matsthāni sarva-bhūtani,* all of them exist in me, but *na ca aham teṣu avasthitaḥ,* I do not remain located in any one of them. 'I' becomes the *ādhāra,* basis, of everything. But I am not *ādheya,* based upon them because they are *mithyā*. I am *satya,* the truth of all of them. They have their being in me but I do not have my being in them. I am not dependent upon them for my existence while they depend entirely upon me for their existence.

One may argue that it is like the situation of a king. The citizens depend entirely upon the king but he does not depend upon the citizens. One is independent, the other, dependent. Similarly if all the worlds are dependent upon you, while you are independent of them, yet there is a difference between the world and you. You have become the *ādhāra* and the world is the *ādheya*.

Bhagavān has covered this by saying that he is *avyakta-mūrti*. Śaṅkara states its significance. An object which has a form is something that can be connected to another object. There is the possibility of *ādhara-ādheya,* a basis based connection. For example, the dish is on the table and the table is on the ground. Since each of these has a form, it can be the *ādhāra,* basis, for another object, which has a form, the *ādheya.*

Now let us consider the relationship between space and an object that has a form. It can be the earth, it can be all the planets. All are based upon, accommodated in space, except space itself. The Lord says, but space also exists in me, consciousness, which has no form whatsoever. If all things exist in space and space itself exists in me, then I have no location. If it is so, what kind of basis-based connection is there? With no location, there is no *ādhāra-ādheya,* basis based, difference. I am self-existent and everything is based upon me.

Those who do not understand this fact may say that *ātmā* is based, located in the *buddhi.* The *buddhi* is the place where you recognise *ātmā,* that is, as consciousness, it manifests there. But it does not mean that *ātmā* is located there. *Ātmā* is that by which everything is pervaded, including your *buddhi, mayā tatam idaṁ sarvam. Buddhi* after all is a *vṛtti* and every *vṛtti* is nothing but *caitanya-ātmā.* A pot *vṛtti* is consciousness plus the name and form, pot. Every *vṛtti* depends upon *caitanya-ātmā* like how the waves depend entirely upon water. But *caitanya-ātmā* has no form that can be located anywhere. So, it is not an object based upon something else. It is *vastu* that has no form and has no connection with anything else; so it is not possible for it to be *ādheya,* based upon something else. It is that in which everything is based. Therefore, Śaṅkara says, the nature of *ātmā* is such that it has no connection whatsoever. Like the water has no connection with the wave. Between *satya* and *mithyā*, there is no connection at all. *Mithyā* does not exist apart from *satya*. One is *adhiṣṭhāna* and the other is a superimposition. Even the *ādhāra-ādheya* difference is not there. The *jagat* is non-separate from me, yet 'I' am independent of the *jagat* because one is *satya*, the other is *mithyā*.

A connection can only be between two things that are *satya*. If *ātmā* is *satya* and if there is any other *ātmā*, which is equally *satya*, then, we can say that one *ātmā* is connected to the other *ātmā*; one is based upon other, one depends upon the other. But there is no second *ātmā* at all. If there were, you should be able to recognise it. Anything you can recognise is an object of *ātmā*, and not *ātmā*. It is because *ātmā* is consciousness which recognises everything. There is only one *ātmā*, which from its own standpoint is non-dual. It is pure *caitanya-ātmā*.

Verse 5

Ātmā is consciousness – it is not connected to anything

न च मत्स्थानि भूतानि पश्य मे योगमैश्वरम् ।
भूतभृन्न च भूतस्थो ममात्मा भूतभावनः ॥ ५ ॥

na ca matsthāni bhūtāni paśya me yogam aiśvaram
bhūtabhṛnna ca bhūtastho mamātmā bhūtabhāvanaḥ (5)

na ca matsthāni bhūtāni – and the beings do not exist in me; *me* – my; *aiśvaraṁ yogam* – connection of mine to the *jagat*; *paśya* – look at; *mama ātmā* – my self; *bhūtabhāvanaḥ* – (is) the creator of the beings; *bhūtabhṛt* – the sustainer of the beings; *na ca bhūtasthaḥ* – and yet not residing in the beings

> And the beings do not exist in me; look at this *aiśvara*, connection of mine to the *jagat*. My Self is the creator of the beings, the sustainer of the beings and yet is not residing in the beings.

First Bhagavān said, '*matsthāni sarva-bhūtāni*, all beings have their being in me.' Now he says, '*na ca matsthāni bhūtāni*, and the beings do not exist in me.' This removes any possible notion of Bhagavān being the *ādhāra* of all these beings. If *ātmā* is only one and everything is dependent upon *ātmā*, there is duality. And Bhagavān would be a huge *saṁsārī* because a *saṁsārī*, after all, is someone with a number of dependants. To rule this out, he completely reverses his language and says, 'All these beings and things do not exist in me.' It is like the clay saying 'The pot exists in me.' Then after thinking it over it says, 'in fact, the pot does not exist in me. All that is in me is clay. I exist in my own right and do not depend upon the pot.' There clay is *satya*, anything else has no independent existence, it is only *nāma rūpa*.

Similarly, every thought is me but in me there is only *caitanya*. If you turn your vision towards *ātmā*, there is no thought there. And for that you need not do anything. When one thought has gone and another is yet to come, what obtains is consciousness, *ātmā*, independent of a thought, independent of the whole *jagat*. That consciousness is the nature of *ātmā* and in its *svarūpa* there are no beings.

Having said this, Bhagavān says something more to make it clear that there is no contradiction in what he has just said.

Look at my connection – my glories

He says, '*paśya me yogam aiśvaram.*' *Paśya* means 'look, understand.' The word '*aiśvaram*' is an adjective to the word *yoga* and means 'that which belongs to Īśvara.' *Yoga* here means connection. The Lord says, *paśya me yogam aiśvaram,* look at my connection (with the *jagat*). This is *yoga,* connection of the cause, *paramātmā* with the effect, *jagat.* In any cause-effect relationship, the cause is independent of the effect while the effect depends upon the cause. This is the reality from the standpoint of *kāraṇa-kārya,* cause-effect. If you go one step further and look at the *kāraṇa,* is there a *kārya*? All that is there is only *kāraṇa* because *kārya* is nothing but *kāraṇa* in another form. Therefore, the Lord says that the entire *jagat* is nothing but himself. The cause of the entire *jagat* is Īśvara; it is all Īśvara's glory, which is why he says, '*paśya me yogam aiśvaram.*'

If this is the nature of *ātmā,* then along with Bhagavān, you can say the same thing. Along with Kṛṣṇa, Arjuna can also say, '*mayā tatam idam sarvam,* all this is pervaded by me,' because he understands that *ātmā* pervades everything and there is no second *ātmā* available. In *ātmā* alone all the beings exist, and at the same time *ātmā* is free from all beings. This is the nature of *ātmā,* and anybody who understands this can say '*paśya me yogam aiśvaram,* look at my connection, my glories.'

All paradoxes are glories. *Ātmā* is the cause of everything and the recognition that takes place about this *jagat* is that, *jagat* is also 'I.' But when the beings do not exist, what do I have to talk about? All I see is Brahman, there is no *jagat* here, *na ca matsthāni bhūtāni*. There is no connection between *ātmā* and *jagat* because there is no second thing belonging to the same order of reality to get connected. This is the *āścarya*, wonder, and which is why he says, '*paśya me yogam aiśvaram*.'

It is a wonder from another standpoint too, which Bhagavān expresses in this paradox. He says, '*mama ātmā bhūtabhṛt na ca bhūtasthaḥ* – My Self is *bhūtabhṛt* but not *bhūtasthaḥ*.' *Bhṛt* means one who sustains or upholds, *bhūtabhṛt* is one who sustains all the beings, *bhūtas*. *Ātmā* sustains all the beings by giving *sattā*, existence, to all of them. Like clay sustains the pot, *ātmā* sustains the *jagat*. At the same time, it is not located in the *bhūtas*, *na ca bhūtasthaḥ*. That is, it is not limited by any of the *bhutas*.

When the Lord says he is *bhūtabhṛt* he is not engaged in this big task of sustaining the world. That is why Lord Viṣṇu is portrayed as *śayānaḥ sarvaṁ bibharti*, lying down he sustains everything, just as *ātma-caitanya* sustains your thought without getting involved in any manner. The meaning is, there is no *saṅga*, connection, in any manner. Further, he is not located in the *bhūtas*. Since *ātmā* has no form, it cannot be *bhūtastha*, residing in the *bhūtas*. That is why he says, 'All the *bhūtas* are located in me whereas I am not located in the *bhūtas*, I am *asaṅga*.'

Bhagavān says, *mama ātmā bhūtabhṛt na ca bhūtasthaḥ*. This word, '*mama*' is in genitive case, which usually indicates a connection. Śaṅkara says here that it is purely in keeping with the common understanding. People look upon the body as themselves and therefore, *mama ātmā* means *ātmā* belonging to the body.

The problem in modern Vedanta is that they superimpose the *ahaṅkāra* upon *ātmā* not knowing the *svarūpa* of *ātmā*. Then they will say, 'You must realise the self, the *ātmā* of yourself, which is other than the self that obtains now. This self is subject to *saṁsāra*, etc., but there is a real self that you should realise.' You first create two selves, then remain two. The truth is that the one who has to realise the self is the self to be realised. There is no other self besides the self that exists right now. The *ahaṅkāra* that claims to be the self is born of error and we are correcting this error by removing ignorance about the self-evident *ātmā*.

So, there is no division. This must be very clear. The mention of *mama ātmā* is purely from the stand point of the superimposition. If you superimpose the body-mind-sense complex on *ātmā*, *ātmā* becomes as good as the body and you get the conclusion, 'I am a human being.' On the 'I,' the body mind-senses are superimposed and thereby *ātmā* becomes a *saṁsārī* who has to now 'realise' the real *ātmā*. Thus there is no '*mama ātmā*,' there is only one *ātmā*. When Kṛṣṇa says, *mama ātmā* there are no two two entities, 'I' and 'mine'. His *svarūpa*, *sat-cit-ānanda* alone is there; there is no other Kṛṣṇa other than that *ātmā*.

Mama ātmā, which is *sat-cit-ānanda-ātmā* is *bhūta-bhāvana*. By a mere thought, with the help of *māyā*, *ātmā* creates everything. *Mama ātmā* makes the whole order of creation evolve and provides it with the sustenance to grow. It is not an agent appointed by any one to take care of the world, like a house-sitter. It is not that Bhagavān created the world and then asked the *ātmā* to take care of it; it is not that some *ātmā* would sustain it but have no *saṅga* because it is not his house. Here, in conjunction with *bhūta-bhāvana*, *ātmā* should be understood as *sat-cit-ānanda-ātmā*.

Sat-cit-ānanda-ātmā through its own *māyā* creates everything. And because all the *bhūtas* are *mithyā*, the Lord can say, '*bhūtabhṛt*, I am the sustainer of all beings,' and '*na ca aham bhūtasthaḥ*, I do not reside in the beings.' And again, that is the reason he can say, '*matsthāni sarva bhūtāni*, all the beings have their being in me,' and in the same breath he can also say, '*na ca matsthāni sarva bhūtāni*, all beings do not exist in me.' It is because they are all *mithyā*. These two verses completely destroy the concepts of duality and creation. The entire creation becomes purely figurative, an *upacāra*.

Then what is created? When you say, '*na ca matsthāni sarva bhūtāni*, there is nothing in me, there is only *ātmā*,' you are not accountable at all for what you created. It is like a person who dreamt and woke up. If you ask him, what he did, he will say that he created a whole world just out of his own thoughts. And if you ask him if that world was separate from him, he will say, 'All of them were in me, *matsthāni sarva bhūtāni*.' If you were to ask him, 'Do you depend upon them?' he would say, 'Not at all, it was my own glory, my own creation. Further more, I am *bhūtabhṛt*, the one who sustains the whole world.' And again if you were to ask him, 'Who created the world?' He would say, 'My self, my *ātmā*, created the entire dream world.' In all this there is no contradiction because in the dream the entire dream world was nothing but the dreamer.

Similarly, Bhagavān says that he creates everything and he sustains everything. Then in the next breath he says, he does not have the task of running the world because there are no beings at all, there is nothing there to sustain. When a person wakes up from the dream and talks about the dream, the dream world he experienced is only from the stand point of the dream. The waker is a single person.

You have to account for a world that is created, sustained etc., only when you accept the world as an independent entity. Only then can you ask,

'Who created the world?'

The Lord would say, 'I created this world.'

The next question is, 'Who sustains the world?'

The Lord says, 'I sustain this world.'

'Then are you dependent upon the world?'

'No. I am not dependent on the world.'

'Is the world dependent upon you?'

'Yes,' the Lord would say.

So, it looks as though he has a great task of sustaining this world. But if you ask him about it, he will ask, 'What task?' It is because in reality there is no world other than Īśvara. All that is here is Īśvara.

Kṛṣṇa is everywhere, or nowhere. He is in no particular place but he pervades the entire *jagat*. That is why he said, '*paśya me yogam aiśvaram*, this is my glory which is to be understood.' With these two verses, *satya* and *mithyā* are very clearly established. 'There is nothing more than me. I am the maker, the sustainer of everything, and I am the one who dissolves everything. In fact, in me there is no world at all. And all that is here in the form of this world is nothing other than me.' Bhagavān says this, and the one who understands the *svarūpa* of Bhagavān as the *svarūpa* of oneself can also say the same.

Everything that was said in these two verses is now illustrated with an example in the next verse.

Verse 6

Kṛṣṇa explains with an illustration

यथाकाशस्थितो नित्यं वायुः सर्वत्रगो महान् ।
तथा सर्वाणि भूतानि मत्स्थानीत्युपधारय ॥ ६ ॥

yathākāśasthito nityaṁ vāyuḥ sarvatrago mahān
tathā sarvāṇi bhūtāni matsthānītyupadhāraya (6)

yathā – just as; *mahān vāyuḥ* – vast air; *sarvatragaḥ* – which goes everywhere; *nityam ākāśasthitaḥ* – always exists in space; *tathā* – similarly; *sarvāṇi bhūtāni matsthānī* – all beings exist in me; *iti upadhāraya* – thus may you understand

> Just as the vast air, which goes everywhere, always exists in space, similarly, may you understand that all beings exist in me.

The word '*yathā*' means 'just as.' Śaṅkara says here it means 'just as in the world.' So, just as in the world *vāyu*, air, *sarvatraga*, which moves from one place to another, *nityam, ākāśasthitaḥ*, always exists in space, *tathā*, in the same manner, all beings exist in me, Īśvara. As *vāyu* moves from Kansas to New York or from there to India, it goes to a new place but not to a new space. *Sarvatra,* means 'everywhere' and *ga* means 'the one who goes.' Thus *vāyu* is called *sarvatraga*. It means that there is no place where he will not go, which is why he is also called *mahān*. The word *mahān* describes the dimension, that is, pervasiveness of *vāyu*. In terms of pervasiveness, *vāyu* is *mahān*, great.

So, too, may you understand that all beings remain in me. Let them go anywhere; they are still in me. Just as how *vāyu*, no matter where it goes, is never away from *ākāśa*, similarly all the *bhūta*s, whatever form they may assume, remain in me.

However, there is no burden imposed upon *ātmā* by all these beings existing in it. There is no imprint left in space by *vāyu*. The space is limitless, all-pervasive, and it is *asaṅga*, unconnected to *vāyu*, even though *vāyu* cannot exist without space. It has its being in *ākāśa* alone and it moves around in *ākāśa*. The example is used only to illustrate that *ātmā* is also *asaṅga*. It is unattached to anything, yet nothing is ever away from *ātmā*. As *vāyu* moves all over but never moves away from space, all the *bhūta*s can move from one place to another, all the worlds may come into being and collapse but they are never away from *ātmā*. If the soul goes from here to *brahma-loka*, the whole movement is in Brahman. The soul is Brahman, the *jagat* is Brahman; there is nothing that is away from Brahman. If the self-conscious being moves from one place to another, the movement is in *sattā*, existence. The soul 'is' and that 'is' is Brahman, *ātmā*. Therefore, it can never go away from Brahman. When you go to *brahma-loka* you are still the same Brahman. Even here, you are Brahman. When you can recognise this here, why should you go elsewhere to recognise it? The whole movements, the entire beings, transactions, and any kind of coming, going and hiding are all in Brahman.

Why does he say that all of them are in Brahman instead of saying all of them are Brahman? It is to make it clear that 'I' remains untouched. Saying, 'in me' is like saying 'in space.' Just as *vāyu* moves in space, leaving no imprint upon space, in the same way, all these beings exist in *ātma-caitanya* and yet leave no imprint on *ātma-caitanya*. May you recognise this clearly, *upadhāraya*.

When Bhagavān says, '*mathsthāni*, they exist in me,' he is talking about *sthiti-kāla*, the period of time when things exist. At the time of their existence, all names and forms have their being in *paraṁ-brahma*, like even the air that moves and has its being in space.

There are three aspects to any created thing, *sṛṣṭi*, its creation, *sthiti*, existence or sustenance, and *laya*, its destruction. Brahman is the cause for all these. If you were to ask, 'What happens during the destruction, *laya-kāle*?'

Verse 7

At the time of dissolution all beings go to my prakṛti

सर्वभूतानि कौन्तेय प्रकृतिं यान्ति मामिकाम् ।
कल्पक्षये पुनस्तानि कल्पादौ विसृजाम्यहम् ॥ ७ ॥

sarvabhūtāni kaunteya prakṛtiṁ yānti māmikam
kalpakṣaye punastāni kalpādau visṛjāmyaham (7)

kaunteya – O Arjuna!; *kalpakṣaye* – at the dissolution of the cycle of creation; *sarva-bhūtāni* – all beings; *māmikam prakṛtim* – to my *prakṛti; yānti* – go; *punaḥ* – again; *kalpa-ādau* – at the beginning of the cycle; *aham* – I; *tāni visṛjāmi* – create them

> All beings, Kaunteya (Arjuna)! go to my *prakṛti* at the dissolution of the cycle of creation. Again, at the beginning of the cycle, I create them.

All beings (sentient and inert), *sarva-bhūtāni,* go to my *prakṛti – māmikaṁ prakṛtiṁ yānti.* He does not say 'to me' but to my *prakṛti.* In saying this, Kṛṣṇa reveals a fact. When one cycle comes to an end it is called *kalpa-kṣaya,* the completion or exhaustion of the cycle. At this time, all beings go into a state of dissolution in my *prakṛti.* We will not translate the word *prakṛti* here.

Again, *punaḥ, kalpa-ādau,* in the beginning of the cycle, *tāni visṛjāmi aham,* I release them, I project them. Here '*vi*' prefixed to the verb *sṛj* in *visṛjāmi* means, 'I create each one as it was in the previous cycle.' So, the creation is the same as it was in all other cycles. To fulfil the *karmas* of the *jīvas*, again the cycle begins. Then it dissolves and from the dissolved state again the creation arises. The created world has its being in me and the dissolved world goes into my *upādhi.* What is this *upādhi* and why should the Lord bring it in? Why should he not say, 'It goes back into me.' A pot, for instance, comes out of clay and goes back to the clay. The clay does not say, 'It goes back to my *upādhi.*'

The existence and dissolution of a given object takes place in the place from which it arises. When the pot is destroyed, it goes back to its cause, the clay. And from that same cause is its creation. From the clay the pot is born, into clay it resolves and while it exists it has its existence in clay.

What is under discussion here is the dissolution of the world into the *prakṛti* of Bhagavān. Since he says, 'It goes into my *prakṛti,*' it can be like saying, 'It goes into my bank account.' I am not my bank account, it is very clear. Similarly here, Bhagavān's *prakṛti* is the place where the created world resolves. He says, 'The existence of the world is in me, *matsthāni,* but its *laya,* dissolution, is into my *prakṛti.*' This seems to be a contradiction because we have seen that if a thing has come from a given material cause, into that it resolves. If from Īśvara the world has come, into Īśvara the world should go back. Instead, he says, 'It goes into my *prakṛti.*' This is not a contradiction but a deliberate expression. We will see why.

Understanding the expression 'my prakṛti'

When Bhagavān says, *matsthāni sarva-bhūtāni,* all these beings have their being in me, are they attributes of *paramātmā*? If so, *paramātmā* has the intrinsic attribute of the *jagat* and is always *saguṇa*. If it is the case, then *paramātmā* can never be free from those attributes. But our experience is entirely different. If we analyse the nature of *ātmā,* we find it is free from all attributes. At any given moment, between two thoughts what exists is *paramātmā,* which is *caitanya* free from any form of limitation. Intrinsically, *paramātmā* is *nirguṇa,* free from attributes. Only because of this is *mokṣa* possible.

If *paramātmā* is intrinsically free from the *jagat,* then when Bhagavān says, *matsthāni,* it exists in me, it is only through some other factor. That factor is what we call *māyā*. It is the *māyā-upādhi* that makes *paramātmā* into Īśvara. Purely due to *upādhi, paramātmā* becomes all-knowledge and all powerful, the creator of everything. Due to a similar type of *upādhi*, you have limited knowledge, *alpajñatva* and so on. As *ātmā*, your *svarūpa* is *sat-cit-ānanda*. It is pure consciousness, which is *satya* and limitless. Then, how do you become one of limited knowledge, limited power, and limited pervasiveness? It is due to *upādhi*. *Upādhi* gives rise to a point of view. You view *ātmā* from the standpoint of your physical body-mind-sense complex and say, 'I am limited,' and so on. It is an unfortunate statement because it is not true. *Ātmā* has not become *alpajña*, it continues to be *sat-cit-ānanda*, which is why I can say *tat-tvam-asi*, you are *sat-cit-ānanda*. If you ask, 'Swamiji, if I am *sat-cit-ānanda*, how do I become *alpajña*?' The question itself is wrong because *sat-cit-ānanda* does not become anything. If you are *sat-cit-ānanda*, you cannot become *alpajña*.

There is a notion that one was originally *sat-cit-ānanda* and gradually over a period of time, due to a number of births, became *alpajña*. Then it has to evolve back. The contention is that we are all in the cycle of evolution. Evolution of what? If *sat-cit-ānanda* is to evolve, what will it become? Now it is limitless, free from attributes. Which part of *sat-cit-ānanda* evolves? How can *sat*, existence, evolve?

The evolution of existence is only destruction. But this is an existence that is limitless. There is no possibility of evolution for such an existence. Can consciousness evolve? Only a thing that has an attribute can evolve. But consciousness, which is pure existence, free from any attribute, cannot evolve. And, as we have seen, it is limitless. Thus, there is no evolution for *sat-cit-ānanda*.

Anything within *saṁsāra* can evolve. You draw an arbitrary line and any development beyond that you can call evolution. The human body may be an evolute because the human mind has a better capacity than the minds of other life forms. But the one who determines this is an evolute, is *alpajña*. And when you say, '*alpajño'ham*, I am of limited knowledge,' that *aham* remains *sat-cit-ānanda*. The property of *alpajñatva*, limited knowledge, is purely an incidental attribute, attributed to you by taking a point of view. For example, a modern artist may draw a table from the perspective of one who is looking at it from a position of lying down. It may not look like a table at all; it is just a perspective. That kind of table is not found anywhere. Similarly, you look at *sat-cit-ānanda* from the perspective of your limping physical body, your ageing brain cells etc., and say, 'I have limited power, limited knowledge, limited pervasiveness,' it is a perspective. Although the drawing had something to do with the table, this perspective has nothing to do with the table. The same is true with *sat-cit-ānanda-ātmā*. If being limited is your view of yourself, it is due to *upādhi* and has nothing to do with *sat-cit-ānanda*. The same *sat-cit-ānanda* appears as though it is *alpajña*. Because it is limitless, there is nothing that is apart from *sat-cit-ānanda*.

As the cause of everything, *sat-cit-ānanda* has to assume the status of being all-knowledge, almighty, whom we call God, Īśvara. But the attributes like, all-knowledge, and almighty are incidental attributes from the standpoint of the *jīva*'s way of looking at the world. And when you look at this world, the same *sat-cit-ānanda* becomes the onlooker as well as Īśvara, the cause of everything. All names are his names and all forms are his forms. Therefore, you have any number of words to describe Īśvara, which is due to *upādhi* called *māyā-upādhi* or *prakṛti-upādhi*.

So, when Kṛṣṇa as Īśvara says, '*sarva bhūtāni*, they are in me,' he is also including the *māyā-upādhi*. Only then can he say, all the beings have their basis in me. He becomes the cause of everything due to *māyā-upādhi*. Through *māyā-upādhi* alone, all the beings have their being in *paramātmā*. By itself, *paramātmā* is free from the creation because it is free from all attributes. So, with *māyā* alone does Bhagavān say, *matsthāni sarva- bhūtāni*. When you look at *paramātmā* as the cause of the entire *jagat*, then *māyā* exists in *paramātmā* as its *śakti*. In *māyā* alone they exist and resolve, and from *māyā* they are again born.

Bhagavān and māyā are not two different entities

Now we have a problem. There is nothing else except *ātmā*, Brahman; it is non-dual. If Brahman has *māyā* in itself, Brahman is one, *māyā* is another and so we have two entities. If fundamentally there are two, there is multiplicity. This is not acceptable because Brahman is *advaya*, non-dual. But when we say 'One is Brahman and the second is *māyā*,' we really do not have this problem. It is because, *māyā* is an interesting word. In Sanskrit, it is defined as follows – *yā mā sā māyā*, that which is not is *māyā*. That is to say, *māyā* has no independent reality. It really does not exist. From one standpoint there is *māyā*, from the other, there is no *māyā*, only Brahman.

If you look at Brahman as the cause of creation, it has *māyā*, which is why it is said, *māyā-śabalam brahma*. From the standpoint of itself, there is no *māyā*, there is only *sat-cit-ānanda*. *Māyā* is not an independent object enjoying a reality like *sat-cit-ānanda-ātmā* because *māyā* is *mithyā*. And *mithyā* does not exist apart from the *adhiṣṭhāna* on which it is dependent on; *mithyā* is therefore, *adhiṣṭhāna-ananyā*. Just like your shirt that has no existence apart from its fabric, similarly, *māyā* is not a substance separate from Brahman. If it exists in its own right, you can say *māyā* and Brahman together create the world and their getting together is the cause for creation. But they are not two independent factors because *māyā* is not independent from Brahman.

This is why we can worship the Lord as male or female. The string of *sahasranāmāvali*, 1000 names, of any *devatā* will invoke that particular *devatā* as the one who is the creator of everything, sustainer of everything, destroyer of everything; in other words, who is everything. Then for the *devī*, the *māyā-śakti*, the goddess, the string of 1000 names will say the same thing. She is the creatrix, the sustainer and the destroyer of everything; in fact she is everything. This is another way of looking at the fact that there is only Īśvara. There is Īśvara from the standpoint of *śakti*, power, and Īśvara without *śakti*. To think of two different entities – Īśvara and *māyā* – has no meaning at all because *māyā-śakti* is not independent of Īśvara. Like the capacity to burn is not independent of fire, *māyā-śakti* is not independent of Brahman, because it is the power of Brahman itself. From the standpoint of viewing Brahman as the cause of everything, you say *māyā-śabalam brahma*, Brahman with the power *māyā*. But there is no problem of duality because one is *satya*, the other is *mithyā*; and *satya* plus *mithyā* is still one, *satya*.

When you stand before a mirror and see your reflection, there appears to be two of you – two heads, two mouths to feed and hundreds of other problems. But you know it is not so. You know there is only one 'you' because you know that the reflection is *mithyā*. One plus one does not make two here. Even if you stand in a house of mirrors and see infinite reflections, yet there is only one 'you.' The only difference is, all the images in the mirror are identical but in *īśvara-sṛṣṭi* no two things look the same, not even two thumbs. The variety is infinite. Moreover, none of the reflections you see in the mirror is taken seriously. You cannot be detracted from or improved upon in a mirror. If you go to one *upādhi*, a concave mirror, and see yourself elongated, or you go to another *upādhi*, a convex mirror, and see yourself widened, you do not get alarmed, you are amused. Why? Because you know it is *mithyā*. If it were real, it would be a problem. Being *mithyā*, there is no problem.

Mithyā undergoes changes; *satya* remains the same. It means, in the *satya-vastu* there are no changes. *Nāma-rūpa*s change, *vastu* does not. It is the cause of all of them. It is the cause that never changes. Therefore, *paramātmā* plus *māyā* does not make two. One reality plus an infinite number of *nāma-rūpa*s is still 'one.' From this standpoint alone Bhagavān says, 'They resolve into me.' Only because of this *mithyā* was it said, *matsthāni sarva bhūtāni*, and from his own standpoint, *na ca matsthāni bhūtāni*. Again he says '*kalpa-kṣaye sarva-bhūtāni māmikāṁ prakṛtiṁ yānti*, again at the end of the *kalpa*, all the beings resolve in to my *prakṛti*.' To say they go back to my *prakṛti* or 'they go back to me, are both right because *prakṛti* has no separate existence other than Īśvara.

When it is proved that creation is *mithyā*, we have to accept a *mithyā* cause, which is *māyā-upādhi*, another word that is used for the *śakti* of Brahman. Because of this alone Brahman becomes the cause.

Brahman however does not undergo any change and is therefore, as we have seen before, *vivarta-upādāna-kāraṇa*. Brahman is both the efficient and material cause. But how can Brahman be the material cause, which must necessarily undergo change to become this variegated world? Even though the creation is non-separate from the cause, Brahman cannot undergo even an apparent change to create this world. We saw that Brahman remains the same and therefore we say it is *vivarta-upādāna-kāraṇa*.

There are two types of *upādāna-kāraṇa*. One is *vivarta-upādāna-kāraṇa* and the other is *pariṇāmi-upādāna-kāraṇa*. When a thing that is the material cause undergoes a change to become the effect, then it is called *pariṇāmi-upādāna kāraṇa*. And if it does not undergo any change to become the effect, it is called *vivarta-upādāna-kāraṇa*. Now, from the standpoint of the world, Brahman is *vivarta-upādāna-kāraṇa* because it is the cause that does not undergo any change. Whatever changes that are necessary are undergone only by *māyā*. Therefore, *māyā* is the *pariṇāmi-upādāna-kāraṇa* for this world. If you say Brahman is the material cause then it is *vivarta-upādāna-kāraṇa*, and if you say *māyā* is the material cause, it is *pariṇāmi-upādāna-kāraṇa*.

So, Brahman undergoes no change and at the same time makes all changes possible. It is like how the rope is the *vivarta-upādāna-kāraṇa* for the snake and consciousness is the *vivarta-upādāna-kāraṇa* for your dream. The dreamer is *caitanya*, the dream world is *caitanya* and the dream experience is *caitanya*. Without the *caitanya* there cannot be any creation and therefore *caitanya* is *vivarta-upādāna-kāraṇa*, and your own memory becomes the *pariṇāmi-upādāna-kāraṇa*. Similarly, Brahman alone is the cause for the whole creation as *vivarta-upādāna-kāraṇa* and *māyā* is the *pariṇāmi-upādāna-kāraṇa*. Thus, through the *upādhi* it becomes *nimitta-kāraṇa*, efficient cause, through the *upādhi*, it becomes material cause, *upādāna-kāraṇa*.

Verse 8

The Lord is also the efficient cause through this māyā upādhi

प्रकृतिं स्वामवष्टभ्य विसृजामि पुनः पुनः ।
भूतग्राममिमं कृत्स्नमवशं प्रकृतेर्वशात् ॥ ८ ॥

prakṛtiṁ svām avaṣṭabhya visṛjāmi punaḥ punaḥ
bhūtagrāmam imaṁ kṛtsnam avaśaṁ prakṛtervaśāt (8)

svāṁ prakṛtim – my own *prakṛti*; *avaṣṭabhya* – controlling; *punaḥ punaḥ* – again and again; *imaṁ kṛtsnaṁ bhūtagrāmam* – this entire group of beings; *avaśam* – necessarily; *prakṛteḥ vaśāt* – by the force of prakṛti; *visṛjāmi* – I create

> Keeping my own *prakṛti* under control, again and again I create this entire group of beings necessarily, by the force of *prakṛti*.

Visṛjāmi punaḥ punaḥ, again and again I create. After the dissolution at the end of each *kalpa*, I again create (Myself). Does that mean I undergo a change? No.

Prakṛtiṁ svām avaṣṭabhya, keeping my own *prakṛti*, my own *māyā-upādhi* in my hands, I create. This is the difference between *jīva* and Īśvara. Īśvara keeps *māyā* under his control, the *jīva* comes under the spell of *māyā* or *avidyā* until he is released from it. Therefore, the Lord says, 'Keeping this *māyā* in my hands, I create again and again, *svām prakṛtiṁ avaṣṭabhya visṛjāmi punaḥ punaḥ*.'

What does he create? *Bhūtagrāmam imaṁ kṛtsnam*, this entire group of *bhūtas* meaning the whole *jagat*. 'What is seen by you, in its entirety I create, *aham visṛjāmi*.' You may ask, 'Why do you do that? All my problems are only because I find myself in this creation. So, why did you create all this?'

Due to the force of prakṛti alone the creation takes place

Avaśam means it is something that has to take place. That is, without any will on the part of Īśvara, this takes place. The question, 'Why did God create the world?' has been asked millions of times. Any answer is only imaginary. The stock answer is that, it is all Bhagavān's *līlā*, a sport for the Lord. But why does Bhagavān need a sport, *līlā*? Is he restless, bored, or lonely? If he is, then how can he be the Lord? He is as much a *saṁsārī* as me, the *jīva*.

The Lord answers this question by saying that, he did not really create anything at all. Only when he has created does he have to answer this question. In the next line he is going to say that he did not create anything. Assuming that there is a creation, we can only say that it came about without any will on his part. How then did it come?

Prakṛteḥ vaśāt, because of the force of *prakṛti* alone the creation takes place. The nature of *prakṛti* is to create. Not only the Lord, but you can also say the same thing. Why do you think about a given thing at a particular time? It is by the force of the same *prakṛti*. If you say, 'I think,' you have a problem; when you say, '*prakṛti* thinks,' you have no problem. What is applicable right now here for you is also applicable to Bhagavān because *ātmā* is common and the *sṛṣṭi* is typical. A given thought is born in your head. That is a *sṛṣṭi* even though you do not will to create a given thought. There is, of course, deliberate thinking but what we are talking about here is a thought that just occurs in your head without your willing. Why did this particular thought occur? Why is it created? It takes place naturally, *prakṛteḥ vaśāt*. Your will is not involved. Then, how can you assume responsibility for it? It is your thought, no doubt, but you have nothing to do with it because you have no will regarding it. This is true for a *jñānī* or an *ajñānī*. Both have nothing to do with the thought that occurs without any willing. So, let it occur and though there may be some cause we are not concerned with it; it is *prakṛteḥ vaśāt*.

An *ajñānī* has another type of thought that is born of his own will. When he wills a given thought, he will of course claim authorship for it. Because he has *ahaṅkāra*, he thinks he is creating the thought. The *jñānī* will also have this type of thought but he looks upon this so called will as a part of *prakṛti*. In his vision, even while thinking, he does not think. '*Paśyan śṛṇvan spṛśan jighran aśnan gacchan.....naiva kiñcit karomi*, seeing, hearing, touching, smelling, eating, walking and so on, I perform no action at all.'[11]

This is the difference between a *jñānī* and an *ajñānī*. Both have the experience of finding themselves with an unsolicited thought – *prakṛteḥ vaśāt*. The *ajñānī* thinks that he created the thought because he thinks he is a *kartā*. Then the confusion is further compounded. He assumes responsibility for the very thought that occurs without his will, and feels guilty about it. Then through therapy etc., he tries to develop some kind of a distance but he still has *ahaṅkāra*. Therefore, the problem is going to recur in one form or another. But there is also deliberate thinking on his part, for which he will certainly claim authorship because he has the notion, 'I am the author.' A *jñānī*, however, has eliminated the notion that he is the author of any action by seeing that *ātmā* is *akartā*. If *ātmā* is *akartā* then because of the force of *prakṛti* alone, thoughts happen. There is no willing or wishing or any kind of action. All these just take place and it is, 'As though I do something, as though I do not do anything.' Things take place 'as though' of their own accord, *prakṛteḥ vaśāt*.

Kṛṣṇa says the same thing. This creation just takes place. This is the answer to the question, 'Why the creation?' The *karmas* of all the *jīvas* form the *prakṛti*. When *pralaya* comes to

[11] *Gītā* 5.8&9

an end, those *karma*s have to find their expression and the manifest creation begins at the beginning of the *kalpa, kalpādau*. Bhagavān brings the creation into being, keeping the *prakṛti* under his control, *prakṛtiṁ svām avaṣṭabhya*. It means that he does not come under the spell of *prakṛti*. 'I' is *sat-cit-ānanda ātmā* and does not will anything to happen. Then who wills? In the presence of Bhagavān with reference to *prakṛti*, there is a will. It is said in the *Taittirīyopaniṣad*, '*so'kāmyata bahusyāṁ prajāyeyeti*...he desired, may I become many.' You can ask, 'Why should he desire?' Then we have to say that desiring is also from the point of view of the *prakṛti* alone, *prakṛteḥ vaśāt*. From the standpoint of *prakṛti*, *ātmā* seemingly desires, which is why Bhagavān says, '*prakṛtiṁ svām avaṣṭabhya*, keeping *prakṛti* under my control.' Without his willing, purely due to *prakṛti* this creation takes place.

It is a creation of great variety because the *jīva*s have to undergo many and different kinds of experiences according to the *karma*s they have earned. Because of that there are varieties of bodies with their own unique *sūkṣma-śarīra*, created according to the *karma* of *jīva*s. Now another question may arise here – when according to their *puṇya-pāpa-karma*s they are given bodies, situations and so on, how is Bhagavān doing anything?

When a king gives money, protection, punishment, etc., according to the services and attitudes of his citizens, he seems to be the one meting out punishment and reward. The same philosophy extends to Bhagavān. If you do the right thing you are rewarded, if you do not do the right thing, you are punished. Even a dog is trained like that. If a person is well behaved, he is the beneficiary and if not, he is adversely affected.

By doing what is proper you are born in a good family, have a good body, and everything goes well for you. Another person is born in a situation full of disadvantages. Each person is affected by his or her own *dharma* and *adharma* which are subject to one's choice. Whenever there is a choice, there is definitely *kartṛtva*, doership. Bhagavān has no such problem because everything that is happening is due to *prakṛti*. He does not really participate in anything. When he says, 'I do not create anything at all,' the word 'I' refers to *sat-cit-ānanda-ātmā* and that is the only *ātmā* there is. In the presence of this *ātmā*, *prakṛti* takes care of everything.

There is one more point to be understood here. And that is, without the presence of *sat-cit-ānanda-ātmā* the *prakṛti* cannot do anything. If we say so, then we will be saying what the *Sāṅkhyas* propound, that is, *prakṛti* does everything and *ātmā* remains unconnected. This is not acceptable. *Prakṛti* and *paramātmā* are not two parallel realities. *Prakṛti* is not independent of *paramātmā*. It is superimposed upon *paramātmā* entirely depending upon *paramātmā* for its existence. *Prakṛti* itself cannot create, and *ātmā* also cannot create by itself; they come together to bring about this creation. But they are not two different entities enjoying the same degree of reality. One is *satya*, the other is *mithyā*. So, there continues to be only one. If this is not understood, we will end up with duality. That is why Lord Kṛṣṇa can say, 'I created everything; I did not create anything.' If it is not understood, it sounds like a contradiction.

In this creation there is a great deal of pain. Bhagavān seems to be responsible for all this. He created man with a wonderful body, senses and mind, and at the same time, he created some mosquitoes etc., to torment him. The human being has to fight against unknown sources of pain throughout his or her life. The one who created this pain must necessarily be affected by all this. Bhagavān says, 'No. Whatever the creation is, it is all due to the force of *prakṛti*, *prakṛteḥ vaśāt*, and I am not involved in it. These *karma*s do not affect me at all.'

Verse 9

I remain unconnected with reference to these karmas

न च मां तानि कर्माणि निबध्नन्ति धनञ्जय ।
उदासीनवदासीनमसक्तं तेषु कर्मसु ॥ ९ ॥

na ca māṁ tāni karmāṇi nibadhnanti dhanañjaya
udāsīnavad āsīnam asaktaṁ teṣu karmasu (9)

dhanañjaya – O Arjuna!; *tāni karmāṇi ca* – and these *karmas*; *mām* – me; *udāsīnavad āsīnam* – who is seated as though indifferent; *teṣu karmasu asaktaṁ* – who is unconneccted with reference to these *karmas*; *na nibadhnanti* – do not bind

Dhanañjaya (Arjuna)! These *karma*s do not bind me who is seated as though indifferent, who is unconnected with reference to these *karma*s.

The Lord says, 'With all its varieties, one superior another inferior, one healthy, another unhealthy, this creation does not affect me because I am unconnected, *asaṅgoham*.' You can join Kṛṣṇa here saying the same, *asaṅgoham*. The reason that Parameśvara is not connected to all these *karmas*, *asaktaḥ teṣu karmasu*, is that, he is resting as one who is absolutely indifferent, *udāsīnavad-āsīnaḥ*. This is an adjective Bhagavān uses to the word *mām,* me, meaning Parameśvara, to make it clear why these *karma*s do not bind.

Udāsīna means the one who is absolutely indifferent. Some one who is neither a *ragī,* one who likes, nor a *dveṣī,* one who dislikes, is called *udāsīna. Āsīna* means the one who is seated. Here Parameśvara is the one who is seated in the very *prakṛti, māyā-upādhi,* exactly like *ātmā* is seated in your *buddhi,* being totally uninvolved in anything that goes on. The *sat-cit-ānanda-ātmā* is seated in your *buddhi,* and is *udāsīna,* one who is indifferent, because it does not choose. It does not choose good *karma* or bad *karma,* a good thought or a bad thought. *Ātmā* does not choose, it just illumines. Therefore, it is *udāsīnavad-āsīnaḥ*.

Asakta means unconnected, without attachment. As *ātmā* is seated in your *buddhi,* here, the one who is seated as the very basis of *māyā,* Parameśvara also remains unconnected, devoid of attachment to the result, devoid of identification with doership. He has no connection to the *karma-phala* nor does he think, 'I am the doer.' *Ātmā* remains absolutely indifferent because it is not subject to any change.

Whenever you see an object, there is a change in your *antaḥ-karaṇa*. If it is something you like, there is a particular modification that takes place. And if it is an irritant, an entirely different type of change takes place. Now if there is an object, which causes no change at all in your *antaḥ karaṇa,* other than the *vṛtti* by which you simply perceive it, the response in the *antaḥ-karaṇa* is neutral, *udāsīna*. Like a perfectly neutral mind, *ātmā* does not undergo any change and is therefore, *udāsīnavad-āsīnaḥ*.

With reference to those *karmas*, *teṣu karmasu*, the three-fold *karmas* of *sṛṣṭi*, *sthiti* and *laya*, Bhagavān says, 'I am not really involved.' He has no sense of being a doer. It is possible for any other person also to have no sense of doership by knowing the same *ātmā*. Parameśvara's *ātmā* is *sat-cit-ānanda* and *jīva*'s *ātmā* is also *sat-cit-ānanda*. With this knowledge, there is no false identification of oneself as a doer.

Again, for *ātmā* there is no connection to the result of an action. Therefore, there is no sense of enjoyership for *ātmā*. The cause for having no connection to *saṁsāra* is simply the absence of these two – *kartṛtva*, doership, and *bhoktṛtva*, enjoyership. If these are there, the whole *saṁsāra* is with you. Just the thought, 'I am *kartā*, I am *bhoktā*,' is enough to bring you into the hold of *saṁsāra*. Freedom from *saṁsāra* is a fact, which is to be discovered. And in this discovery you see that there is no *kartṛtva* or *bhoktṛtva*–doership or enjoyership – in *ātmā*.

There seems to be a contradiction here

These sections of the *Gītā* where some paradoxes are presented to resolve certain other paradoxes are very important. Bhagavān says here, '*bhūta grāmam imaṁ kṛtsnaṁ visṛjāmi*, I create this entire group of beings. It is an expression of Kṛṣṇa assuming the role of Īśvara. He says very clearly, '*visṛjāmi*, I create.' Then he says, '*tāni mām na nibadhnanti*, those *karmas* (of creation, sustenance and destruction) do not bind me.' He himself gives the reason as to why they do not bind him. He says, 'I am seated, within the *upādhi* called *māyā*, like one who is absolutely neutral.' It means he denies all responsibility.

He now says that he is not responsible for these three *karma*s of creation, sustenance, and dissolution, which are continuously taking place in the world and which are imputed to Īśvara, and therefore, they do not bind him.

There seems to be a contradiction here. Generally you cannot say 'I create,' and then also say, 'I am not responsible for this action.' Even if you are forced to perform an action under duress, you still act. You only shift the responsibility to another person. But there is no person other than Īśvara who can induce him to perform an action and to whom he can pass the responsibility. If this is so, he has to assume responsibility for this three fold *karma* of *sṛṣṭi*, *sthiti* and *laya*. But he completely washes his hands off it. He says 'I create, sustain, and dissolve this creation; but I am not affected by the results of these actions.'

Verse 10

Bhagavān resolves this seeming contradiction

मयाध्यक्षेण प्रकृतिः सूयते सचराचरम् ।
हेतुनानेन कौन्तेय जगद्विपरिवर्तते ॥ १० ॥

mayādhyakṣeṇa prakṛtiḥ sūyate sacarācaram
hetunānena kaunteya jagad viparivartate (10)

mayā adhyakṣeṇa – owing to me, the presiding presence; *prakṛtiḥ* – the prakṛti; *sacarācaram* – (the world of) movables and immovables; *sūyate* – creates; *anena hetunā* – because of this reason; *kaunteya* – O son of Kuntī, Arjuna!; *jagad viparivartate* – the world undergoes changes

> With me as the presiding presence, the *prakṛti* creates (the world of) the movables and immovables. Because of this reason, Kaunteya (Arjuna)! the world undergoes changes.

Prakṛti meaning the *prakṛti-upādhi jagat sūyate*, creates this world, consisting of *cara*, things that move, and *acara*, things that do not move. *Cara* and *acara* can refer to all types of sentient beings. Here *acara* meaning stationary life forms like trees and plants and *cara* the life forms that move about. Or *cara* can mean sentient beings and *acara* insentient beings. When Bhagavān says *prakṛti* creates everything, there is a potential problem. If *prakṛti* creates everything, it means Bhagavān, *paramātmā*, has nothing to do with it. If he has nothing to do with this creation, then we have two realities, *ātmā* which performs no action and *prakṛti* which does everything. Then we must ask whether *prakṛti* is inert or sentient. If it is sentient, we have two sentient beings. And, as we have seen, it is not possible to prove the existence of a second sentient being. There is only one source of consciousness; everything else is *anātmā*, object of consciousness. No reasoning will help you establish a second conscious being, nor will perception. They can only establish an object, *anātmā*. And *śruti* is very clear that there is only one source of consciousness, *ātmā*. If this is so, how can an inert *prakṛti* be capable of creation?

The *Sāṅkhyas* call *prakṛti* by the name *pradhāna* and the conscious being by the name *puruṣa* and say that the *puruṣa* is totally unconnected with *prakṛti* and therefore, *asaṅga*. The *asaṅgatva* is total because for the *sāṅkhya*, the *prakṛti* is a reality.

And there is only one *prakṛti*, whereas *puruṣa*s are many. This parallel reality called *prakṛti* accounts for the entire creation, independent of the *puruṣa* who does not participate in the creation of the world.

We cannot accept this because it is against the *śāstra* and also against reasoning. Lot of arguments have been presented in the first and second chapters of the *Brahma-sūtra* refuting the *Sāṅkhya* philosophy. If *prakṛti* creates everything, then what was there before creation? He says all that existed was *prakṛti* and *puruṣa* who is not involved. What was the state of this *prakṛti* as it existed in dissolution? He will say that the three qualities of *prakṛti, sattva, rajas* and *tamas*, were in a state of equilibrium. Then there is a disturbance of the *guṇa*s and *prakṛti* starts creating. The question is, who disturbed this *prakṛti*? Since it is inert, it cannot disturb itself. It cannot think, 'let me create.' And *puruṣa* does not disturb. As there is no other factor to disturb *prakṛti*, how does this creation start?

Bhagavān answers this here saying, '*mayā adhyakṣeṇa*, with me as the presiding presence.' Being blessed by me, *prakṛti* creates this entire *jagat* that is made up of *cara* and *acara* – *prakṛtiḥ sūyate sacarācaram*.' When he says, 'by me,' he means *paramātmā*, pure consciousness. Here *adhyakṣa* means the one who presides. Śaṅkara says that in any situation it is pure consciousness that obtains. Therefore, he says the phrase, '*mayā adhyakṣeṇa*' means '*mayā dṛsi-mātra-svarūpeṇa*, by me the pure consciousness.' This is one of Śaṅkara's favourite words. In the *upadeśa-sāhasrī* he says, this pure consciousness is like space; that is, it has no particular form. Formless consciousness is the *svarūpa*, nature, of *ātmā*. Therefore, when Bhagavān says '*mayā*, by me,' it can only be a self that does not undergo any change whatsoever, which is why he says, *mayā adhyakṣeṇa*. This *prakṛti* presided over by me, creates. It is exactly like your mind and senses become conscious and are capable of creation because of the presence of *ātmā*. Similarly, because of my presence, *prakṛti* is able to create all this.

Śaṅkara quotes a very important *mantra* here:

eko devaḥ sarva bhūteṣu gūḍaḥ sarva vyāpī
sarvabhūtāntarātmā
karmādhyakṣaḥ sarvabhūtādhivāsaḥ sākṣī cetā kevalo
nirguṇaśca

Śvetāśvataropaniṣad 6.11

Ātmā is called *deva* here, and the word *eka* makes it clear that it is non-dual. A non-dual Parameśvara is hidden in all beings, *sarva bhūteṣu gūḍaḥ*. It obtains in the *buddhi* of all beings. But it is hidden in the sense it is not available for perception, but because of which perception takes place. Thereby it is self-evident. The one who is not located in space but is *sarvavyāpī*, all-pervasive, who is *antarātmā*, the inner self of all beings, and the one who presides over all action whether it is the Lord's actions of creation, sustenance, and dissolution or your action, whatever it may be. The one who blesses all the activities yet himself performs no action is *karmādhyakṣaḥ*. And he is *adhivāsa*, the basis of all beings, the one in whom they all have their existence. He is *sākṣī*, witness, *cetā*, the conscious being. From the standpoint of what is witnessed, consciousness has the status of being a *sākṣī*. But itself does not perform the action of witnessing, which is why it is said he alone is, *kevala*, meaning there is no second person, and he is *nirguṇa*, free from all attributes.

Blessed by this ātmā alone prakṛti creates everything

So because of this, because of my presiding over, my lending consciousness to it, the *prakṛti* itself is conscious. Because consciousness inheres in the *māyā-upādhi*, that *ātmā* becomes Parameśvara, the one who does everything and knows everything, and therefore has *sarvakāritva* and *sarvajñatva*. Blessed by this *ātmā* alone *prakṛti* creates everything.

Because of these reasons, *anena hetunā*, the world undergoes all its changes, *jagat viparivartate*. The changes of creation and dissolution, and again changes within creation are all possible because of this alone. They are presided over by me. Therefore, *ātmā* as the Lord can say, '*ahaṁ visṛjāmi*, I create.' And he can also say, 'I do not create.' How? Look at this.

In your own case, when the body is moving, the particular attribute of the body movement is imputed to the one who resides in the body. That is the 'I.' You are the one who is aware of this body and its movements but upon this 'awarer' you superimpose the action of movement. We are not considering *ātmā* as *sat-cit-ānanda* here. We are talking about the *jīva*. This simple *jīva*, seated inside this body does not perform any action even though the actions done by the body are attributed to the *jīva*. It is similar to the statement made by a person riding in a car. Although he performs no action at all, he will impute the attribute of the moving car to himself and say, 'I did 60 miles an hour.' Even if he becomes an Olympic runner he cannot travel 60 miles an hour. This is the property of the car; yet he says that he travelled 60 miles an hour. It is called *āropa*. You superimpose upon your own body a movement of 60 miles an hour, which belongs to the car. Similarly when the physical body is running or walking, the action is superimposed upon the *jīva* and then you say, 'I run, I walk.'

It is the same for Bhagavān. The *adhyakṣa*, the conscious being obtaining in the *prakṛti* makes the whole thing happen. The *prakṛti* aspect undergoes all the changes being blessed by the *cetana-ātmā*, and therefore *prakṛti* performs all the actions.

When it is understood that the action of *prakṛti* is superimposed upon *ātmā*, and that without *ātmā prakṛti* itself cannot create, then you too can say, 'I create, *ahaṁ visṛjāmi*.' Because consciousness itself does not perform any action, you can say, 'I did not create.' In my presence, *prakṛti* performs all the activities. *Prakṛti* or *māyā*, of course, underwent all the changes. I remain in the *māyā-upādhi*, as I always have not been performing any action, *udāsīnavad āsīna*.

It is important to note that Bhagavān includes the entire world here by saying *sacarācaram*. When he says the entire *jagat* is created by *prakṛti* blessed by *ātmā*, which itself performs no action, your body and all the five elements are also included in the *jagat*. They are nothing but the product of *māyā* blessed by consciousness. And the product of *māyā* is not away from *māyā* which itself is not away from *ātmā*. Therefore, there is nothing that is away from *sat-cit-ānanda-ātmā*.

Let us come to your physical body. Is it created or not? Since it is a modification of *prakṛti* or *māyā*, this physical body is also created by *prakṛti*. *Prāṇa*, mind and senses are created by *prakṛti*. And behind them is *sat-cit-ānanda-ātmā*. Therefore, your mind is functioning, being blessed by *ātmā* alone. Every *vṛtti*, thought, enjoys *caitanya-ātmā*. It is the same whether it is individual *sṛṣṭi*, your mind and its thoughts, or total *sṛṣṭi*, the entire *jagat*, because *ātmā* is the same. Behind the whole scene of your personal creation or the total cosmic creation is one *caitanya-ātmā* alone. Therefore, you too can say, along with Bhagavān, 'Blessed by me, *prakṛti* creates this world composed of movables and immovables, *mayā adhyakṣeṇa prakṛtiḥ sūyate sacarāram*.' This is *jñāna*, knowledge. I perform no action; in my presence alone actions take place. The *acetana*, inert, itself cannot create and *cetana*, consciousness, does not create. Inbetween there is the 'so called creation.' Thus inert *prakṛti* blessed by *caitanya-ātmā*, the conscious being, becomes the cause for the entire creation.

So, when Kṛṣṇa says, 'I create,' but at the same time he says, 'I did not do it,' it is exactly like the person seated in the car saying, 'I did 60 miles an hour' and then saying, 'No, I did not do it.' In both the situations, the statements are made from the standpoint of *sat-cit-ānanda-ātmā*. You too can say, 'I thought,' and immediately follow it up with, 'I did not think at all.' It is not denying your responsibility for your actions. Because such denial requires that you accept an action and your doership as real. If you say, 'I am *kartā*, an agent,' then you cannot say that you did the action and at the same time deny that you are responsible. Suppose you have this understanding that you never really performed action even when you performed action, then, when you say, 'I did the action, and I never performed the action,' you are revealing something.

Bhagavān accepts the *karma* when he says, 'I create.' But at the same time he says, 'I did not do it,' exactly like the person seated in the car says, 'Because I was seated in the car, I did 60 miles an hour, at the same time, I did not perform any action.' Both are true. Similarly here, from the standpoint of the *upādhi ātmā* is a *kartā* and from its own standpoint it is purely a blessing, a presence. The self is only a presence of consciousness, in which the mind becomes active, and actions take place.

This is what we saw when Bhagavān said earlier in the fourth chapter, '*karmāṇi akarma yaḥ paśyet sa buddhimān*, the one who recognises actionlessness in actions is a wise man.' That wisdom is being talked about here. The entire *jagat* is changing because of *prakṛti*, which is blessed by me. Therefore, I can say, I create, I sustain, I destroy. And then I can say, I did not do anything because I am like a witness. Thus, all contradictions are resolved.

Śaṅkara describes your own experience here and says, '*dṛṣi-karmatvāpatti-nimittā hi jagataḥ sarvā pravṛttiḥ*, any activity in the world is because it is an object of consciousness.' For example, a desire in your mind is known to you, it is the object, *karma*, of consciousness, *dṛṣi*, in the sense that consciousness lights it up. It lights up any object, even the *ahaṅkāra*, the desirer.

Then the action you do is also lighted up by the same *caitanya*. So, where is the possibility of an action, *pravṛtti,* without consciousness being there? At the same time, consciousness itself performs no action. All the factors involved in an action, the *kāraka*s such as the subject, object, instrument and so on, are lighted up by the same consciousness. It only lights up, performing no action. Therefore, you can say, '*aham akartā,* I am not a doer.' But without the lighting up there is no question of any action. How are you going to fulfil a desire without recognising it? And you have to be there to recognise it. If this is clear, then you see how you can say, 'I did everything, at the same time I did not do anything. I am the *kartā,* I am the *akartā.*'

It is a common misunderstanding that the objective of this knowledge is to eliminate the *ahaṅkāra*. Then the question will naturally arise, 'If I eliminate the *ahaṅkāra,* ego, how will I engage in any pursuit?' We do not eliminate the ego. We say the ego is *ātmā,* but *ātmā* is not the ego. This amounts to an elimination of ego because you think *ātmā* is ego, which is not true. The ego appropriates to itself the status of being 'I,' of being some kind of an independent being. In fact, it is a misappropriation, which only brings in limitation and bondage. It is like losing a million dollar job because of misappropriating some postage stamps. The ego, even though it has no sense of 'I' without the *ātmā,* further appropriates to itself the body, mind and senses, thereby becoming an entity, which is limited. So, we negate that and the ego becomes *bādhita*. Enlightened, one continues to be an entity but at the same time, much more than what one thought one was. Thus, one can say that there is *ahaṅkāra*, and also say that there is absence of *ahaṅkāra*. There is an agent who undertakes activity and there is no activity at all. Both are equally true.

Śaṅkara tells in detail the nature of this activity, *pravṛtti* – 'I enjoy this particular object,' 'I see this,' 'I hear this,' 'I experience this pleasure,' 'I undergo this pain,' 'for the purpose of that alone I will perform this action' and 'I will know this,' and so on. What he wants to show is that the nature of *pravṛtti* is such that it has its being in consciousness. When you say, 'I see,' the fact that you see something, implies knowledge, consciousness. In 'I see,' the seer has its being in consciousness, the sight has its being in consciousness. The object of sight is also non-separate from your consciousness. Once you say, 'I see this,' 'this,' is the object of your sight. How is it away from your consciousness? And therefore, nothing, the seer, seen, sight, is separate from consciousness. Similarly how can you say, 'I enjoy,' unless you light up the enjoyer, enjoyed and enjoyment. So, all this *pravṛtti* – I will perform this action, I will know this object, I know this object, I am seeing this object, I am hearing this object – has its being in consciousness and resolves in consciousness. Once one such *pravṛtti* is over, you are ready again for something else. That also resolves in consciousness and again you are ready for another thing.

It is so intelligent, like a camera, even better. A film is exposed to objects in terms of light and registers an image. But that can happen only once. The film cannot be cleaned and used again; once it is exposed it is finished. Here it is not like that. Look at this. The mind is exposed and the image of the object transpires there. Then it is gone and the light, *ātmā* is there. The eyes require some light as does the camera. But here the light is from within. It lights up the object. Then it is over and ready for the next exposure. Another good thing about this mind is that it can store all the images in the memory so that you can recall them later. Then, after a few days, some of them get erased. If I ask you what you ate the day before yesterday, perhaps if you think it over, you will remember, but definitely not the day a month ago. This erasure is wonderful, otherwise your head will be full of lunches and dinners and varieties of things that you saw or read. Certain important things are always kept in memory. Memory is something amazing. How can it work unless it has the capacity to destroy? But then it has the capacity to automatically remember certain things very clearly. It all seems to be well organised. So, consciousness lights up everything, including memory. Then when it is over, when the mind is cleared, everything is resolved in consciousness. It has its being in consciousness. It has its resolution in consciousness. The *avagati*, end, is a resolution in consciousness. There is a lot more in this, which we will see further.

In the last two verses we saw that *prakṛti* creates the world consisting of things that move and things that do not move. It also sustains and destroys it. Destruction is in the sense of dissolving creation back to itself. Bhagavān says, *prakṛti* can do this only because it is blessed by me. With *paramātmā* as its basis, *prakṛti* creates everything. Without this basis, it cannot be conscious and therefore, cannot create. *Prakṛti*, also called as *māyā*, draws its existence from *paramātmā*, is conscious because of *paramātmā* and therefore, can create by itself. If the word 'I,' *aham* is used keeping the *māyā-upādhi* in view, the Lord can say, '*aham visṛjāmi*, I create.' But in reality, the *aham* is purely *paramātmā* and to say, 'I create' is only a referential statement. Then again, Bhagavān says, '*na ca māṁ tāni karmāṇi nibadhnanti*, these actions do not affect me at all, because I am like one who is absolutely indifferent, *udāsīnavat*.' This is from my own standpoint from where there is no action at all. We have two types of statements here, which understood together is *jñāna*.

Similarly, when you say '*aham karomi*, I do,' all this is involved. The action that obtains in the *upādhi* such as the body-mind-sense complex is superimposed upon the self and then you say, 'I do.' If this is understood, the fact that you do not do anything, even when you seem to do all types of actions, should also be very clear. It is for this reason Bhagavān says that these *karma*s do not bind him.

Śaṅkara poses an interesting question here. When the Lord has no connection to the objects of enjoyment and when there is no other conscious being to be an enjoyer, for what reason does he create the world? If the creation is for another enjoyer, we must first establish that there is another.

Is there another?

The *mantra* that Śaṅkara quoted previously said that there is only one Lord, *eko devaḥ...*,[12] one conscious being concealed in all the beings, *sarva bhūteṣu gūḍhaḥ*. As we have seen earlier,

---

[12] Page 186

it means there is only one self, which by nature is conscious and happens to be this entire creation. There is no multiplicity here at all, *sarvaṁ brahmaiva neha nānā asti kiñcana*. Even the *jagat* is not a second thing because it is *mithyā*, is what the *śruti* says.

Now, suppose you say there are many *ātmā*s. Then we must ask, is the second *ātmā* known to you or not? If you say there is a second *ātmā*, you have to say it is known to you.

How would another be known? By *ātmā*?

If it is known, then we will ask, whether it is known by *ātmā* or *anātmā*? Suppose you say it is known by *ātmā*. To know there is a second *ātmā*, you must be able to see the difference between your own *ātmā* and the second *ātmā*. To do that, you must first see what is the peculiarity in your *ātmā* that makes it distinguishable from the second one. If you look into your *ātmā*, what do you see? White, black?

If you see a black *ātmā* does the blackness belong to *ātmā* or *anātmā*? If it belongs to *anātmā*, how can you say it is 'you?' If it belongs to *ātmā*, how are you going to see it? A property of *ātmā*, which you have to see should be an object. And *ātmā* being yourself, you can never see it as an object. In order to see anything you must have *kartṛ-karma-bheda*, the seer must be different from the seen. So, to look into any particular feature of *ātmā*, you have to divide *ātmā* into two, the seer *ātmā* and the seen *ātmā*. How can you say that *ātmā* is both seer and seen? It is not possible at all. So, you cannot see the features in your own *ātmā* that will distinguish it from another *ātmā*. Thus the difference between one *ātmā* and another cannot be known by *ātmā*.

By *anātmā*?

Then, you have to say it is known by *anātmā*. But *anātmā* is *jaḍa*, inert; it is something that you see. Being inert, *anātmā* cannot see anything at all. Therefore, this difference is not seen by either *ātmā* or *anātmā*. If it is not seen, you cannot prove there is another *ātmā*.

Śaṅkara probes this further. Assuming, for the sake of argument, that this difference exists, is it different or non-different from *ātmā*? If you say it is not identical with *ātmā*, it becomes a *dharma*, property, of *ātmā*, which is *anātmā*. If you say it is identical with *ātmā*, then we have the same problem of establishing how you are seeing it. There is no *pramāṇa* for it because *ātmā* cannot see its own features. It does not have that kind of subject object division.

To summarise, if there are many *ātmā*s, you must be able to distinguish one from the other. And to do that you must be able to establish differences among them. In order to establish the differences, first you must see your *ātmā* having this feature and another *ātmā* having other features. Unless you have established the differences between *ātmā*s, you cannot establish the multiplicity of *ātmā*.

If your *ātmā* is *sat-cit-ānanda*, then what about the other *ātmā*? If you say *ātmā*s are many and all of them are *sat-cit-ānanda*, how can there be another *ānanda* other than this *ānanda*, which is limitless? If one *sat-cit-ānanda-ātmā* is limitless, where is the possibility of another limitless *ātmā*? There is no second limitlessness, which is why you can say along with Īśvara, *mayā adhyakṣeṇa prakṛti sūyate*. That is knowledge. The whole teaching is that you should be able to say along with Lord Kṛṣṇa, 'By me everything is presided over.' Because when he says 'me,' that 'me' is *sat-cit-ānanda-ātmā* and there is only one *sat-cit-ānanda-ātmā*.

Perhaps a second *ātmā* can be inferred.

Even though you do not see *ātmā*, you may argue that you can infer it because a person responds when you talk to him. You are not inferring *ātmā*; you only infer that the mind is present. You never confront another *ātmā*. You confront the body, which is *anātmā*, or even the thought perhaps, by presumption. But the other person is confronting the same thought. Therefore, neither you nor he confronts *ātmā*. Since it can never be confronted, you cannot know another *ātmā* to count as a second.

Unless there is an enjoyer, there is no necessity for a creation. When you create something, either you should enjoy it or someone else should enjoy it. We have just seen that there is only one *cetana-ātmā*. Therefore, no other *ātmā* is available to be an enjoyer. Then who enjoys this world?

Is the creation meant for Īśvara himself?

If *sṛṣṭi* is for its own sake, *paramātmā* should enjoy the *sṛṣṭi* and to do that, it must become an enjoyer. Now to enjoy something, there must be a change on the part of the enjoyer.

Previously he was not enjoying, now he is. Because enjoyment is a state of experience, it is something that did not exist before, exists now and will not exist later. You enjoy for the time being. Enjoyment being a particular mental disposition, *vṛtti viśeṣa*, there must be a *vikriyā* change, into and out of that state. So, *paramātmā* should undergo a change in order to be an enjoyer of the *sṛṣṭi*, which it has created.

Śaṅkara says that Īśvara does not undergo any change whatsoever; he is *avikriya*. So, *paramātmā* cannot become an enjoyer. It is one reason why the creation cannot be for itself.

Further, *paramātmā* does not have any sense of inadequacy that would prompt it to have a thought to create. *Ātmā* is *paripūrṇa*, fullness, limitless. When there can be no desire to become complete, why would he create the world? So, *paramātmā* can neither create nor enjoy the creation. Thus, no one can say anything about the creation of the world.

The question 'why creation' is untenable.

When Śaṅkara asks, 'Why this creation?' what answer can you give? Śaṅkara says, the question and answer are both untenable. If you say that there is only one *ātma-caitanya*, there is no other *bhoktā*, in which case, why do you ask this question? You seem to understand non-duality; so, there is no question. If you understand that only one *caitanya-ātmā* exists, there is no real *sṛṣṭi* for any purpose, and the question, 'Why is there a creation,' is untenable. When even to ask the question is not proper, to answer it is certainly not proper. *Śruti* herself expects this. Elsewhere she says, '*ko addhā veda ka iha pravocat kuta ājātā kuta iyaṁ visṛṣṭiḥ.*[13] Who knows this *jagat*? Who exactly knows every thing? Who is the one who sees the world? There is no *jagat* here to see. Other than *ātmā*, you cannot see the *jagat* and in *ātmā*, you do not see the *jagat* at all. Who would be able to talk about this subject matter? Meaning, who would be able to answer a question like this? Nobody, because there is no *jagat*. Look at this wonder! From where, from where, has this *sṛṣṭi* come? This repetition, as *kuta, kuta*, etc., is for the sake of showing *sambhrama*, perturbation, like when you say, 'Where is he? Where is he?'

Some argue that it is Bhagavān's *līlā*. Then his play is my back pain, my heart attack, my stomach ulcer. What kind of play is that? If he plays and makes me play too, then, we can say Bhagavān is just interested in play; so, he created some others to play with. But it must be play for the others or it is sadism. We see that the world is not play; so, we cannot say it is *līlā*. Even if it were a play, it is for someone who wishes to enjoy. If *ātmā* is *avikriya* then, how can there be *līlā* for *ātmā*? In pure *caitanya* there is no *līlā*.

There is no *prayojana*, purpose in it because Īśvara has no sense of limitation or inadequacy, which would motivate him to create something. So there is no purpose even for Īśvara, much less for *paramātmā*. Īśvara is *ātmā* obtaining in the

---

[13] को अद्धा वेद क इह प्रवोचत् कुत आजाता कुत इयं विसृष्टिः।

kaḥ – who; *addhā* – directly; *veda* - knows (this *paramātmā*); *kaḥ* – who; *iha* – here (with reference to this *paramātmā*); *pravocat* – can talk; *kutaḥ* – from where; *ājātā* – has this (creation); *kutaḥ* – where (is); *iyam visṛṣṭiḥ* – this creation?

māyā-upādhi making *ātmā sarvajña*, omniscient. The omniscient *ātmā* cannot be a desirer because he has no sense of limitation or inadequacy.

When creation is impossible, how to account for it?

Therefore, creation is not possible. So, how do we account for all this? What we call creation is nothing but *māyā*. Anything that is untenable is made tenable by *māyā*. If you ask how *māyā* can make it tenable, that is what *māyā* is; it makes the untenable tenable. This has already been shown by Bhagavān in the fifth chapter, '*ajñānena āvṛtaṁ jñānaṁ tena muhyanti jantavaḥ*, knowledge is covered by ignorance and because of that, living beings are deluded.' The idea is that the whole question arises only from the standpoint of *sṛṣṭi*, creation. Only when you accept a *sṛṣṭi* do you say Īśvara with the *māyā-upādhi* is the cause of creation. Then you can say *ātmā* qualified by *māyā-upādhi* is Īśvara and *paramātmā* without the *upādhi* is the cause that does not undergo any change and is called *vivarta-upādāna-kāraṇa*. That is what is said here, *mayā adhyakṣeṇa prakṛtiḥ sūyate sacarācaram*. *Ātmā*, without giving up its nature, becomes the cause for everything. All this is only from the standpoint of creation, not from the standpoint of *ātmā*.

From the standpoint of ātmā there is no jagat

In *sat-cit-ānanda-ātmā*, there is no *jagat*. So, there is no necessity as to seek an answer as to how this world came about. Since it is not there in *sat-cit-ānanda*, there is no reason to talk about it. It looks as though the *jagat* is one thing and *sat-cit-ānanda* is another. It is not true because when you see the *jagat*, *sat-cit-ānanda* is present. There is no *jagat* separate from *sat-cit-ānanda* but in *sat-cit-ānanda* there is no *jagat*.

The question of how this *jagat* came about does not arise. When I look at the *jagat*, I find that it is not independent of *sat-cit-ānanda*. When this is so, the statements, '*matsthāni sarva-bhūtāni*, all beings are in me,' and '*na ca matsthāni sarva bhūtāni*, the beings are not in me,' are not contradictory but very clear. It means that there is nothing else except me, *sat-cit-ānanda*. So, the *jagat* cannot come from anywhere else; it comes only from *sat-cit-ānanda-ātmā*. There must be some cause and that cause is Īśvara. Therefore, the Lord says, '*mayā adhyakṣeṇa prakṛtiḥ sūyate sacarācaram*, blessed by me, the *ātmā* alone, *prakṛti* creates everything.' Not only does it create everything being blessed by me, it also sustains everything and resolves everything into me. By my grace the world exists.

So the creation is neither for *paramātmā* nor for any other, because there is no other. Therefore, it is very clear, *sṛṣṭi* is not for the sake of any one. You say there is no other *ātmā* except *paramātmā*, which does not require a *sṛṣṭi* at all. You yourself have dismissed the possibility of a *sṛṣṭi* being there; so, why do you ask, 'Why is there a creation?' Once you know this much, you yourself have answered the question. Yet there is something to see here.

When *śruti* says, *ko addhā veda ka iha pravocat kuta ājātā kuta iyam sṛṣṭiḥ*, it is to show that there is no real *sṛṣṭi*. A question and answer are possible only when there is something real. But it is not real. *Prakṛti* itself does not create because it has no existence of its own. *Ātmā* does not create either. Therefore, it is purely by *māyā*; then everything is possible.

The reality is *ātmā* does not create, and *prakṛti* alone cannot create. It has to be presided over, supported by *paramātmā.* Therefore, *prakṛti*'s existence is the existence of *paramātmā.* The *prakṛti*'s capacity to create etc., and the knowledge that is necessary are all due to *paramātmā* alone. *Prakṛti* blessed by *paramātmā* becomes the cause of and accounts for the existence of the creation. Thus Bhagavān says, '*aham visṛjāmi,* I create,' only from the standpoint of *prakṛti.* He himself is not the creator and therefore, says, '*na ca mām tāni karmāṇi nibadhnanti,* those actions do not affect me at all.' You can say the same thing. The body, mind and sense organs, all perform their activities being presided over, being blessed by *ātmā.* But those activities do not bind me at all because between *prakṛti* and *ātmā* there is no real connection. A connection is between two entities enjoying the same degree of reality. Here, one is *satya* and the other is *mithyā.* And *satya* is not affected by *mithyā.* Therefore, *prakṛti* is *āropa,* a superimposition, upon *ātmā.* Because you see everything, there is a *prakṛti,* which is *āropita* upon *ātmā.* It is definitely superimposed because once you say *ātmā* is *paraṁ-brahma,* there is no question of *prakṛti.*

You need to understand these two standpoints because this understanding is *mokṣa.* It is an understanding of your freedom from enjoyership and doership. Everything is connected to *ātmā,* which is the basis of everything. At the same time, *ātmā* remains unconnected. It is always untouched, free from doership and enjoyership. It does not perform action, much less does it enjoy the result of an action. You are already free and all your *karma*s are completely nullified. This is the whole vision.

Therefore, Śaṅkara says here, the 'me' referred to in the verse is the *ātmā* of all beings, which is *nitya-śuddha-buddha-mukta-svabhāva*, by nature always pure, enlightened and free. It is not that the Lord means to say, I am *sat-cit-ānanda-ātmā* for a particular being and not for another. In fact, he says, I am the *ātmā* of all beings. Lord Kṛṣṇa, the one who is saying this, is Īśvara who is *paramātmā*, the *jagat-kāraṇa* which is non-separate from anyone. And it is *nitya-śuddha*, always free from *karmas*, free from *pāpa* and *puṇya*, free form sorrow, etc. And it is *nitya-buddha*, without any ignorance, and therefore, *mukta-svabhāva*, always free. So, you need not purify or enlighten *ātmā* because it is not impure nor does it have any ignorance. You need not free the *ātmā*, because it is not in any way bound. It is omniscient and the cause of the entire creation.

Even though it is the *ātmā* of all beings…

Verse 11

The deluded fail to recognise me

अवजानन्ति मां मूढा मानुषीं तनुमाश्रितम् ।
परं भावमजानन्तो मम भूतमहेश्वरम् ॥ ११ ॥

avajānanti māṁ mūḍhā mānuṣīṁ tanum āśritam
paraṁ bhāvam ajānanto mama bhūtamaheśvaram (11)

ajānantaḥ – not knowing; *mama paraṁ bhāvam* – my limitless nature; *bhūta-maheśvaram* – as the Lord of all beings; *mūḍhāḥ* – the deluded; *mām* – me; *mānuṣīṁ tanum āśritam* – the one who obtains in the human body; *avajānanti* – fail to recognise

> The deluded fail to recognise me, the one who obtains in the human body, not knowing my limitless nature as the Lord of all beings.

Mūḍhāḥ, the deluded, means those who do not have this discriminative knowledge. They have the notion of doershsip and a sense of guilt for all their omissions and commissions. Naturally they have a sense of enjoyership for the results of their actions. These are the people who do not recognise that *ātmā* is *akartā*, non doer, *abhoktā*, non enjoyer, and that things take place as they should. *Ātmā* is only a blessing, a presence. The doership and enjoyership are superimposed upon *ātmā* and do not belong to it. Those who do not have this discrimination completely neglect or disrespect me in the sense that they do not recognise me nor do they think I am to be enquired into or understood. Why? Because *mama paraṁ bhāvam ajānantaḥ*, they do not know my limitless nature. Śaṅkara says that *ātmā* is like space. That is, it is not limited by any particular form or location, always pure and all-pervasive. And *ākāśa* itself is within it. The whole creation is within *ākāśa*; but this is still interior, subtler to *ākāśa* in that it is the basis of *ākāśa* itself. And he is the one who is the Lord of all beings, *bhūtamaheśvara*. Śaṅkara says, he is *svātmā*, one's own self.

He is the one who obtains in the human body. People do not recognise him as such. The people who do not know me, who has taken a human form, *ajñānantaḥ māṁ mānuṣīṁ tanum āśritam*, do not recognise me as Parameśvara, *avajānanti māṁ bhūtamaheaśvaram*. They take me only as the body just as they conclude themselves to be nothing more than their bodies.

And they impute the limitations of the body such as, mortality, etc., to *ātmā* and conclude that they are mortals, subject to all the limitations that the body is subject to. In fact, so intimate is this orientation that no difference is seen whatsoever between the body and *ātmā*. The lot of the physical body is one's own lot. It becomes so ridiculous that one can even say, 'I am white,' 'I am black,' and so on. At least if one says, 'I am fat,' or 'I am tall,' one is describing the body. But when one says, 'I am white' one is referring the pigment of the epidermis and equating it to oneself. This ridiculous state is achieved because one happens to be in this physical body, and takes it as oneself. In doing so, one neglects Parameśvara.

By neglecting Parameśvara one only neglects oneself

If you say that you have other things to do, all of them are only to become the Lord. You try to manipulate the world, to be in control. You want to be Īśvara; you are Īśvara in reality. But you find that you are helpless and some theologies will also tell you that you are eternally helpless, eternally imperfect and therefore, you need the Lord's grace to gain some beatitude. You accept it because you are convinced that you are helpless. Still you have a desire to control because you happen to be identical with Īśvara, who controls the whole creation. Therefore, what you really want is to be yourself. You neglect yourself and you want to be yourself. In other words the very thing you neglect is what you want to be, which is why I say the reality of yourself is not simply metaphysical. It is a value. Here reality and the value are identical. You want to be free; freedom is the reality. You want to be happy;

happiness is the reality, of yourself. This is why *mokṣa-pravṛtti* is entirely different. It is not a philosophical pursuit. It is a life pursuit, a pursuit that gives meaning to life. The purpose of any pursuit is to become free from a sense of lack and the truth is, 'You are already free.' If you do not recognise it and continue trying to be that, you can never succeed. With this limited body and mind you try to be free from a sense of lack. And what you are you neglect entirely.

Bhagavān says, 'I am the one who is seated in this human body, highly worshipful and the one everybody is seeking. And these people do not seek me at all.' What they need to seek is what they are neglecting. This is the *āścarya*, wonder of *māyā*. The one who obtains in this human form was said by Śaṅkara to be always free from any type of *karma*, or ignorance, and therefore, ever liberated, *nitya-śuddha-buddha-mukta-svabhāva*. It is he, the ever liberated one, Bhagavān says, who does not recognise Bhagavān as the truth of himself.

He disregards me, not knowing my *paraṁ bhāva*, limitless nature, which is identical to one's self and, which is Īśvara, the Lord of all beings. Then what do they seek in life? Only me. Not recognising themselves, they begin seeking me, like the tenth man[14]

[14] Once ten people crossed a river. And to start with they were worried if the river will carry them away in its flow. Therefore when they reached the other bank, they wanted to see if all the ten had crossed over safely and so, the leader of the group started counting the people present. He forgot to count himself and got the figure of nine. Immediately panic set in the group that the tenth man was lost. Everybody started wailing and weeping over the loss of the tenth man. The leader was frantically searching everywhere for the lost tenth man, not realising that he was the tenth man. At this point there came a wise man who saw the confusion and panic

or the pauper who is really a prince.[15] The whole problem is one of ignorance.

Necessity for śraddhā and grace

Suppose, you are ignorant of an object. For instance, you insist that charcoal cannot become a diamond. I can perhaps educate you and show you how it becomes a diamond. I can make you understand because it is an object. But if you are ignorant of yourself, while all that you seek – freedom, happiness, freedom from agitation, and so on – happens to be yourself, how will I arrest your attention? How am I going to show you to yourself? It is not possible unless you have *śraddhā* that the self revealed in the *śāstra* does exist. The recognition of that self is possible only when you first recognise it as *asti*.

---

and asked them what the problem was. When he was told that the tenth man was missing, he immediately saw what their problem was. He asked the leader to count again and when he counted nine he pointed out the fact the leader himself was the tenth man he was searching. All his problem of fear, sorrows etc., of losing the tenth man were gone. The problem is the same when one seeks fullness not knowing that fullness is one's own nature. And when the problem is due to ignorance, the only solution to the problem is knowledge.

[15] Once a king was attacked by his enemy and was killed in the battle. His son who was an infant was immediately sent away with a trusted servant in some small town so that his life could be saved. He grew up to be a young man, living on alms. By this time the loyalists of the old king had overthrown the enemy and now came searching for the lost prince. They found him living as a pauper on the streets. They looked for all the necessary evidence and were satisfied that he was their lost prince and told him so. Now this prince, who thinks of himself as a pauper, what does he have to do to become the prince? He has to do nothing. He simply has to know that he is in reality a prince. When the problem is one of ignorance the only solution is knowledge.

Śraddhā is indispensable because you cannot stumble upon this particular fact. You can stumble upon something other than yourself but not yourself.

If someone does not recognise the possibility of such a fact, he cannot accept that the self is free from any sense of limitation. It is the reason why it is said that if a person has an affinity for non-duality, it is only because of the grace of the Lord, *īśvara anugrahāt eva puṁsām advaita vāsanā.*

Out of the sheer despair of one's helplessness in manipulating situations, a person can perhaps become a kind of *bhakta*. But even this much recognition requires Īśvara's grace. A person in distress can remain in distress and just become desperate. One need not resort to Īśvara. It is not necessarily true that someone in distress will become a devotee; one can become mentally ill. If one becomes a devotee, it is only by some grace.

To recognise, 'I am the whole,' requires not just some grace; it requires extraordinary grace because what you seek is not ordinary. It is *advaita;* it is you. Even if it is told, without grace, it will not capture your attention. But if grace is there, it rings true even when you hear it for the first time. It is due to *saṁskāra*. Why should you have that *saṁskāra*? We say it is purely due to the grace of Īśvara. Everyone knows he or she is not the whole. You need no knowledge for that. But it takes a lot of knowledge to recognise your identity with the whole. For this, necessarily, you require grace.

Without that grace they disregard me who is the self of everyone and are destroyed. Śaṅkara says they are lowly people. Even though they were given a thinking faculty, they did not use it. In the next verse Bhagavān describes such people.

Verse 12

Kṛṣṇa describes the people who lack discrimination

मोघाशा मोघकर्माणो मोघज्ञाना विचेतसः ।
राक्षसीमासुरीं चैव प्रकृतिं मोहिनीं श्रिताः ॥ १२ ॥

moghāśā moghakarmāṇo moghajñānā vicetasaḥ
rākṣasīm āsurīṁ caiva prakṛtiṁ mohinīṁ śritāḥ (12)

moghāśāḥ – those of vain hopes; *mogha-karmāṇaḥ* – those of fruitless actions; *mogha-jñānaḥ* – those of useless knowledge; *vicetasaḥ* – who has no discrimination; *ca eva* – indeed; *rākṣasīm āsurīṁ mohinīṁ prakṛtim*[16] – the deluding disposition of *rākṣasa* and *asura*; *śritāḥ* – (they) resort to

> Devoid of discrimination, those of vain hopes, of fruitless actions and useless knowledge, indeed, resort to the deluding disposition of *rākṣasa* and of *asura*.

Moghāśāḥ are those whose hopes are vain idle dreams. Or it can be taken as those who have wasted their grace. It takes certain grace to be born a human being but that grace is wasted if they have not used their will properly.

Mogha-karmāṇaḥ are those whose actions are fruitless. All the *karmas* they do are fruitless because they have not done them for *antaḥ-karaṇa-śuddhi*, preparing them for *ātma-jñāna*.

---

[16] Here we have combined the words together to get the proper meaning of the entire phrase. The meaning of the individual words are as follows: *rākṣasī prakṛtiḥ* – the disposition of a *rākṣasa*; *āsurī prakṛtiḥ* – the disposition of an *asura*; *mohinī* – that which deludes.

Since the end is not very clear to them, the *karma*s they do are useless. In other words, they are not *karma-yogī*s, *mumukṣu*s, who do *karma* to be released from the hold *rāga-dveṣa*s, so that they can recognise *ātmā* is *paraṁ-brahma*. For such *mumukṣu*s everything becomes meaningful because there is an end in view. Marriage is meaningful, family is meaningful. Anything and everything is an *āśrama*, a stage in life, and therefore meaningful. Whereas, the actions of people of vain hopes such as, 'I will do this and I will get this result, etc.,' become meaningless in the final analysis. There are some results, but they are ultimately fruitless, because their hope, which is to be full, is not fulfilled, all because of not recognising Īśvara as *ātmā*.

People have education but not its real result, maturity

Mogha-jñānāḥ are those who have education, even scholarship, but no maturity and so, no recognition of Parameśvara. Education should make you mature enough to recognise Īśvara. It is a part of growing up. You do not pursue something just because your ancestors did it. The hope is that one day you will ask the question, 'What am I doing?' Then you become alive to what you are doing. Otherwise it is a simple routine, within a structure. And any structure gives you a false sense of security because it has no real content. Yet if the structure is not there, you will fall apart. So, in a structured society you can grow well, but if you fall apart without it, you have not grown at all. You need to grow so that you can step into any structure and be a complete person.

Education is supposed to do that, not just make you a bread winner. Even animals are able to find their food and shelter without any schooling. People have lived for ages in the jungles and mountains without any education at all. And they not only lived, they became great-grand-parents and produced such sophisticated people as us. Without modern medicine and technology, they lived adequately enough to keep this population growing. To find food and shelter, you do not require language, culture, music and so on. You do not require anything that you were not born with.

The education you have should make you recognise Īśvara, not just as someone sitting somewhere but as the truth of yourself. Without that, any knowledge a person has is useless because it has not made him mature.

Without maturity, thinking and behavior are deluded

Vicetasaḥ – the people under discussion, with the knowledge they have, are *vicetasaḥ*, people who have no *viveka*. They cannot discern what is proper and improper, *dharma* and *adharma*, leave alone *ātmā* and *anātmā*. They are not able to interpret, in a given situation, what is right. Anything convenient is right. So, what happens to them? They resort to the dispositions of *rākṣasa*s and *asuras*–*rākṣasīm āsurīm caiva mohinīm prakṛtīm śritāḥ* (*bhavanti*).

A *rākṣasa* has a predominance of *rajoguṇa*. He has a lot of ambition that fuels a great deal of activity and vainfulness. In the process of fulfilling his ambitions he destroys anything or anybody that becomes an obstruction because his aim is so important to him. That is a *rākṣasa*. In the business world there are many *rākṣasa*s. The corporate *rākṣasa* will destroy anybody.

He will buy up and assimilate any small rival anywhere. There is no consideration for another life, for another's happiness and so on. This kind of behaviour is called *rākṣasa-prakṛti*. It is all because of non-recognition of Īśvara.

Or he is an *asura,* one whose nature is predominantly *tamas*. Such people will eat or drink anything. There are no rules at all. I knew one person who collected his yoghurt for ten days and kept it on the window sill. The whole building had such a stench that we thought there was a dead rat somewhere. Then we found this yoghurt and asked him what it was for. He was fermenting it for his own consumption! This is called *tamas*.

Bhagavān says that this type of *prakṛti,* behaviour, is *mohinī,* it makes you more deluded. Śaṅkara says, they resort to and advocate complete identity of the body with the self. In their vision, the body and the self are one and the same. 'When the body is gone, I am gone. When the body is okay, I am okay.' Therefore, all you need to do is pamper the body left and right. Feed the senses as long as you can, because they are not going to last. The 70 year old neighbour cannot see, cannot hear, and cannot eat; he cannot do anything. Therefore, make hay while the sun shines; you do not get a second chance. This is their argument. It has no sense at all. The word '*mohinī*' added to the word *prakṛti* makes it to mean more than a mere disposition. They have a philosophy to support their disposition, which is, in turn, a product of their own disposition. It is a philosophy created by a mind that has a predominance of *tamas* or *rajas*. Sometimes they even become religious heads and cult leaders. Cults come up wherever and whenever there is no *vicāra,* no enquiry, no thinking.

Or they can be simple people who do not want to or cannot think. Such people should be encouraged to think. If you can educate a person to think properly that is the greatest gift you can give. Anything less is not enough because he or she then requires further consultation. If you give advice, you will have to give it again. Make them think and discover. This is how people grow.

Śaṅkara says a few things about the dispositions of those of the *rākṣasa*s and the *asura*s. He describes their lifestyles as follows. They say, '*chindhi*, slay him, *bhindhi*, cut him.' In other words, 'Destroy him. Do anything you have to – shoot him, knock him out, level him out – but finish him off.' Then, '*piba*, drink, anything, whatever it is. Even if it is fermented, drink it.' Then, '*khāda*, eat anything that is crawling, flying, walking, swimming; whatever that is available. Just eat it.' Vegetarian food is not what is meant here because that is *svābhāvika*, very natural. Then they say, '*parasvam apahara*, rob the other person's property, do whatever you have to, to get somebody's wealth, somebody's land.' It is similar to a person robbing somebody of their property and then calling oneself a pioneer. Others are all immigrants, aliens, but this one a pioneer. This is amazing to me. It is better to say we immigrated here because we wanted land. We came here and took what we could get. That is being honest and is better than calling ourselves pioneers.

These are the types of actions they do and are also the topics of their conversations. These are the words you hear in an assembly of *rākṣasa*s or *asura*s. Among themselves they talk of their accomplishments in terms of how many people they destroyed, how powerful they have become, what they are eating and what ornaments they have, and so on. If you analyse the topic of any of their conversations it will be one of these. Their activities are cruel. They are destroying themselves because they are incapable of using the grace they have.

Grace is *viveka*. You must tap it and make use of it, otherwise it becomes wasted grace. This is a most deluding *prakṛti*, disposition, and to get out of it is very difficult. You need all the grace you can get.

Śraddhā is what makes the difference in behaviour

Bhagavān says, they are not able to recognise me because they have no *śraddhā*. This is a very important connection to make. In *mīmāṁsā*, there is a rule that if you fail to do certain enjoined daily rituals and duties, you incur *pāpa*, *akaraṇe pratyavāyaḥ*. They have some basis for this contention. But you cannot say that a *karma* not done can produce a result. An action produces a result, not a non-action. If not doing an action produces result, why should you ever do any action? It is against all the laws of *karma*. So, *akaraṇe pratyavāyaḥ* is not to be taken literally. Although not performing an action does not incur *pāpa*, it does create a vacuum, which can be filled by wrong actions that will attract *pāpa*. The idea is that when you do not do the right thing, it will not take long for you to do something wrong because you cannot remain inactive. That is why you must do the right thing.

Suppose, there is no natural tendency, *saṁskāra*, to do what is right – this is where *śraddhā* comes in. Doing the right thing implies not only common sense but much more here because we are talking about religious duties too. Therefore, you require *śraddhā* in the *śāstra* in order to appreciate *puṇya-pāpa,* what is to be done and what is not to be done. With *śraddhā,* there is a greater possibility of doing the right thing. Even though you may still do wrong things, you are committed to doing the right thing. Otherwise, one becomes a person of vain hopes and useless activity, *moghāśāḥ mogha-karmāṇaḥ*. That is the reference Bhagavān makes here, when he says that the people who have no *śraddhā* in the *śāstra* totally disregard him. If they disregard Bhagavān, what will they regard? If they do not regard the *śāstra* there is no *puṇya-pāpa* for them. Therefore, they become *moghāśāḥ mogha-karmāṇaḥ*. This is how the concept of *akaraṇe pratyavāyaḥ* becomes meaningful.

Besides śraddhā, viveka is also required

Now Bhagavān talks about those, on the other hand, who have *śraddhā*. Mere *śraddhā* is not enough because it can induce one to perform *karma*s only for achieving results in this world or later. It means the problem is not clear. They have *śraddhā* alright, but they perform rituals etc., to amass *puṇya* which can be encashed in the future. And all those results are *anitya,* finite. But then, they are satisfied with finite results. They do not think beyond that. Such people, even though they have *śraddhā,* are interested only in *dharma, artha,* and *kāma*. They are working for a better situation in the next world or the next birth. They are not interested in *mokṣa*.

A *mumukṣu* also has *śraddhā*. Along with *śraddhā,* he also has *viveka*. He has the *viveka* to seek *mokṣa*. Śaṅkara says that the following verse is referring to those who are engaged in the pursuit of *mokṣa*. Of the four types of devotees, these are the *jijñāsus*. They recognise *ātmā* as *asti*, existent, and have discerned the fundamental problem. Their whole pursuit is for freedom, *mokṣa*. And it is a pursuit characterised by a committed devotion to the Lord whom they are seeking to know, or whose grace they are seeking. Seeking grace is the initial step. You go one step further when you seek to know.

Verse 13

On the other hand those who are committed to mokṣa seek me

महात्मानस्तु मां पार्थ दैवीं प्रकृतिमाश्रिताः ।
भजन्त्यनन्यमनसो ज्ञात्वा भूतादिमव्ययम् ॥ १३ ॥

mahātmānastu māṁ pārtha daivīṁ prakṛtim āśritāḥ
bhajantyananyamanaso jñātvā bhūtādim avyayam (13)

pārtha – Arjuna!; *mahātmānaḥ tu* – those of noble heart on the other hand; *ananya-manasaḥ* – being totally committed; *daivīṁ prakṛtim āśritāḥ* – being given to a spiritual disposition; *mām* – me; *bhūtādim* – the cause of all beings and elements; *avyayam* – one who is not subject to destruction; *jñātvā* – knowing; *bhajanti* – they seek

> Pārtha (Arjuna)! Those of noble heart, on the other hand, who are given to a spiritual disposition, knowing me as the imperishable cause of all beings and elements and being totally committed to me, seek me.

Mahātmānaḥ tu, on the other hand the *mahātmā*s seek me. A person whose mind is big, whose heart is imbued with love and compassion is called a *mahātmā*, which is why all *sādhu*s are called *mahātmā*s. A *sādhu* is a person whose practice is to help others, *parakāryaṁ sādhnoti*. He does not harm anybody and whenever possible, he will help another person. Helping is natural to him because he is moved by compassion. Such a person is a *sādhu*, a *mahātmā*.

Pārtha, Arjuna, they have a disposition which is very different from the previous ones we have seen. The word '*tu*, whereas' here distinguishes them from those others we saw in the previous verse.

And these *mahātmā*s are *daivīṁ prakṛtim āśritāḥ*, they are people who are given to a disposition in which *sattva* is predominant. These three *prakṛti*s, which he only mentions by name here as *rākṣasī*, *āsurī*, and *daivī*, will be taken later as topics and elaborated upon. *Daivī* means that which is connected to *deva*, the Lord. So, they have godly dispositions in which *sattva* is predominant. It consists of *dama*, self-control, and other qualifications as well as *śraddhā* in oneself and in the *śāstra*. Until one knows, one requires this *śraddhā*.

Śraddhā and viveka work together

Śraddhā is different from faith. Faith remains with you till death and because of which you hope to reach heaven and so on. In Vedanta, faith in the *śāstra* is only pending discovery. Until you discover, you assume it is right. It is presumption but it is highly desirable.

When someone says you are *ānanda*, the whole, the centre of the entire creation and free from all limitations, it is the most desirable. It is exactly what you want to be, which is why you struggle to prove yourself. To whom do you want to prove yourself? In fact, it is only to yourself. Even if you say it is to someone else, it is only because, if in his opinion you are acceptable, then you are acceptable to yourself. It only means in your own estimation you are a nobody, because the limitations are obvious. If you look at yourself through those limitations, naturally you have to prove yourself. And any attempt is not going to remove the limitations. No matter what you achieve, it can give you a healthy self-esteem but it cannot resolve your sense of limitation. The limited person continues to be limited. There is a proverb in Tamil that says if your finger swells, there is a limit to how enlarged it can get. It is not going to swell to the size of a pumpkin. So too, whatever you accomplish, is always going to be limited. If you are already limited, a few more limited embellishments do not make you free from a sense of limitation. Any attempt by a limited individual will definitely be found wanting.

The people who have a disposition characterised by self-control and compassion, seek me. What kind of Me? They seek me who is the cause of all living beings, *bhūtādiṁ mām*. *Bhūtādi* means that which is at the beginning of all elements. Beginning is the cause; so, *bhūtādi* is the one who is the cause of this world. When he says, *bhūtādi*, the cause of this entire world, you can think that it has undergone a change. Once upon a time there was Brahman but now Brahman has become the world. If it is so, only the world is there; there is no Brahman.

To make it clear that it is not so, he says, *avyayam*, changeless. The cause does not really undergo any change to become the world; the change is apparent. Brahman, the cause of the whole creation, retains its nature because the change is purely in terms of *nāma-rūpa*; it is *mithyā*. When the creation is *mithyā*, it requires only a cause that does not subject itself to any change.

Bhūtādim avyayaṁ māṁ jñātvā bhajanti, knowing me as the imperishable cause of the creation, they seek me. How do they know Bhagavān in this way? Here, knowing is only *parokṣa-jñāna*, indirect knowledge, from the *śāstra* and the teacher. Once they have this much knowledge, in order to understand it, they seek.

Their seeking is not a part-time affair. These people are *ananya-manasaḥ*, their minds are not distracted by anything else. Through *viveka* they have lost interest in *dharma-artha-kāma*, and because of *saṁskāra* they seek *mokṣa*. Their disposition is one of self-control and compassion and they have trust in the words of the teacher and the *śāstra*. Their *mumukṣutva* is the result of all their prayers.

The commitment of a seeker

Here a question can be asked. 'If this pursuit is to be done without distraction, what am I to do if I am a family person who has to run a household? As a mother or a father, should I pursue Vedanta or take care of my children?' Whether you pursue this knowledge alone or pursue it along with fulfilling your duties, what counts is your commitment. If commitment is there, whatever you do, this pursuit will not go. It is something like being in love. You are not going to think of your beloved by appointment. It is not that one of the items that you have scheduled for the day is going to be, 'I must think of my beloved.' So whether you are doing your job, your love is not affected; when you love, you are consumed by that love. So too *mumukṣā*, seeking, is what is meant here by being a person who is an *ananya-manas*.

Śaṅkara says such people are not selfish. They don't subscribe to this philosophy of 'me and mine.' They knowingly pursue. It is not simply because someone else whom he or she respects did it and so one is just following in the footsteps. If you follow a beaten track, of course, you will not get lost; that is the beauty of it. But here the path is proper enquiry and if you properly cover all that is to be covered, you cannot but see. Like in arithmetic, if all the steps are followed, the answer must follow. If it is an improper answer, there must be a mistake in the steps. You retrace the steps and correct the mistake. But the correct answer is always the same and certain. This is the track of knowledge. And therefore, knowing full well what they are seeking, they pursue. How do they seek Īśvara is explained further by two more verses.

Verses 14&15

Making proper efforts the jijñāsus seek Īśvara

सततं कीर्तयन्तो मां यतन्तश्च दृढव्रताः ।
नमस्यन्तश्च मां भक्त्या नित्ययुक्ता उपासते ॥ १४ ॥

satataṁ kīrtayanto māṁ yatantaśca dṛḍhavratāḥ
namasyantaśca māṁ bhaktyā nityayuktā upāsate (14)

māṁ satataṁ kīrtayantaḥ – those wo are always appreciating me; *yatantaḥ ca* – and making the necessary efforts; *dṛḍha-vratāḥ* – those whose commitment is firm; *namasyantaḥ ca mām* – and those who remain surrendered to me; *bhaktyā* – with devotion; *nityayuktāḥ* – who are always united to me; *upāsate* – they seek me

> Those who are always appreciating me and making the necessary efforts, whose commitment is firm and who remain surrendered to me with devotion, who are always united to me (with a prayerful heart), seek me.

Satataṁ kīrtayantaḥ māṁ, always appreciating the glories of me, Parameśvara. They always see and appreciate Īśvara's glory, and his glory is not ordinary. All beings, things have their being in him but he is free from all of them; he does not depend upon them for his existence. This is a wonder. Īśvara does not undergo any change and at the same time is the whole creation; he does not do anything and at the same time is the creator, sustainer and destroyer of the entire creation. This is Parameśvara's glory, which they appreciate and praise. The word *kīrtayantaḥ* can also mean *vicārayantaḥ*, those who are always enquiring into Īśvara by *śravaṇa*, *manana* and *nidhidhyāsana*. Who are these people? *Yatantaḥ*, those who make the necessary efforts. What are the efforts here?

Śravaṇa and *manana* are not enough. They have to be backed up by the right kind of mind because it is the kind of mind you have that really accounts for knowledge. A mature mind is necessary and is expressed here by the word *yatantaḥ*, those who take care of their minds properly. How? Śaṅkara paraphrases the word *yatantaḥ* with the following statement – *indriyopasaṁhāra-śama-dama-dayā-ahiṁsādi-lakṣṇaiḥ dharmaiḥ prayatantaḥ*. It is a very clear definition of a *sannyāsī*. *Indriya-upasaṁhāra* means resolution of the sense pursuits, not acting upon one's fancies. Naturally this implies *dama* at the physical level and *śama* at the mental level. You need to have mastery over the mechanical ways of your thinking and the various moods etc., to which you are subjected. Instead of coming under the spell of thinking patterns, you are able to see through them, you have a say over them; in other words you refuse to be led away by them. You do not act upon them. For this you need to have an insight about yourself and also qualities that are necessary to enjoy the mastery such as *śama*, mastery over the mind, *dayā*, compassion, and *ahimsā*, non-injury.

All these show the maturity of the person. Compassion can be natural or cultivated. Here it is cultivated compassion because the person is making an effort, *yatna*. You try to be compassionate, and whenever you lack compassion, looks into what it takes to be compassionate. There is a conscious attempt to maintain this compassion.

Compassion is mentioned again and again by Śaṅkara because compassion towards all living beings is a vow taken by the *sannyāsīs*. *Ahiṁsā*, not deliberately hurting another living being, is the greatest vow taken by a *sannyāsī* at the time of *sannyāsa*. It is the one that characterises him most. All other values like *amānitva, adambhitva, ārjava,*[17] should also be there because they are necessary for the maturity of the *antaḥ-karaṇa* required to gain this knowledge. Therefore, the word *yatantaḥ* refers to those who are making effort to accomplish these virtues, which is why Bhagavān uses the word *yatantaḥ* here.

A *sannyāsī* is called a *yati,* the one who makes effort. He has two things to do. One is the pursuit of knowledge and the other is making effort to mature emotionally if he needs to. He commits himself to *ahiṁsā* and then lives day-to-day, moment-to-moment. Any *Vedāntī* becomes an *adhikārī* only when he or she lives life one day at a time. Otherwise Vedanta does not work. You plan only for one day. Even a plan for the future is only today's plan. Tomorrow you are ready to revise it. That is the life of a *vedāntī*. Naturally there is *yatna,* certain effort, for gaining the *adhikāritva,* qualification, the pursuit of listening to the *śāstra* and so on.

Importance of commitment

And they are *dṛḍhavratāḥ,* whose commitment is firm. Many people are very enthusiastic in the beginning, and then quietly withdraw. But the *dṛḍhavrata*s undertake their pursuits with a commitment. Once they undertake something, they commit themselves to it and pursue unless the evidence is totally against it. The moment you see things are not going well for you, you again study your course – 'What am I heading for?

---

[17] Refer Volume 7 – pages 359 to 382 – Verse 7 of Chapter 13

Is it worthwhile?' If not, sometimes you have to withdraw and re-equip yourself and then start again. When you make a commitment, always make it small. You then do better than what you have committed yourself to. Otherwise you create unnecessary pressures upon yourself and feel defeated most of the time. However here, the *dṛḍhavrata*s are the people who are committed to *mokṣa* and so there is no changing the goal.

Vrata is generally translated as vow. Here it is not exactly a vow but a commitment. You take a vow to accomplish a particular task. But here, a total change is required. They are committed to *mokṣa*, the *parama-puruṣārtha*. So, the other three *puruṣārtha*s, *dharma, artha* and *kāma* do not assail them. That is why in Chapter 13 of the *Gītā*, while enumerating the qualities that are to be cultivated by a *mumukṣu*, the Lord himself mentions *tattva-jñāna-artha-darśana* the capacity to see the truth of this knowledge as unfolded by the *śāstra*, as the last of the qualities. Such people cultivate an understanding of the fact that *mokṣa* is indeed the result of knowledge. It means they have *puruṣārtha-niścaya*; what they really seek in life, is very clear for them. Then the pursuit gains a direction and anything they do becomes highly meaningful. Because they understand that *mokṣa* is the result of *tattva-jñāna*, they have *jijñāsā*. It is not merely a desire for *mokṣa* without direction. They know for sure that the *mokṣa* they seek is in terms of self-knowledge alone and nothing else.

The entire pursuit is going to be determined by how clear you are about what you are seeking. If the human end is very clear to you, you have a direction. The knowledge and everything else involved, becomes something that you love only when this *puruṣārtha-niścaya* is there. If the understanding of *mokṣa* is hazy, there will be confusion and lot of problems, which is why *puruṣārtha-niścaya* is mentioned as one of the values for *jñāna*. Since he has said (chapter 13 verse 11) *adhyātma-jñāna*, knowledge for which the subject matter is *ātmā*, you can conclude that understanding *ātmā*, as a sinner, or as anything else for that matter, is *adhyātma-jñāna*. To avoid this, *tattva-jñāna-artha-darśana* is a very important value. It is the clear understanding that knowledge of the self is liberation. It also includes the understanding that nothing else is required. With the help of *śruti* and through your own *vicāra* in keeping with the *śruti*, you realise that any pursuit is going to be limited. This is *anityatva-niścaya* that results in *vairāgya*, certain dispassion, and the understanding that self-knowledge is the only way out. That kind of understanding of the *puruṣārtha* makes them *dṛḍhavrata*s. They give up everything because they are free from the three types of desires – for progeny, security, and a better situation in the hereafter. They live a life of a mendicant only for *ātma-jñāna*, for *mokṣa*. They are called *dṛḍhavrata*s.

Grace of Īśvara is important

In all this, the grace of Īśvara is important. Therefore, Lord Kṛṣṇa says here, '*māṁ bhaktyā namasyantaḥ*, these are the people who have surrendered to me with devotion. The whole pursuit is done only in an atmosphere of devotion. In such an atmosphere you cannot claim credit for any achievement because you recognise so many limitations. *Namasyantaḥ* are those who surrender, who have a prayerful heart in their pursuit.

People surrender to different things. Some surrender to money, converting it to Īśvara in the form of Lakṣmī or Kubera. They surrender to varieties of things according to the ends they seek, their own likes and dislikes and their *vicāra*. It all depends upon their level of maturity. But here, Śaṅkara says that they surrender to *ātmā*, the self, the one who is Īśa, the Lord of the intellect. They surrender to that *ātmā* alone because they have placed all they have at the altar of *paramātmā*. This is what is to be understood.

We can also take it that they have surrendered to the Lord who is the creator, sustainer and destroyer of the entire world, invoking his grace. Īśvara's grace is here, as is your own grace and the grace of the *śāstra* and the *guru*. Pursuing Īśvara in an atmosphere of *bhakti* is very important, which is why this is not an academic pursuit. Nor is it a purely religious pursuit because there is so much *vicāra*, enquiry, involved. You are enquiring into the words and their meanings, which implies grammar, logic, and so on. It looks very academic but the whole pursuit is value oriented. It is a pursuit in an atmosphere of surrender, *bhakti*, which is why you cannot separate religion from this pursuit. Even though it is not a set of beliefs, but something that has to be understood, then too, Īśvara's grace is necessary here. So, Bhagavān says that these people surrender to me with devotion and seek me with a prayerful heart, *namasyantaḥ ca mām bhaktyā upāsate*.

To recognise Īśvara as *karma-phala-dātā*, the giver of the fruits of action and *karma-adhyakṣa*, the one who presides over all *karmas* is *bhakti*. Any possibility of action is because of Īśvara. So, at both levels, that is, at level of doing the *karma* and at the level of receiving the results, you have an appreciation of Īśvara.

An abiding devotion is adequate

This *bhakti* is abiding for those who are *bhaktyā-nityayuktāḥ*, those who are always connected to me with their abiding devotion. By *dehalī-dīpa-nyāya*[18] the words can be connected to both *namasyantaḥ* and *nityayuktāḥ*. Thus the Lord says that these are the people who are always committed to me with devotion. Being so, they meditate upon me. This is said to point out that only *bhakti*, which is lasting is adequate.

Bhakti can be sporadic, like the *śmaśāna-vairāgya*. When somebody dies and the bereaved goes to the *śmaśāna*, cremation ground, he develops a *vairāgya* towards his pursuits in life. He realises, all that he had worked so hard for, he cannot carry with him and begins to wonder as to what the real meaning of life is. He becomes a great seeker, until he goes home and sees the Wall Street Journal.[19] All his *vairāgya* disappears. Immediately he begins to think about how to increase his wealth. It was just a temporary *vairāgya*. Such a quest for the real purpose of one's life occurs in everybody's head but it is not pursued. Similarly one can have a flame of devotion but it can get extinguished due to inadequate understanding.

---

[18] *Dehalī-dīpa-nyāya* is the analogy of a lamp placed on the threshold. It casts its light both inside and outside of the house. Similarly here the words '*māṁ bhaktyā*' goes with both the words.

[19] An international daily newspaper in English

The prayerful attitude mentioned here is born of understanding. If the understanding is vague, the devotion is subject to waning and waxing, which is why the Lord says, *bhaktyā nityayuktāḥ*, those who are endowed with lasting devotion. Their devotion is for the sake of gaining knowledge of Īśvara. Previously it was said that there are four types of devotees, the one in distress, the one who wants to achieve something, and the third one, the *jijñāsu*. It is the *jijñāsu* who is being talked about here. These *mumukṣu*s, *jijñāsu*s, who are *nitya-yukta*s, want to know the truth of Īśvara because the *śāstra* says, Īśvara is everything.

So Bhagavān says, 'They worship me, they seek me.' How they seek is described in the next verse.

Verse 15

Those who seek me worship me through the ritual of knowledge

ज्ञानयज्ञेन चाप्यन्ये यजन्तो मामुपासते ।
एकत्वेन पृथक्त्वेन बहुधा विश्वतोमुखम् ॥ १५ ॥

jñānayajñena cāpyanye yajanto mām upāsate
ekatvena pṛthaktvena bahudhā viśvatomukham (15)

anye ca api – and there are others too; *jñāna-yajñena* – with the ritual of knowledge; *yajantaḥ* – worshipping; *mām* – me; *viśvatomukham* – who is many faceted; *ekatvena* – as one; *pṛthaktvena* – (and) as distinct; *bahudhā* – in many ways; *upāsate* – they worship

There are others too worshipping me with the ritual of knowledge. In many ways they worship me as the one who is many faceted, as one and as distinct.

Anye, others; they are other than those who are *moghāśāḥ mogha-karmāṇaḥ*. They are *daivīṁ prakṛtim āśritāḥ*, of a spiritual disposition, and *mahātmānaḥ* of noble heart.

And these people, worship me through the ritual of knowledge, *jñāna-yajñena yajantaḥ mām upāsate*. Knowledge alone is the ritual for these people. And the object of this knowledge is Bhagavān. A *sannyāsī* does not perform rituals. When he renounces all his connections with the society, he also renounces rituals like *agnihotra* and so on, which are prescribed for the Vedic society. He has other *karma*s but they are purely contemplative like *japa*, revealing the nature of *ātmā*. The *yajña* done by a *sannyāsī* who has given up rituals is purely for the pursuit of *jñāna*. Just because he does not perform rituals, do not think he is not a *bhakta*. He worships me by invoking me in the form of the pursuit of knowledge. His *yajña* is nothing but *jñāna*.

Māṁ viśvatomukham upāsate means they worship me of many faces. I am the cause of everything, the maker and the material, *nimitta* and *upādāna*. Therefore, I am also the product. I am the *pañca-bhūta*s, five elements, and their products, *pañca-bhautika*s. I am all that you see – the sun, moon, clouds and all the *devatā*s like Indra, Varuṇa and Bṛhaspati. Bhagavān will elaborate on all this later. But he has already pointed out, 'Everything has its being in me, yet I am free from all these beings. Look at my glory, Īśvara's glory, *matsthāni sarva-bhūtāni* *na ca ahaṁ teṣu avasthitaḥ; na ca matsthāni bhūtāni paśya me yogam aiśvaram.*' This is how Īśvara is *viśvatomukha*. *Upāsate* means they seek me through *śravaṇa, manana,* and *nididhyāsana.*

They seek me as *ekatvena pṛthaktvena*. *Ekatvena*, as the one who is in the form of everything and also *pṛthaktvena*, as one who is distinct from everything. When the Lord says, '*matsthāni sarva-bhūtāni,* all beings have their being in me, there is a distinction drawn between the self and not self, *ātma-anātma-bheda*. So too it is said, '*sarvaṁ khalvidaṁ brahma,* all this is Brahman,' '*īśāvāsyam idam sarvaṁ,* all this is to be envisioned as the Lord.' Here, there is the creation, *jagat*, and at the same time, there is the *vastu* which they recognise distinctly. When one contemplates in this manner it is said, '*pṛthaktvena upāsate.*'

Now, look at this with reference to yourself. You are free from all thoughts – from memory, from a piece of knowledge, from any particular thought form. But no thought is free from you. It means you understand a thought as *nāma-rūpa*, name and form, non-separate from the *vastu*. The *nāma-rūpa* is exactly what we call *sṛṣṭi*, creation. You are distinct, *pṛthak,* from *nāma-rūpa* but *nāma-rūpa* is not distinct from you, is not independent of you. B is A, A is not B. Therefore, a given *nāma-rūpa* is not *ātmā*. You need to understand *satya* and *mithyā* properly. Only then is the understanding complete. Therefore, they worship me, both *ekatvena* and *pṛthaktvena*, as everything and as one distinct from everything.

It is said that they worship Īśvara as one who is present in various forms, *viśvatomukha*. What are those forms? In one sentence you can say, I am everything; everything is born of me, sustained by me, and goes back into me. That is indeed Brahman. Or you can say it severally – I am the sun, I am the moon, I am space, I am time, I am the cause, I am the effect. You can repeat the entire dictionary or you can name a few things in order to understand. To simply say, 'I am everything' can be dangerous in that it can be understood in a very shallow manner. So, you sometimes go into the details. Not everything has to be mentioned but sufficient details are necessary to understand *sarvātmatva* properly. That is why we have this *pañca-bhautika*, five-elemental, model. A few details are given in this and in the next chapter.

Verse 16

Bhagavān reveals that he is every aspect of the Vedic ritual

अहं क्रतुरहं यज्ञः स्वधाहमहमौषधम् ।
मन्त्रोऽहमहमेवाज्यमहमग्निरहं हुतम् ॥ १६ ॥

ahaṁ kraturahaṁ yajñaḥ svadhāham aham auṣadham
mantro'ham ahamevājyam aham agnirahaṁ hutam (16)

ahaṁ kratuḥ – I am the ritual; *ahaṁ yajñaḥ* – I am the worship; *ahaṁ svadhā* – I am the food that is offered; *aham auṣadham* – I am food in general; *ahaṁ mantraḥ* – I am the chants; *aham eva ājyam* – I alone am the ghee; *aham agniḥ* – I am the fire (in the ritual); *ahaṁ hutam* – I am the oblation

I am the ritual; I am the worship; I am the food that is offered; I am food in general; I am the chants; I alone am the ghee; I am the fire (in the ritual); I am the oblation.

In this verse, Bhagavān reveals that he is every aspect of the ritual. Since a Vedic ritual is the most exalted *karma*, by saying he is that ritual, he is naturally every other kind of *karma* and anything associated with it.

When you invoke Īśvara as a particular *devatā*, like Indra or Varuṇa, you first light a fire and into it you offer certain oblations, which are to go to the *devatā*. This is called a *yajña*. In a *jñāna-yajña*, you invoke Īśvara alone because every part of the *karma* is non-separate from Īśvara. The fire is Īśvara, the ritual is Īśvara, the offering is Īśvara, the one who performs it is Īśvara, and what you accomplish by that ritual is also Īśvara. It is a *jñāna-yajña*. As we saw in the fourth chapter, when it was said, *brahmārpaṇam brahmahavaiḥ brahmāgnau brahmaṇa hutam*,[20] the language is ritualistic but the vision is *jñāna*. The *arpaṇa*, that by which you offer an oblation, the ladle etc., is Brahman, what is offered, the ghee, *havis*, is also Brahman, where it is offered, the fire, *agni* is Brahman, by whom it is offered, the *kartā* also is Brahman. When you know that Brahman is *akartā*, there is no *kartā*, then the result that is accomplished by this kind of *yajña*, that is, *jñāna* is also Brahman. And the one who accomplishes it sees Brahman in all situations. By understanding that Īśvara is everything, all *karma*s become Īśvara. This is what is meant when we say, '*yat yad karma karomi tat tad akhilaṁ śambho tava ārādhanam*, whatever I do, it is all offered to you, O! Lord.' This can be an attitude or a vision. If it is an attitude, it is *bhakti*. If it is a vision, then it is *jñāna*, the discovery that everything is Īśvara. Here Bhagavān points out that no ritual is free from him.

---

[20] *Gītā* 4.24

The Lord says '*ahaṁ kratuḥ ahaṁ yajñaḥ*. Both *kratu* and *yajña* mean ritual. So, we have to make a distinction here between the two. *Yajña* is a word you can use loosely. Anything, even eating is a *yajña*. But *kratu* is always *śrauta* or *vaidika-karma*, enjoined by or known through the Veda. Lord Kṛṣṇa says, '*ahaṁ kratuḥ*, I am the very *vaidika* ritual and therefore by doing the *vaidika* ritual you are invoking me. But if you understand me, you have understood all *vaidika* rituals. Then you need not accomplish what the *vaidika* rituals can accomplish. That is the whole idea. Because the Lord says, 'I am the *yajña* after saying, 'I am the *kratu*,' Śaṅkara says *yajña* here means *smārta-karma*, any *pūjā* or offering. This is a form of worship that is not enjoined by the Veda but is sanctioned by *smṛti-grantha*s, the secondary books that support the *śruti*. Even *Bhagavadgītā* is considered to be a *smṛti-grantha*. So are works written by informed and qualified people about things based upon *śruti*. From them we have certain *karma*s that are not enjoined directly by the *śruti* but are based upon it. So by mentioning both types of *karma*s, Bhagavān does not omit anything; all types of *karma*s are covered.

Aham svadhā, I am the food offered to the *pitṛ*s, the ancestors. During a ritual to propitiate the *pitṛ*s food is offered to the *brāhmaṇa*s and crows, after invoking the *pitṛ*s in them. That food is called *svadhā*, and the Lord says he is that *svadhā*.

Aham auṣadham, I am the food eaten by everybody. *Oṣadhi* is plants, trees, and creepers; *auṣadha* is what is born of *oṣadhi*. So, food is only vegetarian. Śaṅkara says, rice, maize, oats and so on, are *auṣadhas*. *Auṣadha* can also mean medicine because medicines were mainly herbal. But here the word should only mean food, which is an important part of any ritual.

Then he says, *mantro'ham*, I am the *mantra*s that are chanted when offerings are made to the manes and deities. And I am the *ājya*, the ghee, one of the important oblations that is offered into the fire. Where it is offered, the fire, is also myself, *aham agniḥ*.

Then he says, *ahaṁ hutam*, I am the very ritual itself where this oblation is offered to the various *devatā*s. That very action is me.

Here, in Vedanta, there is only one thing you should know. Where *karma*s are being dealt with, you have a number of things to do. You will never be able to complete them. And there will always be problems because in *karma* there is invariably some omission, or something done wrongly. Then the result that you wanted is quite different from the one you get. Any *karma* is like that. You rarely accomplish what you want. But if you know the *vastu* which is one, you resolve everything. That is why it is called *rājavidyā rājaguhyam*. In the knowledge of one, everything else is included. This one thing an intelligent man would seek.

Verses 17-19

Bhagavān points out a few more things to show he is viśvatomukha

पिताहमस्य जगतो माता धाता पितामहः ।
वेद्यं पवित्रमोङ्कार ऋक्साम यजुरेव च ॥ १७ ॥

pitāham asya jagato mātā dhātā pitāmahaḥ
vedyaṁ pavitram oṅkāra ṛksāma yajureva ca (17)

asya jagataḥ – of this world; *ahaṁ pitā* – I am the father; *mātā* – the mother; *dhātā* – the one who sustains; *pitāmahaḥ* – the grandfather, the uncaused cause; *vedyam* – that which is to be known; *pavitram* – that which purifies; *oṁkāraḥ* – Oṁkāra; *ṛk sāma yajuḥ eva ca* – and the *Ṛk*, *Sāma*, and *Yajur* Vedas

I am the father of this world, I am the mother, I am the one who sustains it, and I am the grandfather (the uncaused cause). I am what is to be known, I am the purifier, I am the *Oṁkāra*, and I am the *Ṛk*, *Sāma*, and *Yajur* Vedas.

I am mother and father – the maker and material of creation

Pita aham asya jagataḥ, I am the father of this world. Here it is a little more than that. Saying he is the father, is saying that he is the creator, the *nimitta-kāraṇa* for this entire world. Then he says, *ahaṁ mātā ca*, and I am the mother. The *prakṛti*, *māyā* is non-separate from me, and therefore, I am also the *upādāna-kāraṇa*, material from which the creation is born. Thus I am both father and mother of this *jagat*.

Once you say father and mother, the next question is, 'Who is his father?' Every child when told that God created the world will ask, 'Who created God?' It is a common question. Seeing that this world is so intelligently arranged, the concept 'there must be some creator' comes to your mind. When you see cooked food, you know somebody has made it. Similarly there must be a creator for this world, which is so well put together.

The next question is, 'Who made God?' Because I have parents, there must be some parents for God too. To negate this idea of imputing a father to Īśvara he says, *aham pitāmahaḥ*, I am the grandfather, meaning I am the uncaused cause. There is no grandfather for me. *Pitāmaha* is also Brahman, the basis of this whole creation. I am also the *dhātā*, the sustainer of the world and the giver of the fruits of actions.

I am the one to be known through all the Vedas

Ahaṁ vedyam, I am the one to be known. Because, by knowing me, the *sat-vastu*, everything is as well known. In fact, I am the only one who can be known fully or totally. Everything else being *mithyā* does not exist on its own; therefore it is available for appreciation only in parts. You can know it only from a standpoint. When you say this is a fern, it is only from a standpoint. A fern is nothing but an arrangement of some particular leaves. And if you analyse the leaf, you discover that it also has constituents. Any one thing, you claim to know in this world, is subject to further enquiry and knowledge and therefore, you have only a point of view. You simply draw a line and assign it a name. So you have only *nāma-rūpa*, but never the final word about anything. Only that which is stable is *vedya*. That is *aham* because it has no standpoint, no parts. And it is *satya*, not *mithyā*, it does not depend upon anything else and therefore, self-existent, self-evident. Without any further revision it can be known as free from all attributes. Knowing, 'I am free from all attributes,' there is nothing more to be known. Thus only *ātmā* can be called the *vedya-vastu*. That alone is worth knowing. And again, by knowing *ātmā* everything is as well known, and there is *mokṣa*, release.

The intellect is always cause-hunting. Even a child will open a clock to find out what is going on inside, what makes it work. This is the cause hunting *buddhi*. You want to know how a thing works. It starts when you are young; where will it stop? Eventually it will lead you to *brahma-vicāra*. You will want to know who is the one who is behind all this. Once your mind starts working on this, when will it come to rest? Only when it comes back to itself appreciating that everything is myself, will it come to rest. Only in this knowledge will it rest. Therefore, the statement, *ahaṁ vedyam* means 'I am *satyaṁ brahma*, knowing which, everything is as well known. All you have to know is *aham* alone is *satya*, and 'everything else' is *mithyā*, which means that I am everything. This knowledge is liberation. Until the *buddhi* knows this, it will keep on searching.

How am I to be known? *Sarvaiḥ vedaiḥ*, I am the one to be known through all the Vedas.

There are lot of things called *pavitra*, that which purifies. But what is it that purifies totally? You are subject to your *raga-dveṣa*s, likes and dislikes, and you may accrue all kinds of *puṇya* and *pāpa* because of the actions they impel you to do. So what will purify you of all this? It is only knowledge of *ātmā*. Therefore, *aham* is *pavitram*, I am the one who, when known, cleanses the *jīva* from every trace of *saṁsāra*.

I am *Oṁkāra*. It is my name. *Om* is great, not as a sound but because the meaning of *om* is myself. It is a great word and sound because it is the name of Bhagavān. The Lord himself says, 'That *om* is myself.'

Now, he goes on to say, I am the *Ṛgveda* , I am the *Sāmaveda*, and I am the *Yajurveda*. Even though there are four Vedas, only these three are used in all rituals. These three are myself. We can also take it to include the *Atharva-veda* and all *smṛti*s, *purāṇa*s and so on. The body of knowledge that is in the form of these Vedas is myself.

He has already said he is the *karma* and the mode of doing the *karma* as well as the one who gives the results of actions. Further, he says:

गतिर्भर्ता प्रभुः साक्षी निवासः शरणं सुहृत् ।
प्रभवः प्रलयः स्थानं निधानं बीजमव्ययम् ॥ १८ ॥

gatirbhartā prabhuḥ sākṣī nivāsaḥ śaraṇaṁ suhṛt
prabhavaḥ pralayaḥ sthānaṁ nidhānaṁ bījam avyayam (18)

(*aham* – I am); *gatiḥ* – the end, the result of actions; *bhartā* – the one who nourishes; *prabhuḥ* – the Lord, the source of all resources; *sākṣī* – the witness; *nivāsaḥ* – the abode; *śaraṇam* – the refuge; *suhṛt* – one who is helpful by nature; *prabhavaḥ pralayaḥ sthānam* – (I am) the one from whom the whole creation has come, into whom everything is resolved and in whom everything has its being; *nidhānam* – in whom everything is placed; *avyayaṁ bījam* – the imperishable cause

I am the result of all actions, the one who nourishes, the Lord, the witness. I am the abode, the refuge and I am the helpful by my very nature. I am the one from whom the whole creation has come, into whom everything is resolved, and in whom everything has its being, in whom everything is placed and the imperishable cause.

I am the *gati*, *karma-phala*, the result of all actions. Any end that is accomplished by a person is me. All *svargādi-lokas*, heavens, are not separate from me. In my *viśvarūpa*, cosmic form, they are all areas of me. There is nothing separate from Parameśvara.

Bhartā, I am the one who nourishes this world. *Bhartā* also is the word for husband because in those days he was the provider. Here Īśvara is called *bhartā* because he supports the world by lending the very existence to it. *Prabhu*, the one who is the master, who has all the glories. There is no other *prabhu* in this world, other than Bhagavān. If one thinks one is rich, then one is mistaken. One's richness depends entirely upon Bhagavān. He is the source of all resources.

Then he says, I am *sākṣī*. Even though I am the *bhartā*, sustainer of creation, *saṁhāra kartā*, one who resolves the whole thing, and *sṛṣṭi kartā*, one who creates it again, yet, I am only a *sākṣī*, I perform no *karma* at all. That is why I am identical with you.

You can always complain to Bhagavān, 'Why did you create me like this? Why did you not place me somewhere else?' Bhagavān will say, '*ahaṁ sākṣī*, I am only a witness; I am not responsible. It is all your *karma*.

The real question is 'Am I created?' Only if you are created, will such questions arise and Bhagavān will answer that it is according to your *karmas*. If you ask, 'Did I come into being,' the answer is 'No.' The *jīva* is *anādi*. Its reality is timeless eternal.

Such a question is answered at different levels. Accepting that you were created, the blueprint is given by no one but you. Īśvara would say, 'There is nothing I can do about it. You can pray to me to modify it but this is how it is now.' When you give the tailor your measurements and in the meantime you put on weight, you will not be comfortable with what you ordered; but it was not the tailor's fault. He gave you what you asked for. If you question, 'Am I created?' you will find that the question resolves into yourself. You realise that you are the *ātmā* that is not created, but which is the cause of everything, which alone is the *sākṣī*. You can also say along with Bhagavān, *ahaṁ sarvasya karaṇam, ahaṁ sākṣī,* I am the cause of everything, but I remain ever the witness.'

There could be a second meaning for the word *sākṣī* and that is, the one who maintains the account of all your actions of omission and commission. Īśvara says, 'You cannot get away from my vision. You may get away from the people's eyes, but not from me. I am the one who is the law of *karma*, who records all that you do.' This is *sarvajña* or *sākṣī*.

Nivāsa means a house, a place where you reside. Here, Śaṅkara says that it is the place in which all beings reside. You live in a house on this earth and the earth lives in the solar system, which lives in the galaxy. And where do the galaxies themselves live? In Me. I am the *āśraya*, abode, of this entire creation because I am *sarvasya adhiṣṭhānam*, the basis of everything.

Śaraṇam means refuge, the ultimate refuge. Going to heaven is only a temporary refuge. From there also you have to move eventually and move back and forth between heaven and earth. What kind of a refuge is it? A refuge is a place where you can relax and from where you will not be buffeted about in *saṁsāra*; this is the ultimate *śaraṇa*. Śaṅkara takes it as a real *śaraṇa*, one that completely relieves you of your sorrow.

Suhṛt. Bhagavān is called *suhṛt*. We saw this before in the sixth chapter. *Suhṛt* is *pratyupakāra-anapekṣaḥ*, one who helps someone without expecting anything, without even being your friend. Out of friendship you might help somebody, then you are only a *mitra* friend. You help out of your affection and empathy for your friend. If he or she suffers you also suffer. Naturally, it is expected that you will help. However, a *suhṛt* is one who has no introduction to you at all. You are absolutely new to the person who is just seeing you now for the first time. That is enough. Whatever the person can give, he or she gives. So is Bhagavān; he is the best friend. You can ask him anything, and you need not even wait for an introduction or a recommendation by an intermediary. You can directly ask as though you have known him for ages. Or, any *suhṛt* is Bhagavān.

Prabhavaḥ pralayaḥ sthānaṁ,[21] I am *prabhava*, the one from whom the whole creation has come, I am the *pralaya*, unto whom everything is resolved, and I am the *sthāna*, in whom everything has its sustenance, its being.

---

[21] *prabhavaḥ - utpattiḥ yasmat; pralayaḥ - pralīyate yasmin; sthānam - tiṣṭhati yasmin*

Nidhānam. A question can be raised, 'As the cause of the creation, does not Brahman undergo modification?' This is answered by saying it is *nidhāna*, the basis in which all causes and effects are placed. That is, Brahman, without undergoing any change, with reference to the *jagat* is called the creator. Because it does not change it is called *nidhāna*, in which everything is placed, meaning superimposed. That is Brahman.

Avyaya bījam, all names and forms that constitute the *kāryas*, effect, are *vyayas* subject to change, to disappearance. The cause, however, is *avyaya*, not subject to disappearance. It means as long as *saṁsāra* is there, the *avyaya-bīja* is there. I am the undifferentiated cause, the *bīja*, seed, from which everything comes. If the *jagat* is looked upon as a sprout, I am its seed or potential form, *avyakta*, undifferentiated. Because he has already talked about the *sṛṣṭi-sthiti kāraṇa*, cause of creation and sustenance, here he specifically refers to *pralaya*. And that cause is *avyaya* because everything goes back into it and comes out of it. In the seed is the unmanifest tree. Similarly here, in the state of *pralaya* is *bījam avyayam* the undifferentiated cause, and that is me.

Further describing how he is *viśvatomukha*, Bhagavān says:

तपाम्यहमहं वर्षं निगृह्णाम्युत्सृजामि च ।
अमृतं चैव मृत्युश्च सदसच्चाहमर्जुन ॥ १९ ॥

tapāmyaham ahaṁ varṣaṁ nigṛhṇāmyutsṛjāmi ca
amṛtaṁ caiva mṛtyuśca sadasaccāham arjuna (19)

tapāmi aham – I heat up; *ahaṁ varṣaṁ nigṛhṇāmi* – I withhold the rain; *utsṛjāmi ca* – and I release it; *amṛtaṁ ca* – and (I am) immortal; *mṛtyuḥ eva ca* – and (I am) also death; *ca* – and; *aham* – I am; *sat-asat* – cause and effect; *arjuna* – OArjuna!

> I heat up the world and I withhold and release the rain. I am immortal and I am also death. I am cause and effect, Arjuna!

Ahaṁ tapāmi, I heat up, I energise, I light up the world. Being the sun, I light up and also heat up this world. Because of heat, water evaporates and the rain begins. It is a cycle. When the earth gets parched, water vaporises. Then, *ahaṁ varṣaṁ utsṛjāmi,* I, the one who heated up the earth, now release the rain, as the law governing rain. Then I hold it back, *nigṛhṇāmi.* This is easily seen especially in India. For eight months I withhold the rain. Then in the four months of the monsoon season, I pour down the rain. In other words, I am the seasons. Seasons are very important. In the network of natural laws, seasons are one of the things we are able to predict. Their predictability is because of the laws and Bhagavān says he is in the form of those laws.

Amṛtam ca eva, I am that *puṇya* because of which the gods become gods and who enjoy certain *ānanda* and immortality.

Mṛtyuḥ eva ca, I am the *puṇya-pāpa* because of which all the mortals come into being and then die. It can also be taken that, 'I am Lord Death, the very principle or law of death. You cannot get away from God. Even if you die, death itself is me. Death is me and *amṛta,* life also is me. In other words, *sat-asat ca aham.* Something that has a form, which you are able to recognise and for which you have a name like pot, tree, leaf, and so on, is called *sat*. *Asat*, in this context, is not a non-existent thing, but what existed before the manifestation of the *nāma-rūpa*, name and form. The manifest form is *sat* and the unmanifest form is *asat*. In other words, the effect is referred to as *sat* here, and the cause is referred to as *asat*. In effect, Bhagavān is saying here that he is both the cause and effect. By this *kāraṇa-kārya-vāda*, cause-effect method, what is pointed out is Bhagavān is *satya* and everything else is *mithyā* which is non-separate from him, that is, Brahman.

The whole *kāraṇa-kārya-vāda* is from the standpoint of the creation, and creation itself is *mithyā*. Later, there will be another statement saying, I am neither *sat*, cause, nor *asat*, effect. At the same time I am both cause and effect. Please understand how important it is to continuously have these two strands of thinking. One is *adhyāropa*, superimposition, 'I am the cause and I am the effect.' The other is *niṣedha-apavāda* a negation, 'I am neither cause nor effect.' Both need to be said, only then the *svarūpa* of *ātmā* will be properly understood.

What is said here is that Bhagavān is the potential cause and the created object and, in fact, is free from all of them because he is the basis for both. The *sat* and *asat*, that is cause and effect in this verse, are both *mithyā*. Since I am both, cause and effect are negated.

Now Bhagavān talks about those who are ignorant of *ātma-svarūpa* but have *śraddhā* in the Vedas, the rituals, prayers, and the after life. Even for this there must be some maturity, though it is not adequate for *viveka*. Bhagavān describes them in the next verse.

Verse 20

The knowers of the Vedas gain heavenly pleasures

त्रैविद्या मां सोमपाः पूतपापा यज्ञैरिष्ट्वा स्वर्गतिं प्रार्थयन्ते ।
ते पुण्यमासाद्य सुरेन्द्रलोकमश्नन्ति दिव्यान्दिवि देवभोगान् ॥२० ॥

traividyā māṁ somapāḥ pūtapāpā
yajñairiṣṭvā svargatiṁ prārthayante
te puṇyam āsādya surendralokam
aśnanti divyān divi devabhogān (20)

traividyāḥ – those who know the three Vedas; *somapāḥ* – those who perform the ritual in which *soma* is offered; *pūtapāpāḥ* – those who are purified of their *pāpas*; *mām* – me; *yajñaiḥ* – with rituals; *iṣṭvā* – having propitiated; *svargatiṁ prārthayante* – they pray to go to heaven; *puṇyaṁ surendralokam* – the world of Indra, which is a result of their *puṇya*; *āsādya* – gaining; *divi* – in heaven; *te* – they; *divyān devabhogān* – the heavenly pleasures of the celestials; *aśnanti* – enjoy

> The knowers of the three Vedas, who perform the ritual in which *soma* is offered and thereby being purified of their *pāpas*, having propitiated me with rituals, they pray to go to heaven. Gaining the world of Indra, which is a result of their *puṇya*, they enjoy the heavenly pleasures of the celestials in heaven.

Traividyāḥ – those by whom the three Vedas, the *Ṛg*, the *Yajus*, and the *Sāma*, are studied. Each Veda is a *vidyā* and together they are called as *trividyā*. The people who have studied the three Vedas are called *traividyāḥ*. These people have learned how to chant them and perhaps also know how to perform rituals.

Somapāḥ – Here is a good example of how a translation can be misleading. The literal translation is, 'Conversant with the lore of the three Vedic texts, *Ṛg*, *Yajus* and *Sāma*, they drink the *soma* juice and are cleansed of their sins by that very drink.' Śaṅkara too says, '*tenaiva soma-pānena pūtapāpāḥ śuddhakilbiṣāḥ*, by drinking this *soma* they are cleansed of their *pāpā*s.' But it is not what is meant here. It is not to be understood that by merely drinking the *soma* they are cleansed of their sins. This is a technical expression. How should it be interpreted? *Somapā*s are those who drink *soma*. There is a ritual called *soma-yāga* that is done for gaining *puṇya-loka*. In the ritual, the juice of a creeper called *soma* is offered to the Lord and the worshippers take the *śeṣa*, whatever is left over, as *prasāda*. Those who perform and participate in the *soma* ritual are therefore called *somapā*s. *Somapā*s are people who have performed these rituals and who have partaken the *soma* as a part of the ritual, and not those who merely drink the *soma* juice. So, technically the word *somapā* stands for the one who has done the *soma-yāga*.

Such people are *pūta-pāpā*s, relatively free from wrong actions. The purification talked about here is not elimination of *rāga-dveṣa*. Because they have *śraddhā* they avoid *niṣiddha-karma*s, actions that are not to be done, and do these *kāmya-karma*s, rituals prompted by desires. There is nothing wrong in it because these *karma*s are *vaidika* and are in keeping with *dharma*. They also perform the daily and occasionally prescribed rituals, which cleanse them of the effects of any wrong actions they may do. Thereby they become *pūta-pāpā*s, cleansed from *pāpās* and are able to do these rituals. They do not do any terrible deeds and whatever small wrongs they may do are neutralised by the prescribed duties, *nitya-naimittika-karmas* which they do diligently because of their *śraddhā* in the Vedas. This is wonderful.

Even though they are doing *kāmya-karmas*, as long as they follow *dharma*, one day, they will gain *viveka*. Now they lack the *viveka* because they are performing these rituals for better *lokas*. They are not *karma-yogīs*. They are prayerful, faithful people, but at the same time, they are only interested in obtaining desired ends like heaven and so on, because they have not properly ascertained what they are seeking. They lack *puruṣārtha-niścaya*. *Artha*, security, *kāma*, pleasures, *dharma*, and *puṇya* become very important to them. All these three *puruṣārthas* are really worthless but they pursue them because they do not know what they are really seeking. Over the shoulders of these pursuits they are aiming at *mokṣa*, freedom. Because they do not pause and ask, 'Am I a seeker? Why am I seeking,' these pursuits become very important.

Māṁ yajñaiḥ iṣṭvā svargatiṁ prārthayante, pray to me, Parameśvara, through the forms of Indra, Varuṇa, Agni, and all the other *devatās*. Having worshipped or invoked me through various rituals like *agniṣṭoma*, what do they request? *Svargati*, going to heaven, or heaven as the very end. They have heard that they will have lot of pleasant experiences there and can remain there for a long time without ageing. It is a kind of relative immortality. This promotional material for heaven is available in the Veda supported by the *purānas*, etc. Naturally, without thinking they pray to me for going to heaven.

Te puṇyaṁ surendralokam āsādya, these people, gaining *surendra-loka*, the world of Indra, Lord of the celestials. This world is called *puṇya-loka* because going there is the result of good *karma*. Heaven is called *puṇya-loka* because it is the result of *puṇya-phala*. *Puṇya* alone is useless; you have to encash it. Even money is the same. You have to convert it into a house, a swimming pool, a Mercedes car, and so on, to enjoy the benefits. This is all *puṇya-phala* is about. The result of *puṇya*, which they gain by various rituals they perform, is going to the heaven called *surendra-loka*. Once they have reached there, what do they do?

Aśnanti, they enjoy, with the eyes and ears. It seems, in heaven, merely seeing satisfies you. If you have hunger, you need not eat at all. The very sight of all the edibles is enough. Then there are more subtle pleasures like music, and so on. In heaven the sense organs are predominant. And their enjoyments are out of the ordinary.

What do they enjoy there? *Divyān devabhogān*, the heavenly objects of enjoyments. *Divyā* is heavenly, not what is known here, Śaṅkara says. The dance and music here in this world is nothing compared to what you will see there. They are *divya-bhoga*s, heavenly enjoyments, not these worldly ones. And where do they enjoy these? *Divi*, in that heaven. They are *deva-bhoga*s meant only for the celestials, not for mere mortals, the worldly ones.

There is a catch in all this, which Bhagavān tells in the next verse.

Verse 21

Such people who are desirous of various objects gain only saṁsāra

ते तं भुक्त्वा स्वर्गलोकं विशालं क्षीणे पुण्ये मर्त्यलोकं विशन्ति ।
एवं त्रयीधर्ममनुप्रपन्नाः गतागतं कामकामा लभन्ते ॥ २१ ॥

te taṁ bhuktvā svargalokaṁ viśālaṁ
kṣīṇe puṇye martyalokaṁ viśanti
evaṁ trayīdharmam anuprapannāḥ
gatāgataṁ kāmakāmā labhante (21)

te – they; *tam* – that; *viśālam* – vast; *svarga-lokam* – heaven; *bhuktvā* – having enjoyed; *kṣīṇe puṇye* – when their *puṇya* is exhausted; *martya-lokam* – the world of mortals; *viśanti* – enter; *evam* – in this manner; *trayī-dharmam anuprapannāḥ* – following the rituals in the three Vedas; *kāma-kāmāḥ* – those who are desirous of various ends; *gatāgatam* – the condition of coming and going, *saṁsāra*; *labhante* – gain

> These people, having enjoyed that vast heaven, enter the world of mortals when their *puṇya* is exhausted. In this manner, following the rituals in the three Vedas, those who are desirous of various ends gain the condition of (repeated) going and coming, *saṁsāra*.

Svarga-lokaṁ viśālaṁ, the vast heaven. The vastness is in terms of plenty, in terms of variety and also in terms of time. *Bhuktvā*, having enjoyed this vast *svarga-loka*, *kṣīṇe puṇye*, when all the *puṇya* is exhausted, what happens to them? *Martya-lokaṁ viśanti*, they are simply dropped down and enter the world of mortals.

They thought they were *amṛta*s, immortals, when they were there. Suddenly they become mortals. They find themselves in another world where everything is different – the body, birth, childhood and all its problems, a place where death looms large, which is full of bugs and people who irritate you, where death is the rule and change is the routine. Thus they enter again the very place from which they sought to escape. They return to square one. If you realise this, you develop *viveka* and *vairāgya*. Such statements are meant to make you turn towards yourself. The *śāstra* always tries to drive you to a corner from where you cannot but seek *mokṣa*.

The cause for these people going to heaven is *puṇya*; so, their stay there will last only as long as *puṇya*, the cause remains. The physical body they enjoy in heaven is earned by previous *puṇya-karma*. And for every experience they have there, they have to encash from their *puṇya*. When the last of the *puṇya* is exhausted, they come back to *martya-loka*, the world of mortals. From this it is very clear that, what is called *amṛta-loka* is really not *amṛta*, immortal. It is here a mistake is often committed. Because heaven is presented in the *śāstra* as *amṛta*, which literally means that which is not subject to death, heaven is misunderstood as eternal. But the immortality here is relative. With reference to your time frame, *svarga-loka* is considered relatively eternal. A day of the *deva*s is much longer than a day here. Most of the theologies have adopted this Vedic concept of *amṛta-loka* as an eternal heaven. But it is referential eternity, not timelessness that is *mokṣa*. This is why when the *puṇya*, that took them to go to heaven and experience the heavenly enjoyments day after day, is exhausted, they come back.

Moreover, they cannot extend their stay by doing new *karmas* and gather new *puṇya* because they have no doership there, only enjoyership. Therefore, they come back.

Evaṁ trayī-dharmam anuprapannāḥ, in this manner, those who follow the rituals enjoined by the three Vedas. *Evam* means 'in the manner that was told in the previous verse,' that is, doing Vedic rituals like the *soma* ritual and avoiding wrong actions. The three fold Veda is called *trayī* here and the word *dharma* refers to *karma*, things enjoined by the three Vedas, like performing a ritual to invoke the Lord or some *devatā* for gaining some *loka* and so on. They are called *dharma* because they are *dharmāt anapetam*, not against *dharma*. These people pursue only legitimate enjoyments.

In the Vedas two things are dealt with – *karma*, which includes meditation, and *jñāna*. Here he is talking only about those who follow the *karmas* enjoined by the Vedas, and not *jñāna*. Even though *trayī-dharma* can include *jñāna*, in this context we have to restrict the meaning to *karma*. *Anuprapanna* means one who follows various *karmas* laid out in the three Vedas. He gives a description of these people.

They are *kāma-kāmāḥ*. *Kāma* can mean desire, the thought process by which you desire an object, or it can mean the desirable object. Here it refers to the desired object. *Kāma-kāmāḥ* refers to those who desire these desirable objects, *kāmān kāmayanti iti kāma-kāmāḥ*. It does not mean desirers of desires. You do not have to desire desires; you have them already. So, *kāma-kāmas* are those who have desires for various desirable ends. The Vedas talk about a variety of things, but you pursue only what you want, according to your *viveka*, maturity.

When you go to the shopping mall, you buy only what you are interested in. A bald headed person does not buy shampoo even though it is on sale! The *kāma-kāmāḥ* have *śraddhā* in and perform the various *karma*s mentioned in the three Vedas but only for various limited ends.

Śaṅkara indicates that *sannyāsa* is not being talked about here even though the three Vedas also discuss renunciation and *mokṣa*. Because Bhagavān has said *kāma-kāmāḥ*,we understand that these people are not interested in*mokṣa*. Otherwise *trayīdharmam anuprapannāḥ* could include *mumukṣu*s also.

Gatāgataṁ labhante, they gain *gata*, going, and *āgata*, coming. They go, and they come back. This is what they gain. It is because they went that they are back. This particular life characterised by going and coming is called *gata-āgata–gataṁ ca āgataṁ ca, gatāgatam*. It means *saṁsāra*. These people who are the desirers of various objects gain only *saṁsāra*. Śaṅkara says that they do not gain any sort of independence or freedom, *na tu svātantryaṁ kvacit labhante*, but remain under the spell of the same *kāma, karma*, and so on. They are helpless because they are caught in the hands of *karma*. Impelled by their own desires, again and again, they do a variety of things. And the *puṇya-pāpa* they gather, require various *janma*s for their fulfilment. So because of *janma* they do *karma*, because of *karma* they have *janma*. Thus they are helplessly caught in this orbit of becoming; all because they have not recognised the truth of themselves. As long as one looks upon oneself as a *kartā*, doer, one does everything necessary for *saṁsāra* to continue. *Kartṛtva*, doership, is the villain of the piece. No matter what they do, the maximum they can achieve is to go to *brahma-loka* which is also within *saṁsāra*. With the help of the *śāstra* they have to give up the notion, 'I am the *kartā*.' It takes place in the wake of knowledge and that is *mokṣa*. Again we see here why the desire for freedom, *mumukṣā*, is so important.

Śaṅkara introduces the next verse as being about those who, on the other hand, are free from desires and have a clear vision of *ātmā*. These are the people who are not committed to the three common pursuits of *dharma*, *artha* and *kāma*, but are committed to the pursuit of *mokṣa*. *Dharma* is less common in the sense that fewer people follow *dharma*. Still fewer are the people who pursue *mokṣa*. Unlike the others, they are not *kāma-kāmas*, desirers. Though *mokṣa* is also a desire, it is born of *viveka* and *vairāgya*. Śaṅkara says, this *mumukṣu* has a clear vision of the goal, which is the knowledge of *ātmā*.

Verse 22

Those who see me as non-separate from them
I take care of their yoga-kṣemam

अनन्याश्चिन्तयन्तो मां ये जनाः पर्युपासते ।
तेषां नित्याभियुक्तानां योगक्षेमं वहाम्यहम् ॥ २२ ॥

ananyāścintayanto māṁ ye janāḥ paryupāsate
teṣāṁ nityābhiyuktānāṁ yogakṣemaṁ vahāmyaham (22)

ye janāḥ – those people who; *ananyāḥ* – (see themselves as) non-separate from me; *māṁ cintayantaḥ* – recognising me; (*mām*) *paryupāsate* – gain me; *teṣāṁ nitya-abhiyuktānām* – for these who are always one with me; *yoga-kṣemam* – what they want to acquire and protect; *ahaṁ vahāmi* – I take care of

> Those people who (see themselves as) non-separate from me, recognising me, gain me. For those who are always one with me, I take care of what they want to acquire and protect.

This is a very famous and often quoted verse. It has an important location. It is about the middle of the ninth chapter, which is in the middle of the eighteen chapters.

This verse can be taken in two ways, as a description of a *jñānī,* a wise man, or as a *mumukṣu*'s approach to the object of his seeking. Śaṅkara takes it as a description of a *jñānī,* based on the words, '*ye ananyāḥ,*' which he says is meant to distinguish these people from the ones Bhagavān has mentioned before in the previous two verses.

Ananyas are those who are not separate from me, the Lord. Does it mean that in the Lord's vision, there are two sets of people, those non-separate from himself, and those who are separate? It is not consistent with all that he has said so far. Therefore, *ananyas* means those who do not look upon 'me' as other than themselves, as another being. They do not see 'me' in one form or another as someone separate from themselves. These are *ananyas* and they are never separate from 'me.'

How is this possible? These are individuals, and how can they be non-separate from Īśvara, the Lord? Śaṅkara says that it is possible due to the fact that the Lord is the *ātmā* of all of them. When this is so, naturally those who recognise the *ātmā* as Parameśvara are non-separate from him. The *ātmā* of Īśvara is the *ātmā* of *jīva*, and it is *caitanya*, *eka*, one, *advitīya*, non-dual, and which is *satyam jñānam anantam brahma*. Those who recognise themselves as such are called *ananyas*.

It is because of the word *ananya* that Śaṅkara has said in his introduction that these are people of clear vision, *samyag-darśīs*. The others are also non-separate from Īśvara but they do not recognise it. The only difference between *samyag-darśīs* and others is recognition and non-recognition, knowledge and ignorance. And that is a vast difference.

These people recognise even the *ahaṅkāra* as Parameśvara. There are some statements that express this. One such statement is, *yatra yatra mano madīyaṁ tatra tatra tava pāda-paṅkajam*, wherever my mind is, there indeed are your lotus feet. It can be a prayer or a statement of fact. At another place it is said, *yatra yatra mano yāti tatra tatra samādhayaḥ*, wherever the mind goes there indeed is *samādhi*, recognising Īśvara. The mind cannot go away from Parameśvara because the mind itself is Parameśvara. It is like someone who wants to get away from space. Where will the person go? There is no such place. This is the way in which these people recognise Īśvara.

Such people, *māṁ cintayantaḥ*, recognising me or enquiring into me, *māṁ paryupāsate*, gain or seek me. And *teṣām*, for them, *nitya abhiyuktānām*, who are non-separate from me at any time, I take care of their *yoga* and *kṣema*. This is one of the most popular statements in the *Gītā* – *yoga-kṣemaṁ vahāmi aham*.

Kṣema is retaining or protecting what you have acquired, *prāptasya rakṣaṇaṁ kṣemaḥ*. In India there is a convention to write '*kṣemam*' at the top left-hand corner of a letter to indicate there is no bad news and everything is fine. If it is a letter informing a death, '*kṣemam*' will be absent. The person has gone. You cannot retain what you do not have; so '*kṣemam*' is omitted. Retention here is always of what is desirable and what you want. Retaining the extra weight that you have gained is not *kṣema*!

Yoga has many different meanings. For example, it can mean the title of a chapter. But when *yoga* and *kṣema* appear together in a compound, the meaning for *yoga* is acquiring what you do not have, *aprāptasya prāpaṇam*. And it must also be desirable to you.

If you look at your life, all your concerns can come under one of these two. What is it that bothers you? Just think of any one thing. It will either be about something you want, *yoga* or something you are afraid to lose, *kṣema*. You have no peace; I want to gain it; *yoga*. You do not have enough money, you want to gain some; *yoga*. You are losing your hair, your health, and you want to retain them; *kṣema*. So *yoga* and *kṣema* indicate a lot about the life of a *jīva*. If *yoga-kṣema* is taken care of, everything is taken care of.

The Lord says, '*nitya-abhiyuktānāṁ yoga-kṣemaṁ vahāmi aham,* I take care of the *yoga-kṣema* for those who are always non-separate from me.' Here Śaṅkara raises a question and answers it. Even other *bhakta*s get their *yoga-kṣema* taken care of by Bhagavān. He is the object of their prayers, and as the *karma-phala-dātā*, he gives the results. So how can you say he takes care of the *yoga-kṣema* of only these *nitya-abhiyukta*s? What does it mean? He says it is true that Bhagavān takes care of the others too but there is a difference with these people.

The object of a devotee's prayer is what is desired by him or her. Look at the previous verse. These people pray and offer rituals to Īśvara for a particular result, heaven. So heaven is the desired object, not the Lord. He is just the means to achieve their end. They will use anyone to get what they want, but they know the local forces are not adequate; and they know that the Lord has *sarvajñatva*, all-knowledge, *sarva-śaktimattva*, all-power, and *sarva-dayālutva*, all-compassion. So they wish to use him to get what they want.

Look at this. *Cintayantaḥ mām*, enquiring into me, *māṁ paryupāsate*, they also seek Īśvara. Then what do they get? Let us consider a *mumukṣu* who wants liberation. He also prays to the Lord, but what is the object of his prayer? It is Īśvara. He wants nothing else but to know Īśvara. He says, 'My object is only to find you and so I pray to know where you are, what you are.' After finding Īśvara what does he want? He says, 'Nothing; only to know that I am one with you.' Such *mumukṣus* do not look upon Īśvara as really separate from themselves. There is a sense of separation for the time being because of ignorance. To resolve it, they are constantly enquiring into the *svarūpa* of Īśvara. They also have doubts, 'If he is non-dual, he is one with me. How can it be? I am such an insignificant being. How can I be Parameśvara, the Lord?' These doubts are there because there is no knowledge, only *śraddhā*. So they seek, *paryupāsate*. How? By *śravaṇa, manana*, and *nididhyāsana*, with devotion and commitment.

The object of their prayer, their pursuit is only Parameśvara. They do not use Parameśvara for gaining limited ends. They are only seeking to know him. This is the difference, Śaṅkara says.

These are the *ananya-darśī*s, the wise people, who do not care whether they are alive or dead. They are not anxious about looking after themselves; nor are they afraid of what will happen to them. They are with Bhagavān, and have no concern for their own *yoga-kṣema*. Their attitude is, whatever happens, happens. Everything, even their desires are in the hands of *prārabdha-karma*, which is non-separate from Parameśvara. Since they recognise the law of *karma* as non-separate from Parameśvara, whatever takes place is Parameśvara for them. They are not using him to protect their *yoga-kṣema*. So their *yoga-kṣema* is taken care of by Bhagavān himself in the form of the laws of *karma*. Hence, they have no concern about their *yoga-kṣema*.

An ordinary *bhakta* is deeply concerned about his *yoga-kṣema*. He has concern because he has doership and centred on this is his entire effort for *yoga-kṣema*. Being what he is, a *bhakta* knows that in spite of all his efforts, he will not be able to get what he wants and retain what he wants to retain. So he looks for help. As a *bhakta*, he performs rituals in order to get and retain what he wants.

A *jñānī*, on the other hand, is not a *kartā*. Who is a *kartā* then? If at all there is a *kartā* it is only Bhagavān. He is the *sṛṣṭi-kartā*, creator, *sthiti-kartā*, sustainer, and *saṁhāra-kartā*, destroyer. That is what Śaṅkara says here.

Mokṣa is only through knowledge of *ātmā* being Brahman, which is the cause of the world. To know this you must enquire and to enquire you must have an appropriate *pramāṇa*, means of knowledge. How are you going to enquire into Īśvara?

Through the *pramāṇa* which is in the form of words. Therefore, enquiring into Bhagavān is enquiring into the words of the *śāstra*. Thus they seek me, they worship me by enquiring into who I am. That is the best form of worship. The *jijñāsu*, whom we are talking about here, are *bhaktas*. Bhagavān gives them an assurance. For those who are so totally committed to me, I will take care of all that is necessary, *yoga* and *kṣema*. What a *jijñāsu* wants to gain and protect is knowledge. Bhagavān will take care of his concern because he is his *bhakta*. The idea is that *śraddhā* will take care of everything.

When *sannyāsīs* give up everything, they do not count upon being taken care of by society, or by anybody for that matter. Society does take care of them in some ways but they do not count on it. They do not think there is a necessity for anybody to take care of them. Things will be taken care of. This is the attitude of the *sannyāsī*. Here, however, Bhagavān assures them, 'I will take care of your *yoga-kṣema*.'

If *yoga* and *kṣema* of the wise are taken care of by Bhagavān, then the seeker's *bhakti* will be free from the concerns of *yoga-kṣema*. Their own commitment to Īśvara will free them from the concerns of *yoga-kṣema*. Because of their commitment to Īśvara, naturally they are not concerned about their *yoga-kṣema*. They know that Īśvara will take care of it. This is expressed as *ahaṁ yoga-kṣemaṁ vahāmi*.

Generally, for one's *yoga-kṣema* one uses a number of forces, one's own powers, knowledge, skills, and the resources at one's command. Often, that is not enough; so, one invokes the Lord as well. There is nothing wrong in it. It shows one is mature enough to recognise Īśvara, but only as a means to accomplish one's *yoga* and *kṣema*. One does not seek to understand the Lord. This is the ordinary *bhakta*.

Whereas, here he says, 'These people do not seek *yoga-kṣema*, they seek me.' Who are they?

Ananyāḥ. Here Kṛṣṇa presents himself as Īśvara or Vyāsa presents him as Īśvara. Either way it is the same. As Īśvara, he says, 'These are the people who are not separate from me. They recognise me as the very *svarūpa, ātmā* of themselves.' They realise there is no separate Īśvara because Īśvara, by nature, cannot be separate from anything, including me. Even looking at it from the physical viewpoint, Īśvara's body will include my body. If the whole creation is taken as Īśvara's body, my body is included. My *antaḥ-karaṇa* is also included. So, even from the standpoint of the body, there is nothing other than Īśvara. From the standpoint of *ātmā, aham,* which is the subject matter here, there is no separation whatsoever. The *jīva* is non-separate from Īśvara. Īśvara's *ātmā* is *jīva* and *jīva*'s *ātmā* is Īśvara. From the standpoint of *māyā-upādhi,* there is Īśvara. But the *ātmā* of Īśvara is nothing but the truth of the *jīva,* the *caitanya ātmā*. And the *jīva*'s *ātmā* is nothing but Īśvara. There is only one *aham,* the limitless *ātmā,* which is the truth of both the Lord and the individual. Those who recognise this identity are called *ananyas*. How did they become *ananyas*?

Māṁ cintayantaḥ, thinking of me, not their own *yoga-kṣema,* they are committed to the pursuit of the knowledge of me, Īśvara. Enquiring into Parameśvara is the aim of their life. They are *jijñāsus*. They are not making efforts for their *yoga-kṣema,* but for the discovery of Īśvara. Śaṅkara presents the *ananyas* as *jñānīs*, *sannyāsīs*. Their *sannyāsa* is not a lifestyle but a renunciation characterised by the knowledge, *aham akartā*, I am a non-doer. They know that they have never done anything, at any time, and they are not doing anything even now while talking. They know that while performing these varieties of action, *paśyan śṛṇvan spṛśan jighran aśnan gacchan svapan śvasan pralapan visṛjan gṛhṇan unmiṣan nimiṣan api*, they do not perform any action. *Paśyan*, seeing, he says, '*aham na paśyāmi*, I do not see.' *Śṛṇvan*, hearing, he says, '*ahaṁ na sṛṇomi*, I do not hear.' What he means is, *ātmā*, the self, the meaning of 'I' being what it is, performs no action. But in its presence all activities take place. I am in the form of consciousness in the presence of which the mind is mind, the senses are senses. 'With the mind desiring, with the intellect deciding, I perform action with the organs of action, *manasā saṅkalpa buddhyā niścitya karma karomi karmendriyaiḥ*.' This is *jñāna*.

Ye janāḥ paryupāsate, those people seek or recognise me in all the states of experience, which is why the prefix '*pari*' is used for *upāsate*. It means at all times, in all states of experience. Who are they? By seeking Parameśvara seriously through *śravaṇa*, *manana*, and *nididhyāsana*, enjoying the *amānitvādi* qualities, they have become *nitya-abhiyuktas*, those whose minds are always awake to me, who have recognised that they are never separate from *ātmā*. Their minds do not come in between themselves and the vision. *Abhiyukta* means endowed with *amānitvādi* virtues. These people have gone through the whole process and therefore have no inhibiting factor to their knowledge. They are *nitya-abhiyuktas*.

Śaṅkara introduces the next verse by raising the objection we saw in detail earlier. Since we say everything here is Īśvara, other *devatā*s are also not separate from Īśvara. So, whether the devotees worship Kṛṣṇa or Rāma, Allah or the Father in Heaven, all of them worship only Īśvara. Nobody worships a *devatā* other than Parameśvara. So, would he not also look after the *yoga-kṣema* of these devotees? Why has Bhagavān singled out the *jñānī* or the *jijñāsu*? It is true, *satyam evam*. But there is a distinction.

Verses 23&24

The Lord blesses even those devotees who worship other deities due to ignorance

येऽप्यन्यदेवता भक्ता यजन्ते श्रद्धयान्विताः ।
तेऽपि मामेव कौन्तेय यजन्त्यविधिपूर्वकम् ॥ २३ ॥

ye'pyanyadevatā bhaktā yajante śraddhayānvitāḥ
te'pi māmeva kaunteya yajantyavidhipūrvakam (23)

kaunteya – Arjuna!; *ye api* – even those; *anya-devatā-bhaktāḥ yajante* – devotees who worship other *devatās*; *śraddhayā anvitāḥ* – endowed with *śraddhā*; *te api* – they also; *mām eva yajanti* – worship me only; *avidhi-pūrvakam* – (but) backed by ignorance

Kaunteya (Arjuna)! Even those devotees who worship other *devatā*s with *śraddhā*, worship me only, (but) backed by ignorance.

Ye api anya-devatā-bhaktāḥ, those for whom God is other than themselves. This is the type of verse a *dvaitī* will misinterpret.

He will translate this as those who are devotees of other *devatās*, and say it is meant to show that Kṛṣṇa alone is God. It is not so.

All the *devatās* are Īśvara. It has been proved that everything is Īśvara; nothing is separate from Īśvara. So, anybody who worships any form, any name, in any mode, worships only Īśvara. These are devotees who do not recognise any of the *devatās* as Īśvara, but only as individual *devatās*.

Yajante, they worship in various modes. How? *Śraddhayā*, with *śraddhā*. Whether the religion is tribal or more sophisticated, all devotees have *śraddhā*.

Kaunteya te api māmeva yajanti, they also worship me alone, Arjuna. The only problem is, their worship is backed by ignorance, it is *avidhi-pūrvakam*. No doubt they are worshipping me, but they do not know me. They think each *devatā* is different from every other, and from me.

I receive their various forms of worship alright, because I am the ultimate recipient through all the *devatās*, but they do not recognise this due to ignorance.

For what reason is it said that their worship is backed by ignorance? The next verse clarifies.

अहं हि सर्वयज्ञानां भोक्ता च प्रभुरेव च ।
न तु मामभिजानन्ति तत्त्वेनातश्च्यवन्ति ते ॥ २४ ॥

ahaṁ hi sarvayajñānāṁ bhoktā ca prabhureva ca
na tu māmabhijānanti tattvenātaścyavanti te (24)

ca – and; *hi* – indeed; *aham* – I am; *sarva-yajñānām* – of all rituals; *bhoktā* – the recipient; *prabhuḥ eva ca* – and the only Lord; *tu* –

but; *te* – they; *na mām abhijānanti* – they do not know me; *tattvena* – in reality; *ataḥ* – therefore; *cyavanti* – fall away

> I am indeed the recipient of all rituals and the only Lord. But they do not know me in reality. Therefore, they fall away.

Aham hi sarva-yajñānām bhoktā, I am indeed the recipient of the offerings of worship, whether it is *śrauta,* a Vedic ritual, or any of the various forms of *pūjā* or *smārta,* prayer. With respect to all of them, I am the recipient. Whichever form they worship, that is me. I am the final altar of their worship.

Prabhuḥ eva ca, and I am the Lord of the *yajña.* A *yajña* produces a result. I am the one who gives that result, the *karma-phala dātā,* not the *devatā* that you invoke. The result may come through the *devatā* but it comes from me alone. I am the ultimate giver. There is no wonder if Africans dance for rain and the rain comes. It is a ritualistic dance and it will bring rain. But the *devatā* that is invoked is myself alone. There is no difference.

The only problem here is that they do not know me in reality, in essence, *na tu mām abhijānanti tattvena.* They do not know what exactly is the nature of Īśvara, who are these *devatā*s, who is this *kartā,* who is the *karma-phala-dātā.* Even though their worship can lead them to *antaḥ-karaṇa-śuddhi,* which can lead them to *mokṣa,* they do not get that result. For that, they need to have some knowledge that there is an Īśvara who is everything and their worship is for *antaḥ-karaṇa-śuddhi,* which can lead them to understand the truth of Īśvara. But they do not have that *jñāna.* So, what do they get?

Cyavanti te, they fall away. They just get simple limited results, not *antaḥ-karaṇa-śuddhi*. For that, a person must be interested in *mokṣa* and understand that prayer is done for *antaḥ-karaṇa-śuddhi*. He alone gets the higher result. When a *karma-yogī* performs a ritual, his disposition is entirely different from that of a *kāma-kāmī*. As we saw before, a *kāma-kāmī* desires certain results and makes use of a particular *devatā* to fulfil them. Therefore, he gets only that much result. He falls away from the higher result, which is the real result of worship because it leads to *mokṣa*. They are worshipping me, but at the same time they do not recognise me. So, instead of gaining limitlessness they get only a limited result. Prayer itself is not defective but its efficacy is reduced by ignorance. If you have *jijñāsā* and do *yajña* with an effort to know Īśvara, you can get *antaḥ-karaṇa-śuddhi* leading to *viveka* and therefore, *mokṣa*. The others fall away from that. However you need to know that all these devotees definitely get results.

Verse 25

No one is denied the result of his or her karma

यान्ति देवव्रता देवान् पितॄन्यान्ति पितृव्रताः ।
भूतानि यान्ति भूतेज्या यान्ति मद्याजिनोऽपि माम् ॥ २५ ॥

yānti devavratā devān pitṛn yānti pitṛvratāḥ
bhūtāni yānti bhūtejyā yānti madyājino'pi mām (25)

devavratāḥ – those who are committed to the gods; *devān yānti* – reach the world of the gods; *pitṛvratāḥ* – those who are committed to the manes; *pitṝn yānti* – reach the plane of the manes; *bhūtejyāḥ* – those who are committed to the spirits; *bhūtāni yānti* – go to the realm of the spirits; *api* – whereas; *madyājinaḥ* – those who worship me; *māṁ yānti* – reach me

> Those who are committed to the gods reach the world of the gods. Those who are committed to the manes reach the plane of the manes. Those who worship the spirits go to the realm of the spirits. Whereas, those who worship me, reach me.

Devavratāḥ devān yānti, those who are committed to the *deva*s in their worship gain the world of the *deva*s. *Devavrata*s are those whose devotion and commitment are to the gods. These are the people who perform *vaidika* rituals to specific gods like Indra and so on. As a result, they go to that plane of experience, *loka,* where those gods are. As we saw, they will stay there only as long as the *puṇya* they have gained from their *karma* lasts. The intention here is to point out the limitation of even good results.

Pitṛvratāḥ pitṛn yānti, those who worship the *pitṛ*s, the ancestors, gain the world of the manes. These are the people who have a disposition, which has predominantly *rajas.* They perform Vedic rituals like *śrāddha* that is done every year on the death anniversary of the departed soul. They also perform *smārta-karma*s that are not Vedic rituals. *Pitṛ* is a mane, a departed soul living in a particular plane of experience, which is more desirable than this world. That plane is called *pitṛ-loka,* and to that plane they go. There they gain the status of a *pitṛ* like *Agniṣvatta. Agniṣvatta* is the name of a mane and they get that particular status when they die.

There is a community in the Coorg district in Karnataka where worshipping the manes is done in a big way. In Tamilnadu there is a movement of *nāstika*s and the followers of that movement reject anything that is Vedic. So, they do not go to temples or perform any Vedic rituals. But they too worship their departed leaders. There were two leaders of this movement who are dead now. Every year their followers go to where they are buried and place flowers, burn incense and so on. They will not say they worship, but it is exactly what they are doing. They are worshipping Īśvara in that form. These are *pitṛvrata*s.

Bhūtejyaḥ bhūtāni yānti, those who worship the *bhūta*s spirits, and various minor *devatā*s like *yakṣa*s, *rākṣasa*s *gaṇas,* and so on, are *bhūtejya*s. Ganeśa as the Gaṇapati is one of these. If you worship Ganeśa as *paraṁ-brahma,* it is different. Then you are worshipping Īśvara. But the people who worship him as Gaṇapati are worshipping him as a *bhūta,* a kind of exalted spirit. They will get only that level of experience. Though it is better than this world, their gain is only limited.

Having said all this, he further says, *yānti madyājinaḥ api mām,* those who are committed to me reach me. Just as these people reach their own ends, consistent with whom they have worshipped, similarly those who worship me will reach me alone. 'Me' means Parameśvara, *paramātmā,* the cause of everything. Śaṅkara says here that *vaiṣṇava*s are those who recognise the Lord as Viṣṇu. Viṣṇu means the one who is all-pervasive and who includes every *devatā*. They recognise me as themselves and thus, reach me.

What do you want now? Do you want to partake a given plane of experience or do you want to be every experience? All experiences are me, nothing is separate from me. So, are those who seek me, recognise me in all the *devatā*s. Their approach, their seeking is entirely different. They are *mumukṣu*s, the ones he described earlier as *ananya*s.

For the same effort, result is less due to ignorance

Here Śaṅkara makes a note. Even though the effort is the same, because they are worshipping me, in ignorance they enjoy only limited results. Effort is common to all of them. In every *yajña* you have to make effort. As all those *devatā*s they worship are me, they are worshipping me. But due to ignorance they do not recognise me as the real recipient of their worship. They think they worship separate *devatā*s for gaining separate *loka*s and thereby limit themselves to that particular experience. The effort is the same as it would be if they were doing rituals for *antaḥ-karaṇa-śuddhi*. But they become the recipients of limited results due to ignorance.

It is like a person who knows that a thing he has is an antique. But he does not know its value. So, he makes a lot of effort to find an antique dealer and finally finds one who gives him a hundred dollars for it. He is happy. But actually its value is more than hundred thousand dollars. So, even though he made the effort required to find the antique dealer, he got a lesser result due to his ignorance.

To say that the Lord is everything, you have to know. Otherwise how can you say it? You do not see the Lord being everything; you have to know. Unless you recognise *ātmā* as *paraṁ-brahma* who is the *nimitta-upādāna-kāraṇa*, you cannot say the Lord is everything; I am everything. If this is understood, then the result is the gain of limitlessness. There is no coming back once you know because the *ahaṅkāra* is gone. You are *mukta*, liberated. All this has been pointed out.

Not only is the result so great, but it is also *sulabha*, easily achieved, because it is already a fact about you. For the sugar to become sweet, what should it do? It simply has to know, 'I am sweet.' Similarly, you have to know, 'I am limitless, *ānando'ham*. It is *sulabha* because it is you. Because you require *antaḥ-karaṇa-śuddhi*, you may think, it requires lots of rituals. No, says Lord Kṛṣṇa.

Then what should I do?

Verse 26

What you offer does not matter – how you offer is important

पत्रं पुष्पं फलं तोयं यो मे भक्त्या प्रयच्छति ।
तदहं भक्त्युपहृतमश्नामि प्रयतात्मनः ॥ २६ ॥

patraṁ puṣpaṁ phalaṁ toyaṁ yo me bhaktyā prayacchati
tadahaṁ bhaktyupahṛtam aśnāmi prayatātmanaḥ (26)

yaḥ – he who; *bhaktyā* – with devotion; *patram* – a leaf; *puṣpaṁ* – a flower; *phalam* – a fruit; *toyam* – water; *me* – me; *prayacchati* – offers; *tad bhakti-upahṛtam* – that which is offered with devotion; *prayatātmanaḥ* – of the person whose mind is pure; *aham aśnāmi* – I receive

He who offers me with devotion – a leaf, a flower, a fruit, water – I receive that offering imbued with the devotion of the person whose mind is pure.

This verse is also oft quoted. What you offer does not matter. It can be a *patra*, leaf, like *bilva* or *tulasi*, *puṣpa*, a flower, *phala*, fruit, *toya*, water. But the action of offering is necessary and how it is offered is also important.

Yaḥ me bhaktyā prayacchati, he who offers to me with devotion. *Bhaktyā prayacchati* means he gives with devotion recognising me as Īśvara. 'I offer this to Īśvara for *antaḥ-karaṇa-śuddhi*, *jñāna* and *mokṣa*.' Then any *karma* becomes *yoga*. There is no entity called *bhakti*. It is only a condition of the mind. When you perform a ritual it is *karma* but *bhaktyā prayacchati* means you do this *karma* with devotion; it is then *karma-yoga*. Any *karma* can be *yoga* if there is *bhakti*. A *pūjā* is *karma*, so is singing, *kīrtana*. It is *vācikaṁ karma*, an oral action. If you do *dhyāna* it is *mānasaṁ karma*, mental action. All of them are *karma*s and with *bhakti* they become *karma-yoga*.

Whose offering is this? *Prayatātmanaḥ*, of a person with the right effort. This is someone whose mind is pure. *Bhakti*, devotion, is an expression of a pure heart. The action is done with a pure heart and in order to gain that pure heart you also perform an act of devotion.

Importance of an act of devotion

The action becomes important here because it produces a corresponding emotion. If the action is not done, the emotion will also disappear. There are actions that cause particular emotions to manifest. The form and the spirit, as I have mentioned earlier, are both important. Suppose there is a form, which is not backed by the spirit. It is a mere form, a dead form. And when the spirit is there, a particular form is not necessary. To make an offering to the Lord, you do not need a physical action. If you have devotion for the Lord you have it. You need no special action to express it. When you have an appreciation of Īśvara, its expression, devotion, is always in you. But the problem is, devotion is not real as long as you think you are a devotee. When there is an *ahaṅkāra*, ego, which thinks it takes care of your *yoga-kṣema* and uses Īśvara as an accomplice, you need an act of devotion. It becomes as important as the spirit of devotion.

As I told you before, if you hate a person, the best way of getting rid of that hatred is to act as though you have love for the person. You may say it is hypocrisy. If your intention is to deceive the person, it is hypocrisy. If your intention is to get rid of the hatred, it is not. You do an act like giving a flower to him daily, for 41 days. The act of giving a flower, in any culture so far on this planet, is a symbol of love or affection. In Indian culture it also indicates respect and devotion. That action, which in your psyche is connected with love and affection, no doubt will come in conflict with your emotion towards the person you hate. But you also want to get rid of this hatred. So, you give the flower and the day comes when you need not do it anymore. In the act of love there is love expressed; so, the opposite emotion, hatred, is converted into love. This is what we call *pratipakṣa-bhāvanā*. In order to eliminate a given emotion you bring in the opposite emotion. If there is hatred, you bring in love. If there is jealousy, you bring in understanding, acceptance, or some kind of admiration. This is how you change.

Here, the act of devotion is as important as the devotion. Only in the act is the devotion manifest and this manifestation is very important. It has to become an all consuming passion; you must become the very content of devotion, which means the *ahaṅkāra* should not be there at all. That is why they ask you to do *pūjā* daily. It need not even be understood. It is just a cultural expression.

Bhagavān is not going to be pleased just because you have offered some flowers. He is not going to be flattered by your act of giving or by your praising him because whatever you can think of, is less than the Lord. It is something like the child who has just learned how to multiply. When his father helps him do his homework, he says, 'Dad, you are a great mathematician.' How does he know? His understanding of a great mathematician is limited by his own knowledge of mathematics. A title should be given by a person competent to give that title. We cannot even spell the word omniscient correctly, what can we really understand when we call the Lord omniscient? From the little knowledge we have, how are we going to appreciate the Lord's omniscience? We have no immediate knowledge of this at all. It can never be immediate knowledge unless we step out of the individual mind. Then each of us can say, 'I am that *sarvajña*.' That is the freedom we can get. With reference to our mind and so on, there is no question of being all-pervasive, all-knowledge, all-powerful. When a *bhakta* praises the Lord, his praise always falls short of what the Lord is. So, the Lord cannot get flattered, much less, can he take what you offer.

When you offer something to the Lord, he does not take it away. If he did, nobody would give anything. But if a priest comes to your house to perform a ritual, he always comes with a bag. At various stages of the ritual, things are offered to him and he puts them in his bag. If the Lord were to take what you offer, he must have a place of his own, like this bag, to keep it. Where can the Lord have a place of his own? To say this is the Lord's place, there must be some place that is not his. Being *sarva-vyāpī,* all-pervasive, all places are his places; being everything there is no place of his own. Whatever you offer remains there. 'Why then do I offer, why do I pray?'

The whole life is an expression of prayer

Often people ask me if the Lord is all-pervasive, if he is in me and outside me, why should I pray? Drop the 'if.' The Lord is everywhere. If you know it, there is no need to pray. But if you do not know, pray in order to get that knowledge. You seem to see yourself as separate from the Lord who is omnipotent, omniscient and who includes you. To that Lord whom you have not understood, pray, 'O Lord! I am told that you are all-pervasive, show me how you are all-pervasive, how am I included in you? If only the Lord is there, then how am I the Lord? Please reveal this to me.'

This act of prayer is as important as the spirit behind it. Without the act there will be no spirit unless you are a *jñānī.*

A *jñānī*'s whole life is an act of prayer. But for a person who is not a *jñānī*, even if the spirit is absent, as long as the act is there, the spirit will come. You cannot perform an act of prayer without the spirit entering into it. It is because prayer is the most voluntary action in the world. It is an action for which the result is not immediate; so, the free will expresses itself in the fullest form. In all other actions you are motivated in one way or another. When you see a go getter, you see a driven person. But if that person simply falls back and offers a prayer, it is definitely voluntary because nobody can make another person pray. Even parents can only ensure that children close their eyes and maybe even utter the Lord's name. But whether you pray is entirely up to you.

As children, we were asked to do a whole set of rituals before and after the *gāyatrī-japa*, which took about fifty minutes. But unless we did them, we would not get our coffee. Therefore, for coffee's sake we were driven to do them. If we are doing something just to please our mother and get our morning coffee, it is only an action, not an act of prayer. But we do pick up the spirit when we perform the act.

If in the act of prayer, there is some spirit, we call it real prayer. In it is our appreciation of Īśvara and our own helplessness. It keeps us sane. The sanest person is one who understands his or her limitations as well as his virtues. One who understands only one's own virtues, is not the sanest. When we appreciate not only our helplessness but also Īśvara as the one who is limitless, our sanity is complete. Then our whole life becomes an expression of prayer.

The spirit of prayer is the same – the form can vary

The importance of prayer is recognised in every religious culture. But each has its own form, which is purely cultural. The prayer is common, how the person prays is prescribed differently. One person may follow a *pūjā* form, step by step, in which *patra*, a leaf, *puṣpa*, a flower, *phala*, a fruit, *toya*, water, are offered. Even if they are not available, one can offer any or all of them mentally. One can even do the whole *pūjā* mentally. But if it is mental *pūjā*, one need not limit one's offering to *patra*, *puṣpa*, *phala* and *toya* alone. Mentally one can offer everything imaginable. But the action is important and that is what Bhagavān points out here. What is recommended in this verse is an act of worship called *pūjā*. One need not do Vedic rituals, only an act of worship in which one offers *patra*, *puṣpa*, *phala* or *toya*.

There is a verse[22] that says that in *kali-yuga* for the people who have impure minds, who do not have rituals prescribed for them, reciting the Lord's name is enough. In every *yuga* peoples' minds are impure. So, this verse embraces those people whose minds are to be purified. Since they have *rāga-dveṣas* and so on, they take to means that are not always proper; they are called *pāpa-dravya-upajīvī*s. If you observe your pursuits, you will notice that when you get something, it is usually at the cost of someone else. There is often some aggression towards others. Therefore, there is *pāpa* involved

---

22 कलौ कल्मषचित्तानां पापद्रव्योपजीविनाम् । विधिक्रियाविहीनानां हरेर्नामैव केवलम् ।
kalau kalmaṣacittānāṁ pāpadravyopajīvinām,
vidhikriyāvihīnānāṁ harernāmaiva kevalam (*Kalisantaraṇopaniṣad*)

in your daily life. Then *kalmaṣa*s, old impurities, cannot be eliminated because daily you gather new ones. You can only eliminate them by doing *nitya-naimittikādi-karma*s like *agnihotra* and other rituals, which are prescribed in the Vedas according to *varṇa* and *āśrama*. But these people do not have any such rituals prescribed for the *varṇa* and *āśrama* they are in. How are they going to rid themselves of *kalmaṣa*, and gain *antaḥ-karaṇa-śuddhi*? The name of the Lord is the only means, *gatir govinda-kīrtanam*. It includes *pūjā, kīrtana* and so on.

Whatever the offering is, it must be *bhakti-upahṛta*, offered with devotion. If you are moved by devotion expressed in the offering of a flower, a leaf etc., with a pure heart, what happens to that offering?

An offering made with devotion is received by Bhagavān

Aham aśnāmi, I eat. Śaṅkara says that this should be taken as *ahaṁ gṛhṇāmi*, I receive it. It means the person gets the result for his action, *antaḥ-karaṇa-śuddhi*. You need not do elaborate rituals. All that is required is recognition, and an act of prayer. The meaning of this verse is that an act of prayer is important and it should be done for the sake of *antaḥ-karaṇa-śuddhi* leading to *mokṣa*. When Bhagavān receives your prayer, you are already blessed.

There is a story illustrating this in *Bhāgavata-purāṇa*. Sudāmā, also called Kucela, was a poor man who lived with his wife and twenty seven children. He and Kṛṣṇa had studied together in the same *gurukula* at the feet of the *ṛṣi* Sāndīpani. Studying under the *ṛṣi* had given him great insight and devotion. Even though he was a *gṛhastha* and had to find food for his large family, he was cheerful and devoted to the Lord. His wife found it increasingly difficult to maintain the family on his meagre earnings. One day she suggested to Sudāmā, that as he had been with Kṛṣṇa at the *gurukula*, he should seek Kṛṣṇa's help. Sudāmā was unwilling to go and ask for charity in the name of friendship. She finally prevailed. After agreeing, Sudāmā started to worry, 'How can I go and meet Kṛṣṇa, my old friend, without a gift? He is no ordinary person, he is more than a king and one should not go empty handed to a king, to a deity or to the *guru – rikta-pāniḥ na paśyeta rājānaṁ daivataṁ gurum*. And I do not have anything to offer to him.' His wife said, 'I have something you can offer him.' She had already saved some beaten rice, called *poha*, from what Sudāmā had brought home. She wrapped all she had, which was about three morsels, in a rag and gave it to Sudāmā. He went to Dvārakā.

Kṛṣṇa, learning that Sudāmā had come, asked that he be escorted into the palace with great respect. He came down to meet Sudāmā at the door, washed his feet and welcomed him into the palace. In those days, if one were a *brāhmaṇa*, the king had to greet the person with respect, and do the prescribed acts of worship. Then Kṛṣṇa asked Sudāmā, 'Did you bring anything for me?' Initially Sudāmā did not say anything, for he thought Kṛṣṇa would take offence at the insignificant gift he had brought. He saw the palace, the riches around, and was aghast within himself as to how he could have come to see Kṛṣṇa with some beaten rice wrapped in a rag. But Kṛṣṇa found the small bundle hidden in his clothes, pulled it out, and began eating from it. He took one mouthful, and then a second one.

Before he could take the third one, his wife, Rukmiṇī, who was standing near him, stopped him. She stopped him because, that very act of eating, *grahaṇa* becomes *anugrahaṇa* bestowal of his grace on Sudāmā. When Kṛṣṇa took the first morsel of rice, there in Sudāmā's village his hut got transformed into a palace. His wife and his children suddenly found themselves in the best of clothes. Rukmiṇī stopped Kṛṣṇa from taking more of the beaten rice, because if he had taken all of it, the whole world would have belonged to Sudāmā!

That is the Lord's *anugrahaṇa.* It becomes available immediately when he accepts an offering. Sudāmā was so overwhelmed by Kṛṣṇa's welcome and the arrangements for his comfortable stay that he forgot to ask Kṛṣṇa for any help. He was just happy meeting Kṛṣṇa after such a long time. He went back to his village, and on reaching, he was not sure whether it was his village or another. Everything was different. Even the ponds that had been dry were full of water. The trees were full of flowers and fruits. He could not recognise the place until his wife and children came out and greeted him. When Bhagavān takes, he just gives.

Even the fact that you can pray is the result of prayer. You try. See if you can really open your heart and pray. You will find it very difficult. With all the pain and cynicism you have inside, it is very difficult to open up. Any number of arguments will come to prove how prayer is useless. So, it takes a number of 'as though' prayers before you can really pray. As I told you, prayer is the most efficacious action that is highly voluntary, where the free will gets its maximum expression. The role of the will is so complete. You are not driven to it, you do it on your own. And its result is assured, which is why Śaṅkara interprets the word *aśnāmi* as *anugṛhṇāmi*.

As a *sādhana* for *antaḥ-karaṇa-śuddhi*, an act of *bhakti* is very important. It will instil devotion because it does imply a degree of surrender and recognition of your limitations. This can lead to helplessness but when it is accompanied by the recognition of Īśvara as limitless, the act of devotion makes this appreciation very real. The attitude of surrender becomes more and more real through the act of surrender. So, the act is as important as the very attitude until the attitude does not come and go. If it is an abiding attitude you need not perform an act of devotion as a means, as we will see in the next verse.

Verse 27

Whatever you do – do it as an offering to me

यत्करोषि यदश्नासि यज्जुहोषि ददासि यत् ।
यत्तपस्यसि कौन्तेय तत्कुरुष्व मदर्पणम् ॥ २७ ॥

yatkaroṣi yadaśnāsi yajjuhoṣi dadāsi yat
yat tapasyasi kaunteya tat kuruṣva madarpaṇam (27)

yat karoṣi – whatever you do; *yat aśnāsi* – whatever you eat; *yat juhoṣi* – whatever ritual you perform; *yat dadāsi* – whatever you give; *yat tapasyasi* – whatever religious discipline you follow; *kaunteya* – Arjuna!; *tat kuruṣva* – please do it; *madarpaṇam* – as an offering to me

Whatever you do, whatever you eat, whatever ritual you perform, whatever you give, whatever religious discipline you follow, Kaunteya (Arjuna)! please do it as an offering to me.

Various actions that you do, whether they are secular or scripturally enjoined, either by the Vedas or by *smṛti*, please do all of them as an offering to me, *kuruṣva madarpaṇam*. Why is this said here?

Generally even though people perform these rituals, prayers, and so on, they do them for their own *yoga* and *kṣema*. The same ritual can be a *kāmya-karma* or a *niṣkāma-karma*. *Niṣkāma-karma* does not mean you do not expect a result. Nobody can perform an action without expecting result. It means you expect no other result except *antaḥ-karaṇa-śuddhi*. You may do anything but if it is no longer a *kāmya-karma*, you do it with an entirely different attitude. What you want is *antaḥ-karaṇa-śuddhi*.

What exactly is the purification? Not to be in the hands of *rāga-dveṣa*s, the two words that really cover all other psychological problems. If you analyse any problem you have, you find it comes under *rāga-dveṣa*s. 'Things did not happen as I wanted; therefore I have a problem. Things do not happen as I want; therefore I have a problem. I do not see that things will not happen as I want, therefore, I have a problem.' So all problems, normal or abnormal, can be brought under *rāga-dveṣa*s.

Connection of prayer and mental purification

Antaḥ-karaṇa-śuddhi is very important and to achieve it, prayer is inevitable. Why, because only a prayerful mind can accept all this. Only on seeing your helplessness, can you forgive yourself. Only understanding yourself very clearly as a limited person can you totally accept that you could only do as much as you did; you could not have done anything better. Perhaps in the order of things this is how it should have been. With this kind of recognition, prayerful attitude, there is serenity. When the mind is settled like this, it can enquire properly. Here Bhagavān is talking about a person who is interested in *mokṣa*. You do *karma* for *antaḥ-karaṇa-śuddhi*. You may do the same action as a *kāma-kāmī* but you do not want anything from it. You want only *mokṣa*, which is non-separate from you. As a *karma-yogī* you renounce the results of your actions, *karma-phala-tyāga*. Though you play roles and perform *karma*s and so on, you do not work for *dharma, artha,* and *kāma*, but work only for *antaḥ-karaṇa-śuddhi*. Or you can be a *sannyāsī* who gives up *karma*s, duties, so that you have no role to play. Both a *karma-yogī* and a *sannyāsī* have recognition of Īśvara and that is called *bhakti*.

Tat kuruṣva madarpaṇam, whatever you do, please offer it to me. It means may you not expect a result of *yoga* or *kṣema*; just do it and let it go to the Lord. It is an expression of your devotion to Īśvara. All you want is *antaḥ-karaṇa-śuddhi*. The very offering brings about inner purification. Therefore, whatever you do, please offer it to me for the sake of *antaḥ-karaṇa-śuddhi* leading to *mokṣa*. Bhagavān is not going to be elated by your offering, rather you are enriched in the process.

Yatkaroṣi, whatever you do. Bhagavān addresses Arjuna directly here. Whatever you do is made into an offering and the result of that *karma* is taken as *prasāda*.

Yadaśnāsi, whatever you eat. It is why, while eating we offer the food saying, *prāṇāya svāhā, apānāya svāhā, vyānāya svāhā, udānāya svāhā, samānāya svāhā* and then finally saying *brahmaṇe svāhā*. It means, unto the Lord who is in the form of *prāṇa*, the respiratory function; *apāna*, the system that throws things out of the body; *samāna*, the digestive system; *vyāna*, the whole circulatory system; *udāna*, the *prāṇa* that ejects the life out of the body at the time of death, I offer this food. *Brahmaṇe svāhā*, to the one who indwells every physical body identified with the total subtle body, *hiraṇya garbha*, I offer this food.

Yat juhoṣi, whatever fire ritual you perform, whether it is a *śrauta-karma* or a *smārta-karma*, or any ritual you perform daily or on special occasions, please offer it unto me. Let it not be for *dharma*, *artha*, or *kāma*. What is important is your attitude. Bhagavān is not going to be flattered by what you do or do not offer. Yet, through association you make your offering more and more real, which creates in you a *bhāvana*, attitude. Viṣṇu is the one who loves ornamentation; he is *alaṅkāra-priya*. Lord Śiva loves a bath; he is *abhiṣeka-priya*. Lord Sūrya loves salutations; he is *namaskāra-priya*. So, you do all this for your own sake, to make your devotion more real. It is only your attitude that counts. Two pieces of wood in the form of a cross mean nothing; every telephone pole looks like it. But it stands for something; so there is *bhāvana*, an attitude; it will work. Nobody will be denied the result of his or her prayer whether one is a Muslim, a Christian, a Jew, a Parsi, a Hindu or anybody. These things must be very clear. Any religion is based on *bhāvana* and it is what makes a person a devotee.

Yat dadāsi, whatever you give as an offering, as charity – gold, food, ghee, clothes and so on. These are things that we generally give to *brāhmaṇa*s, priests, dedicated to a religious life. In former times, they were working for the society and the society took care of them; so, *dāna* was generally for *brāhmaṇa*s. Now you can give anything as *dāna*. Anything you give, do, dedicate them unto Īśvara as a worship.

Yat tapasyasi, any particular religious discipline you undertake. There are varieties of *tapas* like fasting and *japa*.

In all this, Bhagavān says, 'Whatever you do, do it as an offering unto me.' We need to understand these expressions properly. Otherwise what does 'Perform all actions dedicated to the Lord' Which Lord? Where? How? This is the problem.

Here, you need to understand that gaining the knowledge of Īśvara and understanding you are not separate from that Īśvara is *mokṣa*, freedom. To understand this, you need *antaḥ-karaṇa-śuddhi*, and you have to work for it. When *dharma* is Īśvara, even duties are for Īśvara. What is to be done becomes important because it is looked upon as Īśvara and thereby *rāga-dveṣa*s are relegated to the background. Then the special rituals that you perform are meant for no other result than *antaḥ-karaṇa-śuddhi* leading to *mokṣa*. Wanting *mokṣa* means wanting Īśvara because *mokṣa* is non-separate from Īśvara. Knowing, 'I am Īśvara, whose nature is fullness and who is the cause of creation,' is indeed *mokṣa*. When you are seeking *mokṣa*, do not think you are seeking anything other than Īśvara. The various rituals, prayers, and so on, that you perform are all for the sake of *antaḥ-karaṇa-śuddhi*, which is necessary for *mokṣa*, and they are all for Īśvara. The *svarūpa* of *mokṣa* is nothing but Īśvara. So, when you perform these prayers, rituals etc., they are all meant only for Īśvara.

Similarly, the other duties, which you are called upon to do in day-to-day life, are also for Īśvara if they conform to *dharma*. Your likes and dislikes, tendencies and so on, may be opposed to what you have to do. But they are overruled when you conform to *dharma*, because that itself is Īśvara.

For the person who is living his life in this manner, like Arjuna, what will happen?

Verses 28&29

A person with renunciation and karma-yoga is liberated from the bondage of karma

शुभाशुभफलैरेवं मोक्ष्यसे कर्मबन्धनैः ।
संन्यासयोगयुक्तात्मा विमुक्तो मामुपैष्यसि ॥ २८ ॥

śubhāśubhaphalairevaṁ mokṣyase karmabandhanaiḥ
sannyāsayogayuktātmā vimukto mām upaiṣyasi (28)

evam – in this way; *mokṣyase* – you will be released; *karma-bandhanaiḥ* – from the bondage of *karma*; *śubha-aśubha-phalaiḥ* – in the form of desirable and undesirable results; *sannyāsa-yoga-yukta-ātmā* – being one whose mind is endowed with renunciation and *karma-yoga*; *vimuktaḥ* – liberated; *mām upaiṣyasi* – you will come to me

In this way you will be released from the bondage of *karma*, which is in the form of desirable and undesirable results. Being one whose mind is endowed with renunciation and *karma-yoga*, you will come to me liberated.

Mokṣyase, you will be released. From what?

From *śubha-aśubhaiḥ karma-bandhanaiḥ*, the *karma*s that give you desirable and undesirable results. These binding *karma*s have desirable and undesirable results, in other words *sukha-duḥkha*. *Karma* produces two types of results, *śubha-phala*, desirable, and *aśubha-phala*, undesirable. And the *karma*s themselves are bondage because they produce results for the *kartā*, the agent. He is the one who has to experience the *karma-phala* that comes in the form of *sukha* and *duḥkha*. In order to experience them, he must have body, mind, senses, and so on. Therefore, he requires *janma*, birth. Because of *karma* there is *janma*, and because of *janma* there is *karma*.

From all this, Bhagavān says, you will be released. How?

Evam, in this manner, by doing what was described in the previous two verses. Performing actions as a dedication to Īśvara, as it was explained, one becomes *sannyāsa-yoga-yukta-ātma*, whose mind is endowed with *yoga* and *sannyāsa*. This is *mokṣa*. But the person we are discussing is doing *karma*. And all that he does he dedicates unto the Lord, as the Lord himself said in the last verse, *yat karoṣi yadaśnāsi yat tapasyasi*... So, what is the *sannyāsa* here? Śaṅkara makes it clear; it is *sannyāsa* and at the same time, *yoga*. It is *sannyāsa* because he renounces the results of his actions; there is *phala-tyāga*. Everything is done as an offering to Īśvara, *tat kuruṣva madarpaṇam* and he is interested only in Īśvara, nothing else. Īśvara is non-separate from *mokṣa* so, if he is interested in *mokṣa*, he is purely interested in Īśvara. Since he has *karma-phala-tyāga*, it is *sannyāsa*, considering the root meaning of the word rather than the popular meaning, which is a lifestyle of renunciation. It is not the renunciation of *karma*, but an attitudinal renunciation. The context here is the performing of all these rituals, prayers, duties and so on.

Therefore, we are talking about *karma-yoga*. Yet, it is called *sannyāsa-yoga* because there is *karma-phala-tyāga*. He gives up his likes and dislikes and does *karma* only for the sake of Īśvara, not for anything else. The person is committed to Īśvara. So, naturally there is *sannyāsa*. Why is it *yoga*? Śaṅkara says, because the word *karma* is associated with it. And it is *karma-yoga* because the word *sannyāsa* is there. Otherwise it would be only *karma* for the sake of *artha* and *kāma* now; and later it becomes *karma* that binds, *karma-bandhana*, by producing *puṇya* and *pāpa*. These *karma*s, however, do not bind since they create *antaḥ-karaṇa-śuddhi* and through *antaḥ-karaṇa-śuddhi*, you gain *mokṣa*.

There is an order here. The same thing was said in the fifth chapter of the *Gītā*.

योगयुक्तो विशुद्धात्मा विजितात्मा जितेन्द्रियः ।
सर्वभूतात्मभूतात्मा कुर्वन्नपि न लिप्यते ॥

yogayukto viśuddhātmā vijitātmā jitendriyaḥ
sarvabhūtātmabhūtātmā kurvannapi na lipyate Verse 5.7

One whose mind is purified by being committed to a life of *karma-yoga,* who has mastered the body and has the sense organs under control, and who knows oneself to be the self in all beings, (such a person) is not affected even while doing (actions).

This sequence is a style of the *Gītā* and must be understood. Otherwise, it will read as though *karma-yoga* is a means for liberation. This will destroy the whole *śāstra* and create countless problems. Therefore, here you must remember that particular word, *yoga-yukta,* one who is endowed with *karma-yoga*. What does he become? *Viśuddhātmā,* his *antah-karaṇa* is pure, meaning he is no longr in the hands of *rāga-dveṣa*s. Therefore, he is *vijitātmā,* his mind is in his hands and so are his sense organs; he is a *jitendriya*. Such a person becomes *sarvabhūta-ātmabhūta-ātmā*. In time he gains this knowledge and his self is no longer enclosed but is released from the limitations superimposed upon the self. He is the self of all. Even if he performs an action he is not bound by *karma, na lipyate*. This is what is said here.

So, by doing this, you will get released from *karma*. *Karma* generally binds you, but by doing the same *karma* with a change of attitude, it becomes the means for liberation. The binding *karma* becomes non-binding.

The one who does everything for the sake of Īśvara is a *bhakta* and also a *jijñāsu, a karma-yogī, mumukṣu* – all these at once.

Because he is *sannyāsa-yoga-yukta-ātmā,* he has the required qualifications for getting the knowledge. So for him gaining knowledge is easy.

Therefore, *vimuktaḥ mām upaiṣyasi*, liberated, you will come to me, in time. Because he has said *mokṣyase,* you will get liberated, there is a time involved here. Knowledge does not take time. But removing the obstructions does. Being a *karma-yogī,* you gain *antaḥ-karaṇa-śuddhi* and with that mind you are able to understand the *śāstra* and are, therefore, *vimukta*. Living, you are liberated because the mind does not pose any problem insofar as the knowledge of yourself is concerned, which you have gained from the *śāstra*. It is not inhibited by any problem that would be there for want of *karma-yoga*. And uninhibited self-knowledge is *mokṣa*. The teaching is there, *pramāṇa* is there, *vastu* is there and knowledge should take place. It has to take place in your mind. If that mind has a problem, you have to take care of it and it is done by *karma-yoga*.

Living, you are liberated. Then what happens at the time of death? When the body falls at the time of death, you are one with me. What exists is only Īśvara because the notion of *jīvatva*, individuality, is eliminated. The *jīva* has resolved into Īśvara and so you are one with Īśvara, which means that you are Īśvara. Even while alive there is only Īśvara. But because of *prārabdha-karma,* the body-mind-sense complex continues. Therefore, its seeming limitations continue. When the body falls away and the seeming limitations also disappear, there is only Īśvara.

Lord Kṛṣṇa says here, *mām upaiṣyasi*, you will come to me. It is addressed to the *jīva* who is now listening, not to the *sat-*

cit-ānanda-ātmā. Here, 'you' falls short of *sat-cit-ānanda-ātmā*. It goes only up to the *jīva,* the *jijñāsu* and not beyond that. 'You shall come to me' means that there will be no individual, you. You are there as *sat-cit-ānanda-brahma* alone.

This is another expression that can be misunderstood. You have been me, but you come back to me again. As though you are a stranger, you come back to me. It is a figurative expression. There is no coming to Bhagavān or going away from Bhagavān. You are always non-separate from Bhagavān. It is just a matter of recognition.

In the previous verse he says, *yat karoṣi yadaśnāsi yad juhoṣi,* whatever you do, Arjuna, offer it all to me. The one who performs actions for the sake of Īśvara will get Īśvara, whereas the others will not. Then we have a problem. Bhagavān becomes the one who has *rāga-dveṣa*s like any ordinary person. If I praise him, calling him Indra, Candra and so on, I get something out of him. Then if I criticise him, he does not give me anything at all. Today he shows *rāga,* and tomorrow he shows *dveṣa*. Flatter him and he gives me everything. If he is angry, he leaves me out completely. This is what I see in the world. I thought Bhagavān was different who is equal to all people and gives equally to everybody. But it looks as though he too behaves like an ordinary person. I go on doing everything for Bhagavān, then he is pleased and says, 'come back!' What is this? If I care for him, he cares for me. If I do not, he does not care for me. What kind of Bhagavān is he? He should care for me even if I do not care for him. I do not see him doing anything for me nor is he immediately available for me. How can I care for him? I have hundred different cares in my life.

He is said to be all-wisdom, all-love, and all-compassion. In his vision, in his compassion I have done nothing to deserve being neglected by him. Suppose a child happens to kill a cockroach, I do not consider it a sin. It was afraid and it therefore did something. Even if a person commits a small felony, I accommodate him. Our local laws seem to be very kind to the children because they do things in innocence. So what about the almighty Lord who is all-wisdom, who is absolute love and compassion? In his vision what kind of misdemeanor can I commit that will not get his pardon? In fact I must destroy the universe for him to get angry. If I put Mars out of place, turn Jupiter inside out, just spirit the entire Earth away, if I make a mess of his whole home, then he should get angry with me. But these small little things that a human being may do, he should pardon.

I am not like Rāvaṇa who made Lord Varuṇa come and water his garden and wanted Vāyu to come and sweep his floor, and so on. He abused all the *devatā*s and should be punished, all right, but not me, doing my small little thing. What kind of Lord is he, if only when I go on flattering him, he is very kind to me? And if I neglect to say, 'You are *ananta*, you are Kṛṣṇa, you are Rāma, you are this, you are that, etc., he thinks that I am no good and therefore, does not care for me. In my innocence and childishness I may not care for him. But in his wisdom and in his compassion, he should care for me. What kind of God is he if he also has *rāga-dveṣa*s?

It is very clear that such a God is insecure. He has his own fans called devotees. So, he cares for them. And the others, who mind their business and are now grown up, he dislikes.

He should be proud of them. But he wants them always to look up to him, which means he does not want them to grow. He is not even like enlightened parents.

Now, we have simply reduced Īśvara to our level. It is the argument of a *pūrvapakṣī,* an opponent, remember. The answer to this is given in the next verse.

Verse 29

There is no whole-part relationship with Īśvara

समोऽहं सर्वभूतेषु न मे द्वेष्योऽस्ति न प्रियः।
ये भजन्ति तु मां भक्त्या मयि ते तेषु चाप्यहम्॥ २९॥

samo'haṁ sarvabhūteṣu na me dveṣyo'sti na priyaḥ
ye bhajanti tu māṁ bhaktyā mayi te teṣu cāpyaham (29)

sarva-bhūteṣu – in all beings; *ahaṁ samaḥ* – I am the same; *na me dveṣyaḥ asti* – there is no one whom I dislike; *na* (*me*) *priyaḥ* – nor is (anyone) my favourite; *ye bhajanti tu mām* – but those who seek me; *bhaktyā* – with devotion; *mayi te* – they exist in me; *teṣu ca api aham* – and I (exist) in them

I am the same in all beings. There is no one I dislike nor do I have a favourite. But those who seek me with devotion exist in me and I (exist) in them.

Samaḥ ahaṁ sarva-bhūteṣu, I am the same in all beings. I am not someone separate from them. In all the beings I am the same limitless Īśvara because the *ātmā* of everyone is myself alone. In all beings I am available for owning. They need not even come to me; they are me. So, what would be my attitude towards them?

Na me dveṣyaḥ asti, how can I have a *dveṣya,* one who is disliked, when everyone is me? I do not hate myself. I cannot hate myself because I know *aham pūrṇaḥ,* I am complete. To hate oneself, one must be ignorant of oneself. I have no such ignorance. I know that I am everything and when it is so, everyone is myself. There is no separate person at all. Everyone is the same whole person, which is why he is called *puruṣa.* When this is so, there is no person to be hated. You may not dislike some one, but suppose you have a liking for somebody else. That is good enough. It means you are indifferent to others and it also establishes a *tāratamya,* gradation. It is not enough to say, *na me dveṣyaḥ asti,* there is no one for whom I have dislike. Therefore, Bhagavān says, *na me priyaḥ asti,* I have no favourite, no beloved. Human beings are subject to all that but not Īśvara. Then why does he say those who worship him will come to him? If he is giving favours, you can say he gives certain people favours and not others. The problem here is, Bhagavān says, I am all of them. They have to know me. I cannot be more than what I am for them nor can I do more than what I have done already. They themselves are me. They are not separate from me. I am not giving favours to anybody but those who know me get me. It is all according to the law. Even grace is *karma-phala.* They have the free will to earn that grace or not.

Then finally speaking,

Ye māṁ bhajanti bhaktyā, those who seek me, who praise me, who worship me with devotion – all these can be taken as the meaning of the word *bhajanti* – *mayi te teṣu ca api aham,* they exist in me and I exist in them. They exist in me because they seek me. Then they become one with me and therefore, I exist in them. What about others? They are also non-separate from me but they do not seek me with commitment, with devotion, *bhaktyā*. If they do, then I am in them; they are in me. Here you must note that Bhagavān is not speaking with reference to *satya* and *mithyā* as he did earlier when he said *matsthāni sarva-bhūtāni na ca ahaṁ teṣu avasthitaḥ*. Here he is saying that the seeker's *ātmā* is me. Therefore, all the seekers exist in me, and I in them in that both of us are one and the same. Pure *ātmā* is pointed out. He is not talking about the relationship but the identity between *jīva* and Parameśvara. Therefore, I am them and they exist in me. All of them have their being in *ātmā*. When each one says, 'I am so and so' that 'I' is Parameśvara. They all exist in me, one *paramātmā*, and I am in the form of all of them.

Why should he say so?

One may think that they exist in me like the parts exist in the whole. This is what the school of thought called *viśiṣṭa-advaita* says. But this cannot be. There are no fractions of *ātmā* because *ātmā* is always whole. It cannot be fractionated. It is not that from the same fire each one has a spark of divinity. There is no spark here. The spark is the whole. These theologies exist because we have psychological issues. Every one of us wants to belong to somebody because we feel empty inside. We want to be claimed by somebody and therefore, one person says he belongs to a big person, in this case, Viṣṇu. It is purely psychological. There is nothing wrong with wanting to belong to somebody but we are not talking about simple psychological issues here. It is more than that. You do not belong to Īśvara. You are Īśvara.

If you think you belong to Īśvara, then you will also think Īśvara belongs to you. Like this, Īśvara will have one million people saying the same thing. Such people are deluded. When they discover there is another person to whom Īśvara has given the same feeling, their devotion will disappear. Īśvara becomes like the person who was searching for a greeting card and with the help of the shopkeeper finally found the one he was looking for. It said, 'You are the only one I love.' Then he asked the shopkeeper for a dozen of them! Similarly, Īśvara gives every devotee the feeling that he belongs to that devotee. He should; otherwise no one will be a devotee. But among the devotees, each has always an eye upon the other devotee. Each thinks, 'The Lord belongs to me. I am the only one dear to him. That is what he told me.' When one says to the other, 'He told me the same thing,' all the devotion falls apart.

This is what happens if you think you are a fraction of the Lord. This is *viśiṣṭa-advaita*. If everyone belongs to Īśvara and everyone thinks that Īśvara belongs to him, definitely he will have the feeling, 'I am not special to Īśvara, he has general devotees, I am only one of them.' Such devotion will evaporate. There is no belonging. You are Īśvara. There is no question of separation because Īśvara cannot be made into parts so that you have a spark of that Īśvara. Therefore, when you understand, 'I am in all of them, they are in me,' there is no separation.

Bhagavān says, 'I have no *dveṣa* for the people who do not care for me nor do I have *rāga* for the people who care for me. I am available for everyone because in all beings I am the same, *samoham sarva-bhūteṣu*.' It is a question of owning up. The *ātmā* of everyone is Parameśvara. I am not hiding myself from anybody nor I am choosing to reveal myself to someone. I do not extend favours to some and punishment to others. It is all one's own doing.

Having said this, he continues to talk about the nature of commitment to the pursuit of Īśvara, called *bhakti*. Śaṅkara introduces the next verse saying 'Listen to the glory of that devotion.'

Verse 30

Even those with improper conduct who seek the Lord is considered a good person

अपि चेत्सुदुराचारो भजते मामनन्यभाक् ।
साधुरेव स मन्तव्यः सम्यग्व्यवसितो हि सः ॥ ३० ॥

api cetsudurācāro bhajate mām ananyabhāk
sādhureva sa mantavyaḥ samyagvyavasito hi saḥ (30)

api cet – even if; *sudurācāraḥ* – one of highly improper conduct; *ananyabhāk* – being one without a sense of separation; *bhajate* – seeks; *mām* - me; *saḥ sādhuḥ eva mantavyaḥ* – he is to be considered a good person; *hi* – because; *saḥ samyag vyavasitaḥ* – he is one whose understanding is clear

> Even if someone of highly improper conduct seeks me without a sense of separation, he is to be considered a good person because he is one whose understanding is clear.

Api cet sudurācāraḥ, even if he is a person whose conduct is highly questionable. *Sudurācāraḥ* is a person whose conduct, *ācāra*, is highly improper. He omits the things that are to be done and does those things that are not to be done. He is completely unmindful of others' happiness or welfare. Such a totally self-centred person is a *durācāra*. In that, he excels everybody else. There are many criminals but this one excels all of them. Generally the prefix, *su* is not put in conjunction with the prefix, *dur*. But here Lord Kṛṣṇa uses this *su* with *durācāra*. Even though his conduct has been like this, and continues to be like this, he is *ananyabhāk*, one who does not see anything else except Īśvara. Somehow, in spite of all his *durācāra*, because of some previous *karma*, he has discovered some devotion for Īśvara and is committed to the knowledge of Īśvara. Therefore, he has become *ananyabhāk*, one who commits oneself to the pursuit of the knowledge of Īśvara. He seeks me, Parameśvara, even though his *ācāra* is highly questionable.

Then what happens to him?

Sādhuḥ eva sa mantavyaḥ, that person is to be considered a *sādhu*, one whose conduct is good, because his thinking or his understanding is clear, he is well established in the knowledge of Īśvara–*samyag-vyavasitaḥ saḥ*. When his understanding about *jīva* and Īśvara is clear, naturally he should be looked upon as one who is committed to the pursuit of Īśvara and as one who has proper understanding.

If he has such knowledge, how can his conduct be questionable? It is only an argument, which is why *api cet* is there. It is a supposition. Suppose there is such a person. If he is committed to the pursuit of or has understood Īśvara properly as non-separate from *ātmā*, then who can evaluate his conduct? His *ahaṅkāra*, ego, is not there but because of some prior habits picked up, he may continue to do things that are questionable. A story told in the Mahābhārata illustrates this.

One *brāhmaṇa* was sitting under a tree doing his prayers, meditation and *tapas* invoking the Lord. In the process he developed some powers, which he himself did not know about. One day, when he was sitting under a tree, droppings of a crane from the tree top fell on him. He looked at it with angry eyes and the crane was burnt to ashes. Then he knew he had this power. He used to go for *bhikṣā* daily to the same village. Previously he was humble like a *sādhu;* but once he got the power, he became very proud. He went and asked for *bhikṣā* and the woman made him wait for one hour before serving him. He was very angry and asked her how she could make him wait like that. She said that she was doing her duties, which was more important. He said, 'Do you know who you are talking to?' She said, 'Yes I know, but I am no crane.' He asked her how she knew about the crane. And she told him to go and ask a particular butcher. The butcher was busy serving his old and ailing father; so, the *brāhmaṇa* had to wait again. He was furious and asked the butcher why he had made him wait. Then the butcher asked, 'Did that lady send you here?' The lesson here is, do not judge people by what they do. One was a householder and the other a butcher but they were both doing their jobs and were definitely better than the *brāhmaṇa* with all his prayers and meditations.

And he is to be considered a *sādhu* because when he has properly understood, *samyag-vyavasitaḥ hi saḥ* and is pursuing knowledge, his improper conduct is not going to continue.

How can it? If you analyse the *durācāra*, it is either a habit or a real crime. Habit will naturally drop off in time. Crimes are always centred on the person who is insecure, the small 'I.' Because he is highly insecure, his behaviour becomes aggressive. If he has devotion to Īśvara, in the very acceptance of Īśvara his ego gets diluted. And in the pursuit of knowledge of Īśvara, it gets even further diluted. Thereby the tendencies based upon fear, tendencies to cheat, to deceive, to hurt, naturally drop off.

To give an example. When a cotton cluster is thinned out so that it becomes fluffy, all the particles sticking to the cotton drop off. You cannot easily remove them one by one but once the cotton fibres are separated, you find all the particles drop down because there is nothing for them to stick to. So too the ego, once diluted, cannot hold on to these tendencies. They all drop off because fear and selfishness, which are at the centre of all crimes, are due to ego. If that ego is diluted, where is the question of these things sticking there?

Śaṅkara introduces the next verse saying that, having given up improper conduct, which is external, this person becomes a *dharmātmā* because of an inner clarity in understanding of oneself and Īśvara.

Verse 31

Having given up improper conduct,
the person gains inner clarity and peace

क्षिप्रं भवति धर्मात्मा शश्वच्छान्तिं निगच्छति ।
कौन्तेय प्रतिजानीहि न मे भक्तः प्रणश्यति ॥ ३१ ॥

kṣipraṁ bhavati dharmātmā śaśvacchāntiṁ nigacchati
kaunteya pratijānīhi na me bhaktaḥ praṇaśyati (31)

kṣipram – quickly; *bhavati* – he becomes; *dharmātmā* – one whose mind is in conformity with *dharma; śaśvat-śāntim* – eternal peace; *nigacchati* – he gains; *kaunteya* – Arjuna!; *pratijānīhi* – may you know for certain; *me bhaktaḥ* – my devotee; *na praṇaśyati* – does not get destroyed

Quickly he becomes one whose mind is in conformity with *dharma* and gains eternal peace. May you know for certain, Kaunteya (Arjuna)! my devotee never gets destroyed.

Kṣipraṁ bhavati dharmātmā. Dharmātmā means the one whose mind is in conformity with *dharma. Dharma* becomes natural to this person because commitment to *dharma* is part of devotion to Īśvara. An individual does not create the moral order; it is part of the creation. We require such an order because we have the faculty of choice. Once we have that we must have a set of norms for interaction with the world. Otherwise it is a power given to us without proper controls.

So, we do have innate common sense knowledge of this moral order, which is why there is universal agreement about what is fundamentally right and wrong. Besides this, there is cultural right and wrong and situational right and wrong. An interpretation is possible only because there is a universal order, which is a part of the creation. And creation, or what is created by Īśvara, is non-separate from Īśvara; therefore *dharma* is Īśvara. It is not an ordinary thing.

This is something we find only in the *vaidika-śāstra*. Elsewhere *dharma* is purely a mandate, which if you follow, you will be rewarded, and if you do not, you will be punished. This is how all of *dharma* that is values, ethics etc., is presented. But here, *dharma* is non-separate from Īśvara. So, seeking Īśvara is not going to be away from that *dharma*.

Because his mind is committed to *dharma*, he is called *dharma-ātmā*. And *dharma* is always expressed in terms of conduct. Later we are going to see a verse, which says, *sarva-dharmān parityajya*, completely giving up *dharma*, which means *karmāṇi parityajya*, completely giving up *karma* because only where there is *karma* does *dharma* come into play. *Karma* is controlled by *dharma* and has to be in keeping with it. Therefore, *karma* is *dharma*.

Previously he was *durācāra*, now he is *dharmātmā* because of his clarity of understanding, *samyag-vyavastitaḥ hi saḥ*. And because of his devotion to Īśvara, naturally, this change takes place quickly. Even though he was *durācāra* when he started all this, his knowledge and devotion are such that, it consumes all his improper behaviour. Such a person is free from conflict. Therefore, he gains eternal peace, *śaśvat-śāntim nigacchati*. There are different types of *śānti*. Because he does what is to be done and avoids what is not to be done, naturally he gains inner *śānti*. This is relative. But then he already has clear understanding and because of that, he becomes *dharmātmā*. Being a *dharmātmā*, his understanding becomes clearer. As his conduct improves, his clarity also increases. He understands the nature of the self as not subject to modification and therefore, *nitya-śānta-ātmā*. So, this *śaśvat-śānti* is *śānti* that is eternal because it is a peace that is the nature of the self. In spite of thinking, *ātmā* is *śānta*; so, let the thinking take place. That is clarity. Whatever the condition of the mind, it does not become a basis for self-judgement because it does not bring about any change in one's knowledge of *ātmā* being *avikriya*, not subject to change. That is *śaśvat-śānti*. And self-knowledge is called *śānti*.

This knowledge is not sullied by thinking. This is true of any knowledge. If you know what a car is, that knowledge is not in any way affected just because your mind is restless or disturbed. Even when the mind is sad, 1 + 1 is still 2. The nature of knowledge is that it does not get disturbed just because the mind is in a certain condition or the body has become very old or weak. The clarity of knowledge is such that one knows he or she is *śānta* in spite of the mind, not because the mind is *śānta*.

Kaunteya pratijānīhi na me bhaktaḥ pranaśyati, may you know for certain, Arjuna, my devotee does not get destroyed. This is a very famous sentence. Devotee here is the committed person and implies that he or she has recognition of Īśvara. That recognition is a great blessing. It is not all that easy to recognise Īśvara. That there is Īśvara is a great step and then the one who seeks to know that Īśvara is really one whom we call a *bhakta* here. Such a person never comes to a bad lot, whatever his or her conduct has been.

Even with regard to the pursuit, he is very clear about what he is after. And if he appreciates Īśvara, naturally he gains the *śānti*, which is the nature of *ātmā*. And he does not come to destruction, to a bad lot. This is true for any person.

Verse 32

Even those people given to adharma – having taken refuge in me – gain me

मां हि पार्थ व्यपाश्रित्य येऽपि स्युः पापयोनयः ।
स्त्रियो वैश्यास्तथा शूद्रास्तेऽपि यान्ति परां गतिम् ॥ ३२ ॥

māṁ hi pārtha vyapāśritya ye'pi syuḥ pāpayonayaḥ
striyo vaiśyāstathā śūdrāste'pi yānti parāṁ gatim (32)

hi – indeed; *pārtha* – Arjuna!; *ye api syuḥ* – even those who are; *pāpa-yonayaḥ* – born in families given to improper conduct; *tathā* – so too; *striyaḥ* – women; *vaiśyāḥ* – *vaiśyas*; *śūdrāḥ* – *śūdras*; *te api* – they also; *māṁ vyapāśritya* – taking refuge in me; *yānti* – gain; *parāṁ gatim* – the ultimate end

> Indeed, Pārtha (Arjuna)! even those who are born in families given to improper conduct, and so too, women, *vaiśyas* and *śūdras*, taking refuge in me, they also gain the ultimate end.

Pāpa-yonayaḥ are those who happen to be born to parents who are of very improper conduct like people given to crime and so on. It can also be taken as animals etc., because we have stories about such *jīvas* as Gajendra, an elephant, getting *mokṣa*. Caught by a crocodile, he plucked a lotus from the pond and offered to the Lord. Because of his devotion, the Lord helped him release himself from the crocodile. And Jaṭāyu, who was a bird, got *mokṣa* and of course there was Hanumān who was more than a monkey. *Pāpa-yoni* is any birth in which there is a predominance of affliction. For us, *pāpa* is not sin. It is anything that gives us *duḥkha*. Even a mosquito bite is a *pāpa*. If we get a mosquito bite, one *pāpa* has gone.

Śaṅkara takes the word *pāpa-yonayaḥ* as being *striyaḥ vaiśyaḥ* and *śūdrāḥ*. Women undergo more physical and perhaps emotional pain than men; and so a female birth can be considered a *pāpa-yoni*. A *vaiśya*, *śūdra* and so on, do not have a good start in life. A *Vaiśya* does business; so, the motivation to sell something is greater than that to be truthful. He cannot say, 'This is useless but if you want it, you can buy it.' If he can, he is almost ready to become a *sannyāsī*. Therefore, he is considered to be a *pāpa-yoni*.

I[23] do not agree with this. Because the word *tathā*, so too, is there. It is very clear that *strī* and so on, are not *pāpa-yonis*. The verse says, 'Even those who are *pāpa-yonis*, so too, women, *vaiśyas* and *śūdras*, *ye api syuḥ papayonayaḥ tathā striyaḥ vaiśyāh śūdrāḥ*.' And nowhere is it said that *vaiśyas* and *śūdras* are *pāpa-yonis*. The word *pāpa-yonayaḥ* can also mean those who are born outside the four groups of people – *brāhmaṇas*, *kṣatriyas*, *vaiśyas* and *śūdras*.

Or, more correctly, *pāpa-yonis* are those who are born to parents given to a life of *adharma*. But *strī*, woman, who falls within the four groups is also mentioned. So, *strī* cannot be

[23] Swamiji

included in *pāpa-yoni*s here. These would be people like the *cāṇḍālā*s and so on, who come from a tribe that does not conform to any kind of *dharma*. The point is, all of them get liberated. Therefore, the criterion for gaining *mokṣa* is not the parentage or the *varṇa* a person belongs to. Nor is it the *āśrama* the person happens to be in. All these do not really count in gaining *mokṣa*. They count only in determining what kind of duty the person has to perform if the *varṇa-āśrama* system is working. For *mokṣa*, which is in the form of knowledge, these things do not count at all. Therefore, all these people can also gain *parāgati*, the end from which there is no return. It is also an end, which cannot be improved upon; it is the ultimate end, the inner freedom, which is the recognition of *ātmā* being identical with Īśvara.

Verse 33

When such people get liberated, what to talk of others with fortunate births!

किं पुनर्ब्राह्मणाः पुण्या भक्ता राजर्षयस्तथा ।
अनित्यमसुखं लोकमिमं प्राप्य भजस्व माम् ॥ ३३ ॥

kiṁ punarbrāhmaṇāḥ puṇyā bhaktā rājarṣayastathā
anityamasukhaṁ lokamimaṁ prāpya bhajasva mām (33)

kiṁ punaḥ brāhmaṇāḥ – then what to talk of *brāhmaṇas*; *puṇyāḥ* – who have fortunate births; *bhaktāḥ* – devoted; *tathā rājarṣayaḥ* – so too the sage-kings (*kṣatriyas*); *imam* – this; *anityam* – non-eternal; *asukham* – of very little happiness; *lokam* – world of experience; *prāpya* – having gained; *māṁ bhajasva* – may you seek me

Then what to talk of *brāhmaṇas* who have fortunate births and are devoted, so too, the sage-kings (*kṣatriyas*)? Having gained this world, which is non-eternal and of little happiness, may you seek me.

Kiṁ punaḥ brāhmaṇāḥ puṇyāḥ bhaktāḥ, what to talk of *brāhmaṇas* who are born in *puṇya-yonis*? Because of certain *puṇya*, they really have a head start in this pursuit. They are born in a family where there is culture and from the beginning are exposed to rituals etc. When a *brāhmaṇa* boy is eight years old, he is initiated into the study of the Vedas, the *gāyatrī-mantra* and so on. This is not an ordinary opportunity. And of course they must be *īśvara-bhaktās*. They do not fritter away the opportunity they have but with devotion, commit themselves to the pursuit of this knowledge.

It is not where you are but how you are that is important

Bhaktāḥ rājarṣayaḥ tathā, similarly, the *kṣatriyas* who are kings and sages. They also have an advantageous beginning. Bhagavān calls them *rājarṣis*; they are kings, and they are sages, *rājānaḥ te ṛṣayaḥ*. It means they are born in a royal family and they are knowers of Brahman.

Bhagavān has covered everybody. Therefore, it is not where you are, but what you are, that is important. Devotion and commitment is as necessary for a *brāhmaṇa* as it is for the *pāpa-yoni*. And further, no matter what the station in life, the fundamental condition is the same. Bhagavān describes it very clearly.

Anityam asukhaṁ lokam imaṁ prāpya, having gained this world of experience achieved by a human being, which is non-eternal, and of very little happiness. If one is a *śūdra,* one is a human being; if one is a *vaiśya,* one is a human being; if one is a *brāhmaṇa,* one is a human being; if one is a *cāṇḍāla,* one is a human being. Even if one is Hanumān one is like a human being in that one is capable of thinking and not purely controlled by instinct. For all of them this world is the same – *anitya,* non-eternal, and *asukha,* not happy. The world of human beings consists of experiences that are not lasting and not always happy. The '*a*' prefixed to *sukha* here is not negation but conveys the sense of only a little. If there is no *sukha* nobody will want to live. Everyone has some *sukha,* but it is inadequate and *anitya.* Having gained it, one finds it is finite and fleeting.

Śaṅkara says, the status of being a human being, which is the means for fulfilling all the *puruṣārtha*s, is very difficult to gain. The idea is, do not fritter it away. What should you do then?

Mām bhajasva, commit yourself to pursuing knowledge of Parameśvara. Anything less will not satisfy you. You cannot say minus *mokṣa,* which is Parameśvara, this is enough for me. Even though you may think if you get certain thing you will have all you want, but once you get it, it becomes clear that it is not enough. Therefore, everybody is seeking *mokṣa.* To gain that freedom from the sense of limitation, you have to come to 'me,' says Bhagavān. It means you have to know 'me.' Therefore, *mām bhajasva,* please worship or seek me.

Verse 34

Kṛṣṇa tells how one should seek him

मन्मना भव मद्भक्तो मद्याजी मां नमस्कुरु ।
मामेवैष्यसि युक्त्वैवमात्मानं मत्परायणः ॥ ३४ ॥

manmanā bhava madbhakto madyājī māṁ namaskuru
mām evaiṣyasi yuktvaivam ātmānaṁ matparāyaṇaḥ (34)

manmanāḥ – one whose mind is committed to me; *madbhaktaḥ* – who is devoted to me; *madyājī* – who offers rituals unto me; *bhava* – may you become; *māṁ namaskuru* – may you surrender to me; *ātmānam evaṁ yuktvā* – having yourself prepared in this way; *matparāyaṇaḥ* (*san*) – being one for whom I am the ultimate end; *mām eva eṣyasi* – you will reach me alone

> May you become one whose mind is committed to me, who is devoted to me, who offers rituals unto me and may you surrender to me. Having yourself prepared in this way and being one for whom I am the ultimate end, you will reach me, the self alone.

Manmanā bhava, may you become one whose mind is lost in me, is committed to me, Parameśvara. Committed to the Lord means committed to the pursuit of the Lord. Generally, one is committed to various other things in the world that are nothing but *artha* and *kāma* and use the Lord to gain those things. There is nothing wrong with it. But having achieved what you wanted, you are not going to complete the journey towards fulfilment. Therefore, may you choose me straight away as the one to be gained, as the one in whom you lose yourself.

Gain here is in the form of knowledge. So, may you become one whose mind is committed to me.

'*Mad-bhaktaḥ bhava*, may you become one who is devoted to me,' says the Lord. When your mind has to be in the pursuit of the Lord, your love must not be elsewhere. If you are intellectually convinced about the pursuit of *mokṣa* but your heart is distributed in hundred different things, it does not work. You will not have a mind that is seeking the Lord. *Bhakti* here is the emotion of love. *Bhakti* is defined as *prema-svarūpa*, of the nature of love. So, the Lord says, 'May I, Īśvara, the very subject matter of Vedanta become the object of your love.' In other words, may you be a *jijñāsu* where your devotion is for the very knowledge of Īśvara.

Madyājī bhava, may you become one whose rituals, prayers and so on, are offered only for me. It means they are only for the sake of *antaḥ-karaṇa-śuddhi*, whereby is the gain of Īśvara. In every prayer, Īśvara is invoked. But then it is not usually for Īśvara's sake that you perform the ritual. You do it for heaven or some similar end. Even though Īśvara is involved, the purpose is entirely different. Here, Īśvara is invoked only for the sake of gaining him, nothing else. It is excellent. The same prayer is converted into a great *sādhana* because you are invoking Īśvara's grace for knowing Īśvara. You do not want anything less.

Then, the Lord says, *mām namaskuru*, may you surrender unto me. Because the word *kuru* is there, an action is indicated. So, surrender here is *yoga*. Surrendering your doership and enjoyership, may you commit yourself to me. The attitude described here is, 'Whatever is given to me by Īśvara, I am happy with it. All that I do, I do conforming to *dharma* because *dharma* itself is Īśvara. Unto that Īśvara I surrender my personal likes and dislikes.' That is what is called *namaskāra*, surrender.

Evam ātmānaṁ yuktvā, having prepared yourself in this way. When you are doing such actions, it will bring about *antaḥ-karaṇa-śuddhi* and, Śaṅkara says, in this way your mind will be composed and focused. Having focused the mind, *samādhāya cittam*, you surrender unto Īśvara. The mind can be focused on anything but here it is only on Bhagavān.

When this is so, what will happen?

That person becomes *matparāyaṇa*, the one for whom I, Īśvara, am the goal. For him, the ultimate end, the only end is Parameśvara. All because he is *manmanāḥ madbhaktaḥ madyājī* and the one who has surrendered unto me. He has taken refuge in me and thus is called *matparāyaṇa*, one for whom I am the ultimate end; in fact, the only end.

That being so, the Lord says, *mām eva eṣyasi*, you will go to me alone, you will gain me alone. Discovering that *ātmā* is Parameśvara, you will become one with me. This expression, 'becoming one with me,' is always a problem. What is to become one with a person? Do you go somewhere and become one with him? How will you become one with him? Is it a kind of a relationship? Is it a kind of emotional identity or some kind of intellectual identity or a physical identity like an amoeba in your stomach? How exactly does the devotee get identity with Īśvara?

Bhagavān says, 'Because I am the *ātmā* of all beings, coming to me is recognising yourself. When you gain yourself in terms of knowledge, you come to Īśvara.

We have taken the syntax to be, *evam ātmānaṁ yuktvā mām eṣyasi*, having prepared your mind in this way, you will gain me. Here, we have taken the word *ātmānam* to mean the mind. Whereas Śaṅkara says, *evam yuktvā samādhāya cittam evam*, meaning, 'Having gained the composure of mind in this manner…'

And then he says, *ātmānaṁ mām eṣyasi*, you will reach *ātmā* that is myself. And he explains the word *ātmā* as himself, who is the *ātmā* of all beings, *aham hi sarveṣāṁ bhūtānām ātmā* and who is the *parā gati* the ultimate end. Looking at it this way, you get the meaning that your reaching the Lord is reaching yourself because Īśvara is the *ātmā* of all beings.

All this goes along with *kaunteya pratijānīhi na me bhaktaḥ praṇaśyati*, may you know for certain, Arjuna, My devotees never get destroyed. Thus ends the chapter nine with the assurance from Bhagavān that a *bhakta* who comes to know or wants to know Bhagavān in this manner is never destroyed.

ॐतत्सत्।

इति श्रीमद्भगवद्गीतासूपनिषत्सु ब्रह्मविद्यायां योगशास्त्रे श्रीकृष्णार्जुन-
संवादे राजविद्या-राजगुह्य-योगो नाम नवमोऽध्यायः ॥ ९ ॥

oṁ tat sat.

iti śrīmadbhagavadgītāsūpaniṣatsu brahma-vidyāyāṁ yoga-

śāstre śrīkṛṣṇārjuna-saṁvāde rājavidyā-rājaguhya-yogo nāma navamo'dhyāyaḥ (9)

Om, Brahman, is the only reality. Thus ends the ninth chapter called *rājavidyā-rājaguhya-yoga*–having the topic of the king of knowledge, the king of secrets–in the *Bhagavadgītā* which is in the form of a dialogue between Śrī Kṛṣṇa and Arjuna, which is the essence of the *Upaniṣads*, whose subject matter is both the knowledge of Brahman and *yoga.*

And it is not only *brahma-vidyā,* which deals with realities, it is *yoga-śāstra*. It talks about the *antaḥ-karaṇa* and *karmas* etc., telling what one needs to do for purification of the mind. *Dharma*, all disciplines, values, prayer and so on, come under *yoga-śāstra*. In this *yoga-śāstra...*

And this was in the form of a dialogue that took place between Kṛṣṇa and Arjuna, *kṛṣṇa-arjuna-saṁvāda*. In this dialogue, *kṛṣṇa-arjuna-saṁvāde,* is this *navamodhyāya,* nineth chapter dealing with the topic, *rāja-vidyā, rāja-guhya.*

Rāja-vidyā is *brahma-vidyā* and it is *rāja-guhya*, the greatest secret. There are many secrets but this is the *rājā,* king, of all secrets, because even after you are told it remains a secret. And once you understand, it is the most precious.

Chapter 10

विभूति-योगः

Vibhūti-yogaḥ

Topic of glories (of the Lord)

The *Bhagavadgītā* is both *brahma-vidyā* and *yoga-śāstra*. As *brahma-vidyā* it can be reduced to one sentence, *tat tvam asi*, you are that. In this, you need to understand, what this 'you' is, and what 'that' is. To understand any sentence, you must understand the meaning of each word.

The meaning of the word *tat* is Īśvara, the cause of all. 'Who' is this Īśvara? *Tvaṁ-pada* stands for *jīva*. Who is this *jīva*? Enquiry into both must be done.

We saw that the first six chapters of the *Gītā* deal mainly with the meaning of the word '*tvam*, you.' The first chapter depicted Arjuna's sorrow, which is the lot of any *jīva*. Then, discovering in Kṛṣṇa a teacher, he declared himself Kṛṣṇa's student and sought refuge in Kṛṣṇa. In the second chapter Lord Kṛṣṇa teaches him what *ātma-svarūpa* is. The next chapter, *karma-yoga* is also about the *jīva*. The fourth chapter teaches that *ātmā* is *akartā*, which is again teaching the nature of *pratyagātmā*, the inner self. Then the fifth chapter deals with the *jīva*'s renunciation and the sixth chapter is committed to contemplation with reference to *pratyagātmā*, the contemplator.

From the seventh chapter onwards there is a complete change in the presentation of the subject matter. Īśvara, the truth of Īśvara, the glory of Īśvara, is the central topic in these chapters, that is, the next six chapters.

The tenth chapter of the *Gītā*, called *vibhūti-yoga*, presents the glories of Īśvara. Even though he is all-pervasive and is everything, still, the glory of Bhagavān is visible wherever there is a ray of glory.

In India, in ancient times, any good place was dedicated to Bhagavān. A confluence, the coming together of two rivers, is always a wonderful sight. There, you will find a temple. Any mountaintop, from which there is a scenic view, will have a temple. On Rāmeśvaram, the island is a temple. Kanyākumārī is an excellent place where you can see the merging of the three bodies of water, the Arabian Sea, the Bay of Bengal, and the Indian Ocean, each with its own colour. It is a great sight. There you find only a temple, no palace or secular monument.

In the seven hills of Tirupati, there is the famous Bālāji temple. In the Himalayas, in Badrinath, there is a temple. The big snowy peak of Kailāśa is itself worshipped as Lord Śiva. Any unusually good spot, in any spot where the glory of nature is very evident, there is a temple. Even if you build a temple on a very common site, with its exquisite sculptures and imposing towers, it becomes a beautiful place. So, any place of glory or beauty was always given to the Lord, because, it is his beauty.

Śaṅkara introduces this chapter called *vibhūti-yoga* saying, in whichever situation, in whichever object, there is some glory, Bhagavān is to be contemplated upon and appreciated.

The truth of Bhagavān is not easily understood and therefore, must be told again and again. Repetition is valid as long as something has to be understood. If it is to be believed, repetition is meaningless. So Śaṅkara validates the repetition. It is not simple repetition though. There is an elaboration, which also reveals the style of teaching. What you say in passing in one place, you expand upon in another. Previously, the *vibhūti*s, glories, of Īśvara were pointed out in passing and now they are taken up as the main topic. This is how the whole teaching is. In order to cover one topic, you may have to touch on another topic briefly and reserve it for later discussion.

Here, the topic of the glory of Bhagavān is discussed. There is nothing that is not Bhagavān; that is what is going to be told here. In whatever situation, if there is some glory, there the glory of Bhagavān is to be recognised. Something beautiful is not taken merely as a beautiful thing. That beauty is Bhagavān – he is the source of all fame and beauty. For a *bhakta*, an intelligent person who discerns this, Bhagavān alone is famous. Nobody else. Fame, wherever it is, is *bhagavad-vibhūti* alone. To make this clear is this chapter, which is rightly called, *vibhūti-yoga*.

Verse 1

Lord Kṛṣṇa explains why he is going to repeat what he has said

श्रीभगवानुवाच ।
भूय एव महाबाहो शृणु मे परमं वचः ।
यत्तेऽहं प्रीयमाणाय वक्ष्यामि हितकाम्यया ॥ १ ॥

śrībhagavān uvāca
bhūya eva mahābāho śṛṇu me paramaṁ vacaḥ
yatte'haṁ prīyamāṇāya vakṣyāmi hitakāmyayā (1)

śrībhagavān – the Lord; *uvāca* – said;
mahābāho – O mighty armed Arjuna!; *bhūyaḥ eva* – indeed again; *śṛṇu* – listen; *me paramaṁ vacaḥ* – to my words, which reveal the limitless; *yat* – which; *te prīyamāṇāya* – to you who is pleased (by my words); *hitakāmyayā* – for your benefit; *ahaṁ vakṣyāmi* – (which) I will tell

Śrī Bhagavān said:

Indeed, Arjuna, the mighty armed! for your benefit, listen again to my words revealing the limitless, which I will tell you, who is pleased (by my words).

Mahābāhu means literally the one who has two long arms; but here it means a man of might, of glory. Bhagavān is going to talk about his glories and by addressing Arjuna *mahābāho,* he is trying to say, 'The glory that you have belongs to me.' That is what he wants to prove. Later he is even going to say, 'Among the archers I am Arjuna.' Therefore, the glory you have, Arjuna, is my glory. So, mighty armed Arjuna please listen. Why? Because you alone are qualified to listen to this.

Bhūyaḥ eva śṛṇu me vacaḥ, indeed, again listen to my words. The word 'again' stands for repetition of the topic. The topic was the truth of Bhagavān, *bhagavat-tattva*, and also his glories, which were mentioned in the seventh and ninth chapters. There is an adjective *paramam* that has been added to *vacaḥ*, words. How can we translate this word *parama*? As supreme?

Words are not supreme. Śaṅkara says that they are exalted words, *prakṛṣṭa*, because they are meant to reveal the *vastu* that is limitless. The words become *parama* because they reveal the *paramaṁ vastu*, *paraṁ-brahma*.

Yat te ahaṁ prīyamāṇāya vakṣyāmi hitakāmyayā, which I will tell you, who are pleased – pleased with my words. From his looks, eagerness and so on, it is clear that Arjuna is pleased. What he has been waiting for seems to be happening and therefore, Arjuna seems mightily pleased with what is going on right now.

A few hours ago he was not pleased at all. In the first chapter he was definitely not pleased. The weeping was over the moment he said, 'I am your *śiṣya*.' From then on the problem had been transferred to Kṛṣṇa and with that Arjuna had a relief. Afterwards, chapter after chapter, he has been learning. Now Arjuna seems to be highly pleased. Whether he was pleased, it was very clear, Kṛṣṇa was pleased with Arjuna, because he says *prīyamāṇāya*. From your expression, I see you as one who is pleased. Kṛṣṇa presents himself as Īśvara, who is *sarvajña* and therefore, he knows Arjuna is highly pleased now. For your sake who is pleased with my words, *vakṣyāmi*, I am telling this.

Śaṅkara gives an example here, and says that Arjuna is like a person who is highly pleased by drinking *amṛta*, nectar. *Amṛta* is considered to be the sweetest thing, drinking which one becomes immortal physically. It is only a relative immortality; even then there was a war for this *amṛta* between the devas and the *asuras*. It is so sweet that it is the last word in taste.

There is nothing that is more desirable – at once pleasing and immortalising. Generally, anything that is good for your health has to be taken while you block your nose. Healthy and tasty do not go together at all. Only *amṛta* is both.

Amṛta is mentioned in the *purāṇa*s and for Śaṅkara and people like him, who have been dealing with the *purāṇa*s, it is a common word. Therefore, he can use it as an example though it is not exactly an example because it is not directly known to anybody. It is only known indirectly but on that basis Śaṅkara uses it as an illustration. He is qualified to do that because he is also dealing with all these *purāṇa*s while writing his various commentaries. For him it is a household word. But we cannot use *amṛta* as an illustration. We can only understand what Śaṅkara means here when he says explaining the words of the Lord, 'In the way that a person is so pleased by taking nectar, similarly you seem to simply lap up all that I have been saying. Therefore, I am going to tell you, who are pleased, *prīyamāṇāya te ahaṁ vakṣyāmi*.'

Why? *Hitakāmyayā*, with a desire to bring good to you. *Hita* is *mokṣa*. That any *vibhūti*, glory, is Bhagavān and *bhagavat-tattva*, the truth of Bhagavān, is to be understood in order to understand *tat tvam asi*. Understanding this sentence is the greatest *hita, śreyas. Śreyas,* the greatest good you can do for a person, is to make him recognise that he is Īśvara. What better good can you do? Nothing is greater than recognising that you are Īśvara.

Arjuna, with a desire to do good to you I will tell you because I am interested in your welfare. The ultimate thing you can know is *bhagavat-tattva,* the truth of Bhagavān. Even before that, recognising *bhagavad-vibhūti* also is *hita,* beneficial, to you.

Recognising Īśvara's glories benefits you

If you recognise all glories as Īśvara's glories, your pride, your *ahaṅkāra* diminishes. That paves the way for understanding what Īśvara is. What stands between you and Īśvara, after all, is your ego. That ego has to be dilated and then dismissed by knowledge. The dilation of the ego is not easy because knowledge of *śāstra* generally inflates the ego. How do you deflate it?

My ego gets deflated when I understand that anything that makes me feel glorious belongs to Bhagavān. If I say my precious wealth is something that I have gathered with great effort, I cannot say it belongs to somebody else. It is my effort. That is how I become possessive. This sense of ownership gives me some kind of self-esteem. But the very fact that I require self-esteem shows that I do not have much of it. So, how am I going to part with my hard-earned accomplishments and say that the glories belong to Bhagavān?

You do not have to part with anything. Suppose a person is capable of thinking properly. That clarity in thinking is a glory. It is not an ordinary accomplishment; it is the highest achievement you can have as a human being. There is nothing more beautiful than clarity in thinking. If there is such a capacity enjoyed by a given person, then there cannot be pride about it. There can only be appreciation of Īśvara. That very clarity of thinking should help you recognise that all this belongs to Īśvara. There is no personal accomplishment at all. Everything is Īśvara and whatever glory you have is Īśvara's glory. That recognition does you a lot of good, *hita,* even though it is relative.

So, this *vibhūti-yoga* benefits you in a two-fold way. It reveals *bhagavat-tattva,* the nature of Bhagavān, whereby you recognise the full meaning of the sentence *ahaṁ brahmāsmi,* I am the Lord. That is the ultimate *hita,* called *śreyas.* But in order to get *śreyas,* there is a relative *hita* necessary. If you recognise Īśvara's glory, it is altogether different. Whenever you see someone who is extraordinarily gifted, instead of feeling jealous you can say, 'As I have some glories, he also has some. In him Īśvara's glory is expressed better.' When you can look at it this way, your jealousy your pride, your inferiority, etc., will go away. You only recognise the glory of Īśvara wherever you see something beautiful.

Therefore, this is a very important chapter for a seeker. To assimilate what Bhagavān is saying here is essential for maturity.

Bhagavān says, 'Only with a desire to bring good to you, am I telling this. So, please listen.' Why does Bhagavān have to say this here? Perhaps you can get it from somewhere else. Why should he spend his time repeating, 'The glory of the Himalayas is me, the glory of Everest is me, the glory of Gaṅgā is me.' Some pundit can do this. No. If a pundit has to tell this and make it meaningful, he requires validity. That validity can only come from Bhagavān. Therefore, only Bhagavān can speak authoritatively of his glories. This he makes clear in the next verse. Bhagavān says:

Verse 2

Only Bhagavān can speak authoritatively about his glories

न मे विदुः सुरगणाः प्रभवं न महर्षयः ।
अहमादिर्हि देवानां महर्षीणां च सर्वशः ॥ २ ॥

na me viduḥ suragaṇāḥ prabhavaṁ na maharṣayaḥ
aham ādirhi devānāṁ maharṣīṇāṁ ca sarvaśaḥ (2)

suragaṇāḥ – the whole host of gods; *me prabhavam* – my glory of coming into being as this world; *na viduḥ* – do not know; *na maharṣayaḥ* – nor do the sages; *aham ādiḥ hi* – because I am the cause; *devānāṁ maharṣīṇāṁ ca sarvaśaḥ* – of all the gods and sages

> The whole host of gods do not know my glory of coming into being as this world, nor do the sages because I am the cause of all the gods and sages.

Me prabhavam can be taken as my glories, my *śakti*s or my coming into being in the form of this world.

Na viduḥ, they do not totally know. They all know, but not totally. Who? We are not talking about local people here.

Suragaṇāḥ, the whole host of gods – *sura*s are *deva*s like Indra, Varuṇa, and so on. Even they do not know me totally. They may know themselves as *paramātmā,* but still they do not know all the glories of Īśvara. Even Brahmaji can only create, he cannot sustain. And Viṣṇu can only sustain; he cannot create.

That is not his job. Śiva as Rudra can only destroy, not create or sustain. Each one has only one job. Therefore, all my glories, even Brahmaji and so on, do not know.

Not only that, even *maharṣi*s, the great sages, do not know. A *maharṣi* is a great sage – *mahān ca asau ṛṣiḥ*, he is great and he is also a sage. *Maharṣi*s are the ones who know, from whom we get all our knowledge. Even they do not know Īśvara's glories totally. In general they know everything. As *jñānīs* they know the truth of everything as '*ahaṁ satyaṁ brahma*, and everything else is *mithyā*. Everything, known and unknown, is Brahman alone.' That knowledge is *sarvajñatva*, omniscience. But it is different from the omniscience of Īśvara. Īśvara has that omniscience plus all the details of the *mithyā*. These details even the *maharṣis* do not know.

Aham ādiḥ hi devānāṁ maharṣīṇāṁ ca sarvaśaḥ, because I am the cause of all the gods and sages. It is something like the son being told by the father how wonderful his marriage was. It went on for four days. On the first day Bhanumati danced, the second day Ariyakkudi Ramanujam sang, the third day Maharajapuram Santhanam sang, and on the fourth day Semmangudi Srinivasa Iyer came. Hundreds of people came and there was a great canopy. On being told all this, the son asked, 'Why you did not take me?' How can the son ever know all about the marriage directly even though the father describes it so thoroughly? He can only have indirect knowledge born of a description in words, words that have their own limitations experienced both by the speaker and the listener. Words are not always understood as they are meant.

The limitations of language on the part of the listener and the speaker edit, abridge, and distort the very experience that is being described. This is the problem in indirect knowledge. Because he was not there at that time, the son cannot have the same knowledge as the father. Similarly, Kṛṣṇa says, all these devas do not know my glories totally because I am the cause of all these devas and maharṣis.

The creation is presented in the *śruti* as coming about in various ways. Straight away, *yugapat*, everything comes simultaneously from Bhagavān. Or it comes in this order – First *ākāśa*, then *vāyu*, *agni*... And afterwards *sthūla-bhūta*s, the gross elements. An order is pointed out here. Or first comes *hiraṇyagarbha* and afterwards creates everything. There are many modes of creation mentioned in the *śāstra*. But any way you take it, I am the cause, *aham ādiḥ*. In that there is no option at all. Whichever way you look at it, I am at the beginning. Since I am the *ādi*, the cause of both the devas and *maharṣi*s, what can they know about me? Everything they know was taught by me and all that I know they cannot know.

Here Bhagavān is pointing out that he is the most qualified to talk about his own *vibhūti*, glory.

The *maharṣi*s are all human beings. Even though they are endowed with great powers, they are only *jīva*s, mortals. So, are the *deva*s. That is why all of them cannot know my glory. *Prabhava* usually means creation but in keeping with the subject matter of the present chapter, Śaṅkara explains that it refers to the total *śakti*, glory of Bhagavān. They do not know my glories totally because they all have limited knowledge. They may be *deva*s who know a lot more than the mortals here, and the *ṛṣi*s definitely know a lot more than any other mortal. But from the standpoint of *sarvajñatva,* omniscience, all of them are *kiñcijjña*s, of limited knowledge. That is why they cannot know my glories totally, muchless can they talk about them.

Only I am qualified to talk about them. This is called *praśaṁsā,* praise, of the subject matter. What I am going to tell you, only I am qualified to talk of. Thus, Lord Kṛṣṇa introduces himself as Īśvara here. Whether Kṛṣṇa presents himself as *īśvara-avatāra* or Vyāsa presents him as Īśvara, it does not really matter to us. Kṛṣṇa is Īśvara. So, the dialogue here is between Īśvara and *jīva,* Kṛṣṇa and Arjuna.

Who is the one who says he is omniscient?

When this statement is made by Kṛṣṇa, we look upon him as Īśvara. There is no problem in that. But a question arises here. By whom is this statement – I am *sarvajña,* the one who knows everything and therefore, I am going to tell you everything – made? Is it by *sarvajña, sat-cit-ānanda-ātmā,* or is it by the *pramātā,* the knower?

The one who knows is called *pramātā.* When you read this and understand you become the *pramātā* and what is understood becomes the *prameya.* The understanding itself is called *pramā* and the means of understanding, the *pramāṇa.* So, there is a doubt here as to whether the *sarvajña* is *pramātā* or *sat-cit-ānanda-ātmā*. Because in order to be *sarvajña*, you must necessarily have something more namely, an *upādhi* apart from *sat-cit-ānanda-ātmā*, which is knowledge as such, pure consciousness. In that way every *ātmā* is *sarvajña*. But that is not the *sarvajñatva* that is being talked about here. Here when Kṛṣṇa says he knows 'everything,' that requires the knowledge of all the details of *mithyā-jagat*. For that, something else, an *upādhi*, is required. Without that there is no knowledge possible.

And again, he not only said, 'I know,' but also said, 'I am going to tell you in detail.' Having the status of being a speaker and also an all-knowledge person is not possible for *sat-cit-ānanda-ātmā* which does not undergo any change. Omniscience with the knowledge of all the details and being a speaker are not applicable at all to pure *sat-cit-ānanda-ātmā*. Therefore, the one who says this, is not just *sat-cit-ānanda-ātmā*.

Then who is it that knows and speaks? Only the *pramātā*, the knower can know and therefore, can talk. But if you take Lord Kṛṣṇa as a *pramātā*, a knower, then you would be attributing *jīvatva* to him. This is because generally, every knower is a *jīva*. If Kṛṣṇa is also a *jīva* he cannot be omniscient. If he is not omniscient, he would not be qualified to talk about Īśvara's glory. Therefore, the *pramātā* as we know, cannot be the *sarvajña*.

If neither *sat-cit-ānanda-ātmā* nor *pramātā* can be *sarvajña* then who is *sarvajña*? There are two forms for any *jīva* whether it is a *deva*, a human being, or a worm. One is called the *vāstava-rūpa*, what is essentially true. It is not negatable at all. The other is called the *ādhyāsika-rūpa*, a status or role that is assumed, that is superimposed upon *ātmā*. Like an actor who has an essential personality and, at the same time, a role that he plays. Similarly, every *jīva* has a superimposed form and an essential one. This is also true for Īśvara.

Between *jīva* and Īśvara, there is no distinction at all in reality, that is, there is no *vāstavika* difference. Both are essentially *sat-cit-ānanda*. Even the *svarūpa* of a worm is *sat-cit-ānanda*. The *vāstava-rūpa* of any creature – whether a *deva*, a *gandharva* or a *yakṣa*, a human being or a crow – is one and the same *sat-cit-ānanda*. There is no difference whatsoever. When the Lord says *aham* and when the *jīva* says *aham*, that *aham* is one and the same *sat-cit-ānanda*.

Whereas the other form, *ādhyāsika-rūpa*, has the status of being a knower, doer, and so on. It is with reference to this *ādhyāsika-rūpa* that there is a seeming difference between *jīva* and Īśvara. When you bring in the knower, you bring in your *buddhi*, your intellect, the *upādhi* that makes *sat-cit-ānanda-ātmā* to seemingly gain the status of being a *pramātā*.

A *jīva*, to be a knower, must identify with the *buddhi*. So, the *buddhi* determines the incidental status, *ādhyāsika-rūpa* which is superimposed upon *ātmā* and called a knower. But it is not real. So, in the status of being a knower, there is a seeming difference between Īśvara and *jīva*. Even between two *jīva*s there is a seeming difference. The *ātmā* of one person and another are 'both' *sat-cit-ānanda*. But in the *buddhi* there is definitely a difference. So, in the status of being a knower, there is a difference between any two *jīva*s. When a *jīva* is *sat-cit-ānanda*, how does he become a knower? It is only due to the *upādhi*. From the empirical standpoint, he is seer, hearer, thinker, doer and so on. Similarly, with reference to the *vyāvahārika-sṛṣṭi*, empirical creation, Īśvara is also a *pramātā*. Just like a *jīva*, due to the *upādhi* alone, he is a *pramātā*.

There is gradation of knowledge, which is why among individuals, one has knowledge of law while another knows medicine. So a lawyer has to go to a doctor and a doctor to a lawyer. They are both of limited knowledge. What the lawyer knows the doctor does not know, and what the doctor knows, the lawyer does not know.

Now, what about Īśvara? You cannot say what the *jīva* knows, Īśvara does not know. The situation is somewhat like that of a teacher and student. The teacher knows what the student knows, but all that the teacher knows, the student does not. While the *jīva* is *kiñcijjña*, limited in knowledge, Īśvara is *sarvajña*, all-knowledge. Only in that sense can we say that there is gradation of knowledge.

Upādhi accounts for gradation in knowledge

A *jīva* is a *kiñcijjña* because he has *avidyā-upādhi* that seemingly limits the *ātmā*. Whereas Īśvara has an *upādhi*, called *māyā*, which does not limit. On the other hand, it makes *ātmā* omniscient and the cause of the world.

Then, in the expressed form, the *jīva* has a given *buddhi* with which he can know a few things. But Īśvara, through *māyā-upādhi* is *sarvajña*. The *āvaraṇa-śakti*, concealing power, of *māyā* affects the *jīva*. Therefore, he cannot know everything.

Whereas for Īśvara, that *āvaraṇa* does not exist. There is only the capacity to create. Thus, the very *māyā*, which keeps the *jīva* under its spell, becomes a glory for Īśvara. That is the first *vibhūti*. *Māyā* itself becomes the *vibhūti* for Parameśvara, who is not different from *sat-cit-ānanda-ātmā*.

The *buddhi* is limited because it has a location. It operates in a *sthūla-upādhi* depending upon brain cells and so on. Whereas *māyā* is not limited at all because it is the cause of everything.

How do you know this? It is established by the *śāstra*. Therefore, the one who is in the form of Kṛṣṇa is conditioned by *māyā-upādhi*. By his own words in the fourth chapter, Lord Kṛṣṇa presents himself as Īśvara, or Vyāsa presents him as Īśvara.

This being so, the *pramātā*, knower, who is conditioned by the physical body recognised as Kṛṣṇa, has *māyā* as his *upādhi*. Keeping the *māyā* under control, a particular form is born. Since he is an *avatāra*, he is not forced into this birth by the strength of his own *karma*. The assumption of a body is at the will of Īśvara. It is voluntary. And for him there is omniscience, but the gods like Indra are limited in knowledge. Therefore, the devas he talked about in the previous verse, do not know about his glory. They are all *jīva*s enjoying their own limited *buddhi*s; so their knowledge will only be limited.

From the standpoint of *upādhi*, the *jīva* is a *kiñcijjña*, and Īśvara is *sarvajña*. *Sat-cit-ānanda-ātmā* obtaining in a given *upādhi* is *pramātā*, the knower. *Ātmā* alone is called *pramātā*, and not the *upādhi*, that is, not the *buddhi*. The same *sat-cit-ānanda-ātmā* with the *māyā-upādhi* becomes Īśvara, *pramātā* who is *sarvajña*. Viewed from the standpoint of the *upādhi*, the identity between *jīva* and Īśvara is not possible. But the *pramātā* is not real; it is *ādhyāsika*, *mithyā*. Although there seems to be a difference, essentially there is no difference. In reality, the *jīva* is *sat-cit-ānanda-ātmā*, pure consciousness, that is one, non-dual, and so is Īśvara. This identity is revealed by the *mahā-vākya*, *tat tvam asi*.

This relationship between Īśvara and *jīva* is like that of a wave and the ocean. If the wave is told that it is in reality the ocean, it will ask, 'How can I be the ocean? The ocean was there before I was born.' Then the wave realises the implied meaning of 'you' is water and the immediate meaning is wave. Wave and ocean are purely *nāma-rūpa-upādhi*. There is no wave or ocean but merely certain form for which a name is given. On analysis you find both ocean and wave are water. That alone counts. There is no real difference. If you count names and forms, in the ocean there are many waves, breakers, and so on. Now count water and see if there is any additional wave or ocean; all that is there is water. This is the knowledge of non-duality.

Only in the body of Kṛṣṇa is the consciousness conditioned by *māyā*. In our physical bodies, it is the same consciousness conditioned by ignorance, *buddhi*, etc. How do we distinguish this? Kṛṣṇa has a body and so does Arjuna. Arjuna's *ātmā* is *caitanya* and Kṛṣṇa's *ātmā* is also *caitanya*. His *caitanya* is conditioned by his body, mind and senses and our *caitanya* is conditioned by our body, mind and senses. How can we say our *caitanya* is conditioned by ignorance and his is conditioned by *māyā*? Only from the standpoint of limited knowledge, *kiñcijjñatva*, and omniscience, *sarvajñatva*. He knows 'everything' and we do not. There is nothing unknown to him whereas everything is unknown to us except the little we know. And, Kṛṣṇa is talking here about things that a man of limited knowledge cannot talk about at all.

As long as there is *vyavahāra*, empirical life, *jīva* is *jīva* and Īśvara is Īśvara. As *pramātā*s, knowers, there is no identity between *jīva*s, including the *deva*s like Indra and Varuṇa. But from the standpoint of *paramātmā*, there is no difference whatsoever between them as well as between *jīva* and Īśvara.

Even though Īśvara is the *pramātā*, knower, he has *sarvajñatva*, omniscience. Therefore, he can say, 'Even the *ṛṣi*s and the *deva*s do not know what I am going to tell you.' Being omniscient, it is proper for Kṛṣṇa to say so. Even the *deva*s and the *maharṣi*s do not know me because I am the cause of everyone of them and am *sarvajña* while everyone else is *alpajña*.

Now Bhagavān describes himself as the one without birth and as the cause of everything and says that one who knows him in this way gains *mokṣa*.

Verse 3

Bhagavān as the cause of everything

योमामजमनादिं च वेत्ति लोकमहेश्वरम् ।
असम्मूढः स मर्त्येषु सर्वपापैः प्रमुच्यते ॥ ३ ॥

yo mām ajam anādiṁ ca vetti lokamaheśvaram
asammūḍhaḥ sa martyeṣu sarvapāpaiḥ pramucyate (3)

yaḥ – the one who; *mām* – me; *ajam* – who is unborn (not an effect); *anādiṁ ca* – and beginningless (not a cause); *loka-maheśvaram* – who is the limitless Lord of the world; *vetti* – knows; *saḥ martyeṣu* – he amomg the mortals; *asammūḍhaḥ* – being no longer deluded; *sarva-pāpaiḥ pramucyate* – is released from all *pāpas*

> The one who knows me as unborn (not an effect), beginningless (not a cause), and the limitless Lord of the world, he among the mortals, being no longer deluded, is released from all *papas*.

Previously Bhagavān said, 'I am the cause for all the *devas* and the *maharṣis*.' For the *ātmā* of a *deva* or a *maharṣi* he is not the cause because *ātmā* is he. It is for the *upādhi*, because of which you call this *jīva* a *maharṣi* or this one a *deva*, a human being or an animal. For all the *upādhis* meaning body, mind and sense complexes, Īśvara the cause, *ādi*. Creation is only for the *upādhi*.

Because I am the cause of everything, there is no cause for me. Therefore, *aham ajaḥ*, I am unborn. Why? Because, I have no cause, *anādi*. Otherwise *aja* and *anādi* both have same meaning. *Anādi* means the one who has no beginning and is therefore, not born. So, why these two words? I am not born, *aja*, because I have no beginning, *anādi*, meaning no cause. Therefore, the cause for not being born, *ajatva* is *anāditva*, having no cause.

Another way of looking at this is that *aja*, the one who is not born, that is, one who is not an effect. And *anādi* means the one who has no cause, that is, he himself is the cause of everything.

As he is the cause of everything, even of *deva*s and *maharṣis*, there is none other to be the cause of Īśvara. And at the same time he is not born, that is, not an effect.

Śaṅkara takes it this way because Bhagavān has been saying that he is the cause of everything. In this context it is proper to take it this way. *Loka-maheśvara,* the one who is the Lord of all people and who is limitless. Śaṅkara says that he is the one who is not subject to birth, who is not the waker, dreamer, or deep sleeper. He is neither the physical world nor the subtle or causal world. He is the one who is the *adhiṣṭhāna,* basis of all three and the truth of all three, called *turīya*. And he is free from ignorance and its product; he is the Lord, the cause of everything.

The one who recognises Bhagavān as everything is free from delusion

The one who recognises this is an *asammūḍha,* free from delusion. Someone who is deluded takes *sat-cit-ānanda-ātmā,* the cause of everything, as a product. What is free from form is taken as something with a form. What is timeless is taken as subject to time. In other words, *ātmā* is taken as *anātmā*. When you say I am tall, short and so on, the tall or short body is taken as *ātmā*. Upon *ātmā* you superimpose the body, and upon the body you superimpose *ātmā*. The result is a typical *saṁsārī*. Such a person is called *sammūḍha*. *Asammūḍha* means the one who is free from this delusion.

Saḥ martyeṣu asammūḍhaḥ, he is not deluded even though he is one among the mortals; you cannot take him to be a mortal anymore. Such a person is released, *pramucyate*. He is liberated; he gains *mokṣa*.

And *sarvapāpaiḥ*, in terms of all *pāpa*s he is released. There are two types of *pāpa*. One is deliberate, well thought out, the other is a wrong done because of indifference or carelessness. You are supposed to be careful in not hurting etc. If you are not, that carelessness produces *pāpa*. There was a person who was assigned to bring banana leaves for a wedding feast. He had to go some ten miles to get them but that was his job. When the marriage is over, it is very important that all the guests eat and go. Everybody is ready to eat and there are no banana leaves. This person had not brought the banana leaves. When the bride's father asked him what happened to them, he said, 'Oh, it is my mistake. I accept my mistake.' Accepting the mistake cannot solve the problem. When something is to be done, it is to be done. There is no use not doing it and then owning up the mistake. It is an omission due to carelessness. You are supposed to be alert and careful. Even if you unconsciously step on an insect while walking, this is non-deliberate *pāpa*. All these *pāpa*s are neutralised by doing your *nitya-karma*, daily prayers.

Because Bhagavān has said *sarva,* all *pāpa*, it includes *puṇya* also. *Puṇya* is also bondage. It is a golden shackle, binding him to experience some better situation. How is he liberated from all *pāpa*s? Because he is no longer a *kartā*. He recognises *ātmā*, which was always *akartā*, a non doer, but taken as the doer. Because of that, he subjected himself to the various *puṇya-pāpa-karma*s.

Now, recognising the fact that *ātmā* is *akartā*, he is released from *puṇya* and *pāpa*. This is *mokṣa*. The *prārabdha-karma* is there for the time being, but he will be released from that also in time.

Verses 4&5

Bhagavān as the cause of the qualities in living beings

Further, Bhagavān says, 'I am the Lord of all beings because...'

बुद्धिर्ज्ञानमसम्मोहः क्षमा सत्यं दमः शमः ।
सुखं दुःखं भवोऽभावो भयं चाभयमेव च ॥ ४ ॥

अहिंसा समता तुष्टिः तपो दानं यशोऽयशः ।
भवन्ति भावा भूतानां मत्त एव पृथग्विधाः ॥ ५ ॥

buddhirjñānam asammohaḥ kṣamā satyaṁ damaḥ śamaḥ
sukhaṁ duḥkhaṁ bhavo'bhāvo bhayaṁ cābhayameva ca (4)

ahiṁsā samatā tuṣṭiḥ tapo dānaṁ yaśo'yaśaḥ
bhavanti bhāvā bhūtānāṁ matta eva pṛthagvidhāḥ (5)

buddhiḥ – the capacity to understand; *jñānam* – knowledge; *asammohaḥ* – freedom from delusion; *kṣamā* – accommodation; *satyam* – truthfulness; *damaḥ* – restraint in behaviour; *śamaḥ* – mastery over the ways of thinking; *sukham* – pleasure; *duḥkham* – pain; *bhavaḥ* – creation; *abhāvaḥ* – destruction; *bhayam* – fear; *ca abhayam* – and fearlessness; *eva ca* – and further; *ahiṁsā* – not hurting; *samatā* – equanimity; *tuṣṭiḥ* – contentment; *tapaḥ* – religious discipline; *dānam* – charity; *yaśaḥ* – fame; *ayaśaḥ* –

ill-fame; *pṛthag-vidhāḥ* – these many different; *bhāvāḥ* – dispositions (and things); *bhūtānām* – of living beings; *mattaḥ eva bhavanti* – are all from me alone

> The capacity to understand, knowledge, freedom from delusion, accommodation, truthfulness, restraint in behaviour, mastery over the ways of thinking, pleasure, pain, creation, destruction, fear, and fearlessness, and further…
>
> …not hurting, equanimity, contentment, religious discipline, charity, fame, ill-fame – these different dispositions (and things) of living beings – are all from me alone.

Here Bhagavān says, *mattaḥ eva*, all these are only from me. What are they? He tells them one by one, so that nothing is left out. This is why the chapter is called *vibhūti-yoga*. Any glory that you see, any fame in the creation belongs to me. If there is any brilliance or accomplishment in a given person, that belongs to me. If anything is strikingly beautiful, that beauty belongs to me. In the *Purāṇa*s we learn that certain rivers are more sacred than others. That sanctity is only because of me. Therefore, whenever you worship or respect something extraordinary, that respect and worship go only to me because everything is born of me.

Buddhi and *jñāna* both have the same meaning; so, we have to make a distinction here. Śaṅkara says, *buddhi* is the capacity of the *antaḥ-karaṇa* to reveal subtle things, things not available for perception at all. When you say something is beautiful, that beauty is not available for mere sense perception. Yet it is something that you appreciate. Any kind of enjoyment or anything inferentially arrived at is also *sūkṣma,* subtle. Though not available for perception, yet you appreciate its existence. The capacity to reveal such things belongs to the *buddhi.* The one who has that power is called *buddhimān.* He may be a scientist or a musician, but you call him *buddhimān.* He has the capacity to see things that are subtle in nature.

Then, its product is *jñāna.* Those who have *buddhi* gain knowledge of the meaning of the words like *ātmā* and so on. It is called *jñāna,* knowledge. Because the object is there, knowledge of it is possible. That object is born of me. And knowledge is born of me because being *sarvajña,* all-knowledge is with me. Any time you come to know something, it has come from me. Since omniscience is already there, you do not produce any knowledge, you only remove the ignorance with reference to a given object. Thus, knowledge is 'born.' You may think that you have produced certain knowledge. Bhagavān says, 'No, it has come from me.' The very faculty of knowing is from me and the knowledge itself is born of me. If you see this, your *ahaṅkāra* gets diminished.

Asammoha is freedom from delusion. Whenever an object appears in front of you, if it is known as it is, without any distortion, it means that you pursue the knowledge with discrimination. This is called *asammoha.* If you come to a hurried conclusion without discrimination, it is called *sammoha.* You see a rope and you jump thinking it is a snake. This is *sammoha.* *Asammoha* is deliberately, without hurrying, looking into things and understanding them as they should be understood. You keep an open mind and explore and understand; then there is *asammoha*.

You should know that the senses, the mind, etc., can deceive. They are capable of distortion and do not really present objects as they are. Your perception can be born of your own fear and anxiety and so on. You can even project things that are not there at all. Therefore, proper understanding is very important. It will make you alert. That *asammoha* is also from me, Bhagavān says.

Kṣamā – Suppose you are scolded by somebody or are subjected to verbal or physical abuse, you will not be affected by it if you have *kṣamā*. *Kṣamā* is a state of mind in which you do not internalise those things. If someone is angry, you have to deal with his anger. But if, in the process, you become angry, you are internalising the problem. Not internalising is *kṣamā*. If somebody is angry, you confine his anger to him. Try to understand why he is angry and do what has to be done. That is dealing with it. The mind that does not undergo any internalisation in situations, which are not very pleasant is said to have *kṣamā*.

Satyam – Here Śaṅkara gives a definition of *satya*.[1] Here he has taken the word *satya*, not as an ontological word talking

---

[1] सत्यम् – यथादृष्टस्य यथाश्रुतस्य च आत्मानुभवस्य परबुद्धि-संक्रान्तये तथैव उच्चार्यमाणा वाक् सत्यम् उच्यते ।

Satyam – yathādṛṣṭasya yathāśrutasya ca ātmānubhavasya parabuddhi-saṅkrāntaye tathaiva uccāryamāṇā vāk satyam ucyate.

about the reality of something, but as referring to the value of truthfulness in the spoken word. The spoken word should be true to something that is seen or heard or experienced by you. And in that manner, that is, exactly as it was seen or heard, it should be conveyed to another mind in order to make the other mind understand it exactly as you understood. Something was heard or seen or experienced by you. Therefore, you can talk about it. Not that you should go about talking to others about everything. It is not necessary. But when you want to, please say it honestly. As it was experienced directly through your own sense organs or as it was reported to you by somebody else or even experienced by you subjectively, in the same manner it is to be spoken of, for the purpose of making another person understand. That is called *satya*.

All these belong to an order, a moral order, uncreated by the individual. It is all Bhagavān's creation. *Satya, dama, śama,* are all Bhagavān's creation and when we have them, we are in harmony with the creation and with Bhagavān. So, what we speak is what we know. *Satyaṁ vada*, be truthful. Then it should also be pleasing, *priyaṁ vada*. We make a prayer for this, *jihvā me madhumattamā*, let there be honey on my tongue. May I speak in a way that pleases, that does not hurt anyone.

Only a teacher can say hurtful words, nobody else. He has to say the truth and when he does, it is not always very pleasant. But even he has to say it in a way that does not frighten the person away. Though he sometimes has to say something unpleasant he has to say it in a pleasant way. Therefore, be truthful, but do not be indifferent to your discretion. All these, Bhagavān says, emanate from him alone.

Dama is discipline with reference to external organs. It is control at the level of expression, a capacity not to be carried away by an action, which has already arisen in your mind. Having arisen, it can be carried out either perceptually or by an organ of action. The capacity to refrain from that is called *dama*.

Śama, a mastery over the very ways of thinking. You do not yield to certain patterns of thinking, which you know are harmful or useless. You get certain space because of which you are able to have a mastery over the ways of thinking. This is called *śama*. When *śama* is there you do not need to practise *dama* because it follows automatically. There is no problem. But in the absence of *śama*, you do require *dama*.

Sukha, inner pleasure or happiness. Even *sukha,* Bhagavān says, is born of me. It means there is nothing you can claim as your own. These are desirable things and they are all from me alone.

Even undesirable things are from me, he is going to say later. But here he emphasises desirable things because undesirable things do not cause a problem in terms of inflating your ego. But Bhagavān makes it clear that whenever you get desirable things, which can cause pride, this pride is meaningless. This is what he wants to prove. Wherever there is something praiseworthy, the source of that is me. Therefore, you cannot be proud about it. In one form or another the *ahaṅkāra* wants to survive. So, Bhagavān says that whatever you accomplish, the accomplishment belongs to me. It is my glory, my fame. As an individual there is no fame unless you say, 'I am the

Lord.' Then you are not an individual. You can say, 'Everything is mine.' But purely at the individual level you have to recognise all glories or accomplishments as *vibhūti*s of Īśvara.

Duḥkha, affliction, Bhagavān says, is also from me. Any pain is according to the law of *karma*, which is myself. And, therefore, it also comes from me.

Bhāva, creation. Any creation is from me. Even though you may be the father of a child and may say the child is born of you, in fact, it is born of me, Bhagavān says. I saw a cartoon of Bhagavān as a kid trying to make a chicken. He had all the genes in a test tube; then the tube broke and all the genes got scattered everywhere. In the cartoon they show him with a question mark! He is God and he is wondering what to do! It is very revealing. Putting together all these genes to make a chicken is not an ordinary thing. So, if anybody thinks that I am the doer, it is meaningless. The hen can think she created the chick, the rooster can say he is the author. But Bhagavān says, 'I am the author.' Even a creation within the creation is from Bhagavān. That is the idea.

Abhāva has different meanings. The prefix '*a*' can be used in the sense of *abhāvārtha*, total absence, *alpārtha*, inadequacy, or *viparyayārtha*, in the sense of opposite. When you say there is no light, it can mean darkness. Or it can be inadequate light. Here Śaṅkara takes it as opposite, *viparyaya*. Why? Because Bhagavān has said *bhāva*, creation. If creation is from Bhagavān, its opposite, destruction takes place because of Īśvara alone. That there is the possibility of destruction is because of me alone.

Destruction means destroying something that is created. There is a law that governs life and because of that law, life continues. Because of the same law, life goes. The law is Bhagavān and that is why he says, 'Destruction is also from me.'

'*Bhaya*, fear, is also from me,' Bhagavān says. Because, the source of fear is the vastness of the creation, and its irrevocability. Certain things such as death and time are irrevocable, you can never reverse them, and that inevitability causes fear. Death and time are also Bhagavān. So, all *bhaya* is caused by him. You can avoid this *bhaya* if you hold on to Īśvara but if you think you are going to take care of things, *bhaya* comes. As long as an individual thinks that he is an individual, separate from everything else, there will be fear. Īśvara himself becomes *bhaya-kāraṇa*, the source of fear.

The *Taittirīyopaniṣad* says, *vāyu*, air, moves because of fear of Īśvara, and the sun rises because of this fear alone; in other words, because of Īśvara's mandate. Agni and Indra both do their jobs; Agni keeps burning and Indra rules the heaven all because of Īśvara's mandate. Even Lord of Death is on the move because of Īśvara.[2]

Abhaya, fearlessness. The same Īśvara, if you do not look upon him as separate, is *abhaya-kāraṇa*, the very source of fearlessness. Both fear and fearlessness are from Īśvara. If Īśvara is not known to you, the whole world is separate from you

---

[2] भीषास्माद्वातः पवते भीषोदेति सूर्यः भीषास्माद् अग्निश्चेन्द्रश्च मृत्युर्धावति पञ्चम इति। (तैत्तिरीयोपैषद् २.८.१)

bhīṣāsmād vātaḥ pavate bhīṣodeti sūryaḥ bhīṣāsmād agniścendraśca mṛtyurdhāvati pañcama iti (*Taittirīyopaiṣad* 2.8.1) because to know Īśvara is to know everything is Īśvara. If this is not known, the fear will start from cockroaches. If it is known, there is no fear at all.

Ahiṁsā, not hurting another living being deliberately. How do you know *ahiṁsā* is from Īśvara? Is it revealed in a scripture? Otherwise, how can you prove that anything came from Īśvara? *Ahiṁsā* does not need to be revealed because it is known to us. It is revealed already by common sense. The law is there. We all know. We do not want to get hurt nor do we see anyone else wanting to get hurt. Therefore, *ahiṁsā* exists as an integral part of the moral order. The moral order is part of the creation. It does not need to be mandated by Īśvara in some scripture. If such a thing happens to be there, it is universal. If it is universal, it is not man-made; it is from Īśvara. Therefore, Bhagavān says, *ahiṁsā* is from me.

They are all from 'me.' And they are also good for gaining 'me,' because when you follow them, you are in harmony with the universal order that is 'me.'

Samatā, sameness of mind whether you get something desirable or undesirable. *Tuṣṭi,* contentment. When you gain something you have a sense of satisfaction. A gain does not necessarily leave you with a sense of satisfaction. It can be a source for greed. The more you get, the more you want. That sense of *alam,* having enough, is called *tuṣṭi,* contentment with what you have. If contentment is there, you become the master of any desire you have. A desire that comes out of contentment is a luxury. It becomes your endowment. Because you are capable of desiring, you desire. It is not that you desire in order to be content. You have a contentment out of which desires come, so that all activities become expressions of Īśvara. 'Contentment,' Bhagavān says 'is born of me.' That particular frame of mind called contentment is because of the predominance of *sattva*. And *sattva* is *māyā*, which is of Īśvara. Therefore, contentment is from me alone.

Tapas refers to religious austerities. Śaṅkara says, that disciplining the body backed by control of the sense organs is called *tapas*. Suppose you find that things are not going according to your will because of your own limitations and find yourself carried away by various situations, then you decide you are going to take charge of your life by undergoing a religious discipline. That is what is called *tapas*. Any difficulty you willingly undergo for the purpose of some other accomplishment is called *tapas*. But it should be for *antaḥ-karaṇa-śuddhi* or *antaḥ-karaṇa-naiścalya*, or any other spiritual or religious goal. Any pain you undergo for that purpose becomes *tapas*.

That also, Bhagavān says, is from me, because various disciplines bring about certain definite results. That law, which connects the means to the result, is from me. When you strike a matchstick, there is flame. Īśvara says it is from me. Striking the matchstick is *sādhana* and the flame that results is *sādhya*. This law is from me; it is me. *Tapas* is *sādhana*, the result is the *sādhya*. And there is invariability in the result; if you do this *tapas* you get this result. It means there is a *sādhana sādhya* connection. Therefore, it is from Īśvara.

Dāna means giving. Śaṅkara says, *dāna*, giving should be according to your capacity. This is a very interesting qualification.

You should not cross your limit. You give, up to your limit but if you cross it, somebody else has to give you *dāna*. To give to your limit, no further, is called *dāna*. This capacity to do *dāna* is definitely from Īśvara. It is not something everyone can do. Only those who can give, give in charity. Charity requires certain culture, certain maturity and humility. That disposition to give is a particular *puṇya*. To give, you have to have that. Thus, people who can give, keep giving. There are some people who cannot give at all. There are still others who give and complain about it all the time. And then there are people who can give and forget about it. This is *dāna*. There is also another important factor involved in *dāna* – that is the recipient, *pātra*, the one to whom you are giving. You must make sure that the recipient is worthy. Śaṅkara says that it should be proper distribution, *sama-vibhāga*. Propriety in distribution implies selection of the recipient.

Yaśas means fame. Śaṅkara says fame born of *dharma*, *dharma-nimitta-kīrti* is the real fame. This is also from Īśvara. How can one say Īśvara gives fame? If a person has fame, why is he famous? Suppose it is because he did a lot of charity and people recognise him as a good and great man. Now the recognition is because of the good he has done. It means there is such a thing as good, which is recognised universally. That good is Bhagavān. That is law, the universal law. So, this person is good to all and therefore he becomes famous. But suppose no one cares for what he or she did; they think it is all silly. Then one will not become famous; instead, one will be considered an idiot. And again, suppose one's charity is in the form of going to New York city and distributing cocaine.

Everyday the person buys one hundred thousand dollars worth of cocaine and distributes it. He may become popular among certain people. But that is not the *kīrti* meant here, which is why Śaṅkara says *dharma-nimitta-kīrti*. But notoriety is also from Bhagavān.

Ayaśas means ill-fame. Here the particle '*a*' is used in the sense of opposite, *viparyaya*. It is not anonymity here, though that also is from Bhagavān. Śaṅkara says that it is fame born of improper action, *adharma-nimitta-kīrti*. Like Al Capone;[3] he is also famous for doing things that are not proper. Why do people look upon him as one who did improper things? Because there is such a thing as propriety, which is created by Īśvara. And naturally, there is the other side of the coin, impropriety. Whoever follows that becomes notoriously popular.

All these various things that Bhagavān has mentioned so far are connected to living beings, *bhūtānāṁ bhāvaḥ*. And they are *pṛthagvidhāḥ*, many and varied. Bhagavān says, 'All these many and varied things connected to living beings are from me alone.'

How is it that they are from Bhagavān? Does he arbitrarily distribute them? No. Śaṅkara says, *svakarma-anurūpeṇa*, all these take place according to one's own *karma*, one's own efforts. And that law of *karma* is from me. So, in that form, everything is from me alone. Śaṅkara introduces this one word to explain that in spite of the disparity we see in *karma*, there is no

---

[3] Capone, Al (1899-1947), gangster of the prohibition era.

partiality on the part of Bhagavān. It is all *svakarma-anurūpeṇa,* according to one's own *karma* which includes both present effort and past *karma.* Together they are the basis for all these various things, *bhāvas*. They do not come from us, but from Īśvara. Further...

Verse 6

Bhagavān as the cause of the sages and manus

महर्षयः सप्त पूर्वे चत्वारो मनवस्तथा ।
मद्भावा मानसा जाता येषां लोक इमाः प्रजाः ॥ ६ ॥

maharṣayaḥ sapta pūrve catvāro manavastathā
madbhāvā mānasā jātā yeṣāṁ loka imāḥ prajāḥ (6)

maharṣayaḥ sapta – the seven *ṛṣis*; *pūrve* – of yore; *catvāraḥ manavaḥ* – the four *manus*; *tathā* – as well as; *madbhāvāḥ* – those whose minds are resolved in me; *mānasāḥ jātāḥ* – born of (my) mind; *yeṣām* – of these; *imāḥ prajāḥ* – are all these living beings; *loke* – in the world

The seven *ṛṣi*s of yore as well as the four *manu*s who have their minds resolved in me, are born of my mind, and of whom are all these living beings in the world.

Pūrve means people who lived in the remote past, long, long ago. At the beginning of the creation in a particular cycle, there were seven *maharṣi*s – Marīci, Aṅgiras, Atri, Pulastya, Vasiṣṭha, Pulaha and Kratu.[4]

---

4 This is the generally accepted list of the *saptarṣi*s. But at some places the name Bhṛgu replaces that of Aṅgiras. And again the names of *saptarṣis* varies with each Manvantara.

According to the *purāṇa*s there are 14 *manus*[5] and we are now under the rule of the Manu called *vaivasvata*.[6] In chapter 4 of the *Gītā*, Bhagavān says, this *yoga* I taught to Vivasvān. His son is called Vaivasvata-Manu. In each *manvantara* Manu's period, only four of them have the status of being the ones that create the people, *prajā*. And because of that reason they are special and therefore, Bhagavān mentions them. And in the present *manvantara* those four are Brahma-sāvarṇi, Rudra-sāvarṇi, Dharma-sāvarṇi, and Dakṣa-sāvarṇi. All of them, and the seven *ṛṣi*s, Bhagavān says, are *madbhāvāḥ*.

Madbhāvāḥ, Śaṅkara says, are those whose *bhāvana*, disposition or mind, is resolved in me, Bhagavān. It means they have become one with me, being enlightened people. And they are endowed with the powers of Viṣṇu, meaning Īśvara.

Mānasāḥ jātāḥ, they are all born by mind alone. They are directly born by Īśvara's mere *saṅkalpa*. These *catvāraḥ mānavaḥ* and *sapta-maharṣayaḥ* are the direct children of Īśvara according to the *purāṇa*s. What we see in the *purāṇa*s is confirmed by Bhagavān Kṛṣṇa here.

Yeṣāṁ loke imāḥ prajāḥ, of these are all the living beings in the world. First, the *manu*s were created and then the *ṛṣi*s. After the *ṛṣi*s, the sons of *ṛṣi*s. From them are born, all the living

---

[5] The 14 Manus are – Svāyambhuva, Svārociṣa, Uttama, Tāmasa, Raivata, Cākṣusa, Vaivasvata, Sāvarṇi, Dakṣa-sāvarṇi, Brahma-sāvarṇi, Dharma-sāvarṇi, Rudra-sāvarṇi, Raucyadeva-sāvarṇi and Indra-sāvarṇi.

[6] The period of each Manu's rule is one-fourteenth of a day of Brahma, 4,320,000 human years; so, one day of Brahma consists of 14 Manu-periods. The period of each Manu is divided into four sub-periods, each under different rule.

beings in this world, under the mandate of *Manu*, which is why human beings are called *mānavāḥ*. And they are also descendants of *ṛṣi*s. That is why everyone has a *gotra*. 'All of them,' Bhagavān says, 'are from me.'

Verse 7

The one who knows the glories of Bhagavān is endowed with unshaken vision

एतां विभूतिं योगं च मम यो वेत्ति तत्त्वतः ।
सोऽविकम्पेन योगेन युज्यते नात्र संशयः ॥ ७ ॥

etāṁ vibhūtiṁ yogaṁ ca mama yo vetti tattvataḥ
so'vikampena yogena yujyate nātra saṁśayaḥ (7)

etāṁ mama vibhūtim – this glory of mine; (*mama*) *yogaṁ ca* – and (my) connection with that; *tattvataḥ* – in reality; *yaḥ vetti* – the one who knows; *saḥ* – he; *yujyate* – is endowed; *avikampena yogena* – with unshaken vision; *na atra saṁśayaḥ* – there is no doubt about this

The one who knows, in reality, this glory of mine and my connection with that, he is endowed with unshaken vision. There is no doubt about this.

Vetti tattvataḥ means he knows in reality, as it is. He knows this glory of mine that has been so far told, *etāṁ vibhūtiṁ mama*. *Etāṁ*, Śaṅkara says, gives the sense of what was said so far. *Vibhūti* is what has come from or emanated from Īśvara.

Mama yogam ca, and he knows my association with all of them. He knows not only my glories but also my connection to these *vibhūti*s in reality. How is the Lord connected to his glories? Īśvara is *saccidānanda-svarūpa*. So, what connection can he have? The connection between the glory and Īśvara is exactly the connection between your own *ātmā* and your limited knowledge. The connection is like this – the other is, the one is; the other is not, the one is. This is the connection between *satya* and *mithyā*. Through *māyā* are all the connections. There is no other connection. Only *māyā* connects *paramātmā* and any glory that is manifest. The one who knows that, knows *satya* and *mithyā*. If he knows Īśvara and his glory in reality, he knows what is *satya* and what is *mithyā*, naturally.

Once he knows that, there will be advantages for him at different levels. Simply, accepting Īśvara as the one who is the source of all glories in others and me will free me from a lot of problems. If someone sees a person sing very well and understands that it is Bhagavān's glory, then he cannot be jealous of that person. If he is able to sing well, his own glory will not give him a big ego. He avoids pride, jealousy, hatred, etc. simply by attitude. This attitude brings about certain composure, *antaḥ-karaṇa-śuddhi* and steadiness of mind, *antaḥ-karaṇa-naiścalya*. Then if he comes to know these glories, how they come about and how Īśvara is connected to them, he himself *avikampena yogena yujyate*, is endowed or connected with an unshaken vision.

The clarity of the vision of *ātmā* as Parameśvara, the *samyag-darśana*, Śaṅkara says, is well rooted and steady, *sthira*. The one who recognises me and my glories properly and the connection of me with the glories etc., is endowed with an uninhibited vision, a vision that does not shake. *Yoga* here means the vision. Any other *yoga* will be shaky.

Na atra saṁśayaḥ, there is no doubt in this. If you understand Īśvara, his glories, his connections and so on, properly, that is enough. Then you know yourself. *Īśvara-darśana* is *ātma-darśana*. There is no other *darśana* of Īśvara, which is why it is not merely experiential. To know silence is not enough. That silence has to be understood. Similarly, Īśvara and the connection between Īśvara and *jagat* has to be understood. Understanding Īśvara means understanding the whole *jagat* as Īśvara. You have to understand the whole *jagat*. And if you have to understand the *jagat* as something born of *paramātmā*, *caitanya-ātmā*, then the connection has to be understood properly. If that connection is understood, you understand *satya* and *mithyā*. This is liberation. This *īśvara-darśana*, which is *ātma-darśana* is given here by pointing out the glories.

Bhagavān thus introduces his own chapter, a chapter of his glories, with these verses. Because the word *yoga* is used, we need to clarify the meaning. *Yoga* can be anything. Therefore, Bhagavān gives the meaning in the next verse.

Only knowledge can be unshaken. Appreciation of the Lord as the cause of the world is not enough. The connection must be clear. Does the creator really become a creator? What type of creation is it? All these are to be understood. Only then can you understand Īśvara. The degree of reality enjoyed by the creation is to be understood first. If it is understood, the status of the creator is also very clearly understood. When this is so, a person will be endowed with this unshaken vision.

Verse 8

Nature of this clear vision

अहं सर्वस्य प्रभवो मत्तः सर्वं प्रवर्तते ।
इति मत्वा भजन्ते मां बुधा भावसमन्विताः ॥ ८ ॥

ahaṁ sarvasya prabhavo mattaḥ sarvaṁ pravartate
iti matvā bhajante māṁ budhā bhāvasamanvitāḥ (8)

ahaṁ sarvasya prabhavaḥ – I am the creator of everything; *mattaḥ sarvaṁ pravartate* – because of me everything is sustained; *iti matvā* – thus knowing; *budhāḥ* – the wise men; *bhāva-samanvitāḥ* – endowed with vision; *māṁbhajante* – gain me

I am the creator of everything and because of me everything is sustained. Thus knowing, the wise men endowed with vision gain me.

Ahaṁ sarvasya prabhavaḥ, I am the cause for the creation of everything. *Aham* here means *paraṁ-brahma*, the one who is called Vāsudeva. We have seen the word Vāsudeva before, that in which alone all have their being. Like pots have their being in clay, the *jagat* has its being in the self-existent *sat-vastu*. Everything else depends entirely upon that. And there is only one thing that is self-existent, that is *ātmā*. The self alone is self-existent; everything becomes evident to it. So, what is self-evident is self-existent. Therefore, anything not self-evident cannot be called self-existent. Without my obliging the *vastu* with my perception, inference, and so on, it is self-evident and this self-evident *ātmā* alone is self-existent. It is called Vāsudeva, that in which everything has its being.

Thus, *ahaṁ sarvasya prabhavaḥ*, I am the cause of everything. *Prabhava* means the source of creation; so, I am the cause for the creation of everything.

Somebody may create something, but then, its care may fall to someone else. Like modern parents. They are the cause for the children alright but then somebody else takes care of them. Similarly, Bhagavān may create everything and then appoint somebody else to be in charge of it.

To negate this idea, Bhagavān says, '*mattaḥ sarvaṁ pravartate*, because of me everything is sustained. This *jagat* continues to exist and is sustained by me. A created object sustains itself for a length of time undergoing partial changes and finally a total change, in the form of disappearance. A human body changes partially. The person you saw ten years ago you may now see as bald but you can still recognise him. Later after death, the body disintegrates. So, you find activities of sustenance and disintegration taking place with reference to each and every object. There is no real destruction. There is only disintegration or partial disintegration of a particular form. This is the *jagat* characterised by its sustenance, its changes, and its disintegration. Then there are the results and their enjoyment. This includes the experiences of pleasure and displeasure, the places of enjoyments and activities, which produce *karma-phala*s that provide situations for enjoyment. All these constitute what we call *jagat*. And Bhagavān says, 'I am not only the cause for the coming into being of this creation, I am also the cause for its sustenance. Because of me alone everything exists and behaves in its own way.'

Iti matvā thus knowing, that this whole *jagat* that they encounter is from me alone, *māṁ bhajante budhāḥ*, the wise men gain me, recognise me, know me. Śaṅkara defines the wise men here as *avagata-paramārtha-tattvah*, by whom the truth of everything is understood as nothing but *paramātmā*.

Bhagavān describes these wise men as *bhāva-samanvitāḥ*, those who are endowed with *bhāva*. The word *bhāva* has different meanings. We have to see the context. Here it is vision. What vision? The definite knowledge of the reality in the form of the understanding, 'I am Brahman.' The meaning of the word 'I' is Brahman the limitless, which is *jagat-kāraṇa*. Those who have that clear vision are called *bhāva-samanvitāḥ*.

Māṁ-bhajante, they gain me. They become one with me because between Īśvara and the *jīva*, there is no essential difference. Īśvara is nothing but *paraṁ-brahma*, *jīva* is also *paraṁ-brahma*. This identity they gain. Further…

Verse 9

Those who have this clear vision are one with me

मच्चित्ता मद्गतप्राणा बोधयन्तः परस्परम् ।
कथयन्तश्च मां नित्यं तुष्यन्ति च रमन्ति च ॥ ९ ॥

maccittā madgataprāṇā bodhayantaḥ parasparam
kathayantaśca māṁ nityaṁ tuṣyanti ca ramanti ca (9)

mat-cittāḥ – whose minds are in me; *madgata-prāṇāḥ* – whose living is resolved in me; *bodhayantaḥ parasparam* – mutually teaching each other; *kathayantaḥ ca mām* – and talking about me; *nityam* – always; *tuṣyanti ca* – they are satisfied; *ramanti ca* – and they revel

> Those whose minds are in me, whose living is resolved in me, teaching one another and always talking about me, they are (ever) satisfied and they revel (always).

They know Īśvara as the cause of the creation and the truth of that Īśvara as themselves. Understanding the *kāraṇa-kārya,* cause effect, is the basis of the whole teaching. The effect is inseparable from the cause, which is Brahman. Therefore, the effect is inseparable from Brahman. Because it is inseparable, the effect is *mithyā;* it is only apparent.

Therefore, the entire *jagat* which includes the body-mind-sense complex is a product and is *mithyā*. So, between the cause and the effect, the relationship is very peculiar. The cause is *satya,* that which exists independently, and the other, which is *mithyā* depends upon that independently existent principle. Like pot and clay; like your shirt and its cloth. If you analyse it, the cloth is *mithyā,* the thread is *satya,* the thread is *mithyā,* the fibre is *satya,* fibres are *mithyā,* particles are *satya.* Like this you can go on and on. Then what is *satya*? That which does not depend upon anything else. Is there such a thing? Yes, that is Brahman. Thus through this *kāraṇa-kārya-viveka,* the teaching takes place here.

By knowing that Īśvara is everything, they become one with Īśvara. How is that? This second step is interesting. The first step is knowing Īśvara as the maker and the material cause and therefore, that the effect, the creation is non-separate from him.

This is the knowledge of Īśvara. Knowing it, you come to recognise you are that Īśvara. This is the second step. If Īśvara is everything, your physical body is Īśvara, your mind is Īśvara and your senses are also Īśvara. What is not Īśvara? If everything that is created is Īśvara, perhaps consciousness is not Īśvara because it is not created. You cannot say that because what was there before creation was *sat* alone.

If consciousness is uncreated, that cannot be different from the *sat*, the *svarūpa* of Īśvara. So, *sat* and *cit* are the same. Knowing Īśvara, you become one with Īśvara. This is not an ordinary statement. First it is presented as though something else is the cause. Afterwards, if you analyse the whole thing, it ends up that you are the cause. Your isolation, the separation between the Lord and yourself is simply swallowed in the vision of Īśvara. Therefore, the vision of Īśvara is the vision of yourself, the vision of the whole.

Maccittāḥ – those whose minds are in me, Parameśvara. With their knowledge, the mind naturally is non-separate from *paramātmā* and therefore, cannot go away from *paramātmā*. People often complain that they understand but then their mind goes away. But understanding is never away from the mind. The understanding is that the mind is never away from *ātmā*. That is understanding that nothing is away from Brahman. For those who understand, the mind is never away from me, the whole, because satya is *ātmā*. And it sustains the mind.

Madgataprāṇāḥ – In this expression, the word *prāṇa* is taken to represent all the sense organs. They are all awake to Īśvara.

Therefore, these people are called *madgataprāṇas*. Even though they perceive things distinctly, these wise men see something more. What the eyes see is a form and this form is distinct from every other form. That they see. But then, they see something more because they also appreciate that the object perceived, the perception and the perceiver all have their being in one consciousness, which is self-existent. If there is no ignorance with reference to this fact, one becomes *madgataprāṇa.* Although all the sense activities take place, they are never away from Parameśvara. The perception of the sense organs is not a hindrance to the knowledge of the self. So, being in the world does not in any way hinder the vision of the self. And not going through experiences is not going to bring about the vision. Ignorance is the hindrance, not perception. Those who do not have that hindrance are *maccittāḥ madgataprāṇāḥ*. In other words, Śaṅkara says that even for one second their lives are not away from Īśvara.

Prāṇa is also breathing and therefore can stand for *jīvana,* living. So, *madgataprāṇas* are also those whose living is non-separate from Īśvara. Their life is resolved in Īśvara. It means there is no division of spiritual life and material life for them. Some people have a peculiar philosophy that life has two separate compartments as spiritual and secular. There are no such compartments. Everything is one whole alone.For one who knows, life is non-separate from this vision. Whatever you know about yourself is what you are and if that happens to be the whole, how are you going to be away from it? Do what you will, you cannot be away from it because the one thing you can never be away from, is yourself. You can be away from one object or the other, but never from yourself. Those who understand this clearly are *madgataprāṇas*, *maccittas*.

Ramanti, they revel. How? *Parasparaṁ bodhayantaḥ*, mutually teaching each other. What else can they do? Those who want to learn, they teach. *Māṁ kathayantaḥ ca*, talking about the glories of me, Parameśvara. When do they do this? They do it always, *nityam*.

Kathayantaḥ is different from *bodhayantaḥ*. *Bodhana* implies a class situation or a discussion. *Kathana* is just descriptive. There is no teaching. When you describe the glories of the Lord – his knowledge, his strength and so on, it is called *kathana*. In talking about 'me,' whether teaching or describing, they discover a joy and in that they revel, *ramanti*, and enjoy satisfaction, *tuṣyanti*. Revelling does not require anything but Parameśvara.

He has used two words here, *ramanti* and *tuṣyanti*, which have a similar but slightly different meaning. *Ramanti* is with reference to the external world; so, it involves people here. *Tuṣyanti* is with reference to oneself. They have found satisfaction; so they do not need to go after things in order to be happy.

There are two ways of going after things. One can go after things for happiness or one can happily go after things. Going after things to discover happiness generally does not work. And if one is happy with oneself as a person, then one need not go after things. It does not produce any result for oneself. But then, one can do things joyfully.

Śaṅkara gives an example of how they revel in talking about Īśvara. Suppose a person is with someone very beloved to him. What would be the joy he discovers in conversing with, in being in the company of his beloved? With such a joy or more, the one who appreciates Īśvara revels in sharing his understanding of Īśvara.

This can include even those who do not have that knowledge but discover their joy in teaching and sharing what they see of the glories of the Lord. Even when you see a beautiful flower, you can simply say the flower is beautiful or you can see something more than that. The beauty of the flower is the glory of Īśvara. Wherever there is any ray of glory, anything striking, that is where Īśvara is present for you to recognise.

This verse can be about the wise men or the *jijñāsus*, those who want to be wise and who are after this knowledge. They share with others whatever they have come to know and in the process, they discover further clarity.

Only when you discuss what you think you know, do you discover what you do know. Clarity takes place only when you begin to part with the knowledge you have, sharing it with another person. Because there is a pair of eyes looking at you, they become a check for you. If there are any fallacies in your thinking, it will become very clear. Any vague areas in your thinking also become very evident. If you commit a mistake, those eyes will reveal that something is wrong. When you see that, your mind becomes alert. It begins to discover those areas of vagueness. The sharing of knowledge can also be mutual, in a discussion among seekers. Both are part of *brahmābhyāsa*, the *sādhana* for knowing Brahman, which is not different from yourself. There is no other *sādhana*. It is not something that is going to emerge at some time in the heat of meditation. The self is you. It is never hidden at any time. The only thing that covers it is ignorance. Therefore, listen and reflect on what you have understood by sharing it with others and in discussions among yourselves.

Verse 10

Those who are committed to me gain me

तेषां सततयुक्तानां भजतां प्रीतिपूर्वकम् ।
ददामि बुद्धियोगं तं येन मामुपयान्ति ते ॥ १० ॥

teṣāṁ satatayuktānāṁ bhajatāṁ prītipūrvakam
dadāmi buddhiyogaṁ taṁ yena mām upayānti te (10)

teṣāṁ satatayuktānām – for those who are always committed to me; *prīti-pūrvakaṁ bhajatām* – seeking with love; *taṁ buddhi-yogam* – that vision; *dadāmi* – I give; *yena* – whereby; *te mām upayānti* – they reach me

> For them who are always committed to me, seeking me with love, I give that vision whereby they reach me.

Teṣāṁ satatayuktānāṁ, for those who are always committed. Those who are seeking in this manner were previously called *nityayuktas*, always committed to me, not just in the morning and/or evening. Īśvara is not just one of the irons in the fire for them. Their priorities are clear. They have assimilated their experiences and understand exactly what they are seeking. Seeking the truth of everything is not a pastime; it is their life. And they do not see any other pursuit that is worthwhile. They are mature.

Such people have a love for the knowledge of Īśvara. What started as a curiosity becomes a desire because you cannot accept ignorance once you know that there is something to know. That is why, as I told you, if you want to make somebody miss his sleep, tell him that you have a great secret to tell him, and that you will tell him tomorrow morning! Once one knows that there is something to know, one cannot but try to know it. It becomes a desire. Afterwards, this *jijñāsā*, a desire to seek knowledge becomes a love for knowledge. Once it becomes love for knowledge, then they revel, *ramanti*, they enjoy satisfaction, *tuṣyanti*. Then you will not ask, 'Swamiji, when will this seeking end?' Nobody asks, 'When will this love end?' In love, you are always happy, especially if that love is for knowledge. As long as it is a desire, it is fraught with pain because there are impediments in fulfilling a desire. Once it transforms into love for knowledge, then it is a matter of revelling. Impediments do not count.

Bhagavān says, to those seeking with love, *ahaṁ dadāmi*, I give. What do I give? *Buddhi-yoga*, the vision of myself. When you are seeking Īśvara, he has to give; he has to reveal himself. Therefore, he says, 'I give them that *buddhi-yoga*, the vision of truth, the vision of me, through which they reach me, they become one with me.' The followers of *Hare Kṛṣṇa* movement and other *dvaita* schools of thought would translate these words as, 'I will give them the grace whereby they will come to me. Where? In *Golokabṛndāvan* or any other heaven. Previously, Kṛṣṇa was here; then, he transferred himself to *Goloka* where he has been waiting for these people to come.

Because you are always singing the glories of Īśvara, you are a special invitee there. You go there and play with him. But when he plays with the others, you will have to wait – the same old problem that the *gopī*s faced. Previously, when Kṛṣṇa was playing with one *gopī*, another *gopī* would be very jealous. These are our original problems. This problem, which was here on earth, *Bhūloka*, will also be there in *Golokabṛndāvan*. I do not know, which *śāstra* refers to *Golokabṛndāvan*. No *Upaniṣad*s talks about it. *Goloka* can be translated as the light, *loka*, of words, *go* – the meaning of the words of *śruti*.

When the Lord says, 'I give this clear vision,' it is just an expression. You can say he gives and you take; but after all, Īśvara is the *ātmā*. So, where is the question of his giving anything and to whom? The *buddhi-yoga* is gained and in this, the object is nothing but *ātmā*, which is Parameśvara. The Lord himself is the object of that knowledge. Therefore, when he says, '*dadāmi*' he means, 'I give them this *buddhi-yoga* whereby they recognise me, they come to me.'

There is also an element of grace involved in all of this. The *pratibandhaka*s, obstructions, in gaining this clear vision are numerous. Therefore, Bhagavān says, those who seek me are assured of the grace they will need. Because those who seek me, *jijñāsus*, are also *bhakta*s. The very pursuit is *bhakti*.

Naturally it is able to produce certain grace. Meditation upon Īśvara, besides being a part of the means for knowing, is also *karma*. *Dhyāna* is mental activity and is therefore able to produce *karma-phala*. That *karma-phala* is called grace. Anything *adṛṣṭa*, if it is favourable to you, is grace or *puṇya*.

Grace is gained by this very pursuit and because they are *jijñāsu*s, they are considered *bhakta*s, devotees; so, the act of devotion involved in their pursuit produces certain grace. They say that even if you just repeat the *Gītā* without studying it, it becomes a prayer. Similarly, the *Upaniṣad*s can be repeated daily as a prayer because the words all come from Bhagavān and describe Bhagavān. If they are repeated with *śraddhā*, it is a prayer and it has a result. So, it can also be taken that gaining this vision requires the grace of Īśvara.

If you were to ask, 'Why do you give this *buddhi-yoga* to your devotees? What stands as an obstacle to gaining this clear vision, for destroying which you are giving this *buddhi-yoga* for your devotees?' Kṛṣṇa answers in the next verse.

Verse 11

Remaining in the buddhi as the very truth,
I only remove the ignorance

तेषामेवानुकम्पार्थमहमज्ञानजं तमः ।
नाशयाम्यात्मभावस्थो ज्ञानदीपेन भास्वता ॥ ११ ॥

teṣām evānukampārtham aham ajñānajaṁ tamaḥ
nāśayāmyātmabhāvastho jñānadīpena bhāsvatā (11)

teṣām eva – for them alone; *anukampārtham* – out of compassion; *ātma-bhāvasthaḥ aham* – I, obtaining in the thought of (their) mind; *jñāna-dīpena bhāsvatā* – by the shining lamp of knowledge; *ajñānajaṁ tamaḥ* – delusion born of ignorance (lack of discrimination); *nāśayāmi* – I destroy

> For them alone, out of compassion, I, obtaining in the thought of (their) mind, destroy the delusion born of ignorance by the shining lamp of knowledge.

Teṣām eva, for those seekers who are seeking nothing but *śreyas*, there is freedom from being a *jīva, mokṣa*. How will they get this *śreyas*?

Anukampārtham, out of sheer compassion. Bhagavān will give them this *śreyas*. Compassion is grace here, which is evoked by your own *karma*, or prayer.

How will he give them this *śreyas*? *Ātma-bhāvasthaḥ*, being present in their own minds, he will give them this *śreyas*. *Ātma-bhāvastha* is a very interesting word. The simple meaning is, the one who resides in the thought in the mind. *Ātmā* here refers to the *antaḥ-karaṇa*, the mind, and *bhāva* refers to *vṛtti*, the thought modification. So *ātma bhāvastha* is one who obtains in the *vṛtti*, in the thought of everyone. By using this word, Bhagavān removes a possible misconception arising from his saying '*dadāmi*, I give.' When he says, 'I give,' you can go away with the idea that Īśvara is located somewhere from where he hears your petition and answers. This tendency to put a distance between yourself and Īśvara is a continuing problem. Whenever Bhagavān says *dadāmi* etc., this problem arises. To counteract it he says here, *ātma-bhāvasthaḥ aham*, I am the one who obtains in the *vṛtti*, in the very thought of the seeker as *paramātmā*. I obtain in your mind as '*aham, aham, aham,*' purely in the form of consciousness. As Īśvara, I shine in the form of your own *svarūpa*. Later in chapter 15, he will say, '*sarvasya ca ahaṁ hṛdi sanniviṣṭaḥ*, I obtain in the *hṛdi*, heart, in the *buddhi* of everyone.' Here the same thing is conveyed by saying, '*aham ātma-bhāvasthaḥ*.'

Obtaining as the very essence of every thought what does Parameśvara do? *Nāśayāmi*, I destroy. Because of the seriousness and devotion of their commitment, certain conducive condition is created in the minds of the *jijñāsus*. In that conducive condition, called grace, *aham nāśayāmi*, I destroy. What does he destroy?

Tamaḥ, darkness, Śaṅkara says, it is *moha-andhakāra*, delusion. Bhagavān says, 'The delusion of darkness I destroy.' This delusion is born of ignorance, *ajñānaja*. Or you can call it *aviveka*, lack of discrimination. Due to lack of discrimination there is a false notion of the self being the body, mind, and so on. And again the reverse, the notion of the body-mind-sense complex being the self. These false notions about yourself, which in one word we call *mithyā-pratyaya*, I destroy, *aham nāśayāmi*. Who is this *aham*? Not someone somewhere, but the one obtaining as the very essence of the *vṛtti* the truth of any thought. How does he destroy?

Jñāna-dīpena bhāsvatā, by the shining light of knowledge. The destruction of delusion does not require any weapon. All that is involved is a simple lighting of a lamp. When the whole problem is ignorance and delusion, what you require is a flame of knowledge that leaves no dark corner anywhere in your *buddhi*. That is why the adjective *bhāsvatā* is used for *jñāna-dīpena*. It is not knowledge clouded with doubts and vagueness but a shining smokeless flame of knowledge that leaves nothing to be desired. It leaves no shadows of ignorance in your mind. 'By that lamp I destroy,' says Bhagavān, 'You do not destroy, I do.' This is another interesting thing.

In a confluence, when the river reaches the ocean, you have no idea whether the river flows into the ocean or the ocean reaches out and enters the river. You will find that for a mile at least from the ocean, the river water is saline. You can sometimes even see the flow of the river reversed as in a tidal bore.[7] Thus, you find you do not know whether the river is reaching the ocean or the ocean is reaching out to the river. That is what is said here; the knowledge reaches out to you as it were.

Do we gain knowledge of ātmā or is it given?

You will find both kinds of expressions in the *śāstra*. One is that you recognise me or reach me, gaining this knowledge through your own pursuit. But in fact you do not gain this knowledge. In every other knowledge there is a subject, a *jñāna-kartā*, a knower, involved and there is also an object of knowledge involved. For example, in the knowledge, '*ayaṁ ghaṭaḥ*, this is a pot,' the pot is an object that is objectified by you through your mind. Because you are the one who

---

7 A high, often dangerous wave caused by the surge of a flood tide upstream in a narrowing part of the lower course of a river where its current is met by the tides.

objectifies the pot, you say, 'This is a pot, *ayaṁ ghaṭaḥ*. ' In this, the subject is not cancelled; it is retained and the object is known by the subject. It is true in all forms of knowledge. But, when it comes to *ātma-jñāna* the *kartṛtva* itself is destroyed. The notion that I am the knower is destroyed by the knowledge that I am pure consciousness, which is Brahman, *ahaṁ śuddhaṁ kevalaṁ caitanyaṁ brahma*. The *ahaṅkāra* itself is resolved into a flame of knowledge.

The reason there is no *kartā* involved in this knowledge is that the *pramāṇa* is not in the hands of the *ahaṅkāra*. However, when you use perception as a means of knowledge, the perception is in your hands; you are the *kartā*. Using the means of knowledge known as perception, you see pot, tree, and so on. Similarly, *anumāna*, inference, implies a *kartā*. Only presupposing the existence of the subject, the knower, does inference operate. In the statement, 'I infer,' there is a subject. *Arthāpatti*, presumption, another form of inference, also presupposes a knower. Then the knowledge of the absence of something, like your not having a pot in your hand, *kara-tale ghaṭaḥ nāsti*, is arrived at through the *pramāṇa* called *anupalabdhi*, which also implies the existence of the knower. By *anupalabdhi* you gain the knowledge that a thing does not exist. It involves a *kartā*. So, does the knowledge gained through *upamāna*. You may be told that a bison is like a water buffalo. You know what a water buffalo is but not a bison. The *upamāna*, illustration, of the water buffalo gives rise to indirect knowledge of a bison. When you see a bison, remembering the illustration of the water buffalo, you gain direct knowledge of the bison.

All this implies a subject. So, the subject is never cancelled. When you know about a cell, an atom, or a particle, the subject is involved. Even if you know something about your psychological past, there too the subject is involved. You make inferences such as, 'I am responding to this in this way because of what happened to me before.' That inferential connection is made by the *kartā*, the subject.

In fact, in all these, the subject is untouched. But when you expose yourself to the *śabda-pramāṇa*, particularly Vedanta, the *kartā* does not operate. Once it has placed itself in a situation where such knowledge can take place, it does nothing further. Like a river that has come to a point from where it sights the ocean. After that it does not do anything. The ocean takes care of it. It is the same here. Your going to a teacher and exposing yourself to the teaching is all done by your own will. It does not happen automatically. You have to place yourself in a condition from where knowledge can take place. Then *śabda*, the words, take over.

The sentence that gives the knowledge is, *tat tvam asi*. In the process of understanding this firstly, the meaning of the word *tvam*, you, is analysed properly and then, *tat*, Īśvara, is also analysed properly. Then the *akhaṇḍa-artha*, the meaning of identity that is involved in the sentence is recognised. What does that recognition do? First let us understand how the recognition takes place. It has to occur in the *buddhi* because that is where the ignorance is destroyed by the *buddhi-vṛtti*, eliminating the notion that the self is merely the subject. The subject is the self, but the self is not the subject. The knower-known-knowledge are one and the same. Where is the subject, where is the object? *Ātmā* is free from all three of them. It is Brahman.

This recognition that the self is Brahman, swallows the subject. So, how can you say that you gain it? Through the *śāstra*, Īśvara alone gives this knowledge. You do nothing to gain it. Since the *ahaṅkāra* is not involved, it is proper to say that Īśvara gives you this knowledge. Even though in the previous verse the Lord said, 'I give this vision, *ahaṁ buddhi-yogaṁ dadāmi*,' here he says, 'In fact I do not give anything. Remaining in the *buddhi*, as the very truth of the *buddhi-vṛtti*, I only remove the ignorance, *ajñānajaṁ tamaḥ nāśayāmi*.'

Dadāmi is now replaced by *nāśayāmi*. One is positive, the other negative. In the positive expression, there can be a division. Someone is giving; someone is receiving. Because division implies duality, there is the possibility of a wrong understanding that there is a giver and that Īśvara gives. It can look as though something positive is given, some kind of knowledge is superimposed upon or thrown into the *buddhi*. It is not like that. In fact, there is no giving involved. Bhagavān is only destroying ignorance. Knowledge is not something that happens. What really happens is that ignorance, *ajñāna*, is removed. Then why do we have such expressions as 'gaining knowledge?' Because a *vṛtti* is necessary to destroy ignorance, we say knowledge occurs. But knowledge does not occur. What happens is that the *vṛtti* is produced and it destroys ignorance. Knowledge is not created; *ajñāna* is removed.

That is why this whole process is a process of *nivṛtti* and not *pravṛtti*. *Pravṛtti* implies a *kartā*. In this *nivṛtti*, the *kartā* itself is negated. The removal of ignorance of the self being Brahman is what is called knowledge here. Positively nothing happens.

If knowledge is something that can be positively given, and it is given to someone who is ignorant, that person will remain ignorant. Knowledge would merely get superimposed upon him. The truth is that knowledge always is. You only remove the ignorance that conceals it. And knowledge is always true to the object. *Ātmā* is Brahman. If that Brahman is limitless, it is limitless all the time. And the knowledge of it is also as true as the 'object.' If Īśvara is omniscient, then all-knowledge exists already. No new knowledge is ever created. In your mind it may not exist but to correct that, all we have to do is bring in the particular *buddhi-vṛtti* that is able to destroy ignorance. To know that *ātmā* is Brahman, you bring in the *buddhi-vṛtti* that will destroy self-ignorance. There can be obstacles to that; so, to remove them, you require grace. From that perspective Bhagavān can say, 'I give this vision, *ahaṁ buddhi yogam dadāmi*.

The dawn of knowledge is like the lighting of an oil lamp

Śaṅkara explains very beautifully this imagery of the lamp taking it as an oil lamp. A lighted oil lamp implies a few things such as oil, wick, flame, and oxygen and Śaṅkara explains all the parts of the analogy.

What is the oil for this lamp? Śaṅkara says that the oil, *sneha*, is *bhakti*, devotion and cheerfulness. *Sneha* can also mean affection or love. What is the difference between love and devotion? Where there is respect and reverence with love, there is *bhakti*, devotion. Love, when it is for Īśvara, involves certain supplication, a surrender and looking up to. This appreciation and respect is implied in *bhakti*. Thus love, with respect and reverence is *bhakti*. Śaṅkara says that the wick of the lamp must be *abhiṣikta*, soaked with the oil, *sneha*, which is cheerfulness and *bhakti*.

I[8] find that spiritual seekers become very serious. There is some sadness about them. I have seen some of these people who have dedicated their lives to certain organised religions for the pursuit of God. They are so frightened, all because they see their thoughts as either virtuous or sinful. Thoughts are just thoughts, neither good nor bad. Only actions are right or wrong because they produce results. But then, if one deliberately meditates upon or prays for the fall of someone, then it is an act, a mental act. We take it as a *karma*. Thus there are no good or bad thoughts; there are only thoughts and there are proper or improper actions, be they mental, verbal, or physical. Only if one understands this, can one be cheerful. And, this is not an ordinary thing to understand. Thus, to light this lamp of knowledge the wick has to be soaked in the oil of cheerfulness and devotion to the Lord.

What is the wick for this lamp? The wick is the preparedness of the *Buddhi* purified by the study of the *śāstra* with a proper attitude and all other disciplines under the tutelage of a *guru*. The wick obtains in the lamp of the *antaḥ-karaṇa*. This lamp should be protected from strong winds. Śaṅkara says, the

[8] Swamiji

strong winds, which may blow off this lamp are the binding likes and dislikes. But then, the flame has to be sustained by air. That air, Śaṅkara says, is the *buddhi-vṛtti* that recognises the identity between *jīva* and Īśvara, accomplished by constant contemplation.

Having listened to the words of Kṛṣṇa on the glories of Īśvara, Arjuna now asks a question. The important thing to understand here is that the *Gītā* is a dialogue. Its subject matter is primarily to be understood; very few things are meant for belief.

The main issues are to be understood and some of them like values, attitudes and so on, are to be understood and lived up to. So, there is certain will involved here. But when Bhagavān talks about realities, they are purely to be understood. Even beliefs require some understanding. Since there is a lot to be understood, there is a dialogue. And now Arjuna makes a request to the Lord.

Verses 12-16

Arjuna reveals his understanding of what has been taught

अर्जुन उवाच ।
परं ब्रह्म परं धाम पवित्रं परमं भवान् ।
पुरुषं शाश्वतं दिव्यमादिदेवमजं विभुम् ॥ १२ ॥

आहुस्त्वामृषयः सर्वे देवर्षिर्नारदस्तथा ।
असितो देवलो व्यासः स्वयं चैव ब्रवीषि मे ॥ १३ ॥

arjuna uvāca
paraṁ-brahma paraṁ dhāma pavitraṁ paramaṁ bhavān
puruṣaṁ śāśvataṁ divyam ādidevam ajaṁ vibhum (12)

āhustvām ṛṣayaḥ sarve devarṣirnāradastathā
asito devalo vyāsaḥ svayaṁ caiva bravīṣi me (13)

arjuna – Arjuna; *uvāca* – said;

bhavān – O revered one! you are; *paraṁ-brahma* – limitless Brahman; *paraṁ dhāma* – the light of all lights; *paramaṁ pavitram* – the most purifying; *sarve ṛṣayaḥ* – all the sages; *devarṣiḥ nāradaḥ tathā* – including Nārada, who is the sage among gods; *asitaḥdevalaḥ vyāsaḥ* – (and) Asita, Devala, Vyāsa; *tvām āhuḥ* – talk of you as; *puruṣaṁ śāśvatam* – the eternal being; *divyam* – not of this world; *ādidevam* – the source of all the gods; *ajam* – unborn; *vibhum* – all-pervasive; *svayaṁ ca eva* – and indeed, you yourself; *bravīṣi me* – tell me (so)

Arjuna said:

Revered One! You are limitless Brahman, the light of all lights, the most purifying. All the sages, including Nārada, the sage among gods, Asita, Devala, and Vyāsa talk of you as the eternal being, not of this world, the cause of all the gods, unborn and all-pervasive. And indeed, you yourself tell me so.

Having listened to Kṛṣṇa through these chapters, Arjuna has an understanding of the topic. He now speaks from his understanding. All the sages talk about you, O! Kṛṣṇa, as being *paraṁ dhāma*. *Dhāma*[9] is used here in the sense of light. As light helps you to see things, so too this is the light of all lights, the light of consciousness. You are the source of all consciousness. You are consciousness. With *dhāma* in the sense of abode, you are the most exalted end reaching which there is no further end possible or necessary.

Then he says, you are, *bhavān*, *pavitraṁ*, *paramam*. There are a lot of things, which purify the mind and bring solace to it. But how can you ever completely purify the *antaḥ-karaṇa* that is subject to *puṇya-pāpa-karmas*. Nothing can get rid of these except the knowledge of Īśvara. Therefore, you are the *pāvana*, the one who is most purifying. The knowledge of the Lord, when he reveals himself, destroys the *jīva*, the individual, who feels isolated, frightened and bound. In the wake of knowledge of the Lord the *jīvatva*, the feeling of isolation is destroyed. It is because the knowledge of the Lord is knowing that 'I am non-separate from the Lord.' Here, the knowledge is that the subject, the knower, the knowledge and the object of knowledge are one and the same. If it is knowledge of myself then the object of knowledge is myself. The knowledge is as true as myself and the subject is myself. So, the one who knows is also myself. Here the subject, object and the knowledge are all one. Therefore, by that knowledge Īśvara completely purifies a *jīva*. The *saṁsārī* who is a limited individual subject to birth and death is totally released. There is nothing more purifying, *pāvana*.

---

[9] The word *dhāma* is derived from the root *dhā*. Here it has the meaning of *raśmi*. It also has the meaning of 'abode'.

Then Arjuna goes on to say that all *ṛṣi*s talk of you as, *puruṣaṁ nityaṁ śāśvatam*. The word *puruṣa* has two meanings. The one who is enclosed by the body-mind-sense complex is called *puruṣa*, and *puruṣa* is also that which fills up everything. So, when you repeat this word, '*puruṣaḥ puruṣaḥ*, *puruṣa* is *puruṣa*,' it becomes a *mahā-vākya*. If you say, *puruṣo'haṁ puruṣaḥ*, it means the one who obtains in the body-mind-sense complex, seemingly enclosed, is indeed the limitless *puruṣa*, filling up everything. *Puruṣa* being limitless, is not bound by time, and is therefore *śāśvata*. *Divya* means something of an exalted nature that is not of this world, *alaukika*. It is unlike anything we know. When we have no example to explain something extraordinary, we use the word *divya*. *Ādideva* means the one who was there before the beginning of all the *deva*s, the god of gods, their very source. And he is *aja*, the one who is unborn, not subject to birth at all. He is the cause of everything, *vibhu*, all-pervasive, the one from whom everything has come and who sustains everything in the sense that his mandate is followed by everybody.

People who say all this about Kṛṣṇa are those who know. In every generation there will be a few. Arjuna says that what he had said in the previous verse about Kṛṣṇa is not only his personal observation, but that of the sages, who really knew this subject matter and whose opinion you cannot dismiss. Also he says, all the *ṛṣi*s of *deva-loka*, including *devarṣi* Nārada, say the same thing. Other *ṛṣi*s like Asita, Devala and Vyāsa also say that this is what you are. They may all say so, but suppose the person himself says he is not Bhagavān.

Not here. Therefore, Arjuna says, 'Even you yourself have told me that you are Īśvara, *svayaṁ eva ca bravīṣi me*.'

And Arjuna goes on to say,

सर्वमेतदृतं मन्ये यन्मां वदसि केशव ।
न हि ते भगवन्व्यक्तिं विदुर्देवा न दानवाः ॥ १४ ॥

sarvam etad ṛtaṁ manye yanmāṁ vadasi keśava
na hi te bhagavan vyaktiṁ vidurdevā na dānavāḥ (14)

keśava – O Lord Keśava!; *sarvam etad* – all this; *yat māṁ vadasi* – which you have told me; *tat ṛtaṁ manye* – I consider true; *hi bhagavan* – indeed, O Lord!; *na devāḥ* – neither the celestials; *na dānavāḥ* – nor the *rākṣasa*s; *te vyaktim* – your manifestation; viduḥ – know

All this, which you have told me, Keśava (Kṛṣṇa)! I consider true. Indeed, neither the celestials nor the *rākṣasa*s know your manifestation (they do not know what you are), O Lord!

All the descriptions given by these *ṛṣis,* I consider to be true. What you have been saying to me (in the earlier chapters) and what others have said, I consider to be *ṛta*, absolutely true.

Even though both these words, *ṛta* and *satya* mean truth, there is some difference between them, especially when they are used together. When a fact is described by words and there is no difference between what the words mean and what the fact is, that is *satya* or *ṛta*. If the two words, *satya* and *ṛta*, are used together, either it is repetition or they have different meanings. In that case, *satya* is the truthful expression of something as you see it. What you express outside is as you see it inside, it is *yathārtha-bhāṣaṇa*, and it is called *satya*. But suppose you do not see correctly. Sometimes what you think is the truth turns out to be false because of your lack of knowledge. What you think as true is really false, though your expression of it is true to what you know. That is *satya*. But if what you see is accepted by the *ṛṣis* and is in keeping with the *śāstra*, that is *ṛta*. If what you see is *ṛta*, it is a truth that can never be negated. So, *ṛta* is more powerful than *satya*. Here the two words are not used together. And Arjuna uses only the word *ṛta*. Therefore, when Arjuna says that he considers what Kṛṣṇa has said to be *ṛta*, he is saying that there can be no doubt about these words at all and that they are absolutely true.

In the next line he says, 'O Bhagavān! neither the celestials, *deva*s nor the *rākṣasa*s, *dānava*s, know of your person, *vyakti*. You are the cause of everything, but they do not see you at all. Everybody sees the effect, the creation, but nobody sees the cause thereof.'

Arjuna continues and in the process reveals the knowledge he has gathered so far.

स्वयमेवात्मनात्मानं वेत्थ त्वं पुरुषोत्तम ।
भूतभावन भूतेश देवदेव जगत्पते ॥ १५ ॥

svayam evātmanātmānaṁ vettha tvaṁ puruṣottama
bhūtabhāvana bhūteśa devadeva jagatpate (15)

puruṣottama – O the most exalted being!; *bhūta-bhāvana* – the creator of all beings! *bhūteśa* – the ruler of all beings!; *devadeva* – the Lord of the gods!; *jagatpate* – the Lord of creation!; *tvaṁ svayam eva vettha* – you yourself know; *ātmanā* – with your own mind; *ātmānam* – (your) self

> You (yourself) know yourself with your own mind, Puruṣottama (Kṛṣṇa)! The creator of all beings! The ruler of all beings! The Lord of the gods! The Lord of creation!

वक्तुमर्हस्यशेषेण दिव्या ह्यात्मविभूतयः ।
याभिर्विभूतिभिर्लोकानिमांस्त्वं व्याप्य तिष्ठसि ॥ १६ ॥

vaktum arhasyaśeṣeṇa divyā hyātmavibhūtayaḥ
yābhirvibhūtibhirlokān imāṁstvaṁ vyāpya tiṣṭhasi (16)

divyāḥ – the extraordinary; *hi* – indeed; *ātma-vibhūtayaḥ* – the glories of yourself; *yābhiḥ vibhūtibiḥ* – those glories by which; *imān lokān* – these worlds; *vyāpya* – pervading; *tvaṁ tiṣṭhasi* – you remain; *aśeṣeṇa vaktum arhasi* – you are capable of telling in full

> You indeed are capable of telling in full the extraordinary glories of yourself, the glories by which you remain pervading these worlds.

Arjuna confirms the opinion of the *ṛṣi*s that Kṛṣṇa is Īśvara. Then he tells why Kṛṣṇa alone is qualified to talk about all those glories by which he remains covering the entire universe. Though there are others to talk about it, you are the most eligible, Arjuna says.

Tvaṁ svayaṁ vettha, you yourself know, not being taught by anybody. What does he know? *Ātmānam*, you know the truth of yourself. How? *Ātmanā*, through your own mind, which is why you speak of yourself as Īśvara all the time. Śaṅkara says here, that you know yourself as one who has knowledge, overlordship, strength, and power that leave nothing to be desired. In short, you know yourself as Īśvara, Puruṣottama, the one who is exalted among the *puruṣa*s.

He is addressed as *bhūta-bhāvana*, the one who creates all the beings with their body-mind-sense complexes. For each being he creates a unique *sthūla-sūkṣma-śarīra* appropriate to their *karma*. And not only does he create all beings, he also takes care of them; so, he is called *bhūteśa*, the ruler of all beings. Then he is addressed as *devadeva*, the Lord of all the gods and *jagatpati*, the Lord of this entire creation. All these are appellations of the Lord.

Vaktum arhasi aśeṣeṇa, you are capable of revealing without leaving anything out. What is revealed is *ātma-vibhūti*s, your own glories, which are not of this world, *divya, alaukika*. The word *ātmā* shows that this refers not only to the Lord but to yourself. Arjuna is implying, 'You know about me, *ātmā*, and you can talk about all the glories of *ātmā* which you know so well.'

Yābhiḥ vibhūtibhiḥ lokān imān tvaṁ vyāpya tiṣṭhasi, all these glories by which you stand pervading all these worlds, only you are eligible to talk about. Arjuna says later, 'I am still not satisfied with what you have been saying about yourself. You talk not just about your glories but mine too, which you can see.

All of us want to listen to our glories. So, tell me more.' Lord Kṛṣṇa does not simply tell Arjuna that he, Kṛṣṇa, is everything; he proves the fact that he is everything. And Kṛṣṇa also implies that Arjuna, or anyone for that matter, can know that he is also not different from Īśvara Then all these glories would apply and belong to him too. It is not flattery, but a statement of fact.

So, even when it is not understood it has a ring of truth and logic to it. Here you have facts that elevate you; the more you listen, the more you want to know. You always love to gaze at yourself in the mirror, much more than is necessary. There is self-love in you because *ātmā* is something you cannot but love. It is intrinsically *ānanda,* fullness. Because you have some insight about that, you cannot give up the hope that one day you are going to be wonderful. So, when someone holds up a word mirror and makes you see that you are everything, you can never be tired of it.

Arjuna says, 'Listening to these nectar like words, which reveal your glories and therefore, mine, I have no satisfaction, *tṛpti.* So, please tell me more about these glories. For those of us who cannot directly appreciate you, which are the places and things in which your glory is so pronounced that it can become an object of meditation?' Thus Arjuna asks for further description. Lord Kṛṣṇa says, 'It is very difficult to do this and even if I describe it for days, it will not end. Yet, I will make an attempt to say a few things.' Then, in the eleventh chapter he makes a drastic revelation by giving Arjuna a vision of the cosmic form.

Verses 17&18

Arjuna requests Lord Kṛṣṇa to reveal his glories

कथं विद्यामहं योगिंस्त्वां सदा परिचिन्तयन्।
केषु केषु च भावेषु चिन्त्योऽसि भगवन्मया ॥ १७ ॥

kathaṁ vidyām ahaṁ yogiṁstvāṁ sadā paricintayan
keṣu keṣu ca bhāveṣu cintyo'si bhagavan mayā (17)

sadā paricintayan – always contemplating; *kathaṁ vidyām aham* – how can I know; *tvām* – you; *yogī* –the greatest of the *yogīs*, Lord!; *keṣu keṣu ca bhāveṣu* – and in which forms; *cintyaḥ asi* – are you to be meditated upon; *mayā* – by me; *bhagavan* – O Lord!

The greatest of the *yogīs*! Ever contemplating, how can I know you? In which forms are you to be meditated upon by me, O Lord!

Here he says, '*sadā paricintayan*, always contemplating, how can I know your glory?' All we see around us are only objects. To appreciate Īśvara, the *puruṣa*, because of whom the object is an object we have to go behind the objects and see beyond what we can physically perceive. It is purely a vision of the *buddhi*; so, it is with *jñāna-cakṣu*, the eye of wisdom, that we have to see. Meditation upon Īśvara, *īśvara-dhyāna*, is seeing the glories of Īśvara, *īśvara-vibhūti-dhyāna*.

Then Arjuna asks the Lord, '*keṣu keṣu ca bhāveṣu cintyaḥ asi*, what are the objects in which you are to be meditated upon?' There are many objects and beings in the universe; in some of them the Lord's glories are particularly manifest.

These are identified as special by the Vedas or Purāṇas. Also, certain objects by convention and some people by their deeds become popular. The glory, which made them popular is Īśvara and thus they become a focus of meditation.

So, Arjuna says, 'O Lord! Tell me all those glories in which you are specially manifest, where you can become the object of meditation.' It is true that the Lord is manifest in everything but the glories of some objects and people stand out in creation. The value in any of these glories is Īśvara and the absolute value, *pratyagātmā* is also Īśvara. A value in anything is always connected to a being. If there is an intrinsic value to a reality, then that intrinsic value belongs only to Īśvara.

Here the value is not imagined or superimposed, as it is in gold, for example. Gold has two values, the superimposed and the intrinsic value. That it is shiny, malleable, rare, and rust proof is its intrinsic value. The monetary value is superimposed. But its intrinsic value minus our projections is Īśvara's glory. It is the basis for *īśvara-dhyāna*. I eliminate my projections and appreciate Īśvara's glory as identical with the object's intrinsic value. That value is the glory of Īśvara.

Therefore, please tell me in which objects I can see you like this.

विस्तरेणात्मनो योगं विभूतिं च जनार्दन ।
भूयः कथय तृप्तिर्हि शृण्वतो नास्ति मेऽमृतम् ॥ १८ ॥

vistareṇātmano yogaṁ vibhūtiṁ ca janārdana
bhūyaḥ kathaya tṛptirhi śṛṇvato nāsti me'mṛtam (18)

vistareṇa – in detail; *bhūyaḥ* – again; *kathaya* – please describe; *ātmanaḥ yogam* – the wonder of yourself; *vibhūtiṁ ca* – and the glory; *janārdana* – O Lord!; *hi* – because; *amṛtaṁ śṛṇvataḥ me* – for me the listener of this nectar; *tṛptiḥ na asti* – there is no satisfaction

> Please describe (to me) again in detail the wonder and the glory of yourself, Janārdana (Kṛṣṇa)! because I, the listener of this nectar, have no satisfaction.

As Īśvara, the Lord, you have unique capacities like omniscience and omnipotence, called *yoga* in this verse. These manifest in the creation as *vibhūtayaḥ*, glories, like the sun and the moon, which are the glories of your power. Again, O! Janārdana, please describe to me in detail your glory, *vistareṇa vibhūtiṁ bhūyaḥ kathaya.*

Janārdana[10] is the one who destroys people of improper conduct, *duṣṭa-janān ardayati iti janārdanaḥ.* Here destruction means to discipline, by giving *karma-phala.* There are two meanings for the root *ard* in the word Janārdana. One is *gamana*, going, the other is *yācana*, asking for or requesting. Śaṅkara gives two meanings for Janārdana using both senses of the root. In the sense of *gamana*, he is the one who makes all the *asuras*, those who are opposed to the *devas*, go to unpleasant places like *naraka.* By the law of *karma*, which is non-separate from him and is mandated by him, he sends them to *narakādi lokas*.

---

[10] अर्दतेः गतिकर्मणो रूपम्। असुराणां देवप्रतिपक्षभूतानां जनानां नरकादिगमयितृत्वात् जनार्दनः। अभ्युदय-निःश्रेयसपुरुषार्थ प्रयोजनम् सर्वैः जनैः याच्यते इति वा। (शङ्कर भाष्यम्)

Taking the second meaning of the root, he is the one who is propitiated by all people, either for limited results or for the limitless, *niśśreyas*. Limited results, *abhyudaya*, are prosperity, pleasures and so on. Any desirable end other than *mokṣa* is called *abhyudaya*. Janārdana is the one that all these people pray to for both types of results. In a prayer there are two objects. The primary object is what you are asking for and the secondary object is whom you are asking. For a *saṁsārī*, the two are separate. But a seeker prays to the Lord to know the Lord. So, the two objects become one. The person from whom all this is asked, be it *abhyudaya* or *niśśreyas*, is called Janārdana, *janaiḥ ardyate yācyate yasmāt saḥ janārdanaḥ*.

Please describe your glories to me, the listener, because the description is like *amṛta*, nectar, to my ears. *Amṛta* is anything that satisfies you or gives you happiness. Śaṅkara says that Arjuna refers to the words coming out of Kṛṣṇa's mouth as *amṛta*. 'For me, there cannot be enough of it, *tṛptiḥ nāsti me*.' The more he hears, the more he wants to hear.

Verses 19-39

Lord Kṛṣṇa recounts his glories

श्रीभगवानुवाच ।
हन्त ते कथयिष्यामि दिव्या ह्यात्मविभूतयः ।
प्राधान्यतः कुरुश्रेष्ठ नास्त्यन्तो विस्तरस्य मे ॥ १९ ॥

śrībhagavān uvāca
hanta te kathayiṣyāmi divyā hyātmavibhūtayaḥ
prādhānyataḥ kuruśreṣṭha nāstyanto vistarasya me (19)

śrī bhagavān – Śrī Bhagavān (The Lord); *uvāca* – said;
hanta – well now; *kuruśreṣṭha* – O the best of the Kurus; *te* – to you; (*ye*) *divyāḥ ātma-vibhūtayaḥ* – the glories of mine that are divine; *tāḥ kathayiṣyāmi* – (those) I will tell; *prādhānyataḥ* – in keeping with their prominence; *hi* – because; *me* (*vibhūtinām*) *vistarasya* – for the detailed description (of my glories); *antaḥ na asti* – there is no end

Śrī Bhagavān said:

Well now, Arjuna, the best of the Kurus! I will tell you my divine glories in keeping with their prominence; because there is no end to a detailed description of my glories.

अहमात्मा गुडाकेश सर्वभूताशयस्थितः ।
अहमादिश्च मध्यं च भूतानामन्त एव च ॥ २० ॥

aham ātmā guḍākeśa sarvabhūtāśayasthitaḥ
aham ādiśca madhyaṁ ca bhūtānām anta eva ca (20)

guḍākeśa – O the master of sleep, Arjuna!; *aham ātmā* – I am the self; *sarva bhūtāśaya-sthitaḥ* – who resides in the hearts of all beings; *ca* – and; *aham* – I am; *bhūtānām* – of all beings/things; *ādiḥ* – the cause; *madhyaṁ ca* – and the sustenance; *antaḥ eva ca* – and the resolution

Guḍākeśa (Arjuna)! I am the self, who resides in the hearts of all beings and I am the cause of the creation, sustenance, and resolution of all beings/things.

Hanta is an expression of wonder or pleasure. Kṛṣṇa is happy that Arjuna has asked him this. He says, '*te kathayiṣyāmi*, I will explain to you these special heavenly glories, *divyāḥ ātma-vibhūtayaḥ*.' There is no end to my glories, they are endless, *nāsti antaḥ vistarasya me*. Therefore, I will enumerate them in keeping with their importance, *prādhānyataḥ*.

Śaṅkara explains, it is not possible to narrate all of them without leaving anything out. Even in one hundred years the list would not come to an end. Therefore, Bhagavān says that he would tell Arjuna, a few important ones among them.

Firstly, you said you want to meditate. Then meditate upon yourself for I am yourself, *aham ātmā*. Instead of glorifying Īśvara, just know yourself, for you are that Īśvara and all the glories belong to you.

Guḍākeśa is the one who has mastered sleep. The word *guḍākā* means sleep. One who has mastered this *guḍākā* is *guḍākeśa*. Śaṅkara says *jita-nidra*[11] where *nidrā* means *tamas*; he is the one who has mastered *tamas* and is alert. There is another meaning of *guḍākeśa*; the one who has matted hair – *guḍa* means thick or matted and *keśa* means hair.

Arjuna asked Bhagavān as to which are the objects in which he is available for meditation and Kṛṣṇa says, '*aham ātmā guḍākeśa*, I am *ātmā*, the self in you Arjuna.' The *pratyagātmā*, *aham*, in Arjuna is Bhagavān and the name form Arjuna is

---

[11] गुडाका निद्रा तस्याः ईशः गुडाकेशः जितनिद्रः। (शङ्कर भाष्यम्)

only an *upādhi*. Since all glories belong to Bhagavān, and *aham* is Bhagavān, all glories of Bhagavān also belong to the *pratyagātmā*. The primary statement of the *śāstra* is that the *vastu* is *pratyagātmā*. 'Secondly, with reference to *avastu* which is *mithyā*,' the Lord says, 'I am *jagat-kāraṇa*, the cause for everything. And I am the one who obtains in the *buddhi* of all beings, *sarva-bhūta-āśaya-sthita*, as the *pratyagātmā*. So, first you have to recognise me as yourself.'

The statement, *aham ātmā guḍākeśa sarva-bhūta-āśaya-sthitaḥ* is an equation. That *ātmā* which obtains in the *buddhi* of all beings, I am. The predication is between *aham* and *ātmā* where the adjective to *ātmā* is *sarva-bhūta-āśaya-sthita*. That *ātmā*, which resides in the heart of all beings, I am. *Aham* here means Īśvara. So, Īśvara is predicated to *ātmā*. This *ātmā* obtaining in all beings is *paramātmā*. That I am, *aham asmi*. If you want a primary form of contemplation upon Īśvara, then contemplate on the *pratyagātmā*. *Nididhyāsana* is another *aṅga* of *śravaṇa*, the *śāstra-vicāra* which is the real means for knowing. Śaṅkara says that it is to be meditated upon always, *nityaṁ dhyeyaḥ*.

Bhagavān says, 'In all the various objects that I am now going to narrate to you, I should be meditated upon. I am available for appreciation there.' How is this so?

Aham ādiḥ bhūtānām, I am the efficient and material cause of the creation, the one because of whom the creation of all things takes place. Then *madhyaṁ ca*, I am the sustaining cause, *sthiti-kāraṇa* of all the *bhūtas*, beings. The sustenance of all beings is because of me. And I am *antaḥ*, the cause into which they resolve. In the end they come back to me, the material cause, *upādāna-kāraṇa*. This being so, any object is me and can be meditated upon as me. Any value, which is intrinsic in the manifested form, is me, like sugar in the sugarcane. You may love sugar. That is your personal value. But in the sweetness in the sugar you can see Bhagavān because it is this sweetness that makes sugarcane what it is. With this understanding you can see that Īśvara is available for invocation in any object that has some glory. Being the *abhinna-nimitta-upādāna-kāraṇa*, nothing is separate from him. There are countless names and forms, all of which are available for meditation. But then you only see your ego surfacing as an admirer with reference to certain objects. The source of that admiration is nothing but Īśvara seen by your ego as it assumes the form of an admirer.

Since Īśvara is the cause for creation, sustenance and dissolution, naturally anything here is an object of meditation. Īśvara can be invoked in any given form. Yet in certain places he is invoked more easily.

आदित्यानामहं विष्णुर्ज्योतिषां रविरंशुमान् ।
मरीचिर्मरुतामस्मि नक्षत्राणामहं शशी ॥ २१ ॥

ādityānām ahaṁ viṣṇurjyotiṣāṁ raviraṁśumān
marīcirmarutām asmi nakṣatrāṇām ahaṁ śaśī (21)

ādityānām aham – among the *ādityas*; *ahaṁ viṣṇuḥ* – I am Viṣṇu; *jyotiṣām* – among the luminaries; *raviḥ* – the Sun; *aṁśumān* – the one who has rays; *marutām* – among the *maruts*; *marīciḥ asmi* – I am Marīci; *nakṣatrāṇām* – among the luminaries seen at night; *ahaṁ śaśī* – I am the Moon

> Among the *āditya*s I am Viṣṇu; among the luminaries I am the Sun, the one who has rays; among the *marut*s I am Marīci, and among the luminaries seen at night I am the Moon.

वेदानां सामवेदोऽस्मि देवानामस्मि वासवः ।
इन्द्रियाणां मनश्चास्मि भूतानामस्मि चेतना ॥ २२ ॥

vedānāṁ sāmavedo'smi devānām asmi vāsavaḥ
indriyāṇāṁ manaścāsmi bhūtānām asmi cetanā (22)

vedānām – among the Vedas; *sāmavedaḥ asmi* – I am the *Sāmaveda*; *devānām* – among the gods; *vāsavaḥ asmi* – I am Indra; *indriyāṇām* – among the means of knowing; *manaḥ asmi* – I am the mind; *bhūtānāṁ ca* – and of the embodied beings; *cetanā asmi* – I am the faculty of cognition

> Among the Vedas I am the Sāmaveda; among the gods I am Indra; among the means of knowing I am the mind, and of the embodied beings I am the faculty of cognition.

In the *purāṇa*s, Vedas, you will hear of various objects suitable for contemplation upon Īśvara. From the standpoint of the *purāṇa*s, among the twelve *āditya*s, I am Viṣṇu. Īśvara viewed from the standpoint of sustenance is Viṣṇu. Here Viṣṇu is the name of one of the *āditya-devatā*s,[12] known to us through

---

[12] The *āditya*s are twelve in number and they are: Dhātā, Mitra, Aryamā, Rudra, Varuṇa, Sūrya, Bhaga, Vivasvān, Pūṣā, Savitā, Tvaṣṭā, Viṣṇu.

the *purāṇas*. Each *āditya*, Sun, sustains life within its sphere but Viṣṇu is the all-pervasive sustainer of even the *ādityas*. And here Bhagavān says, I am that Viṣṇu.

From the standpoint of the world, among the luminous bodies in the sky the brightest is *ravi*, the sun, the one who has *aṁśumān*, rays. The sun is the centre of our solar system, the energising factor because of which the earth has life. So, among the luminous bodies I am the life giving sun. In the *śruti*, there are several *devatās* mentioned. Among them are the *marut-devatās*. Among these *marut-devatās*, I am Marīci. Among the luminous bodies visible in the night sky, *nakṣatras*, I am *śaśī*, the moon, the brightest. There is another interpretation of this. *Nakṣatra*[13] means the place one goes to. Due to the efficacy of certain rituals, one goes to *lokas*, which are called *nakṣatras*. Among all these *nakṣatras*, *candra-loka* is one of the better ones. But this *candra-loka* is different from *candra*, the moon.

In all these, the one who obtains is Īśvara and his *vibhūti* is what is pointed out here. The glory of the *devatās* or the glory of the luminaries is nothing but the glory of Īśvara. So, the topic is not which *devatā* is to be worshipped but that an object is what it is because of the glory of Īśvara. This is what is to be understood here.

Among the Vedas, I am the *Sāmaveda*. All four Vedas talk of the glories of Īśvara. In each, the first portion discusses *karmas* or rituals and the law of *karma*, which is non-separate from Īśvara.

---

[13] *Nakṣate gacchati* - goes, *yajamānaḥ* – the performer of the rituals; *etat* - to this place; *iti nakṣatraḥ*.

It reveals the Lord as the one who presides over the law of *karma*, *karma-adhyakṣa*, and as one who is the *karma-phala-dātā*, the one who gives the results of action. For the performance of a ritual, *puṇya* is the *karma-phala*. Something that is the cause for a favourable result, but considered by you as luck because it is not visible, the *śāstra*s call it *puṇya*. It can be gained by the performance of certain rituals. That a particular ritual will produce a particular result is Īśvara's mandate. Therefore, in that very *karma* is Īśvara. The *sādhana*, the means, is Īśvara and the *sādhya*, the end that is sought, is Īśvara. The entire *karma-kāṇḍa* talks indirectly of Īśvara in this way. The *jñāna-kāṇḍa* reveals Īśvara directly. So, all the Vedas talk about Īśvara. 'Among them, I am *Sāmaveda*,' says the Lord. In the *Sāmaveda* all the *mantra*s are sung, that is, they are recited in a simple musical form. This 'singing' is more than mere recitation. Therefore, the *Sāmaveda* stands out among the recited Vedas. Another reason, though weak, is that the *Sāmaveda* has the famous *mahā-vākya*, *tat tvam asi*. So, Bhagavān says, 'Among the Vedas I am the musical and pleasing *Sāmaveda*.'

'Among the various *deva*s, I am Indra.' Indra is the Lord of the *deva*s, the most exalted among them. His elevated status is due to Īśvara alone. So, the glory of Indra is Īśvara. In Indra who is the most exalted of *deva*s we invoke Īśvara.

There are different types of *indriya*s, sense organs; the *karmendriya*s, organs of action, and *jñānendriya*s, the organs of knowledge. 'All of them,' Bhagavān says, 'are me.' 'But among them I am the mind,' because all senses have the mind as their basis. It is through the mind that we gain the knowledge of the world and through the mind we order the *karmendriyas* to perform their actions. The mind is behind the sense organs as a receiving organ that receives data from all sense perceptions. And it is the seat of desires that are fulfilled by the *karmendriyas*. Both, the sense organs of perception and the organs of action, depend upon the mind. Therefore, the mind is also considered an instrument, *karaṇa*. Among all the *indriyas*, *karaṇas*, I am the mind, the one that is most important, without which none of the others can function. Wherever there is such importance, there is the glory of Īśvara. The glory of the mind is Īśvara.

Then, 'Among the embodied beings, *bhūtanām*, I am the *buddhi,* the faculty of cognition.' The capacity to enquire and understand, which is manifest through the *buddhi,* is Īśvara. There is nothing more beautiful than clarity of knowledge. Bhagavān says, 'I am that *cetanā*.' *Cetanā* implies not only clarity, but free will. It is the highest form of *prakṛti*'s manifestation. If you accept a process of evolution, *prakṛti* reaches a point of fulfilment the moment the *upādhi* gains the faculty of choice, *buddhi*. There is an in-built faculty for a child to grow to become an adult. It is a biologically mechanical process involving no special will. It is called *bhāva-vikāra*. But once the will is given, *prakṛti* has fulfilled itself and does not help you in your growth any further. You have to use the will you have been given, to grow into a mature person. And you can grow up to the point where you discover you are infinite. It is the highest manifestation of Īśvara as a being.

रुद्राणां शङ्करश्चास्मि वित्तेशो यक्षरक्षसाम् ।
वसूनां पावकश्चास्मि मेरुः शिखरिणामहम् ॥ २३ ॥

rudrāṇāṁ śaṅkaraścāsmi vitteśo yakṣarakṣasām
vasūnāṁ pāvakaścāsmi meruḥ śikhariṇām aham (23)

rudrāṇām – among the Rudras;[14] *śaṅkaraḥ ca asmi* – I am Śaṅkara; *vitteśaḥ* – (I am) Kubera, the Lord of wealth; *yakṣa-rakṣasām* – among the *yakṣa*s and *rākṣasas*; *vasūnām* – among the *vasus*; *pāvakaḥ ca asmi* – I am fire, the purifier; *meruḥ aham* – I am Meru; *śikhariṇām* – among the snow-peaked mountains

> Among the Rudras I am Śaṅkara; I am Kubera among the *yakṣa*s and *rākṣasa*s; among the *vasu*s I am Fire, and among the snow-peaked mountains I am Meru.

Now Bhagavān talks about the eleven Rudras found in the *purāṇa*s and the *śruti*. 'Among them, I am Śaṅkara.' Earlier he told us that he is Viṣṇu, the sustainer, among the *āditya*s. Now he reveals that he is Śaṅkara, the destroyer among the Rudras. *Śaṁ karoti iti śaṅkara*, the one who blesses is called Śaṅkara. In the tradition he is looked upon as Śiva and worshipped for *mokṣa*, as the destroyer of ignorance and its product, *saṁsāra* and *duḥkha*. In the word *Upaniṣad,* the root *sad*

---

15 The Rudras are eleven in number. The names of the eleven Rudras are given differently in different *purāṇa*s. They are; Aja, Ekapāda, Ahirbudhnya, Tvaṣṭā, Rudra, Hara, Śambhu, Tryambaka, Aparājita, Īśāna and Tribhuvana.

means that which causes the disintegration of *saṁsāra* by putting an end to ignorance, *avasādayati*. Because destruction is involved, Śiva is always worshipped by the one who wants *mokṣa*. *Śam* means *maṅgala*, that which is auspicious, the final end. By destroying ignorance, he gives the ultimate end, which is *mokṣa*. And there is nothing more auspicious than *mokṣa*.

'*Ahaṁ vitteśaḥ*, the presiding deity of wealth,' says Bhagavān. That is not Lakṣmī. She is wealth itself and is Īśvara's glory. When you look at Īśvara from the standpoint of wealth, then Īśvara is Lakṣmī, the *śakti* of Īśvara. But the presiding deity of wealth is Kubera. So here, *vitteśaḥ* is Kubera, one of the *yakṣas*. '*Yakṣāḥ* and '*rakṣāḥ*[15] are groups of celestials. Among them, I am Kubera.' There is yet another group – a group of eight *vasus*.[16] 'Among them, I am the god of fire, *ahaṁ pāvakaḥ*.' The god of fire is called *anala* because he burns everything; he never has enough, *alaṁ na vidyate yasya*. He is also called *pāvaka* because by burning he purifies everything.

Then he talks of the mountains. There are two types of *śikharīs*, mountains, those with peaks, and *aśikharīs*, those without peaks. Here Bhagavān refers to mountains that have peaks. 'Among them, I am Meru.'

---

[15] *Rakṣāḥ*–a particular sect of *asuras*. *Rakṣitavyaṁ śarīram asmāt iti rakṣaḥ*, the one from whom one's body has to be protected.

[16] The *vasus* are eight in number – Dhara, Dhruva, Soma, Ahas, Vāyu, Agni,Pratyuṣa and Prabhāsa.

पुरोधसां च मुख्यं मां विद्धि पार्थ बृहस्पतिम् ।
सेनानीनामहं स्कन्दः सरसामस्मि सागरः ॥ २४ ॥

purodhasāṁ ca mukhyaṁ māṁ viddhi pārtha bṛhaspatim
senānīnām ahaṁ skandaḥ sarasām asmi sāgaraḥ (24)

pārtha – O Arjuna!; *purodhasāṁ ca* – and among the priests; *mukhyam* – the chief; *bṛhaspatim* – Bṛhaspati; *māṁ viddhi* – may you know me to be; *senānīnām* – among the commanders-in-chief; *ahaṁ skandaḥ* – I am Skanda; *sarasām* – among the water reservoirs; *sāgaraḥ asmi* – I am the ocean

Pārtha (Arjuna)! May you know me to be Bṛhaspati, the chief, among the priests. Among the commanders-in-chief I am Skanda, and among the water reservoirs I am the ocean.

Puraḥ means 'in future.' So, *purodhas*[17] is the one who helps you gain *puṇya* in the future, by performing rituals and so on. That is a priest. Even kings bow down to priests. Yet among the priests there is one who is above all the rest – Bṛhaspati, the *guru* of Indra, the king of the *deva*s. Even the king of *deva*s bows to Bṛhaspati, the *guru* of *deva-loka*. I am that Bṛhaspati who is the chief, *mukhya*, among the royal priests.

Senānīnām,[18] among the commanders in chief who lead the army, I am Skanda. Skanda is Lord Subrahmaṇya. In the *purāṇas*,

---

[17] *puraḥ, agre* (in future) *yajamānaṁ dadhāti*, helps the one who performs the ritual in gaining *puṇya iti, purodhas*.

[18] *senāṁ nayati svavaśam āpādayati iti senānī*, the one who leads the *sena*, the army, that is, the one who keeps the army under his control.

he is referred to as the general of the *devas*, *devasenādhipati*. Lord Subrahmaṇya is also called Skanda or Ṣaṇmukha and is invoked for protection from any type of fear. So, here Īśvara is invoked as one who protects and the glory of that Skanda is Īśvara's glory.

There are two types of water reservoirs. One is created by God, the other by man. Among the God-made water reservoirs, which are stationary, *sarasām*, I am the ocean, *sāgara*. This does not include the flowing rivers, which he talks of later. So, here he says, among the natural stationary water reservoirs I am the mighty ocean.

महर्षीणां भृगुरहं गिरामस्म्येकमक्षरम् ।
यज्ञानां जपयज्ञोऽस्मि स्थावराणां हिमालयः ॥ २५ ॥

maharṣīṇāṁ bhṛguraham̐ girām asmyekam akṣaram
yajñānāṁ japayajño'smi sthāvarāṇāṁ himālayaḥ (25)

maharṣīṇām – among the sages; *aham bhṛguḥ* – I am Bhṛgu; *girām* – among the words; *ekam akṣaram asmi* – I am the single syllable *om*; *yajñānām* – among the rituals; *japa-yajñaḥ asmi* – I am the ritual of *japa*; *sthāvarāṇām* – among the mountains; *himālayaḥ* – the Himalayas

Among the sages I am Bhṛgu; among the words I am the single syllable *om*; among the rituals I am the ritual of *japa*, and among the mountains, the Himalayas.

Among the ancient *maharṣis*, Bhṛgu was considered to be the greatest. He is mentioned in the *Taittirīyopaniṣad,* which says Bhṛgu who was the son of Varuṇa got this knowledge from his father. Here Bhagavān says I am this Bhṛgu.

Gīḥ means speech. Śaṅkara says that, here it refers to 'words.' Among the many words, *girām*, in all languages, there is one all inclusive word of one single syllable. That is *om*. Phonetically, the word *om* does not belong to any language. It is a universal sound consisting of three sounds – A U M. When anybody opens his mouth and makes a sound, it is '*a*.' When he closes his mouth and makes a sound, '*m*' is the sound produced. The same '*a*' becomes '*u*' when the mouth is rounded. So, these are sounds that come naturally to any human being, and all other sounds are modifications of '*a*.' All words are combinations of these sounds and all names are words in all languages. So, *om*, the name of the Lord, is a single syllable representing all words.

It is a perfect name for the Lord. How, otherwise, are you going to give him a name? If you give him one name you are excluding all other names – as though they are not the names of the Lord. This is the difference between the Lord and an object. When you say apple, it means only one object and excludes all others. All other fruits and all other objects are excluded. Similarly if you say Rāma, then Kṛṣṇa, Śiva, you, and everybody else are excluded. So, the Lord's name has to be such that it includes all names, which is why in prayer we repeat a given name 108 times. The Sanskrit letters from '*a*' to '*ha*' are 54 in number when you include certain forms of letters, which are not generally counted. All names are names of the Lord and all names are but words, which in turn are letters.

If you count the letters in ascending order, *ārohaṇa*, then in descending order, *avarohaṇa*, they amount to 108. Within this alone all words are possible. Therefore, if you repeat one name 108 times, you have symbolically repeated all the names of the Lord, known and unknown. That is for Sanskrit. Then phonetically, all sounds in all languages are between '*a*' when you open your mouth and '*m*' when you close it. The letter '*u*' stands for all other sounds inbetween. So, we have *om*. When you say '*om*' all names are included. So, the whole *jagat*, the apparent form of Īśvara, the Lord, is covered. Once you have said *om*, you require nothing more because it is a non-linguistic phonetic symbol for the Lord.

The Lord is one and non-dual containing within himself all things, which are expressed by *om*. So, *om* stands for the non-dual one and among the words, I am *om*. That is why *oṁkāra* is the sound symbol, *pratīka* for meditation upon Īśvara.

'*A*' stands for the waking world, '*u*' for the thought world and '*m*' for the unmanifest. It starts with *sṛṣṭi*, creation, and resolves into Brahman. *Om* is thus a word symbol for meditation upon *paraṁ-brahma* It is also a word through which you understand *paraṁ-brahma*. Thus, it becomes both a word revealing Brahman and a verbal symbol for meditating upon Īśvara. *Om* as a word means that which protects and sustains everything, *avati, rakṣati*. In that sense, *om* is the name for Īśvara.

There are many rituals called *yajña*s for which you require a number of ingredients. You need fire. And when you light one, some small creatures, living in the wood you offer, may be unwittingly destroyed. You need money to buy the things required to perform the *yajña* and that money you obtain by competing in the world. In doing so, you hurt somebody. Your gain is necessarily at the expense of someone else's gain. So, in the process of performing the ritual, you unwittingly hurt or destroy many things. To offset these *pāpa*s you have to say a few extra prayers. All rituals and prayers help in acquiring *antaḥ-karaṇa-śuddhi*. But among them, *japa-yajña*, mental repetition, of the Lord's name is the greatest because you do not harm anything. So, among all these various *yajña*s I am this *japa-yajña* that incurs no *pāpa.*

Sthāvarāṇāṁ himālayaḥ, among the mountains, I am the Himalayas. Here, he talks about the mountains that may or may not have peaks. *Sthāvara* means that which does not move. So, among these immobile mountains, I am the Himalayas, *ālaya*, an abode of *hima*, snow. The distinction of the Himalayas among all the mountains is the vastness of their ranges.

The Lord continues to describe his glories as they express in various exalted beings. He has chosen what is famous in the *purāṇa*s and the *śruti*s and all that is popular in the world. Later Lord Kṛṣṇa says, 'among men I am Arjuna.' Wherever there is excellence, that excellence belongs to the Lord.

अश्वत्थः सर्ववृक्षाणां देवर्षीणां च नारदः ।
गन्धर्वाणां चित्ररथः सिद्धानां कपिलो मुनिः ॥ २६ ॥

aśvatthaḥ sarvavṛkṣāṇāṁ devarṣīṇāṁ ca nāradaḥ
gandharvāṇāṁ citrarathaḥ siddhānāṁ kapilo muniḥ (26)

sarva-vṛkṣāṇām – among all the trees; *aśvatthaḥ* – (I am) the ficus religiosa, the sacred tree; *devarṣīṇāṁ ca* – and among the celestial sages; *nāradaḥ* – (I am) Nārada; *gandharvāṇām* – among the *gandharvas*; *citrarathaḥ* – I am Citraratha; *siddhānām* – among the *siddhas*; *kapilaḥ muniḥ* – (I am) the sage, Kapila

> I am the sacred ficus tree among all the trees; among the celestial sages I am Nārada; among the *gandharvas* I am Citraratha, and among the *siddhas* I am the sage Kapila.

The *aśvattha* tree, made famous by the *śruti* and the *Gītā*, symbolises the entire *saṁsāra*. The twigs of the *aśvattha* tree are used in the *vaidika* fire rituals and the tree itself is worshipped by people who want children. The neem tree that grows along with the *aśvattha* tree is considered its wife and generally couples wanting children perform the marriage of these two trees. So, among the trees, *aśvattha* is the most sacred and therefore, the Lord says here that among all the trees, I am the *aśvattha*, every part of which is worshipped. There is even a *śloka* on this in which Brahmaji is invoked in the root of the tree, Viṣṇu in the middle, and Śiva at the top and then they are worshipped there – *mūlato brahmarūpāya madhyato viṣṇurūpiṇe agrataḥ śivarūpāya vṛkṣarājāya te namaḥ*.

Then he talks of *ṛṣis*. There are two types of *ṛṣis*, those who are *manuṣyas*, human beings, and those who are *devarṣis*, gods. *Ṛṣi* means the one who knows. They are also called *mantra-draṣṭās* because all the *veda-mantras* are seen in the minds of *ṛṣis*. For every *mantra* there is a *ṛṣi* who received it.

Sage Viśvāmitra, for example, is the *ṛṣi* for the *gāyatrī-mantra*. *Ṛṣi*s are involved in every part of the Veda and among all the *ṛṣi*s, Bhagavān says, I am Nārada. In all eighteen *purāṇa*s, Nārada appears quite often. Here Bhagavān says that the greatness enjoyed by Nārada is his.

There are different types of celestials. Among them, are the *gandharva*s, a group of art and music lovers. 'Among these *gandharva*s I am Citraratha,' says Bhagavān. Citraratha was one of the sixteen sons of Kaśyapa who was a king and a great artist.

Among the ones born wise, *siddha*s, I am Kapila says Bhagavān. There is a beautiful story in the *Bhāgavatapurāṇa* about Kapila. As a young boy, he teaches *brahma-vidyā* to his mother, Devahūti.

उच्चैःश्रवसमश्वानां विद्धि माममृतोद्भवम् ।
ऐरावतं गजेन्द्राणां नराणां च नराधिपम् ॥ २७ ॥

uccaiḥśravasam aśvānāṁ viddhi mām amṛtodbhavam
airāvataṁ gajendrāṇāṁ narāṇāṁ ca narādhipam (27)

aśvānām – among the horses; *uccaiḥśravasam* – Uccaiḥśravas; *amṛta-udbhavam* – born of the churning for nectar; *gajendrāṇām* – among the elephants; *airāvatam* – Airāvata; *narāṇāṁ ca* – and among men; *narādhipam* – the king; *māṁ viddhi* – may you know me as

Among the horses may you know me as Uccaiḥśravas, and among the elephants as Airāvata, (both) born of the churning for nectar, and I am the king among men.

'Among the horses I am Uccaiḥśravas,' says Bhagavān. It is Lord Indra's horse. There is a famous story in the *purāṇa*s in which the *deva*s and *asura*s churn the ocean of milk to extract *amṛta*. Using mount Mandara as the churning rod and the serpent Vāsuki as the churning rope, the *deva*s and *asura*s churn this ocean. During the churning a lot of things came out, one of which was this particular horse. It was given to Indra. Because it was born of the ocean, which produced the nectar or because it was born when the churning for *amṛta* took place, it is *amṛtodbhava*. Here, *amṛta* means *kṣīra*, milk; and *udbhava* means that which was born of; therefore, *amṛtodbhava* means born of milk, here milky ocean.

Airāvata is the name of a white elephant born of Irāvān. It was also produced from the churning of the ocean for *amṛta*. *Irā* means water, *tadvān* means one who has that, therefore, *Irāvān* means one who has water, the ocean. Born of Irāvān is Airāvata. It is the only one of its kind and it also belongs to Indra. 'Among all the elephants, I am Airāvata.' Then among the human beings, I am the ruler, *narādhipa*, in other words, the king. All the power and pomp of the king belong to me. The crown, which makes him a king, is me.

आयुधानामहं वज्रं धेनूनामस्मि कामधुक् ।
प्रजनश्चास्मि कन्दर्पः सर्पाणामस्मि वासुकिः ॥ २८ ॥

āyudhānām ahaṁ vajraṁ dhenūnām asmi kāmadhuk
prajanaścāsmi kandarpaḥ sarpāṇām asmi vāsukiḥ (28)

āyudhānām – among the weapons; *ahaṁ vajraṁ* – I am Vajra; *dhenūnām* – among the cows; *kāmadhuk asmi* – I am the wish-fulfilling cow; *prajanaḥ ca asmi kandarpaḥ* – I am Kandarpa, the god of love who is the cause for progeny; *sarpāṇām* – among the poisonous snakes; *vāsukiḥ asmi* – I am Vāsuki

> Among the weapons I am *Vajra;* among the cows I am the wish-fulfilling cow (Kāmadhenu). I am Kandarpa (Manmatha), the god of love, who is the cause for progeny. Among the poisonous snakes I am Vāsuki.

Among the various weapons I am *vajra-āyudha*. Made from the bone of a great *maharṣi* clled Dadhīci, it is the most powerful of all weapons. And it too belongs to Indra. So, among all the weapons I am the most powerful *vajra-āyudha*.

There are thousands of cows that give milk. But Kāmadhenu gives anything you ask from it. So, among the givers nobody can give like Kāmadhenu. It also came out of the ocean while it was being churned for *amṛta* and it belonged to sage Vasiṣṭha. There is a story in which King Viśvāmitra, travelling through the forest with his soldiers and retinue, came to Vasiṣṭha's cottage. Vasiṣṭha, though living in a simple hut, was able to feed the king and all his soldiers through the bounty of the Kāmadhenu. When King Viśvāmitra came to know of this, he wanted to have the Kāmadhenu. Vasiṣṭha told him that the cow would yield only to a *brāhmaṇa.* Viśvāmitra vowed he would become a *brāhmaṇa.* But the cow did not yield anything. As long as he had *rajas* expressing as anger, greed, and so on, nothing happened. Finally King Viśvāmitra understood and gave up everything and became a *maharṣi* himself. This is the story of Kāmadhenu. And the Lord says, among givers, I am Kāmadhenu.

Prajanaḥ is the cause for progeny. In the parents of children, I am Kandarpa, the God of love. He is the presiding deity of the love that is behind progeny. *Prajana* is adjective to Kandarpa. We have to add, 'In the parents of children.' Parents are not the cause of progeny. It is Kandarpa, the god of love, who is the cause of progeny. And the glory of Kandarpa is the glory of the Lord, and not that of Kandarpa.

Then among the poisonous snakes I am Vāsuki. Vāsuki, as we have seen, was used to churn the ocean for *amṛta*. It is a very long snake found in *deva-loka* whose very breathing will destroy people. So, it is a source of great fear. That source of fear and that poison is nothing but me. There is nothing that is separate from me.

अनन्तश्चास्मि नागानां वरुणो यादसामहम् ।
पितॄणामर्यमा चास्मि यमः संयमतामहम् ॥ २९ ॥

anantaścāsmi nāgānāṁ varuṇo yādasām aham
pitṝṇām aryamā cāsmi yamaḥ saṁyamatām aham (29)

nāgānām – among the many-headed snakes; *anantaḥ ca asmi* – and I am Ananta (the king); *yādasām* – among the gods of water; *ahaṁ varuṇaḥ* – I am Varuṇa (the king); *pitṝṇām* – among the manes; *aryamā ca asmi* – I am Aryamā (the king); *saṁyamatām* – among those who enforce discipline; *ahaṁ yamaḥ* – I am Yama

I am Ananta among the many-headed snakes, Varuṇa among the gods of water, Aryamā among the manes, and among those who enforce discipline I am Yama.

There are one-headed and many-headed snakes according to the *purāṇas*. 'Among the many-headed, I am Ananta, Ādiśeṣa a great devotee of Lord Viṣṇu who had one thousand heads. Lord Viṣṇu reclines on the coils of Ādiśeṣa, the original spring mattress!

Yādasām, among the presiding deities of rivers such as Gaṅgā, Yamunā, etc., I am Varuṇa. Varuṇa is the Lord of water and is therefore, exalted among the presiding deities of rivers etc. His glory is again that of the Lord.

Among the celestial manes, I am Aryamā. People who live a religious life but do not perform the *vaidika* rituals such as *agniṣṭoma* become celestial manes called Agniṣvātta and so on, otherwise known as *pitṛ*s in general. Their king is Aryamā. This glory of Aryamā is of Īśvara.

Among people who enforce the law like the police and judiciary, I am Lord Yama, the Lord of death. Nobody can go past him. The power he has, which makes him the feared Lord of death, is nothing but me.

प्रह्लादश्चास्मि दैत्यानां कालः कलयतामहम् ।
मृगाणां च मृगेन्द्रोऽहं वैनतेयश्च पक्षिणाम् ॥ ३० ॥

prahlādaścāsmi daityānāṁ kālaḥ kalayatām aham
mṛgāṇāṁ ca mṛgendro'haṁ vainateyaśca pakṣiṇām (30)

daityānām – among the *asura*s who are born of Diti; *prahlādaḥ ca asmi* – and I am Prahlāda; *kalayatām* – among things that reckon; *ahaṁ kālaḥ* – I am time; *mṛgāṇāṁ ca* – and among the wild animals; *ahaṁ mṛgendraḥ* – I am the king of animals, the lion; *pakṣiṇām* – among the birds; *vainateyaḥ ca* – and I am Garuḍa

> I am Prahlāda among the *asura*s who are born of Diti. Among things that reckon, I am the Time; among the wild animals I am the lion, and I am Garuḍa among the birds.

The one who is born of Diti is a *daitya*. A descendent can be regarded either from the maternal or paternal standpoint. Here it is from the standpoint of the mother. The son of Kuntī, Kaunteya is another example of mentioning the descendent from the standpoint of the maternal side. The sons of Diti are all *asura*s. The *asura*s and their progeny are called *daitya*s. Among them, there was one who, even though he was a son of an *asura*, was a *bhakta* of Nārāyaṇa. That was Prahlāda. He continuously repeated the Lord's name in spite of his father, King Hiraṇyakaśipu's order and his teachers' efforts to teach him otherwise. Hiraṇyakaśipu had ordered in his kingdom that he alone should be worshipped as God and no other God should be worshipped. Everyone had to repeat the words, *hiraṇyāya namaḥ* and worship him as God. Prahlāda refused to do that and continued to say Lord Nārāyaṇa's name, *oṁ namo nārāyaṇāya.* All attempts to make Prahlāda accept Hiraṇyakaśipu as Īśvara including attempts to kill him failed.

One day, his father asked, 'Where is this Nārāyaṇa of yours?'

'Everywhere' said Prahlāda.

'Is he in this pillar?'

'Yes,' said young Prahlāda.

Then Hiraṇyakaśipu kicked the pillar. He had tried to ensure that he would be immortal by securing a special boon. The boon was that he cannot be killed by a human being or animal, neither during day nor at night, neither inside nor outside the house, neither by a wet nor dry instrument, etc. So, when the pillar broke open, Lord Viṣṇu came out in the form of Narasiṁha with the head of a lion and a human body. He came at twilight, *sandhyā-kāla*, when it was neither day nor night. He sat on the threshold so that he was neither inside nor outside. And since Hiraṇyakaśipu should not touch the ground, Narasiṁha put him on his lap and killed him without violating any of the conditions of the comprehensive boon. Later he enthroned Prahlāda. 'That Prahlāda who is a great *bhakta* among the *daitya*s, I am,' says the Lord.

There are many people who keep accounts. Among all of them, I am the Time that is ticking away constantly. There is nothing that escapes the reckoning of Time. That Time I am.

Among all the wild animals living in the forest, I am the king of them, the lion or tiger. The lion is not afraid of any animal. A tiger, though it may kill a lion cub, will never voluntarily engage in a fight with a lion. It will run away. But a lion will not run away even from a tiger. Sometimes the lion is wary of an elephant. But it is relatively fearless and can kill an elephant too. There are many forests where, in the absence of lions, the tigers, if they are there, become the rulers. The word *mṛga* means a wild animal whose habitat is the forest. What we should understand here is this. Bhagavān says that the fearlessness and the power in the king of animals are 'me.'

Next he says, among the flying creatures or birds, I am Garuḍa. Garuḍa is the son of Vinatā as is Aruṇa. Therefore, he is called Vainateya and is a devotee of Viṣṇu. Garuḍa flies very high where even vultures cannot go. It looks like an eagle with a white band around its neck and sighting it is a good omen. The capacity to soar to such heights and fly so beautifully are its special features. This *vibhūti* of Garuḍa is nothing but me, says Bhagavān.

पवनः पवतामस्मि रामः शस्त्रभृतामहम् ।
झषाणां मकरश्चास्मि स्रोतसामस्मि जाह्नवी ॥ ३१ ॥

pavanaḥ pavatām asmi rāmaḥ śastrabhṛtām aham
jhaṣāṇāṁ makaraścāsmi srotasām asmi jāhnavī (31)

pavatām – among the purifiers; *pavanaḥ asmi* – I am air; *śastrabhṛtām* – among those who bear weapons; *ahaṁ rāmaḥ* – I am Rāma; *jhaṣāṇām* – among the fish; *makaraḥ ca asmi* – I am the shark; *srotasām* – among the rivers; *jāhnavī asmi* – I am Gaṅgā

> Among the purifiers, I am Air; I am Rāma among those who bear weapons; among the fish I am shark, and among the rivers I am Gaṅgā.

Pavana is another name for Vāyu, air. Among the various purifying agents, *pavatām*, I am Vāyu, says Bhagavān. It is Vāyu that keeps the atmosphere clean and it also has a life giving quality. It provides carbon-dioxide for the plants and oxygen for man. That cleansing, life giving capacity is I.

Among those who wield weapons, I am Rāma who is an *avatāra* of Viṣṇu himself. The *avatāra* in this human body of Rāma had great prowess. Even with one arrow he could dry up the ocean and perform incredible feats because his arrows had extraordinary powers. Since there are other powerful *avatāra*s also named Rāma, like Paraśurāma and Balarāma, Śaṅkara says, Dāśarathī Rāma, who was the son of Daśaratha.

*Jhaṣa*s are fish and other varieties of sea animals. Among them, I am *makaraḥ*. The word *makara* can refer to any large aquatic animal such as crocodile, shark or a whale. A shark has a great capacity to devour. Its whole body seems to be full of teeth. The crocodile is also very powerful. And there is nothing like a whale for size, strength and beauty. It is the elephant of the waters. 'That *vibhūti* of the shark or whale or a crocodile, I am,' says Bhagavān.

Among the rivers I am Jāhnavī, otherwise known as Gaṅgā. Her water is always fresh. It is said that no bacteria can thrive in Ganges water. Whether it is so, every Hindu home has a pot of Gaṅgā water, which never spoils. And through association and the circumstances of her birth, Gaṅgā stands for knowledge. She is said to have come from Lord Śiva's head. And there are hundreds of stories associated with her as a source of knowledge and purification. In India every river is worshipped. But Gaṅgā has a special place. It is not just a river, but *jñāna-*

gaṅgā, the unbroken flow of knowledge itself. One dip is said to remove all sins. That is the *śraddhā* people have for Gaṅgā. She is looked upon as a *devatā*.

सर्गाणामादिरन्तश्च मध्यं चैवाहमर्जुन ।
अध्यात्मविद्या विद्यानां वादः प्रवदतामहम् ॥ ३२ ॥

sargāṇām ādirantaśca madhyaṁ caivāham arjuna
adhyātmavidyā vidyānāṁ vādaḥ pravadatām aham (32)

arjuna – O Arjuna!; *sargāṇām* – of creations; *aham* – I am; *ādiḥ* – the beginning; *antaḥ ca* – and the end; *madhyaṁ ca* – and the middle; *eva* – indeed; *vidyānām* – among the disciplines of knowledge; *adhyātma-vidyā* – I am the knowledge of the self; *pravadatām* – of those who discuss; *vādaḥ aham* – I am the discussion leading to truth

> Arjuna! I am indeed the beginning, the middle, and the end of the creations. Among the disciplines of knowledge, I am the knowledge of the self. Of those who discuss, I am the discussion leading to truth.

Sarga here can be any activity. Of the various actions you may perform like talking, eating, and so on, I am the beginning, the middle and the end. The act of creation, the action that protects and sustains, and the action of destruction are the three most important of all actions. Or, you can interpret it this way. The beginning of any action is the thought of doing it, *saṅkalpa*. I am the very *saṅkalpa* of every action. The *kriyā*, process of doing it, is also 'myself' and so is the *phala*, result. There is nothing else besides me.

Among the various disciplines of knowledge, I am *adhyātma-vidyā*, the knowledge centred on the *ātmā*; in other words, the knowledge that reveals the nature of *ātmā* and knowing which you know everything as well. This is the only *vidyā* that completely frees you from ignorance, because you are not ignorant. You are *sat-cit-ānanda-svarūpa*.

Among the three different types of discussions, *vāda, jalpa,* and *vitaṇḍā,* I am *vāda,* discussion to discover the truth. In *jalpa,* each participant wants to convince the other of his view. The discussion is not to find the truth, but only to prove one's point, like a discussion between two believers. In *vitaṇḍā,* anything one of the participants says is judged wrong by the other. It is a personality clash and has nothing to do with finding out the truth. The whole point is to prove the other person wrong. While *jalpa* is fanaticism, *vitaṇḍā* is an ego trip. The third is *vāda,* discussion to find out the truth. Whether you contribute to the discussion or just listen, the purpose is to discover the truth. Such fact finding discussions are real discussions and this is what is referred to here. In fact finding discussions we want to discover what is really there and what is there is Īśvara. In the other two types of discussion, there is only *ahaṅkāra* and one's own mental cobwebs. There is no truth. *Vāda,* on the other hand, leads you to the discovery of Īśvara. And Bhagavān says, '*vāda* is me.' The fact finding capacity in the dialogue of those who discuss is 'me.' Here the sixth case in the word *pravadatām* has the meaning 'of.'[19] Therefore, 'I am

---

[19] In this section, two types of sixth cases have been used. One is '*śeṣe*' and the other is '*nirdhāraṇe*.' *Śeṣe* has the meaning of 'of' and *nirdhāraṇe ṣaṣṭhī* has the meaning of 'among.'

the *vāda*, the very fact finding discussion of those who discuss, *pravadatām*.' The prefix *pra* before *vadatām* tells us that the persons who are discussing are committed to *vāda*, not other forms of discussion.

An account of the glories of Īśvara continues. Even though there is nothing separate from him, wherever there is excellence, whether it is in terms of knowledge, beauty, or prowess, and so on, that excellence should be viewed as Īśvara's. This applies not only with reference to people but to places as well.

We saw that Bhagavān said, 'Among the words, *girām*, I am *oṁkāra*.' *Om* is a word, which includes phonetically all words in all languages. Because all forms are the Lord's form and all names his name, the word *om* is a perfect name for the Lord.

Now the Lord talks about the most important letter among the letters in the beginning of the following verse.

अक्षराणामकारोऽस्मि द्वन्द्वः सामासिकस्य च ।
अहमेवाक्षयः कालो धाताहं विश्वतोमुखः ॥ ३३ ॥

akṣarāṇām akāro'smi dvandvaḥ sāmāsikasya ca
aham evākṣayaḥ kālo dhātāhaṁ viśvatomukhaḥ (33)

akṣarāṇām – among the letters; *akāraḥ asmi* – I am the letter '*a*'; *sāmāsikasya ca* – and among the compounds; *dvandvaḥ* – (I am) the *dvandva*; *aham eva* – I am indeed; *akṣayaḥ kālaḥ* – the perennially eternal time; *ahaṁ viśvatomukhaḥ dhātā* – I am the all-pervasive giver (of *karma-phala*)

Among the letters I am '*a*', and I am the *dvandva* among the compounds. I am indeed the perennially eternal time. I am the giver (of *karma-phala*) who is all-pervasive.

Akṣarāṇām aham akāraḥ asmi, among all the letters I am the letter '*a*.' The first sound is '*a*' and through the modification of that basic sound come all other sounds of letters in all languages and dialects. Therefore, among all the letters, I am the basis. The excellence in that basic sound is me. Without that sound emanating from the voice box, where is the possibility of language? The greatest musical instrument ever made is the human voice. All other instruments have notes, but lyrics and *bhāvanā* can come only through the human voice. There, the basic sound is '*a*.' So, the Lord is manifest in the form of '*a*.' Every other sound is a modification of that. Because he is that basic sound, in all sounds Bhagavān is there. Nothing is away from him.

In all languages there are compounds. In English we have words such as house keeping, blue-eyed, work place, foot path, etc., which are compounds. They are all formed through usage. But in Sanskrit, compounds are formed by rules. So, you can make a compound, which, if properly formed, can theoretically be understood by anybody else.

Two beautiful features of the Sanskrit language are the compounds and the *taddhita* or nominal derivatives. For example, the word, *ārṣa* means that which belongs to the *ṛṣi*s. Vedanta is *ārṣa*. It does not belong to anybody in particular. *Ārṣa-vidyā* is a compound. It is *ārṣa*, born of sages, and it is *vidyā*, knowledge.

As an example of compounds made in the Sanskrit language, here we can look at a beautiful compound – *kaṭākṣa-kiraṇa-ācānta-naman-mohābdhaye.*[20] It is one word. All these words, *kaṭa, akṣa, kiraṇa, ācānta, naman, moha* and *abdhi,* make up this one word. There is only one declension at the end – *moha-abdhaye. Kaṭa* means a corner and *akṣa* an eye; so, *kaṭākṣa* means corner of the eye, a glance. If you look at someone through the corner of your eye, you illumine the person by your sight. So, this side-glance being like a *kiraṇa,* a ray of light, is *kaṭākṣa-kiraṇa.* These rays mentioned here, like the rays of the sun, not only light up things, but also dry up things. What do they dry up? They dry up the *mohābdhi. Moha* is ignorance and delusion and *abdhi* is ocean. *Mohābdhi* is the ocean of ignorance and delusion. It is dried up by being *ācānta,* sipped up. So, the whole ocean of ignorance and delusion is dried up by the ray of one side-glance. Whose glance? Whose else can it be except Īśvara's? Our glance does not even dry up the tears, let alone the ocean. Here, I am not even asking for a direct look from the Lord. Just a glance is enough for me. Because he is infinite, my sorrow is nothing. *Kaṭākṣa-kiraṇa* amounts to grace. The rays of whose glance dry up the entire ocean of delusion, for whom? *Namaskṛtānām,* for those who have surrendered to him. To get the glance you have to go to him.

This verse continues and ends in two more compounds – *ananta-ānanda-kṛṣṇāya jagan-maṅgala-mūrtaye,* salutations to that Lord Kṛṣṇa, who is limitless and all joy, whose very form is a

---

20 *Advaita Makaranda* Verse 1

blessing to the world. All these are compounds. The one who is *ananta,* limitless, *ānanda,* all joy, Kṛṣṇa – to that Kṛṣṇa, my salutations. Kṛṣṇa never had any sorrow, unlike Rāma who behaved as though he were a human being. Rāma is the Lord expressing in the form of *dharma* and Kṛṣṇa is the Lord expressing in the form of *ānanda. Ānanda* attracts. It is the only attraction in the world and the Lord is that *ānanda. Jagan-maṅgala-mūrti* is the one whose very form is a blessing to the world.

There are even longer compounds than these. The beauty of Sanskrit is that in one compound you can express so much. They are divided into four main groups – *avyayībhāva, tatpuruṣa, bahuvrīhi* and *dvandva.* In the *avyayībhāva* compounds, the first word is an indeclinable and is the most important. Take the word *upakumbham,* which means 'near the pot.' Here the first word, *upa* is the predominant word. In a *tatpuruṣa* compound, the last word is important as in *rājapuruṣa,* the employee of the king. Here the second word, *puruṣa* is important because the compound refers to the *puruṣa,* the man who belongs to the king. In a *bahuvrīhi* compound, another word, a word that is not in the compound, is the most important, *pradhāna.* The compound refers to a word that is outside the compound. That is, it is an adjective to another word. Suppose I say, '*eka-karṇam ānaya.*' *Eka* is one, *karṇa* is ear, and *ānaya* means bring. Should you chop one ear off the first person you see and bring it? No. *Eka-karṇa* is a person who has only one ear. So, it means, 'Bring the one-eared person.' This is *bahuvrīhi.* Most of the compounds in the *Gītā* are like this. And the fourth is the *dvandva*. It is different. In the word '*rāmalakṣmaṇau*' which is more important? Here both are equally important. If you want to see Bhagavān in a compound, analyse a *dvandva* compound. Among the compounds I am the *dvandva*, the compound where all words are equally important. The idea is, the Lord is equally present in everything. Rāma is the Lord, Lakṣmaṇa is the Lord because the Lord is the same in all beings, *samo'haṁ sarva bhūteṣu*. I am equal in all beings and in the *dvandva* compound you can see this fact about me totally. Therefore, I am the *dvandva* among the compounds.

Then he says, *aham eva akṣayaḥ kālah*. There are two meanings given for *kāla*. Here there is no sixth case, no 'among,' as we have been seeing like in, among the letters I am '*a*' or 'of' as in 'of those who discuss, I am the discussion.' Here, Bhagavān is simply expressing himself. Where there is no sixth case it means that he is talking about his *mahattva*, greatness. *Akṣaya* means that which does not come to an end. In the relative field of *saṁsāra*, time does not come to an end. In a sense, it is a continuous flow. Of course in *paramātmā*, there is no time. But within the framework of the *jagat*, time is continuously flowing and in it, all things come and go. So, I am that time, which is perennially eternal.

Or, Śaṅkara says this statement means, I am the time, which is eternal, because of whom time is born, but who is timeless. I am *akṣayaḥ kālah*, I am timeless, the truth of time and the very creator of time.

Dhātā ahaṁ viśvatomukhaḥ. *Viśvatomukha* means the one whose faces are everywhere. He is all-pervasive. And he is *dhātā, vidhātā* giver of *karma-phala*s to all the beings according to their *karma*s; the one who ordains everything. It is not an arbitrary one sided giving. For each action, a specific result has to be given. The Lord says, I am doing that. My laws produce all the results. For all actions, right and wrong, I give the results. And he is qualified to do that because he is *viśvatomukha,* all-pervasive. The idea is that there is nothing that takes place outside the scope of his vision. So, every result is true to the *karma* that produced it.

While everything is the manifestation of the Lord, there are areas of excellence. These are the places where you can appreciate the Lord. If you just appreciate the object, you miss out on something. But in appreciating the object as a glory of the Lord, you connect yourself to the whole. Otherwise you connect only to an object in a subject object relationship. In recognising Īśvara's glory, you are immediately connected to the Lord, the total. Therefore, wherever there is an expression of excellence, Bhagavān says, please understand that it belongs to me.

मृत्युः सर्वहरश्चाहमुद्भवश्च भविष्यताम् ।
कीर्तिः श्रीर्वाक् च नारीणां स्मृतिर्मेधा धृतिः क्षमा ॥ ३४ ॥

mṛtyuḥ sarvaharaścāham udbhavaśca bhaviṣyatām
kīrtiḥ śrīrvāk ca nārīṇāṁ smṛtirmedhā dhṛtiḥ kṣamā (34)

mṛtyuḥ – death; *sarva-haraḥ* – that takes away everything; *ca aham* – and I am; *ca bhaviṣyatām* – of those yet to be; *udbhavaḥ* – the cause of prosperity; *ca nārīṇām* – and among feminine words; *kīrtiḥ* – fame; *srīḥ* – wealth; *vāk* – speech; *smṛtiḥ* –

memory; *medhā* – intelligence; *dhṛtiḥ* – fortitude; *kṣamā* – equanimity

> I am Death that takes away everything, and I am the cause of prosperity of those yet to be. Among the feminine words[21] I am fame, wealth, speech, memory, intelligence, fortitude and equanimity.

Mṛtyuḥ is that which puts an end to something. Śaṅkara says there are two types of death. One takes away wealth and so on, *dhana-hara*. It can include your title, land, possessions, money and so on. Then there is *prāṇa-hara*, the one who takes away your life.

Here, which *mṛtyu* is Bhagavān talking about? He makes it clear by saying *sarva-hara*, the one who takes away everything. If he takes away money etc., you can always gain that money back. Or, even if you do not, without money you can gain some knowledge and thereby still be happy. So, there is no way that *mṛtyu* can rob you of your happiness by taking away *dhanādi*, wealth etc. But if it takes away your life, what can you do? Therefore, *mṛtyu* is called *sarva-hara* – *sarvaṁ harati iti sarva-haraḥ*. One who takes away is *hara*. But then with the word *sarva* as a modifier, it means that he is the one who takes away everything. Bhagavān says there is no *mṛtyu* except me. Therefore, Lord Death is also myself alone.

Previously he spoke of himself as Lord Yama who enforces discipline, '*yamaḥ saṁyamatām aham*.' This is based on the

---

[21] Sanskrit words for fame etc., are feminine. They are valued by all.

root '*yam*' having the meaning of control. Since this aspect of Yama was mentioned before, here *mṛtyu* is the one who puts an end to everything.

Or, I am the Lord in the form of the destroyer, who resolves everything into myself at the time of *pralaya*. I am the sustainer, I am the creator and I am also the *saṁhāra-kartā*. At the time of total dissolution he destroys everything and brings it back to himself. *Sarva-hara* then is Rudra who is pointed out here is also not separate from Īśvara.

Then again *udbhavaḥ* is that which happens in plenty and in a desirable way. Śaṅkara translates it as *abhyudayaḥ*, prosperity. Any pleasant experience, whether it is a world of experience or a comfort gained through some wealth etc., is called *abhyudaya*. There are two desirable ends for a human being, *abhyudaya* and *niśśreyasa*. *Niśśreyasa* means *mokṣa* and is the most desirable. Anything other than *niśśreyasa* is *abhyudaya*; therefore, *dharma*, *artha* and *kāma* become *abhyudaya*, because they are other than that which is the most desirable.

Not only the *abhyudaya*, but the cause for it is also me. All the *dharma*, *puṇya* and so on, is born of me alone. Do not think that you have created it. It is my law and is therefore gained only because of me. And anything created by me is non-separate from me. If anyone has gained anything in terms of *dharma*, *artha* or *kāma*, that is myself. The result is myself and I am the cause for the gain of that result. The connection between *sādhana* and *sādhya*, the means and the end, is created by me and therefore, I am the cause of the *abhyudaya*.

Udbhavaḥ bhaviṣyatām, I am the prosperity of those who are going to gain prosperity in the future. Even the *puṇya* you think you have gathered today, you have not. I am the one who is gathered by you and the capacity to gather is also myself.

Then again, among the words in the feminine gender, *nārīṇām*, I am *kīrti*, *srī*, *vāk*, *smṛti*, *medhā* and *kṣamā*. *Kīrti* is fame born of *dharma*. *Srī* means wealth, health, knowledge, everything desirable. *Vāk* is speech that is *hita*, good; *satya*, truthful; and *priya*, pleasant. This is all implied in *vāk* because he is talking about something exalted. *Smṛti* here is the capacity to remember. *Medhā* is the power to receive, retain, and reflect upon knowledge. If there is *medhā* there will also be *smṛti*.

Dhṛti is fortitude or courage. *Kṣamā*, though it is often translated as forgiveness, is more of a capacity of not getting disturbed. Whether there is praise or censure, the mind does not undergo any significant change. For praise, there is no elation and for censure, no depression. Among all the words in the feminine gender, I am these qualities.

Śaṅkara says, even if somebody has a shade of these such as fame, or some wealth, which he looks upon himself as being fulfilled, that is the Lord. Suppose one has some capacity to speak. He gives a simple after dinner talk and is so happy when everybody praises him. That *kīrti*, *srī*, *vāk*, and so on is me. All these belong to me because I have all of them in absolute measure.

बृहत्साम तथा साम्नां गायत्री छन्दसामहम् ।
मासानां मार्गशीर्षोऽहमृतूनां कुसुमाकरः ॥ ३५ ॥

bṛhatsāma tathā sāmnāṁ gāyatrī chandasām aham
māsānāṁ mārgaśīrṣo'ham ṛtūnāṁ kusumākaraḥ (35)

tathā – so too; *sāmnām* – among the *sāmas*; *bṛhatsāma* – the Bṛhatsāma; *chandasām* – among the metres; *ahaṁ gāyatrī* – I am Gāyatrī; *māsānām* – among the months; *aham* – I am; *mārgaśīrṣaḥ* – Mārgaśīrṣaḥ (November-December); *ṛtūnām* – among the seasons; *kusumākaraḥ* – the spring (the one that brings forth flowers)

So too, I am the Bṛhatsāma among the *sāmas*; Gāyatrī among the metres; among the months, Mārgaśīrṣa, and among the seasons, the Spring.

The *sāmas*, the *mantras* that are sung, are sung in different styles each of which has a name. One of them is more difficult and more melodious than the others. That is called Bṛhatsāma. Therefore, among the *sāmaveda-mantras*, I am Bṛhad. Only certain *mantras* are sung in this particular manner. Those *mantras* together with the style are called Bṛhatsāma.

There are many metres, *chandas*, in the Veda such as *uṣṇik*, *anuṣṭup*, *triṣṭup* and so on. Among them, I am *gāyatrī*. Generally a verse in the *anuṣṭup* metre is called a *śloka* and has 4 *pādas* of 8 letters, *akṣaras*, a total of 32 letters. In the Veda, *gāyatrī-chandas* has 3 *pādas*, each having 8 *akṣaras*, a total of 24 letters.

The *gāyatrī-mantra* is as follows; *tat savitur vareṇyam* is the first *pāda* of 7 syllables; *bhargo devasya dhīmahi* the second *pāda* of 8 syllables; *dhiyo yo naḥ pracodayāt* is the third *pāda* of 8 syllables. *Om* is added at the beginning and the *mantra* will have 24 syllables. So the 24 *akṣaras*, syllables are: *oṁ tat sa vi tur va re ṇyam bhar go de va sya dhī ma hi dhi yo yo naḥ pra co da yāt.* The Lord says, among the various meters, I am *gāyatrī*.

Why is it *śreṣṭha* more exalted than the rest? The first *mantra* of *Ṛg-veda* is in *gāyatrī-chandas* and for every *devatā* there is a *mantra* in *gāyatrī-chandas*.

Śaṅkara says that it is this *mantra* that is popularly called *gāyatrī-mantra*. There are many *mantras* in the *gāyatrī* metre but this particular one is called *gāyatrī*. Like the word Rāma. Even though it has its own etymological meaning, when it is said, it is understood to mean Daśaratha's son. It is called *rūḍhi*, the popular meaning.

When you say Gandhi, only one Gandhi is understood; others have to be qualified by their first names. Similarly here, *gāyatrī*, though it is just a metre, is understood as this well known *mantra*.

I am this *mantra* not only because it is popular. Its meaning is the entire *brahma-vidyā*. Let us look at it. *Om* is Bhagavān. *Bhūr*, *bhuvaḥ*, *suvaḥ*, are the three worlds, gross, subtle and unmanifest, *sthūla*, *sūkṣma* and *kāraṇa prapañcas*. *Om* is all three; it includes everything.

Tat, that (Lord), *vareṇyam* is the most worshipful. *Dhīmahi* means 'we meditate' upon that Lord, as a *sādhana*, or we recognise that Lord, which is knowledge. This *mantra* in fact is chanted first as a *sādhana*. Later, when it is understood, it is contemplated upon. We contemplate upon *devasya savituḥ*, the one who is self-effulgent and all-knowledge. The one who is all-knowledge is symbolised by *savitā,* the sun because in the sun's brilliance, there is no trace of darkness, a symbol for ignorance. The sun is always likened to the Lord because it has no taint of darkness, unlike the moon, which has patches. *Yaḥ,* that Lord, who is *bhargaḥ,* all-knowledge, *pracodayāt,* may he brighten, *naḥ dhiyaḥ,* our minds. This is prayer. In contemplation we have the meaning – the all-knowledge Lord, as the self, illumines our minds.

This *gāyatrī-mantra,* in a succinct form, holds a lot of meaning. Once you know this *mantra,* it is said that you have as well studied all the Vedas. A child who has been initiated into the *gāyatrī-mantra,* after prostrating to an elderly person or a scholar, gets up and introduces himself in this manner – 'I am born in the family of this *ṛṣi,* (Bhāradvāja etc.) and I follow this *dharma-sūtra* (*āpastamba-sūtra, bodhāyana-sūtra* etc.) for the purpose of performing various rituals.' Then he will say, 'I have studied this branch of the Veda (*ahaṁ yajuśśākhādhyāyī, ṛkśākhādhyāyī* or *sāmaśākhādhyāyī*).' This practice is still maintained by the *brāhmaṇas*. He may never have opened the Veda but he can legitimately say this because *gāyatrī* chanting is considered equivalent to the study of one Veda. When he says, *ahaṁ yajuśśākhādhyāyī,* it is not true because he has never studied the *Yajur-veda*. But then he has been initiated into *gāyatrī* and therefore, he is acquitted of any falsehood. Chanting the *gāyatrī* transforms a person into a *brāhmaṇa.*

Among the months, *māsānām,* I am the Mārgaśīrṣa. With the end of this month, the southern solstice comes to an end. During this month, the sun goes to the house of Capricorn, *makara.*

This month is astrologically conducive to religious activities. I make this month auspicious.

Among the seasons, I am the spring. Everything bursts forth at that time. All the trees seem to be waiting for it. The spring is called *kusumākara* because this season makes all the plants to flower. Also it is the season that is enjoined by the Veda for the performance of an important fire ritual, *jyotiṣṭoma – vasante vasante jyotiṣā juhoti.*

द्यूतं छलयतामस्मि तेजस्तेजस्विनामहम् ।
जयोऽस्मि व्यवसायोऽस्मि सत्त्वं सत्त्ववतामहम् ॥ ३६ ॥

dyūtaṁ chalayatām asmi tejastejasvinām aham
jayo'smi vyavasāyo'smi sattvaṁ sattvavatām aham (36)

chalayatām – among those that deceive; *dyūtam asmi* – I am the game of dice; *tejasvinām* – of the brilliant; *aham tejaḥ* – I am the brilliance; *jayaḥ asmi* – I am the victory (of the victorious); *vyavasāyaḥ asmi* – I am the clarity in thinking (of those who have that clarity); *sattvavatām* – of those whose natuure is predominantly *sattva*; *sattvam aham* – I am the *sattva-guṇa* (the contemplative disposition)

> I am the game of dice among the things that deceive; of the brilliant I am the brilliance. I am the victory (of the victorious). I am the clarity in thinking (of those who have that clarity). Of those whose nature is predominantly *sattva*, I am that *sattva-guṇa* (contemplative disposition).

Chala is anything that has an element of deception. Among those things that make you incur loss, I am the game of dice. Dharmaputra lost everything in a game of dice. The Veda prohibits playing with dice. It says, *akṣaiḥ mā dīvya,* do not play with dice.

I am that brilliance of people who have brilliance in any field of knowledge. Whatever brilliance they enjoy, it does not belong to them, but it is tapped from the original source, *ātmā,* which is limitless in terms of power and knowledge. Everything you have tapped is from that source. *Sat-cit-ānanda ātmā* being Īśvara has all the potential. In a given *upādhi,* there cannot be infinite brilliance because we are talking in terms of manifestations, not *svarūpa.* In essential nature, you are non-separate from Īśvara because the self is limitless. That is a different thing altogether.

But in the manifest form, in the *antaḥ-karaṇa,* there can only be limited brilliance, *tejas.* Therefore, at any time, in any *antaḥ-karaṇa,* the brilliance is the manifestation of Īśvara. So the Lord says, of the brilliant, I am the brilliance. I am the victory of the victorious, the success of the successful. In people who have clear understanding, I am that clarity of understanding.

Then of those in whom *sattva* is predominant, that *sattva* I am. Everyone is a composite of *sattva, rajas* and *tamas. Sattva* accounts for contemplativeness, enquiry, knowledge, and happiness. *Rajas* for ambition, energy and so on. *Tamas* for dullness. If *sattva* is predominant in a person, he will not feel, 'I am *sāttvika.*' That is a manifestation of *rajas. Rajas* is also the

Lord, but it is not a *vibhūti* as *sattva* is. The expression of *sattva*, his contemplative disposition, Bhagavān says, is myself.

We are talking about *dhyeya*, an object of meditation; so, we view Īśvara as a quality that we consider desirable, a virtue. Wherever there is such a virtue, it is Īśvara's glory alone. This is appreciated and meditated upon.

वृष्णीनां वासुदेवोऽस्मि पाण्डवानां धनञ्जयः ।
मुनीनामप्यहं व्यासः कवीनामुशना कविः ॥ ३७ ॥

vṛṣṇīnāṁ vāsudevo'smi pāṇḍavānāṁ dhanañjayaḥ
munīnām apyahaṁ vyāsaḥ kavīnām uśanā kaviḥ (37)

vṛṣṇīnām – among the Yādavas; *vāsudevaḥ asmi* – I am Vāsudeva (Kṛṣṇa); *pāṇḍavānām* – among the Pāṇḍavas; (*aham*) *dhanañjayaḥ* – (I am) Arjuna; *munīnām api* – and among the seers; *ahaṁ vyāsaḥ* – I am Vyāsa; *kavīnām* – among the sages; *uśanā kaviḥ* – the preceptor Uśanā

> Among the Yādavas, I am Vāsudeva (Kṛṣṇa); among the Pāṇḍavas, I am Arjuna; among the seers I am Vyāsa, and among the sages, the preceptor Uśanā.

Bhagavān has been speaking of himself as Īśvara, the one who is everything. Now he talks of himself as an *avatāra.* With a physical body he is called Vāsudeva, son of Vasudeva. Among the people belonging to the *vṛṣṇikula*, the Yādavas, *ahaṁ vāsudevaḥ*, I am Vāsudeva. Here he is speaking of himself as Vāsudeva with a *kārya-karaṇa-saṅghāta*, not as Parameśvara. The physical body-mind-sense complex, which was recognised among the Yādavas as Kṛṣṇa is who I am. Because of the great excellence that was there in terms of knowledge, power and so on, as we see in the life of Kṛṣṇa in Bhāgavata and Mahābhārata, we know that he was an exalted being. That excellence in the *kārya-karaṇa-saṅghāta* makes him stand out among the Yādavas.

Among the Pāṇḍavas, I am Dhanañjaya, the one who won many kingdoms and great wealth. Arjuna was considered the most accomplished among the brothers in archery, logistics, and so on. It means that Kṛṣṇa is saying, 'I am you.' The prowess and versatility that you have are manifestations of Īśvara's glory, my glory.

It was to Arjuna that the Lord chose to teach the *Gītā*. He could have chosen any of the others but he found Arjuna to be the most qualified. And again it was only Arjuna who asked for it also.

Among the scholars and seers, people who have the capacity to think and retain, *munīnām*, I am Veda-Vyāsa. It was he who wrote the *Mahābhārata*, authored the eighteen *Purāṇa*s and edited the four Vedas. Originally there were many branches of the Vedas all preserved by oral tradition. Vyāsa collected and compiled the *mantra*s into four different groups; so, they could be preserved. Each family was to retain one Veda and there was a rule that one was supposed to study one Veda and hand it over to the next generation. In dividing them up, Vyāsa made it easy, so that one Veda could be studied in twelve years. He is called Veda-Vyāsa, the compiler of the Vedas – *vedaḥ vyasyate anena iti veda-vyāsaḥ*.

He also wrote the *Brahma-sūtra*s that deal with the subject matter of *vedānta-śāstra* analytically, tackling opposing views and thereby establishing the vision of Vedanta. Because of this work, Vyāsa is called *sūtrakāra*. Śaṅkara is *bhāṣyakāra*. The tradition holds that Lord Śiva himself was Śaṅkarācārya and Lord Nārāyaṇa was Bādarāyaṇa, Vyāsa. We salute both of them since they are the links in this tradition. Thus Vyāsa occupies the most exalted place among the sages. Without him, we would not have retained anything. He is a very important sage in the Vedic tradition.

Kavi means the one who is able to see all three periods of time, past, present and future. Among such people who are capable of seeing things beyond the human intellect, I am Uśanā, Śukrācārya. He was the *guru* of all the *asura*s. It was Uśanā that they would consult. They would not listen to him, however, so, they always ended up in trouble. Uśanā was also famous for his work on ethics, *Śukra-nīti*.

दण्डो दमयतामस्मि नीतिरस्मि जिगीषताम् ।
मौनं चैवास्मि गुह्यानां ज्ञानं ज्ञानवतामहम् ॥ ३८ ॥

daṇḍo damayatām asmi nītirasmi jigīṣatām
maunaṁ caivāsmi guhyānāṁ jñānaṁ jñānavatām aham (38)

damayatām – of people who enforce discipline; *daṇḍaḥ asmi* – I am the discipline; *jigīṣatām* – of those who want success; *nītiḥ asmi* – I am justice; *maunaṁ ca eva asmi* – and I am silence; *guhyānām* – among the secrets; *jñānavatām* – of those who have knowledge; *ahaṁ jñānam* – I am that knowledge

> I am the discipline of those who enforce discipline. I am justice of those who want success and I am silence among the secrets. Of those who have knowledge, I am that knowledge.

Damayatām of those who enforce discipline, giving punishment to those who transgress, I am the discipline. If you have self discipline, Bhagavān says, I am that very discipline. If you lack self-discipline, it needs to be imposed. I am the one who enforces discipline.

Jigīṣatām, of those who are desirous of victory and are working for it, I am the *nīti*, the order. When you achieve victory, it must come within the framework of justice. Otherwise, it cannot be considered a victory. Success won at the cost of justice is not meaningful for a mature person, because for him, the means is as important as the end. For a morally retarded person, only the end is important. Justice is not only important in victory; it is also essential. Before, Bhagavān said, in the victorious, I am victory. Here he says where there is success, I am the justice, the order, which brings success.

Among the secrets, I am *mauna*, silence. Among the devices employed to maintain secrecy, silence is the best. Any secret that you divulge will eventually come back to you – and in another form. Silence is the only sure way of keeping a secret. So, it is the best form of secrecy.

Of those who have self-knowledge, I am the *svarūpa*, the knowledge itself. Knowledge and Īśvara are not two different things and I am the very form of that knowledge.

यच्चापि सर्वभूतानां बीजं तदहमर्जुन ।
न तदस्ति विना यत्स्यान्मया भूतं चराचरम् ॥ ३९ ॥

yaccāpi sarvabhūtānāṁ bījaṁ tad aham arjuna
na tadasti vinā yatsyānmayā bhūtaṁ carācaram (39)

yat ca api bījam – and also, that which is the cause; *sarva-bhūtānām* – of all beings/things; *tad aham* – that I am; *arjuna* – Arjuna!; *na tad asti* – there is not; *bhūtaṁ cara-acaram* – (any) mobile or immobile/sentient or insentient thing; *yat syāt* – which can exist;*mayā vinā* – without me

> Arjuna! I am also that which is the cause of all things. There is no mobile/sentient or immobile/insentient thing that can exist without me.

Bīja literally means seed but is often used in the sense of cause. Since a seed is the cause for the tree, by implication it is used for cause in general. There are many causes and effects. *Bhūtānāṁ madhye* among the various causes, I am the cause of all beings or of all things. *Bhūtas* can be taken as the elements – *ākāśa, vāyu, agni, āpaḥ, pṛthivī* – or as beings. That which is the seed of all these is, in other words, *jagat-kāraṇa*.

Among all the causes, each is a cause only from the standpoint of its effect. From another standpoint that cause itself becomes an effect for some other cause. So, what is the real cause, *bīja*? It should be an uncaused cause. *Prakṛti* can be said to be *sarvabhūtānāṁ bījam* because it has no cause. But because *prakṛti* has no existence independent of *ātmā*, Īśvara is the ultimate cause of everything. Therefore, he says, *sarvabhūtānāṁ bījam* (*prakṛtiḥ*) *aham asmi*, I am the material cause for everything. Now to sum up the topic of *bhagavad-vibhūti* , the glory of Bhagavān, he says, without me there would not be any *bhūta* neither *cara*, those that move, nor *acara*, those that do not move at all – *na tat asti bhūtaṁ cara-acaraṁ yat syāt mayā vinā*. The whole creation is made up of what moves and what does not. This is one way of looking at it. In another way, sentient is *cara* and insentient, *acara*. If *acara* means merely immobile, it will include a sentient tree also. Whichever way it is taken, without me, there are no such things that could exist. That means if I am not there, there is no object at all.

If Parameśvara is *sat*, the efficient and material cause, which object is away from that material cause? Without me, the *sat*, if there is an object, it will be *nirātmaka* or *śūnya*. It will have no existence at all. Wherever there is an existent object, that object is non-separate from the *kāraṇa*, which is existence. Every product entirely depends on the cause and the final cause is Īśvara.

Bhagavān has gone on listing his glories and now comes to the point where he has to say that he cannot continue because the list is endless.

Verse 40

There is no end to my extraordinary glories

नान्तोऽस्ति मम दिव्यानां विभूतीनां परन्तप ।
एष तूद्देशतः प्रोक्तो विभूतेर्विस्तरो मया ॥ ४० ॥

nānto'sti mama divyānāṁ vibhūtīnāṁ parantapa
eṣa tūddeśataḥ prokto vibhūtervistaro mayā (40)

parantapa – O the scorcher of foes, Arjuna!; *mama divyānāṁ vibhūtīnām* – to my extraordinary glories; *na antaḥ asti* – there is no end; *tu* – but; *eṣaḥ vibhūteḥ vistaraḥ* – this detailed narration of (my) glories; *mayā* – by me; *uddeśataḥ* – taking into account a few important ones; *proktaḥ* – was told

> There is no end to my extraordinary glories, Arjuna, the scorcher of foes! But this detailed narration of glories was told by me taking into account a few important ones.

Kṛṣṇa addressed Arjuna here as Parantapa, the one who is always victorious against the opponents.

O! Arjuna, the glories not easily seen in the world, the *vibhūti*s which are *divya*s, my brilliant manifestations, have no end – *mama divyānāṁ vibhūtīnāṁ na antaḥ asti*. Since there is no end to them at all, I have to end it. Therefore, I am ending it here.

What has been related here is a brief account of the vast extent of my glories. The full particulars can never be given because the list is endless. I could only tell a few things.

If that is so, why did he start? Because the intention was to make one understand *bhagavad-vibhūti*, and not to complete the list of *vibhūti*s. I want you to understand that wherever there is any brilliance, that indeed is mine. If you ask me why I said this, it is purely to establish this general rule, which is told in the next verse.

Verse 41

Any glory – may you know – is born of a fraction of my glory

यद्यद्विभूतिमत्सत्त्वं श्रीमदूर्जितमेव वा
तत्तदेवावगच्छ त्वं मम तेजोंऽशसम्भवम् ॥ ४१ ॥

yadyadvibhūtimatsattvaṁ śrīmadūrjitameva vā
tattadevāvagaccha tvaṁ mama tejoṁ'śasambhavam (41)

yat yat – whatever; *vibhūtimat sattvam* – existent thing that has glory; *śrīmat* – that which is endowed with any form of wealth; *ūrjitam eva vā* – that which is indeed mighty; *tat tat eva* – every one of that; *mama tejoṁ'śa-sambhavam* – born of a fraction of my glory; *avagaccha tvam* – may you know

Whatever existent thing there is, which has glory, which is endowed with any form of wealth, or that which is mighty, every one of that, may you know, is born of a fraction of my glory.

Any existent thing in this world that has some glory, whether in terms of knowledge, power, beauty, some brilliance, skill, or any fame, that, Bhagavān says, is *śrīmad*. *Śrī* can be attraction or beauty, *kānti*; it can also be *nīti*, justice; *kīrti*, fame; *dhana*, wealth; *dhānya*, food; *santāna*, children; *gṛha*, domestic happiness; *saubhāgya*, any sense of well being; *vara* a boon; or *vidyā*, knowledge. These are the different forms of Lakṣmī known as *Śrī*. *Śrīmad* is that which has *Śrī*. It covers everything. In fact, all glories are covered by the '*Śrīmad*.' That '*Śrīmad*' is Bhagavān.

Anything powerful, distinguished, and arresting is *ūrjitaṁ*. *Avagaccha*, may you understand that each one of them, *tat tad eva*, arises from only a part of my *tejas*. *Tejas* here means splendour, the *bhaga* in Bhagavān.[22] Bhagavān is six fold, belonging to Īśvara, as we have seen before – *śrī*, absolute wealth; *aiśvarya*, absolute overlordship; *yaśas*, absolute fame; *vairāgya*, absolute dispassion; *jñāna*, infinite knowledge; and *vīrya*, absolute power, the power of creation, destruction, and sustenance.

All glories are born of this six fold sovereignty, *aiśvarya*, which attempts to classify the infinite affluence of Īśvara, briefly called *bhaga*.

The creation of all these glories is from only a fraction of my *tejas*. Not *tejas* directly but from only *tejo'ṁśa*, a fraction of the infinite glory of Bhagavān. Only a part of that Īśvara is manifest in all these glories. In fact the *jagat* is nothing but an *aṁśa*, a part, of Īśvara. Even though the Lord is partless, because of *māyā* it appears manifold, like partless space seems to be divided into pot space, room space etc., and these are called part of the total space.

The idea is that everything here is only projected by *māyā*, *māyayā kalpitam*. Arjuna, please understand, each one is born of only a fraction of my glory. There is no exception to this.

---

[22] Refer to the definition of the word Bhagavān in Volume 1 - page 42

Now there is one problem when we say that anything that has any glory whatsoever is born of a fraction of Bhagavān's glory, meaning it is only one manifestation of Bhagavān, the total power of Īśvara. Then what about all other things? There are countless people who were born and gone, whose names are not remembered at all except by the bereaved. There are millions of people in different generations and a lot of things in the world, animals and so on, whose names are not known to anybody, which are not recognised as having some special excellence. Do you say they are not born of your *tejas*, your *bhaga*?

This we must understand well. These glories, which are a fraction of this six-fold absolute virtues – knowledge, wealth, supremacy, power, fame, and dispassion are mentioned only for meditation on Īśvara in these particular forms, as *āditya* and so on. That is one meaning.

Another is this. These verses are meant to establish a general rule that wherever there is *vibhūti*, it is Īśvara's *vibhūti*. No one particular person has gained anything, which he can legitimately claim as his own. Once it is Īśvara's *vibhūti* no person can become an object of your jealousy because jealousy is possible only when he has achieved it and you have not.

Now if you look upon everything as Īśvara's glory, you will find that glory in many forms. Every blade of grass is Īśvara's glory; the sun, moon, and stars are all Īśvara's glory. And if anybody is able to sing or dance, it is all Bhagavān's *vibhūti*. In one place an aspect of it manifests more and in another less, but it does not make any difference at all. It is all Īśvara's glory.

And if you recognise his glory, you become Bhagavān's *vibhūti*. Even the capacity to appreciate beauty is a glory of Īśvara. Many wonderful manifestations of Īśvara go unrecognised for want of people's capacity to appreciate. Unless you have that perceptive ability you are not going to see something glorious. So, many great men go unrecognised and many a good book goes unread just because the author is not known. There are countless such things that are never recognised.

Although some singers become popular, for every one of them there are many more who are equally good or better but never become known. I know one person, at least, who is so accomplished in playing the *vīṇa* that she would have excelled over anybody. But she is not known. Only those in her home and those who are closely connected to her have the privilege of hearing her music. There are a number of people like this. Thus, wherever there is a manifestation of glory it is Īśvara's glory. Sometimes it is known, sometimes not.

As a devotee you cannot be jealous of Īśvara if you understand Īśvara

To discover the glory of a person, you require certain capacity to appreciate. If you are able to become jealous of someone, it is only because you are able to perceive the glory of that person. Otherwise, how are you going to become jealous? That capacity to see is your glory. Where is a musician if there is no *rasika*, connoisseur? Someone who enjoys that music is necessary. When you know that all glories belong to Īśvara, you can no longer be jealous. You can be jealous of an individual, but not Īśvara because jealousy is only possible between similars, not dissimilars. You cannot be jealous of Īśvara any more than you can be jealous of an eagle because it soars so high. You may wish to fly like an eagle, that is possible, but you can never be jealous of the eagle. Because it is unlike you.

Similarly, Īśvara does not belong to the human species; so, where is the question of your being jealous of Īśvara? This rule helps eliminate your jealousies, the friction in your personal relationships. *Vibhūti-yoga* is a very beautiful chapter to help you discover this attitude.

If there is a person who is free from jealousy, that person is a saint, because jealousy can appear in a hundred different subtle forms. Even among *sādhu*s I see it. They are jealous of one another's popularity. In fact, I find the more popular you are, the more likelihood of your knowing less or knowing wrongly. It is difficult to be popular if you know profound things. Because when you talk it is going to be profound and that is not going to be popular. To be popular you have to tell some stories, some jokes and use some catchy expressions even though they do not mean anything. You can be a gorilla and be popular. In Milwaukee there was a popularity poll and the winner was Samson, the gorilla in the local zoo! Sitting there quietly he became popular. So, popularity is meaningless.

You must repeatedly read this chapter *vibhūti-yoga*. Wherever there is any brilliance, any skill, you should be able to appreciate it as Īśvara's glory. Any intelligent person should be able to do that. It does not require great knowledge to see that these capacities that we have are all given to us. Nothing is really created by anybody. Simple observation of our own life, of our own powers will reveal that everything is given to us. The whole world is given. What is it that is created by us? If we have a power to create, to bring things together, that is also given. What is created by us is nothing. The more we see this, the more objective we will find our ego. And an objective ego is as good as non-existent – even if it is not enlightened. That is the devotee's ego, which is good enough to discover *ātmā*. It becomes pure and can therefore, discover *gūḍha- ātmā*.

Even if such an appreciation of Īśvara's glories is incomplete in the beginning, afterwards it becomes real. If you keep bringing it to mind, even though you do not see it, it becomes real – because it is a fact, not a superimposition. Even if you do not understand totally at first, later it becomes more and more clear. Though the profundity may not be very clear, that forced appreciation is good enough. As in friendship or love, suppose you are not able to discover love, if you can force yourself to say something nice, you will find yourself beginning to discover love. Any act of love will make you discover love. Similarly here, even though it is incomplete at first, it becomes real. Nothing can stop it because it has its basis in truth.

So, as a devotee you cannot be jealous of Īśvara and if you understand Īśvara, it is all you. If you step out and see the whole *jagat* as Īśvara, then you are that Īśvara because there is no Īśvara other than *sat-cit-ānanda-ātmā*; therefore, it is all your glory alone.

What about those things that are not recognised as glories? In answer to this Bhagavān says, in fact, the entire *jagat* is nothing but my glory and is still only one-fourth of my total glory, *pādo'sya viśva bhūtāni*. Three fourths is lost in your heart as *paraṁ-brahma, tripādasyāmṛtaṁ divi*. In the *caitanya-ātmā* three fourths is gone. All fourteen worlds, seven above and seven below are only one-fourth. This is just an expression to say that the entire *jagat* does not account for the infinite.

Verse 42

I pervade this entire world with just one part of me

अथवा बहुनैतेन किं ज्ञातेन तवार्जुन ।
विष्टभ्याहमिदं कृत्स्नमेकांशेन स्थितो जगत् ॥ ४२ ॥

athavā bahunaitena kiṁ jñātena tavārjuna
viṣṭabhyāham idaṁ kṛtsnam ekāṁśena sthito jagat (42)

athavā – on the other hand; *bahunā etena jñātena* – by this knowledge of many and varied things; *kiṁ tava arjuna* – what is accomplished for you, Arjuna; *viṣṭabhya* – pervading; *idaṁ kṛtsnaṁ jagat* – this entire world; *ekāṁśena* – with just one part (of me); *ahaṁ sthitaḥ* – I remain

On the other hand, by this (incomplete) knowledge of many and varied things what is accomplished for you, Arjuna? (May you know that fully) I remain pervading this entire world with just one part (of me).

Athavā means, or let us put it this way. I said everything that has *vibhūti* is born of a fraction of my glory, *tejoṁ'śa-sambhavam*. From that you may conclude that only those things that have *vibhūti* are born of me and others are not. So, *athavā*, means 'to put it correctly.'

By this knowledge of manifold things, various things, *bahunā etena jñātena* – like among the trees I am the sacred ficus, among the rivers, I am Gaṅgā – what is accomplished for you Arjuna, *kiṁ tava* Arjuna? Not much is accomplished because my *vibhūti* is endless. It is, therefore, not possible for me to complete this list. Śaṅkara says it is a knowledge that leaves a lot to be desired, *sāvaśeṣeṇa jñātena*. Since it is an incomplete knowledge of Īśvara's glory, what is accomplished?

In fact, what Bhagavān wants to say is that you must understand just this one thing – that everything is Bhagavān. Bhagavān says, 'All of this is only a part of me; in fact, I remain pervading this entire world by only one part of myself – *aham idaṁ kṛtsnaṁ jagat ekaṁśena viṣṭabhya sthitaḥ*. This *jagat* being *mithyā*, requires me, the *upādāna-kāraṇa*, to give reality to it.

The *jagat* one knows, one experiences is only a part of it. Whether *sūkṣma-prapañca*, subtle, or *sthūla-prapañca*, physical, whatever you see is only *aṁśa*, one part, of Īśvara. Three fourth is lost in your *buddhi*. That is the truth of yourself, the limitless, the infinite. It is not literally three-fourths but an expression to convey that this makes it complete. The three-fourths is that without which this one-fourth, the *jagat*, is incomplete. Because the *jagat* is non-separate from Brahman, it is said to be one fourth of that whole. Śaṅkara quotes the *mantra* that expresses this, *pādo'sya viśva bhūtāni*. His one-fourth is all this – all eyes are his eyes, etc. But still, three fourths is beyond time and space, *tripādasyāmṛtaṁ divi*. The source is lost in the sense that it is not available for your objectification. Therefore, what is really to be seen is the three-fourths that is partless infinite. Obviously there is a poetic approach to the topic here.

Brahman is *niraṁśa*, not subject to division. This apparent division is created for understanding.

ॐतत्सत् ।

इति श्रीमद्भगवद्गीतासूपनिषत्सु ब्रह्मविद्यायां योगशास्त्रे श्रीकृष्णार्जुन-संवादे विभूति-योगो नाम दशमोऽध्यायः ॥ १० ॥

oṁ tat sat.
iti śrīmadbhagavadgītāsūpaniṣatsu brahma-vidyāyāṁ yoga-śāstre śrīkṛṣṇārjuna-saṁvāde vibhūti-yogo nāma daśamo'dhyāyaḥ (10)

Om, Brahman, is the only reality. Thus ends the tenth chapter called *vibhūti-yoga* – having the topic of glories (of the Lord) – in the *Bhagavadgītā* which is in the form of a dialogue between Śrī Kṛṣṇa and Arjuna, which is the essence of the *Upaniṣads*, whose subject matter is both the knowledge of Brahman and *yoga*.

Alphabetical index of verses

Books by Swami Dayananda Saraswati

Public Talk Series :

1. Living Intelligently
2. Successful Living
3. Need for Cognitive Change
4. Discovering Love
5. The Value of Values
6. Vedic View and Way of Life

Upaniñad Series :

7. Muëòakopaniñad
8. Kenopaniñad

Prakaraëa Series :

9. Tattvabodhaù

Text Translation Series :

10. Çrémad Bhagavad Gétä
    (Text with roman transliteration and English translation)
11. Çré Rudram
    (Text in Sanskrit with transliteration, word-to-word and verse meaning along with an elaborate commentary in English)

Stotra Series :

12. Dīpārādhanā
13. Prayer Guide
    (With explanations of several Mantras, Stotras, Kirtans and Religious Festivals)

Moments with Oneself Series :

14. Freedom from Helplessness
15. Living versus Getting On
16. Insights
17. Action and Reaction
18. Fundamental Problem
19. Problem is You, Solution is You
20. Purpose of Prayer
21. Vedanta 24x7
22. Freedom
23. Crisis Management
24. Surrender and Freedom
25. The Need for Personal Reorganisation
26. Freedom in Relationship
27. Stress-free Living
28. Om Namo Bhagavate Väsudeväya
29. Yoga of Objectivity

Bhagavad Gétä

30. Bhagavad Gétä Home Study Course
    (Hardbound - 9 Volumes)

Meditation Series :

31. Morning Meditation Prayers
32. What is Meditation?

Essays :

33. Do all Religions have the same goal?
34. Conversion is Violence
35. Gurupürëimä
36. Dänam
37. Japa
38. Can We?
39. Moments with Krishna
40. Teaching Tradition of Advaita Vedanta
41. Compositions of Swami Dayananda Saraswati

Exploring Vedanta Series : (*väkyavicära*)

42. çraddhä bhakti dhyäna yogäd avaihi ātmānaṁ ced vijānīyāt

Books translated in other languages and in English based on Swami Dayananda Saraswati's Original Exposition

Tamil

43. Veeduthorum Gitopadesam (9 Volumes)
    (Bhagavad Gétä Home Study Course)
44. Dänam

Kannada

45. Mane maneyalli Adhyayana (7 Volumes)
    (Bhagavad Gétä Home Study Course)
46. Vedanta Pravesike

Malayalam

47. Muëòakopaniñad

Hindi

48. Ghar baithe Gétä Vivecan (Vol 1)
    (Bhagavad Gétä Home Study Course)
49. Antardåñöi (Insights)
50. Vedanta 24X7
51. Kriya aur Pratikriya (Action and Reaction)

English

52. The Jungian Myth and Advaita Vedanta
53. The Vedantic Self and the Jungian Psyche
54. Salutations to Rudra
55. Without a Second

Biography

56. Swami Dayananda Saraswati
    Contributions & Writings
    (Smt. Sheela Balalji)

Distributed in India & worldwide by
MOTILAL BANARSIDASS - NEW DELHI
Tel : 011 - 2385 8335 / 2385 1985 / 2385 2747

Also available at :

ARSHA VIDYA RESEARCH AND PUBLICATION TRUST
32 / 4 Sir Desika Road
Mylapore Chennai 600 004
Telefax : 044 - 2499 7131
Email : avrandpt@gmail.com
Website : www.avrpt.com

ARSHA VIDYA GURUKULAM
Anaikatti P.O.
Coimbatore 641 108
Ph : 0422 - 2657001
Fax : 0422 - 2657002
Email : office@arshavidya.in
Website : www.arshavidya.in

ARSHA VIDYA GURUKULAM
P.O.Box 1059. Pennsylvania
PA 18353, USA
Ph : 001-570-992-2339
Email : avp@epix.net
Website : www.arshavidya.org

SWAMI DAYANANDA ASHRAM
Purani Jhadi, P.B.No. 30
Rishikesh, Uttaranchal 249 201
Telefax : 0135 - 2430769
Email : ashrambookstore@yahoo.com
Website : www.dayananda.org

Other leading Book Stores:

Chennai:	**044**
Motilal Banarsidass	24982315
Giri Trading	2495 1966
Higginbothams	2851 3519
Pustak Bharati	2461 1345
Theosophical Publishing House	2446 6613 / 2491 1338
The Odessey	43910300
Bengaluru:	**080**
Gangarams	2558 1617 / 2558 1618
Sapna Book House	4011 4455 / 4045 5999
Strand Bookstall	2558 2222, 25580000
Vedanta Book House	2650 7590
Coimbatore:	**0422**
Guru Smruti	948677 3793
Giri Trading	2541523

Trivandrum:	**0471**
Prabhus Bookhouse	2478 397 / 2473 496
Kozhikode:	**0495**
Ganga Bookhouse	6521262
Mumbai:	**022**
Chetana Bookhouse	2285 1243 / 2285 3412
Strand Bookstall	2266 1994 / 2266 1719/ 2261 4613
Giri Trading	2414 3140

Made in the USA
Las Vegas, NV
10 August 2023

75924605R10273